WOMEN AS IMAMS

WOMEN AS IMAMS

Classical Islamic Sources and Modern Debates on Leading Prayer

Simonetta Calderini

I.B. TAURIS
LONDON • NEW YORK • OXFORD • NEW DELHI • SYDNEY

I.B. TAURIS
Bloomsbury Publishing Plc
50 Bedford Square, London, WC1B 3DP, UK
1385 Broadway, New York, NY 10018, USA
29 Earlsfort Terrace, Dublin 2, Ireland

BLOOMSBURY, I.B. TAURIS and the I.B. Tauris logo are trademarks of Bloomsbury Publishing Plc

First published in Great Britain 2021
This paperback edition published in 2022

Copyright © Simonetta Calderini, 2021

Simonetta Calderini has asserted her right under the Copyright, Designs and Patents Act, 1988, to be identified as Author of this work.

For legal purposes the Acknowledgements on p. ix constitute an extension of this copyright page.

Series design by Adriana Brioso
Cover image: Muslim women take part in Eid al-Fitr prayers.
(@ SIMON MAINA/AFP/Getty images)

All rights reserved. No part of this publication may be reproduced or transmitted in any form or by any means, electronic or mechanical, including photocopying, recording, or any information storage or retrieval system, without prior permission in writing from the publishers.

Bloomsbury Publishing Plc does not have any control over, or responsibility for, any third-party websites referred to or in this book. All internet addresses given in this book were correct at the time of going to press. The author and publisher regret any inconvenience caused if addresses have changed or sites have ceased to exist, but can accept no responsibility for any such changes.

A catalogue record for this book is available from the British Library.

A catalog record for this book is available from the Library of Congress.

ISBN: HB: 978-1-8386-0618-3
       PB: 978-0-7556-3714-0
       ePDF: 978-0-7556-1803-3
       eBook: 978-0-7556-1802-6

Typeset by RefineCatch Limited, Bungay, Suffolk

To find out more about our authors and books visit www.bloomsbury.com and sign up for our newsletters.

To Dr Delia Cortese
The most brilliant and generous colleague and friend

CONTENTS

Acknowledgements	ix
Prologue	xi
INTRODUCTION	1

Part I
THE PAST

Chapter 1
PRAYER LEADERSHIP, IMAMS AND WOMEN: DEFINING THE
CONTEXTS AND SETTING THE ISSUES ... 23
    Prayer and women: Purity and leadership ... 24
    The imam as prayer leader ... 31

Chapter 2
CONGREGATIONAL PRAYERS: WOMEN LEADING WOMEN ... 51
    Setting the narrative context: Umm Salama ... 51
    *Hadith*s on female prayer leadership and Sunni jurisprudence ... 62
    Shi'i positions on female *imama* of women: Identity, shared
        issues and esoteric interpretations ... 77

Chapter 3
CONGREGATIONAL PRAYERS: WOMEN LEADING MEN ... 97
    Setting the context ... 97
    Women as prayer leaders of men: Umm Waraqa and Ghazala ... 99
    Legal arguments on women leading men in prayer ... 116
    Ibn al-'Arabi and female *imama* ... 122

Part II
THE PRESENT

Chapter 4
PRESENT DEBATES AND PRACTICES ... 137
    Some current cases of women imams of women ... 140
    Some current cases of women imams of mixed congregations ... 159
    Contemporary arguments and debates on female imams of men ... 165
    Uses of the past in contemporary debates ... 171

CONCLUSION 191

Glossary 197
Bibliography 201
Index 221

ACKNOWLEDGEMENTS

The research for this book was made possible by grants from the Arts and Humanities Research Council for my project 'The Contexts and Discourses of Arguments in Favour and Against Female Ritual Leadership and Religious Authority in Islam' (2008) and from the Southlands Methodist Trust Fund (2018). I thank the University of Roehampton London, School of Humanities, for giving me periods of research leave and funding to enable me to participate in national and international conferences.

I am grateful to a number of institutions for inviting me to conferences and lectures to present the findings of my research: The George Mason University, Virginia, USA and its Ali Vural Ak Center for Global Islamic Studies (2014); the Fondazione Bruno Kessler e Scienze Religiose of the University of Trento, Italy (2013); the Institute of Isma'ili Studies for organizing a panel at the MESA conference in Denver, Colorado (2012); and the Università degli Studi di Napoli L'Orientale, Italy for the international conference 'Sapienza Fede e Dialogo' (2018). I thank the Digby Stuart Research Centre and University of Roehampton for sponsoring and facilitating an international conference there in 2012, 'Women, Authority and Leadership in Christianity and Islam', and my colleague Professor Tina Beattie, who co-organized it with me.

Throughout my research work, I greatly benefited from the collection and facilities of the Aga Khan Library and the efficiency and support of all its staff, its Head Librarian Dr Walid Ghali, Waseem Farooq, Shah Hussain, the ever helpful Khadija Lalani, Alex Leach and Pedro Sanchez. I also benefited from other libraries, including the British Library and that of the School of Oriental and African Studies, University of London.

My gratitude goes to the many colleagues and friends who supported me over the past ten years; first of all Dr Delia Cortese, without whose advice and support this book would not have been completed, then to the three anonymous reviewers of the draft of this book, particularly the one who produced 13 pages of helpful comments and queries. As part of my research I was fortunate to know several inspirational women such as Professor amina wadud, and those who welcomed me in their communities of faith, among them chaplain Mrs Rukhsana Shah, all the congregants of the Inclusive Mosque Initiative, London and of the Women's Mosque of America, Los Angeles. Lastly a warm thank you to all those who gave advice on specific aspects of the book: Mrs Yasmin Amin, Dr Carolyn Baugh, Dr Nadia Duvall, Ms Narguess Farzad, Prof Robert Gleave, Dr Sumaiya A. Hamdani, Mr Russell Harris, Dr Shuruq Naguib, Dr Nuha al-Shaar, and many more.

I acknowledge the staff of I.B. Tauris and the Bloomsbury Publishing editorial team for their assistance, in particular Sophie Rudland for her constant support and encouragement, and Tom Bedford for his help with copyediting.

My everlasting thanks go to my husband, Piers Jackson, who not only put up with the ups and downs of this project as well as the papers and books scattered in every corner of the house, but also patiently read and sharply commented upon each draft of this book. To my daughters, Clementina and Violetta, for encouraging me all the way in their selfless conviction that this was an important endeavour, although one that took away so much time from our having fun together.

PROLOGUE

During the spring of 2009, having just attended a meeting in London at the House of Commons on interfaith issues, I and a number of other participants were congregating outside the lecture room. I introduced myself to a notable Muslim *shaykh*, who was surrounded by a conspicuous retinue and who, after the formal introductions, presented himself as Chair of an organization representing over half a million imams of India. When I asked him whether any of those imams were female, time stood still, his face frozen in bewilderment, and, without uttering a word, he turned his face away from me and busied himself conversing with other men. Members of his retinue soon dispersed. Only one of them, unseen by the others, came back to ask me whether women imams actually existed. To my answer in the affirmative he retorted that his *madhhab* (legal school) surely did not consider it permissible for a woman to lead prayer. When I asked him whether he was a Maliki, he replied that he was a Hanafi. Well, I said, for most classical Sunni and Shi'i legal scholars it is permissible for women to lead other women in prayer; as for the Hanafis, for some it is *makruh* (disliked), but still permissible.

It would have been too much to even mention the possibility of women leading mixed congregations, such as the 2005 mixed prayer led by amina wadud, but I did refer as a textual precedent of a female imam to the *hadith* on Umm Waraqa, which I was then working on. Still doubtful, he left, and I remained there, pondering how representative those half a million, all-male imams were of the Muslim population in India at that time of over 160 million, more than half of whom were women.

That one member of the *shaykh*'s entourage gave me a glimmer of hope that someone was curious enough to enquire about the remote possibility that there could be women imams. I took that single step as a good omen for me to continue my research and eventually expand it into a book to address and answer some of the questions on female leadership in prayer and consider how far the past informs the present. I thought it would be a book aimed at those who, like the man in the *shaykh*'s retinue, wanted to know more, perhaps even beyond received general knowledge.

INTRODUCTION

Preliminaries

It is well-known that *salat*, the prescribed ritual prayer to be performed five times a day, is one of the 'five pillars' required of all Muslims. In the Qur'an, *salat*, like the other pillars, is prescribed to both men and women who, as specifically explained in one verse (Qur. 33.35), are equally to reap reward from their individual fulfilment of religious duties. While various elements of the prayer are indicated in the Qur'an, such as its main ritual actions, the direction of prayer and the ablutions that precede it, there is no explicit indication of the need for prayers to be led. This is, however, specifically and extensively discussed in the *hadith*s, the records of the deeds and words of the Prophet Muhammad and his Companions. There, it is explained that a prayer, performed by more than one person, needs to be led by an imam. What was a seemingly straightforward act of devotion became, from the first centuries of Islam, a platform of ritual discussion of a social nature. When dealing with the performance of prayer, its location, its staging and issues of visibility, various concerns about the interaction between men and women came to the fore.

This book brings to light the hidden history of a current debate in Islam that revolves around one core question relating to this ritual interaction: can a woman lead prayer? Since the standard answer Muslims typically offer to this is 'no, she cannot', this book should maybe end here. What makes it worthwhile writing is that this emphatic 'no' is in fact preceded by a long, complex and rich history of opinions about female prayer leadership. These include outright prohibition, dislike, permissibility under certain conditions and, though rarely, unrestricted sanction or even endorsement.

From the first century of Islam the issue of women's leadership in prayer emerged as a very complex one that occupied the minds of theologians and jurists alike. In handling what would escalate into a thorny question, the varied answers which in turn cascaded onto aspects of doctrine and social mores became more and more varied, contradictory, nuanced and contested. The question of women's leadership in prayer has therefore a 'history'. By uncovering hitherto forgotten or sidelined voices in these debates and revisiting famous ones, this book will trace that history in a way that has never been *comprehensively* and *multifacetedly* done before.

This book discusses the ways in which – and reasons why – scholars of the past engaged in debates on female prayer leadership. To have these debates gathered, critically analysed and historically contextualized in a collective study is important because, thus far, although they have informed current debates on female *imama* (prayer leadership), they have been used selectively depending on modern agendas and biases. Presenting the variety of opinions discussed in the past offers instead the opportunity to address the question of female *imama* today in a less polarized manner, thus opening up room for opportunity and change, if not necessarily in practices then at the very least in attitudes.

While women are central to this work, this is not a book on gender. It is the study of an aspect of religion where women play a major part. This is not primarily a book about the history of the gender issues that framed the acceptability or not of women's leadership in prayer. It is, instead, about the history of how and why pre-modern Muslim theologians and jurists informed their debates on prayer leadership around issues that were shaped by, or came to shape, or had become part of, gender discourses since early Islam. Also, the debates discuss women but these discussions are enmeshed in the broader theme that is of real and primary concern for writers and exegetes, i.e. the performance of prayer, and specifically the correctness of its procedure and its validity.

While resting mostly on evidence from *hadiths* and from works on Islamic jurisprudence, this book does not fall into the *hadith* studies or Islamic jurisprudence categories. Its focus and aims are not to evaluate the *hadiths* in order to determine their authenticity – that is, whether they can be considered as the actual words and deeds of the Prophet and his Companions – nor their historicity. Rather, it analyses *hadiths* relevant to female prayer leadership which have been reported and used in doctrinal-legal literature as evidence of scholarly positions in order to identify the underlying discourses and developments in debates. This book appraises the positions of diverse legal schools and the facets and developments of legal discourse, as well as discussing the principles and methodologies of some representatives of Islamic jurisprudence. However, it is not confined – nor limited – to Islamic legal studies methodologies and theoretical frameworks, but positions itself at the interface between various approaches and interpretative keys.

The most important compilations of *hadiths* mentioned in this book date from the 9th and 10th centuries. They include the so-called Six Canonical Collections of Sunni *hadiths*, particularly featuring those compiled by Muhammad al-Bukhari (d. 870), Muslim ibn al-Hajjaj (d. 875) and Abu Dawud (d. 889). Moreover, the 10th and 11th c. main collections of Shi'i traditions on the authority of the Shi'i Imams are used, specifically those by Muhammad al-Kulayni (d. 940–1), Muhammad Ibn Babawayh (d. 991) and Abu Ja'far al-Tusi, known as Shaykh al-Ta'ifa (d. 1067). Later collections are also referred to as evidence of developments in the debates. *Hadiths* are the second source of authority in Islam used by scholars to formulate laws for Muslims to live by, in accordance with the *sunna* of the Prophet and his Companions and, additionally for Shi'is, the words and deeds of their Imams. In this capacity – after a process of scrutiny – what is narrated in *hadiths* functions as legally binding precedents of practice that a Muslim must follow to ensure her/his adherence to Islamic principles in life as revealed by God in the Qur'an via his Prophet, who is the ultimate role model for all Muslims.

The second body of literature this book primarily rests upon is that of Islamic jurisprudence (*fiqh*), the aim of which is to ground legal practice in theological perspectives. This is the tool through which, from the 9th century onwards, exegetes were able to translate the revealed divine guidance into legal theory and practice for the Muslim community to live by. Religious law (shari'a) is divided into *'ibadat*, laws regulating acts towards God, and *mu'amalat*, laws regulating human mutual relations. *Salat* is primarily dealt with in the *'ibadat* section of legal literature.

Legal positions will be presented and analysed here within the framework of the legal schools (*madhhab*, pl. *madhahib*) which gradually emerged from the middle of the 8th century as local centres, and so reflect the geographical diversity of customs. The two centres mentioned most in this book are those around, first, Medina and the Hijaz region, and second, around Basra and Kufa in Iraq. They not only developed their own trajectories but also influenced each other. While Kufa was the centre from which the school of Abu Hanifa (d. 767) emerged, Medina was the centre which produced Malik ibn Anas (d. 795). It is al-Shafi'i (d. 820), a pupil of Malik, who is ascribed responsibility for the systematization of a procedure for legal reasoning which relied on the Prophetic *sunna* as an authoritative source of law. A group centred around the figure of Ibn Hanbal (d. 855) developed later, which also had its roots in Medina. By the end of the 10th century these four Sunni schools were well-established. This book also makes use of legal literature from other branches of Islam such as the Shi'a, as represented by scholars of its Twelver and Sevener subgroups, as well as Zaydis. Legal scholar representatives of the Ja'fari legal school included here are 'Allama al-Hilli (d. 1325) and the already mentioned Shaykh al-Ta'ifa. The former was responsible both for the systematization of the evaluative methods in *hadith* literature and for making reasoning (*'aql*) the central feature of Shi'i jurisprudence. A representative of Shi'i Isma'ili jurisprudence is al-Qadi al-Nu'man (d. 974).

This book primarily charters the complex and ambivalent use of *hadith*s in Islamic jurisprudence when it came to deliberating on the position of the law regarding women as leaders of prayer. These exegetical processes and legal deliberations could not be detached from the historical and social context in which the theologians and jurists formulated them. Accordingly, to trace this context, in this book recourse will be made to the input of those historians, chroniclers, biographers etc. who in many ways were the barometers for the attitudes and world views of their times.

The time span considered here, in Part 1 of the book, ranges from the time of the *hijra*, the Prophet's migration from Mecca to Medina in 622 – that is the moment identified as the formal start of the Muslim community – to the 12th century, with some references to developments up until the 14th century. During this period we will encounter women as leaders of prayer in the main centres of an empire that, after the death of the Prophet Muhammad and the four caliphs governing the Muslim community from Medina, known as al-Rashidun (632–661), gradually expanded from Arabia eastwards to the Middle East and Central Asia, and westward through the Mediterranean and North Africa to the Iberian peninsula. Ruling over this vast empire were the Sunni caliphal dynasties of the Umayyads (661–750) of Damascus and the 'Abbasids (750–1258) from Baghdad, but also, in time, local rulers, the Umayyads of al-Andalus (711–1492) and various Shi'i dynasties. One important absentee from this periodization is the Ottoman period (1299–1923). This is due mainly to the lack of access to Ottoman archives and documents, the perusal of which would have taken the trajectory of this book beyond its intended scope. An examination of Ottoman sources would no doubt yield a vast amount of information that would deserve a separate study altogether. Part 2 of this book covers from the late 19th century up to today, and spans across the countries of the former Islamic dynasties and empires as well as China, the USA and Europe.

Moving from Part 1 to Part 2 of the book, an important shift will take place that will be marked by a deliberate change in the choice of wording to indicate women as imams. In Part 1 we use expressions such as, for example, 'women leading prayer' or 'women acting as imams', because the reported instances of these occurrences show, irrespective of the type of source, that these women were by and large instructed in or delegated prayer leadership roles. In short, they acted in response to a higher (male) command or need.

In Part 2, in contrast, we mostly find women who have been elected or chosen as their leader by a community of faith with whom they share, among other things, a specific understanding of religious leadership. Others succeeded previous male imams and self-consciously recognize themselves in the *imama* role. There are also those women imams who, on the strength of their knowledge, spiritual attainment and Qur'anic-based commitment to gender justice, have chosen to be imams. They do so without asking for anyone's permission to lead prayer, except the consensus of those who choose to follow them. There are women imams today who are appointed by a secular state institution as representatives of a community of Muslims. Moreover, there are those who operate outside conventional religious institutions, and either create their own or are given licence by administrative bodies that, while nominally religious, operate and are organized along secular lines. Finally, there are female imams who appoint themselves to prayer leadership based on their own understanding of textual authority and precedents as well as their own spiritual trajectory of self-realization.

Some prefer to call themselves faith leaders or Muslim community representatives, but to all intents and purposes these women are female imams; they are called as such by their supporters, as well as their detractors, and therefore this is how they will be mainly referred to in Chapter 4 of this book.

At the same time the use of the term 'imam', when applied to women, will be extended to encompass a broad range of meanings to better reflect not just what a female imam does, but what it means to them – and the groups they lead – to be in that role. As a consequence, we will explore the changes in the terms that frame the debates on female imams in the way they are currently carried out. Current debates are no longer conducted as seen in Chapters 2 and 3 as a function of the law, but they become debates about Islam and women's rights, political agency, as well as female ritual participation and community authority sharing.

Issues and aims

The focus of this book is on Muslim women's prayer leadership, an issue that is specifically treated in *hadith* collections and Islamic legal works under the topic of *salat* prayer, specifically of congregational prayers (*salat al-jama'a*).

The first part of the book traces some theologico-legal arguments and narratives formulated during the so-called formative period of Islam (from the 8th to 10th century CE) but it also extends to the post-formative period of Islamic thought. Part 2 analyses current opinions and debates and the extent to which they are informed by the past. Prayer leadership is primarily intended as the formal role or the office of 'being an imam' as a concrete activity, but also, especially in Part 2 of this book, as one expression of Muslim women's religious authority.

The legal literature examined here typically reflects the opinions of the five main Islamic legal schools: the Sunni Hanafi, Maliki, Shafi'i and Hanbali, as well as the Ja'fari Shi'i school. In most Islamic legal texts, past and present, prayer leadership by women is framed within the issue of the validity of prayer for the person whom the woman leads. Cases referring to male and female gender binaries are usually enriched with reference to those individuals with fluid sexual identity, such as the omnipresent examples of the *khuntha*, an umbrella Arabic term used to indicate a range of identities from hermaphrodite and intersex to an effeminate person. Gender social hierarchy, gender separation and gender-related propriety all inform these legal debates: overall, given certain conditions and notwithstanding differences among and within legal schools, 'qualified' male imams can lead everybody, *khuntha* can lead women and intersex individuals like themselves, while women may only lead women. As the focus of this book is on the history of the debates about women as imams, issues of non-binary gender identity are not explicitly addressed, although Part 2 on the modern period provides examples of inclusive mosques where such issues are directly relevant to prayer leadership.

When analysing legal literature texts, a highly relevant yet very complex question to address is the extent to which we can infer the practice of prayer from the theory about prayer leadership. Scholarly opinions on this issue are varied, their positions depending on diverse methodological concerns but also geographical and historical contexts. A definite answer is impossible to gauge, even in the presence of seemingly textual evidence, due to the reliability and various agendas of the sources consulted. However, even within the more theoretical aspects of legal literature, related social issues can be inferred or detected, issues such as female access to mosques, the rituals and other activities women could and did perform there and, in practice, the way they negotiated time and space with male worshippers.

This study is not restricted to the analysis of *hadith*s or legal sources. Historical texts, including chronicles, will also be explored when reporting social and other past practices related to women and prayer. Marion Katz has already shown that women who in pre-modern times are reported to have attended mosques did so for several reasons, both religious and profane, and at varied times, days and occasions, which 'should not be conflated with that of their participation in specific activities, such as Friday prayer'.[1]

Salat can indeed be performed anywhere as long as the place is clean, and for the Friday prayer, unlike men, women are not required in any case to attend at a mosque. Though building in part on Katz's seminal work, this book departs from it by deflecting the focus away from the issues arising from the relationship between the female body and the ritual space, and instead pursues a hitherto untrodden direction by centring directly on debates about female leadership in prayer.

An underlying issue related to female leadership of prayer in pre-modern times is that of whether the events referred to in the texts corresponded to, arose from, or were at all representative of ritual practice. In Part 1 we will discuss this point when exploring the episodes of women acting as imam during and after the time of the Prophet.

Bearing in mind that the possible 'recovery of the past' could be attempted both on the 'basis of documents and the absence of documents',[2] we might be tempted to infer that lack of specific information in the sources about women leading prayer does not necessarily imply absence of women acting as imams during the pre-modern era. Could this lacuna of references in pre-modern sources also be linked to the nature and location where such a leadership might have occurred? Women could have been praying and leading prayer in places other than the mosque, for instance at home, at shrines or in prayer grounds. They could have done so during specific festivals or celebrations, a type of participation which legal or historical literary sources were not keen on promoting, or indeed interested in reporting. Additionally, writers have primarily recorded mosque activities in conjunction with the most normative of mosque rituals: the Friday congregational prayer, which may affect the inclusion of references to women and the diversity of uses and rituals that women performed in the mosque.

Furthermore, it is commonly the case that chroniclers and historians focused on writing about urban rather than rural settings and, as far as mosques are concerned, references to large city mosques overwhelm those of village and small neighbourhood mosques.[3] All these considerations contribute to questions over the overall accuracy, representativeness, extent and range of extant information about women's usage of mosques, and women's ritual performance inside or outside of them.

Given the considerable time span this book covers, special attention will be paid to the changes in the understandings and uses of terminology and semantic developments denoting female leadership and terms connected to it. Obviously, at the heart of this investigation is the term 'imam'. Wherever possible, terms in connection with prayer leadership are qualified and contextualized to alert the reader to the importance of locating them in their own historical, theological and 'sectarian' contexts.

Important considerations related to female prayer leadership are those of meaning and understanding of what constitutes female religious authority, including the extent of this authority, its acknowledgement, modes of acquisition and expressions. Some of the questions this book will address are: on what ground did the leadership of a woman in prayer lie? Was it a *de facto* authority or was it acknowledged, and if so, by whom? Was it acquired, 'granted' or was it 'taken'?

Have these bases and modes of authority changed over time? Are they still relevant to today's debates on Muslim women leading prayer?

While historical references to, or even records of, women leaders of prayer during the pre-modern period are limited to very few individuals, relatively more can be found about women who performed some tasks or roles usually associated with that of the imam, among them preaching and imparting religious education. Included in this study is a sample of such religious and ritual leadership roles. Some, but by no means all, of these activities, did or may have taken place in mosques.

The central and recurrent theme of this book is the use of 'tradition' and a re-appropriation of the past through texts and narratives which exhibit legitimizing and authorizing functions. Such a re-appropriation is particularly evident in the final chapter of the book, where both progressives and conservatives cite what they present as the normative past in order to endorse the authoritativeness of their respective arguments and actions. However, throughout the book, whether explicitly stated or implicitly alluded to, whether it is the past that re-appropriates a real or idealized 'past', or a present that re-appropriates both, this appropriation, with its multiple layers, remains the underlying thread through the variation of interpretations and narratives.

It will be shown and argued that, unlike some loud claims to the contrary, this 'tradition' is not fixed and unchanging, but an evolving discourse which is historically, socially and doctrinally embodied about what constitutes 'the past'. As aptly argued by cultural anthropologist Talal Asad (1986), this is a 'discursive tradition' with an extended lifespan as it references the past, is embodied in the present and is projected to shape the future.[4] Tradition is therefore not simply an imitation, repetition or replication of the past, but a process, a relationship between the present and the past.

Islamic history scholar William Graham identified this relationship of connectedness or continuity with the past (typically, the Prophetic past) as 'traditionalism' or, in his own terminology, *ittisaliyya*, and identified it as not just a feature, but as a deep structure within Islam.[5] From a rather different perspective, for Asad, the starting point for an anthropological study of Islam is the concept of a discursive tradition 'that includes and relates itself to the founding texts of the Qur'an and the *Hadith*'.[6] Given that a discursive tradition is relational and interpretative, it will therefore account for, and include, variations and even rejections of 'tradition', yet, provided those 'foundations' are parts of the discourse, it will still be within the fold of Islamic tradition.[7]

Another viewpoint on the uses of the past in relation to notions of time is that propounded by Aziz al-Azmeh who identifies two registers of historicity in medieval Islamic literature. One of them he defines as typological, whereby an event, originally reported as part of a chronological sequence, becomes paradigmatic and is taken away from chronological time into the 'perspective of eternity'. Examples he provides of the appropriation of past events by myth are related to the 'origin' of some ritual practices, but also to historical events such as, for instance, the battle of Badr.[8] As will be explained in Chapter 3 of this book, this battle had both historical and typological value in the context of narratives linked to prayer leadership, *jihad* and martyrdom. The appropriation of the past is also an important link between the textual interpretation of the past and the legitimization of the scholarly elite whose remit is that of carrying out such an interpretation.

Especially relevant, but not exclusive, to Part 2 of this book on the modern cases of female imams is a further thread of enquiry as to the extent to which, and the ways in which, scriptural, normative and pre-modern sources are used in present debates. A common goal among current scholarship and activism in the fields of social justice, gender justice and human rights in Islam is to invoke and re-construct what is believed to be the 'perfect' normative Islamic past. Is the rationale behind this attempt to 'unveil' and include the past in its historical or theological context, to actualize and re-live the past or to validate and legitimize essentially modern claims? While the recourse to the ideal past has been a constant of theological discourse, its use has been channelled through established interpretative norms. Are these norms adhered to, or even referred to, in current debates on female leadership of prayer? And who are the spokespeople and actors in such a debate? In other words, who has, or claims to have, the authority to interpret and use the past?

It will be argued that authority, being relational by definition, is varied and multifaceted, and that, over the centuries, the authoritative bodies of individuals have indeed undergone adaptations and changes, which seem more pronounced since the modern era began.[9] With post-modernity, globalization, enlarged access to information and, to a more limited degree, to knowledge, new scholars and spokespersons are emerging to claim, project and exert authority, all using their own version of the past as a tool of legitimacy. The possible danger is all too clear to see; the consequences of such an enlargement of information and its users, who, lacking the linguistic, interpretative and critical tools, might indeed mistake the imagined past for the historical past. On the other hand, enlarged access has led to a much more varied array of voices contributing to the overall debate.

Even though this book is concerned with leadership of the congregational *salat*, a proviso should be included. It is not assumed that ritual group prayer is uniform among all Islamic communities throughout time, nor that the figure of the imam as prayer leader is required in all cases of congregational prayer. For some minority Muslim communities, for instance, it is the prayer reciter who embodies a leadership role as the one starting the prayer or a specific form of ritual where prescribed words or actions might not be the norm. This will be detailed particularly in Part 2 of the book . One of the aims of this book is to include, as far as possible, a cross-section of examples – and the arguments which surround them – of female ritual leadership to reflect the diversity within Islam.

Methodology, theoretical framework

A book that relies on a variety of sources and attempts to bridge the past and the present by evaluating the use of the past in subsequent and current debates necessarily requires flexible, interdisciplinary and inclusive methodological approaches. To investigate the Islamic past, textual-hermeneutical, contextual and overall historical approaches will be predominant. For present debates, a blend of discourse analysis and critical discourse analysis is used to best identify the formulation of constructed gender identities and roles, particularly leadership roles. There is constant recourse, in various sections of this book to gender discourse, which is understood as the social construction of gender identity at a particular time in history by a specific group of scholars or prominent individuals, and expressed through legal, theological and other approaches. But gender discourse does not define or restrict the discussion and interpretation of the findings. The book remains interdisciplinary as it hopes to eschew the dogmatism of paradigms and agreed-upon principles of a single discipline or research method; its underlying focus is the analysis of specific historical, religious/theological and, where applicable, social backgrounds and their developments. Scholars, chroniclers, reporters and the 'real actors' themselves, the prayer leaders, whether women or men, are all conditioned by their own environment, language and backgrounds in formulating, rejecting or exemplifying specific agendas.

In keeping with most discourse analysis approaches, this book deals with the analysis of language as text, especially in its written formulation, but also, in some cases, through speech and performance. It shares with discourse analysis core research questions, such as the relation between text and context, between discourse and power, but it also looks at the discourse of the past as constructed memory. Like critical discourse analysis, it is multidisciplinary. Unlike some positioning within critical discourse analysis, however, the writer of this book, though aware of her own academic and historical conditioning, does not take a socio-political activist stance. The aim of this work is therefore not that of 'change through critical understanding'[10] but of uncovering and re-inscribing in present debate cases and voices from the past, that were previously unknown, neglected or even deliberately overlooked. It is hoped that such uncovering will impact upon current and future discourse to evidence one or the other side of arguments about female leadership. At the very least, this work will have filled the gap of the perceived lack of instances of women as imams past and present. The inquisitive man in the *shaykh*'s retinue mentioned in the Prologue will have been given examples in this book to answer his own question.

A substantial part of this work is devoted to the scrutiny of legal positions and arguments in selected formative, post-formative and modern legal texts about women leading prayer. It is hoped that, for a more general audience, this focus will redress some preconceptions about shari'a being primarily concerned with social matters (marriage, inheritance etc.) (*muʿamalat*), and not also with religious duties (*ʿibadat*). The two are far from being divorced from one another, as will be shown throughout this study. As far as possible the aim is to include a variety of positions not only among different legal schools but also to note developments of currents within them. Selected legal texts are examined for evidence of factors such as socio/geographical attitudes, social contexts and agendas, which might have influenced or determined specific opinions. The selection criteria for such texts include the high number of citations from them in contemporary and later debates due to their being widely considered as representative of specific legal schools or, conversely, exhibiting alternative minority opinions.

Some of the angles and research questions identified and discussed by Judith Tucker in her perceptive 2008 monograph *Women, Family and Gender in Islamic Law*[11] about ways in which Islamic law has 'constructed' gender will be applied in Chapters 2 and 3 of this book. I use caution, however, in replicating modern concepts drawn from feminist legal theory to interpret pre-modern texts. One of those is Tucker's question of how the law 'discriminated' against women. Jurists did not see different rulings on the basis of gender as discriminatory, but as reflecting gender differences which they saw as sanctioned by utterances of revelation. Some jurists did show awareness of changed social and historical circumstances and identified some rulings and practices concerning women and ritual prayer during the Prophet's time as being no longer applicable in their own times. However, this awareness was used as evidence to limit the exercise of female ritual agency or leadership in congregation, not to extend it.

Another of Tucker's angles of enquiry is the process of silencing and quieting of women, which comes to the fore in this book when precedents of female ritual agency among the Prophet's wives and Companions are recalled by modern activists as examples of gender 'egalitarianism' in early Islam. Issues of female agency in modern times will also be discussed in Chapter 4, bearing similar cautionary considerations as voiced by Saba Mahmood,[12] and since shared by a number of scholars, about the risk of equating female agency with resistance to patriarchal norms. As some cases, for instance geographically specific women-only mosques, will show, female agency may instead result in endorsing and justifying patriarchal values and hierarchies, as exemplified by female exclusion or gender separation in religious ritual, rather than integrated participation in it.

The legal reasoning behind a sample of arguments for or against women leading prayer will be examined especially in Chapters 2 and 3. The level of interaction and relative authority of the factors determining legal conclusions is difficult to gauge or to generalize about. There are various factors contributing to reaching a legal opinion, such as scriptural and other textual sources, precedent, or social-communal, even individual, considerations. Are some of these factors more authoritative than others? Is the balance different in each case depending on context and circumstances? Is the understanding of what is included in 'scriptural sources' fixed and commonly agreed?[13] The issue of selectivity is of paramount importance in this study; a case in point is the specific choice by a scholar of one of different versions of a *hadith*, for example in the Umm Waraqa narrative. This is but one example of selective evidence to support a pre-determined argument.

Studies on Islamic ritual have evolved considerably over the last century and individual and congregational prayer are no exception. Critiquing the traditional Islamic theological narratives of rituals and prayer, some scholars have raised questions about whether, for instance, the five daily prayers and communal prayer were *coterminous* with the deeds and words uttered by the Prophet himself. Was there an internal development with reference to prayer as implied by the Meccan-Medinan periods, with their Qur'anic language, style, focus and themes? Was such a process even slower, extending to the time after the Prophet Muhammad?[14] Such considerations are relevant, for instance, to the understanding of the term 'imam' in the Qur'an, the meanings associated with it in the *hadith*s and when the roles and functions of the imam as prayer leader emerged and developed within the early community of Muslims.

Increasingly relevant for modern cases of women imams is the study of prayer as not only the spiritual inner act, but also as a public performance of religious leadership. Such a performance can become an innovative act in itself, through which new realities can be experienced, communicated, established and, for some, eventually validated and approved as normative. From this perspective, Judith Butler's conceptualization of gender 'performativity', whereby performance reiteration can produce norms,[15] is of some relevance, especially in Chapter 4 of this book with reference to modern case studies of women imams.

The sources and state of studies

Scriptural and exegetical sources

The most authoritative primary sources in Islamic theology and jurisprudence, the Qur'an and the *sunna*, will be introduced as being normative for individual scholars, but also as an object of critical analysis. Especially for those Qur'anic verses and *hadith*s which scholars and activists alike present as evidence in the debates on the legitimacy of female leadership, reference will be made to issues of composition, dating, redaction and interpretation; whenever possible, the latter will not be confined to Sunni exegesis.

For the *hadith*s, additional issues of reliability, authenticity and historicity will be considered. There is a substantial literature about the extent to which *hadith*s can be accepted as reliable sources, with arguments ranging from historical scepticism to exclusive reliance on the Qur'an as a source of authenticity. Asma Afsaruddin (2007) summarises the current position of 'careful and responsible scholars' as that of an overall consensus that 'the traditional historical, biographical, and prosopographical works together constitute an invaluable and indispensable source for the study of the formative period of Islam'.[16] A few decades earlier, Fazlur Rahman, while acknowledging the limitations of some *hadith*s, had carefully expressed an underlying awareness of the wide-ranging implications and consequences for the 'whole fabric of Islam' if *hadith*s were to be rejected altogether as historical sources.

To solve this potential *impasse*, scholars including F. Rahman and J. Brown distinguish between historical accuracy and legal efficacy of *hadith*s. In other words, even though a *hadith* might not have been historically accurate and, for some, was known to be 'weak', nevertheless, it could still have been recognised as an effective legal precedent. This is particularly relevant to the topic of the present book, where a number of *hadith*s which some past and present jurists deemed as weak are nonetheless widely used in Islamic legal literature. Moreover, the evaluation of their reliability is not fixed but fluctuates with time and according to individual experts and schools. Hence, the very citation of *hadith*s as precedents has historical value in as far as these *hadith*s are seen as representative of the concerns and debates taking place during a particular period of time in a specific context.[17] In this study, notwithstanding issues of authenticity, historical accuracy and reliability, weak *hadith*s can still be considered authentic records of how scholars perceived and understood the past.

The *al-Sira al-Nabawiyya* (The life and times of the Prophet Muhammad), mostly in its redaction by Ibn Hisham (d. 828 or 833), is not as legally authoritative as the previous sources, not being itself a primary source of Islamic law. Nevertheless, the *Sira* is referred to, especially in Chapter 1 with reference to the Prophet's earliest 'paradigmatic' guidance in the performance of prayer. Not unlike the above-mentioned approach to the use of *hadith*s as sources, historical significance does not equate with historical accuracy of the events as narrated or reported. Thus, the *Sira* is taken as constructed literature, reflecting the theological and communal-social concerns and understandings from the perspective of its time of origin, with its own aims and target audience.[18] What *hadith*s and the *Sira* have in common is an underlying understanding shared by Muslim scholars of approaching the early history of Islam and, for Muslim exegetes, the Qur'an itself through the framework of the life of the Prophet Muhammad.

As the issue of leadership of prayer is not explicitly treated in the Qur'an, the *tafsir* (scriptural exegesis) genre is not widely represented in this study. In some instances, however, *tafsir* works are used to clarify semantic developments of core terms such as 'imam', or to illustrate the sources of scholarly arguments, such as those on the status of Mary, the mother of Jesus, as prophet or on her performance of prayer. Moreover, relevant sources belonging to the *Asbab al-Nuzul* (occasions of Qur'anic revelation) literary genre are also employed, particularly when they refer to individual women as instrumental in prompting the revelation of some Qur'anic verses (see Qur. 33.35 in Chapter 2). As argued by a number of scholars such as Andrew Rippin, the *Asbab* works had several functions, one of which was to provide a narrative context to specific Qur'anic passages and, overall, to historicise the Qur'an by grounding it in the life of the Prophet.[19]

Legal sources

This study aims to be inclusive of a variety of sources not only from the four canonical Sunni legal schools but also from some Twelver Shi'i, Zaydi and Isma'ili legal traditions. The legal debates examined are concerned with female prayer leadership of a female-only or of a mixed congregation. One of the main concerns expressed in the legal arguments is the validity of the prayer of the person who is led by a woman acting as imam. These arguments are often intertwined with considerations about female ritual purity, but also with political or judicial female leadership, and underpinned by the interpretation of female legal capacity. Hence, specific laws on worship often overlap with laws on social interaction, one set being used to validate – or exemplify the application of – the other, and, ultimately, conveying similar theoretical frameworks of expected gender roles.

Given the extent of the period covered in this study, and the focus on the uses of the 'past', both formative and post-formative legal literature is included. The difficulty is acknowledged of pinning down the opinions and the rationale behind the statements, attributed to, or reported from, several authorities of the formative period.

Beyond the legal framework what will be presented here are also philosophical-mystical argumentations, which also contribute to the debates on female leadership of prayer. The greatest and most influential Sufi of all time, Ibn al-'Arabi (d. 1240) will be showcased as the main example of this method of argumentation.

State of studies

Works focusing on female prayer leadership, which include academic studies as well as more general arguments and counter-arguments on the topic, have multiplied exponentially since amina wadud's 2005 New York defiant prayer leadership, from the front, of a mixed congregation of men and women. Indeed, as will be detailed in Chapter 4, wadud's 2005 event was pivotal both in terms of stimulating academic and broader debates on women, leadership and governance in Islam but also in setting a precedent for the establishment of organizations and 'mosques' in different parts of the Islamic and non-Islamic world where women lead prayer.

The New York event had been 'announced' beforehand by an online article written by a then PhD candidate, Nevin Reda. Based on the analysis of Qur'anic passages, selected *hadith*s and legal arguments of some (now extinct) early Sunni schools, Reda's argument is that in early Islam there was no explicit prohibition on women leading men in prayer. For Reda, this arose during the 9th–10th century along with an increase in female segregation and withdrawal from the public space.[20]

In response to Reda's argument and wadud's prayer leadership event, a group of mainly US-based Muslim scholars uploaded online in 2005 a *Collection of Fatwas* which they present as evidence of scholarly legal consensus on the lack of permissibility of women imams of mixed prayers.[21] Their evidence is gathered from selected, yet widely circulated and well known *hadith*s and Sunni legal sources. Their arguments are only partially constructed according to classical legal and exegetical frameworks and are pervasively enriched by current political and social concerns. Most contributors not only show limited critical approach to the *hadith*s but also little awareness of contextualization of the legal sources as they refrain from any explanation of the rationale for the rulings beyond the literal meaning of their selected texts. Arguments by some individual scholars from this compilation will be analysed in the final chapter of this book, as will a contrasting view on the topic of female ritual leadership by Jamal al-Banna (d. 2013), who is chosen as one example among several current supportive voices in favour of Muslim women's ritual leadership of mixed congregations. Al-Banna opens up his critique of positions against female leadership and female authority in general within the broader issue of patriarchal readings of the text but also of current socio-political concerns and agendas behind them. Particularly relevant for this book is Banna's understanding and use of the past in current debates.[22]

The works by amina wadud have provided a theoretical and theological reference point for most current academic and broader debates on ritual female leadership in Islam, though her actions and activism have thus far constituted her greatest impact. Both will be discussed at several junctures in this book. wadud's elaboration of the hermeneutical framework of the '*tawhidic* paradigm of horizontal reciprocity' has partly informed the justification for, and application of, gender egalitarian practice in a Muslim ritual context. This *tawhidic* paradigm is wadud's (feminist) hermeneutical approach to the Qur'an which interrogates the patriarchal reading of the Qur'anic verses and proposes, instead, a gender egalitarian reading of the Qur'an. Not being specifically focused on the contextualization of individual legal or theological sources, her works are here complemented by a number of studies which apply diverse approaches to the study of gender attitudes in formative and post-formative legal rulings or theological teachings.

In the developing field of studies on Islamic ritual and piety, the work by Daniella Talmon-Heller is a successful example of interdisciplinary research combining philological, social-historical and anthropological approaches.[23] Foundational works such as those by Norman Calder and Gerald Hawting on the development of prayer constitute the theoretical basis with which to frame more specifically gender-focused studies. Among the latter are Christopher Melchert's concise study on female access to mosques, and, more recently, the aforementioned survey by Marion Katz of Sunni legal discourse about women's mosque attendance, which has brought to the fore a degree of evolution of normative assumptions about gender.

Another diachronic study, with a focus on women and group prayer in Hanafi legal rulings, is that by Behnam Sadeghi, who identifies internal developments in the justifications of those rulings but expresses scepticism about inferring from legal theory social practices or developments in gender attitudes. Sadeghi singles out legal inertia as the main factor that perpetuates the law through time and sees received laws as the starting point of juristic elaboration, the main task of which is to reconcile those laws with scriptural sources. Significant for the present study is Sadeghi's recognition of regional differences in early legal positions on women's prayer. These are evidenced and supported by the findings in this study which, unlike Sadeghi's, is not confined to one particular Sunni school, and by previous research on the origins of *hadith* transmitters of the Umm Waraqa *hadith*.[24]

A well-organized survey of post-formative Sunni legal sources is that by David Jalajel,[25] whose main aim is to determine the origins of particular legal rulings. Jalajel includes, among the factors contributing to the legal rulings against female ritual leadership, not only hermeneutical and juristic principles in conjunction with scriptural sources, but also, like Sadeghi, legal inertia, informed by a strong conservative legal tendency to preserve inherited legal rulings. Equivalent surveys of Shi'i or Sufi sources on the topic of women and prayer are still a *desideratum*, though notable ethnographic studies have been conducted featuring rituals among modern Shi'i women or their religious authority and training in seminaries in current contexts.[26] As for sources on Sufism and gender leadership, beyond specific studies on Ibn al-'Arabi's understanding of female spiritual authority, there is increasing research on current expressions of female religious leadership among Sufi women, including on ritual performance and roles.[27]

For the contemporary period a number of studies relevant to the subject of women and ritual leadership have been very useful reference points for the compilation of some sections of Chapter 4. The first are the various chapters in the edited work by M. Bano and H. Kalmbach (2012)[28] on female leadership and authority in the mosque, but also in the madrasas, with a focus on the emergence, consolidation and impact of female leadership. In it are examples of women exegetes, preachers and ritual leaders, spanning Islamic countries and Muslim minority communities in non-Islamic countries. The volume edited by Bano and Kalmbach, which includes diverse contemporary expressions of female leadership, would be useful to read alongside this book. It illustrates, through modern examples, a variety of shared issues arising from the pre-modern sources analysed in the first three chapters of this book. Specific to women mosques in China are the ethnographic monograph by Maria Jaschok and S. Jingjun (2000) and the anthropological work by Élisabeth Allès (2000),[29] while the ethnographic study by Saba Mahmood (2005) is influential for the issues it raises about non-reformist developments for women's leadership, in which feminist terminology and discourse are examined and critiqued with reference to the Egyptian women's mosque movement.

The underlying thread running throughout this book is the way in which the past has been used to justify arguments in favour of or against female leadership in prayer. Of relevance to this theme have been the seminal works by Jonathan Plumb (1969), on how authority is legitimized though the past, and Hobsbawm and Ranger (1983), on how the past can be used to forge communal, national (and in our case religious) identities. In addition to Asad's influential concept of 'discursive tradition', discussed above, and the subsequent refinements and elaborations by scholars such as Graham (1993) and Ovamir (2007), of particular significance for the present study is the work by Fentress and Wickham (1992) on how group identities structure collective memory as well as questions about a hypothetical, distinctive female view of the past.[30]

Current research on the uses of the past in an Islamic context has been recently presented in a series of stimulating colloquia as part of the wider international project 'Understanding Shari'a' (2016–18) led by Robert Gleave, which was very beneficial especially for the final chapter of this book. The project's interdisciplinary approaches and findings enriched the analysis of how various formulations of the concept of a 'perfect past' inform debates and diverse programmes of change or reform of the 'imperfect present' in Islamic legal thinking.[31]

The structure of the book

This book is subdivided into two parts: Part 1, 'The Past', comprising three chapters, and Part 2, 'The Present', comprising one long final chapter. The subdivision is mainly but not exclusively chronological, with Part 1 setting out foundational issues, scriptural narratives, sources, their contexts and relevant debates in the formative and post-formative period of Islamic history. Part 2 focuses on present examples of women imams and ensuing debates, along with an ongoing analysis of the extent to which, and the different ways in which, current debates are informed by their uses of the past as a legitimizing precedent.

Chapter 1 provides the background context for the understanding of terminology, narratives and concepts which are recurrently employed or referred to in this book. Some of the most common terms such as imam and mosque seem deceptively simple; in fact, they can be specific but also polysemic, depending on context and time. The foundational narratives, such as the account of the Prophet's performance of prayer in its development over time, along with his role as prayer instructor and then as prayer leader, constitute the basis of theological, legal and to a degree 'political' past and present debates on the legitimacy of female leadership. Such debates are informed by varied understandings and elaboration of concepts of legitimate authority and acknowledged leadership, of what makes ritual leadership legitimate and the effect of female purity on the validity of ritual leadership. It will be argued that theological and legal discussions on prayer leadership often occur in conjunction with discussions on political leadership as they share underlying discourses on hierarchical constructs based on piety and knowledge, as well as social status, tribal affiliation or genealogical origins. The prerequisites for being an imam, the imam's roles and characteristics are presented diachronically to show theological, legal, historical and socio-political developments and adaptations. The framing questions informing this chapter include whether semantic developments can be identified in some key terms linked to ritual authority; the extent to which bases and modes of ritual authority have changed over time; and whether some of the qualities or requisites for being an imam may reflect specific social, ethnic, sectarian or other contexts.

Chapter 2 focuses on the theological and legal arguments surrounding female leadership of a women-only congregation. It uses the oppositional narratives on two of the Prophet's wives – 'A'isha and Umm Salama – as a starting point for broader issues of textual interpretation, the selection and use of *hadith*s in legal sources and the legal opinions by Sunni and Shi'i scholars. The arguments presented to justify varied legal positions on women as imams are analysed with a focus on their uses of the past as a legitimizing device. The research questions of this chapter include whether oppositional narratives can be a means of portraying – or be a reflection of – community conflicts of a sectarian-political nature, and the extent of the agency of the individual women featured in these narratives in shaping their own legacy.

Chapter 3, on the debates on women leading men in prayer, introduces the cases of two women who are reported to have led men in prayer. It engages with critical analysis of *hadith*s about Umm Waraqa, as well as with historical methods, to contextualise narratives on Ghazala al-Haruriyya. Exegetical methods are linked to the construction and development of legal arguments against and those 'not against' women leading men in prayer. Framing questions that feature are: the extent to which we can assume a link between legal theories and ritual practices, as well as the significance of the narratives in identifying the different bases on which the authority of the two female 'leaders' rests.

Finally, Chapter 4 includes not only the narratives on, but also the voices of, female imams. Its sources are not confined to the literary and academic but embrace various media, including social media. The chapter begins with an overview of the developments of the status, characteristics and roles of imams in contemporary societies, particularly in those countries where Islam is a minority religion. In answer to the question of the inquisitive man at the House of Commons, the chapter evidences numerous cases of women imams of women only, or of mixed congregations, in countries such as China, across the Arabian Sea and Indian Ocean, South Africa, the USA and in Europe. The well-known figure of amina wadud, who led Friday prayers for mixed congregations, is given special prominence for the impact she has had, and continues to have, upon theological, legal and wider debates, and upon the exponential increase in academic scholarship on female leadership in Islam. wadud's 2005 prayer leadership event and her hermeneutical methods have been pivotal not only in sparking debates in very diverse circles, but also in leading to the emergence and spread of inclusive mosques in several parts of the world, where women imams lead prayer and cite her example as a significant and legitimizing precedent. The coverage of the activities of these women imams by a variety of media is also analysed in Chapter 4.

Framing questions such as 'On what bases does ritual leadership lie?' and 'How is leadership acquired, and how it is expressed?' are addressed in this chapter within the current context of women imams whose voices, unlike in the pre-modern examples, directly contribute to the formulation and response of such questions.

A sample of contemporary contrasting positions on female *imama* is discussed from the angle of the main subtext of this book: i.e. how the past is selected, adapted, reformulated and applied in current debates. Reflecting changed contexts and expressions of female religious leadership in modern times, the concluding part of the final chapter identifies and analyses four main modalities of making use of the past. Though the use of the past is shared by both modern female religious leaders, scholars and activists opposing their leadership, attention is paid to the different ways in which this is done, and the different agendas it serves.

Notes

1   Katz, Marion Holmes. *Women in the Mosque: A History of Legal Thought and Social Practice*. New York: Columbia University Press, 2014, 5.
2   Le Goff, Jacques. *History and Memory*. New York: Columbia University Press, 1992, 182 (1st edn 1977).
3   Katz, *Women in the Mosque*, 6.
4   Asad, Talal. *The Idea of an Anthropology of Islam*. Washington, DC: Center for Contemporary Arab Studies, Georgetown University, 1986, 14: 'an Islamic discursive tradition is simply a tradition of Muslim discourse that addresses itself to conceptions of the Islamic past and future, with reference to a particular Islamic practice in the present'.
5   Graham, William A. 'Traditionalism in Islam: An Essay in Interpretation'. *Journal of Interdisciplinary History* 23, 3 (1993): 495–522.

6 Asad, *The Idea of an Anthropology of Islam*, 14.
7 See in this respect the examples of two applications of Asad's argument to modernist interpreters of Islamic tradition in Ovamir, Anjum. 'Islam as a Discursive Tradition: Talal Asad and His Interlocutors'. *Comparative Studies of South Asia, Africa and the Middle East*, 27, 3 (2007), 663–7.
8 al-Azmeh, Aziz. *The Times of History: Universal Topics in Islamic Historiography*. Budapest and New York: Central European University Press, 2007, on Badr see 32, 73.
9 For a selection of scholars who have addressed issues of change and development in authoritative bodies in Islam see Zaman, Muhammad Qasim. *The 'Ulama in Contemporary Islam: Custodians of Change*. Princeton, NJ: Princeton University Press, 2002; Krämer, Gudrun and Sabine Schmidke (eds.). *Speaking for Islam: Religious Authorities in Muslim Societies*. Leiden: Brill, 2006; and Mandaville, Peter. 'Globalization and the Politics of Religious Knowledge'. *Theory, Culture & Society* 24, 2 (2007): 101–15.
10 Van Dijk, Teun A. 'Principles of Critical Discourse Analysis', *Discourse and Society* 4, 2 (1993): 252. For a comprehensive overview of the developments of discourse analysis and the features of critical discourse analysis, see Wodak, Ruth and M. Meyer. 'Critical Discourse Analysis: History, Agenda, Theory and Methodology'. In *Methods for Critical Discourse Analysis*, edited by Ruth Wodak and M. Meyer, 1–33. London: Sage, 2009.
11 Tucker, Judith E. *Women, Family, and Gender in Islamic Law*. Cambridge: CUP, 2008.
12 Mahmood, Saba. *Politics of Piety: The Islamic Revival and the Feminist Subject*. Princeton, NJ: PUP, 2005, 9, 64; also Tucker, *Women, Family, and Gender in Islamic Law*, 34.
13 For a succinct critical comment about the notion of textual sources in legal reasoning as signs which become normatively meaningful through the intervention of the jurist, see Farahat, Omar. 'Review of B. Sadeghi's The Logic of Law Making in Islam'. *Journal of Law and Religion* (2014): 3. www.academia.edu/7331550/Review_of_Sadeghis_The_Logic_of_Law_Making_in_Islam (accessed 28 May 2020).
14 For the theory that Friday prayer was instituted gradually after Muhammad's death, especially during the Umayyad period, see the early 20th century German scholar Becker, C. H. 'On the History of Muslim Worship'. In *The Development of Islamic Ritual*, edited by Gerald Hawting, 49–74. Aldershot: Ashgate, 2006, this is a translation into English of a paper delivered in 1912. Most scholars contemporary to Becker, such as Goldziher, agreed with the traditional narrative that the rituals of Islam, including prayer, had already been established during the Prophet's lifetime.
15 Butler, Judith. *Bodies That Matter: On the Discursive Limits of 'Sex'*. New York: Routledge, 1993.
16 Afsaruddin, Asma. *The First Muslims: History and Memory*. Oxford: Oneworld, 2007, xx; and Rahman, Fazlur. *Islam*. Chicago and London: University of Chicago Press, 1979, 64–7. Among others, see also Brown, Jonathan. 'Did the Prophet Say It or Not? The Literal, Historical, and Effective Truth of Hadiths in Early Sunnism'. *Journal of the American Oriental Society* 129, 2 (2009): 259–85; Sayeed, Asma. *Women and the Transmission of Religious Knowledge in Islam*. Cambridge: CUP, 2013; and Calderini, Simonetta. 'Classical Sources on the Permissibility of Female Imams: An Analysis of some Hadiths about Umm Waraqa'. In *Sources and Approaches across Near Eastern Disciplines*, edited by Verena Klemm et al., 53–70. Leuven: Peeters, 2013. Academic debates about the historicity and reliability of *hadith*s are referred to on several occasions throughout this book, though they could not be expanded, due to word limit, to a devoted section.

17 Rahman, Fazlur. *Islamic Methodology in History*. Karachi: Central Institute of Islamic Research, 1965, 44–5, 71; Brown, 'Did the Prophet Say It or Not?' 259–85.
18 For scholarly debates on the nature of *Sira* as literature and its historical value see Motzki, Harald (ed.). *The Biography of Muhammad: The Issue of the Sources*. Leiden: Brill, 2000.
19 For a critical approach to the functions of the *asbab al-nuzul* genre see Rippin, Andrew. 'The Function of *Asbab al-Nuzul* in Qur'anic Exegesis'. *Bulletin of the School of Oriental and African Studies* 51, 1 (1988): 1–20.
20 Reda, Nevin. *Women Leading Congregational Prayers*. Canadian Council for Muslim Women. [2005]. www.ccmw.com/documents/WomenLeadership.doc (accessed 31 May 2005; no longer available); and 'Women in the Mosque: Historical Perspectives on Segregation'. *American Journal of Islamic Social Sciences* 21, 2 (2004): 77–97, esp 93.
21 Assembly of Muslim Jurists of America. *A Collection of Fatwas and Legal Opinions on the Issue of Women Leading Prayer*. 5 April 2005 / 25 Safar 1426. www.abc.se/home/m9783/ir/d/fwlp_e.pdf (accessed 28 May 2020).
22 Al-Banna, Jamal. *Jawaz Imamat al-Mar'a li'l-Rijal*. Cairo: Dar al-Fikr al-Islami, 2005.
23 Among Daniella J. Talmon-Heller's publications, see *Islamic Piety in Medieval Syria: Mosques, Cemeteries and Sermons under the Zangids and Ayyūbids* (1146–1260). Leiden, Boston: Brill, 2007.
24 Sadeghi, Benham. *The Logic of Law Making in Islam: Women and Prayer in the Legal Tradition*. Cambridge: Cambridge University Press, 2013. See also Calderini, 'Classical Sources on the Permissibility of Female Imams', 53–70, esp 63–5.
25 Katz, *Women in the Mosque*; Jalajel, David Solomon. *Women and Leadership in Islamic Law: A Critical Analysis of Classical Legal Texts*. Oxford, New York: Routledge, 2017.
26 In addition to the 1965 work by Fernea, E. *Guests of the Sheik: An Ethnography of an Iraqi Village*. New York: Anchor Books, and her subsequent ethnographic studies on female ritual performances, see also Torab, Azam. *Performing Islam: Gender and Ritual in Iran*. Leiden, Boston: Brill, 2006; Deeb, Lara. *An Enchanted Modern: Gender and Public Piety in Shi'ite Lebanon*. Princeton, NJ: PUP, 2006; Kunkler, Mirjam and Roja Fazaeli. 'The Life of Two Mujtahidahs: Female Religious Authority in Twentieth-Century Iran'. In *Women, Leadership and Mosques*, edited by Masooda Bano and Hilary Kalmbach, 127–60. Leiden: Brill, 2012; Pierce, Matthew. 'Remembering Fatimah: New Means of Legitimizing Female Authority in Contemporary Shi'i Discourse'. In *Women, Leadership and Mosques*, edited by Masooda Bano and Hilary Kalmbach, 345–62. Leiden: Brill, 2012.
27 Beyond studies on Ibn al-'Arabi's interpretation of the 'feminine' and his position on female spiritual leadership – such as Shaykh, Sa'diyya. *Sufi Narratives of Intimacy: Ibn 'Arabi, Gender, and Sexuality*. Chapel Hill, NC: The University of North Carolina Press, 2012 – for Sufi women, prayer leadership and rituals see Raudvere, Catharina. *The Book and the Roses: Sufi Women, Visibility, and Zikir in Contemporary Istanbul*. London: IB Tauris, 2002; Sharify-Funk, Meena, William Rory Dickson and Merin Shobhana Xavier. *Contemporary Sufism: Piety, Politics, and Popular Culture*. London: Routledge, 2018; and the ethnographic study on Sufi *muqaddamat* in Senegal by Hill, Joseph. *Wrapping Authority: Women Islamic Leaders in a Sufi Movement in Dakar, Senegal*. Toronto: University of Toronto Press, 2018; see also interview with Senegalese academic and politician Penda Mbow in Guardi, Jolanda and Renata Bedendo. *Teologhe, Musulmane, Femministe*. Cantalupa (To): Effatà Editrice, 2009, 128–30.
28 Bano, Masooda and Hilary Kalmbach (eds.). *Women, Leadership, and Mosques: Changes in Contemporary Islamic Authority*. Leiden: Brill, 2012.

29 Jaschok, Maria and Shui Jingjun. *The History of Women's Mosques in Chinese Islam*. Richmond: Curzon, 2012 (1st edn 2000); Allès, Elisabeth. *Musulmans de Chine: Une Anthropologie des Hui de Henan*. Paris: Éditions de l'École des Hautes Études en Sciences Socials, 2000.
30 Plumb, John Harold. *The Death of the Past*. Basingstoke, New York: Palgrave/Macmillan, 2004 (1st edn 1969); Hobsbawm, Eric and Terence Ranger (eds.). *The Invention of Tradition*. Cambridge: CUP, 1983; Fentress, James and Chris Wickham. *Social Memory: New Perspectives on the Past*. Oxford: Blackwell, 1992, esp. 137–14 on women's historical consciousness.
31 Gleave, Robert (PI). *Uses of the Past: Sharia and Gender in Legal Theory and Practice*. Bergen, Exeter, Gottingen and Leiden, 2016–18. www.usppip.eu/ (accessed 14 June 2020).

Part I

THE PAST

Chapter 1

PRAYER LEADERSHIP, IMAMS AND WOMEN: DEFINING THE CONTEXTS AND SETTING THE ISSUES

Introduction

This chapter is a survey of issues in pre-modern Islam which are at the heart of debates on prayer leadership with specific reference to women. They include definitons of authority, leadership and guidance, concepts and understandings of ritual purity. The term imam is analysed in its varied uses and scriptural references and is shown, depending on context, to be used to indicate ritual but also political leadership. Some of the prerequisites for being, or being recognized as, a legitimate imam have become in time, especially in Islamic jurisprudence, increasingly complex and varied. Two of them, moral excellence (*fadila*) and precedence in submission and service to Islam (*sabiqa*) have been studied within the context of political leadership and found to be interrelated with prayer leadership. For this reason, in the present book, while the emphasis will be on prayer leadership, due consideration will also be given to the political connotation of the role of imam. The two prerequisites, of excellence and precedence, will be tested against the field of ritual leadership when analysing, in the next two chapters, the reports of Umm Salama, 'A'isha and Umm Waraqa, whom the sources present as having led prayer. A short survey of the pre-modern ideal roles of the imam will also provide the basis for comparison with modern roles to be explored in the final chapter of this book.

The framing questions for this chapter are: the extent to which any semantic developments can be identified in some key terms linked to ritual authority; and whether the bases of ritual authority have changed over time and, with them, the imam's roles, qualities or prerequisites for being an imam.

Almost three centuries after the Prophet Muhammad received his first revelation, the great Sunni Muslim historian Abu Ja'far al-Tabari (d. 923) completed his universal history. In it, he recorded in great detail the events of the Prophet's life, among them, those linked to what al-Tabari defines as the first among the duties of a Muslim: *salat* (worship, prayer). In discussing how prayer came about, al-Tabari relies on the literary accounts of the biography of the Prophet in the *Sirat al-Nabi* by Ibn Ishaq (d. 768), by using a redaction which is different from the more famous later edition by Ibn Hisham (d. 833).

Al-Tabari recounts that after the Archangel Gabriel had shown the Prophet how to worship, Muhammad 'went to Khadija and performed the ablution for her in order to show her how to purify herself for prayer, as Gabriel had shown him. She performed the ablution as he had done and then he led her in prayer [*salla biha*] as Gabriel had led him [*salla bihi*], and she followed his actions'.[1] As the first to have believed in the truthfulness of her husband's divine mission, Khadija is presented as not only the first 'convert' to Islam but also the first believer to be instructed on how to pray and be led in prayer by the Prophet. The ritual requirements for her worship and the manner of its performance are thus identical to those of the Prophet himself. Hence, not only the ritual 'duty' of worship, but also its performance, are shown to be the same for all believers, irrespective of gender. While the pre-eminence of Khadija's character is uncontested among Muslim scholars past and present, her exemplary role as worshipper has not been sufficiently explored. Though the above account could be viewed as an example of 'gender equality' in ritual performance at the inception of Islam, it could, however, also be reflecting a hierarchical model in ritual leadership. God (through Its genderless angel) instructs and leads the Messenger, a man, who, in turn, instructs and leads Khadija, a woman, his wife.

The above account sets the stage to address the following questions: in which contexts do we find women singled out in the act of prayer in early Islam? To what extent have historians and scholars, reporting about prayer in early Islam, included the religious, political and social context in which that prayer was taking place? And more specifically, what is meant or understood by ritual leadership? Is it a form of instruction and of guidance on the part of the 'leader', an imitation by the person being led, as described above in the *Sira* account? Are the rules of leading prayer dependent upon specific spatial, social and other factors or are they beyond these variables? The answers to these questions will provide the background to Chapter 2 on pre-modern debates on the permissibility of women leading women, as well as to Chapter 3 about women leading men. They will be revisited in Chapter 4, when discussing the uses of past precedents in current debates on female *imama*.

Prayer and women: Purity and leadership

Ritual purity has been associated with Islamic prayer from its very inception. The Qur'anic references to ritual purity have been typically linked, among other verses, to the Medinan verse 4.43, 'Do not approach prayers … if you are in a state of major impurity (*junub*) … until you have fully washed', as well as 5.6, 'when you are about to pray, wash your face, and your arms … and if you are in a state of *junub*, purify yourselves'. Thus, it could be deduced that being in a state of ritual purity is foremost among the conditions for the prayer to be valid for the worshipper. In works of *tafsir*, Qur'anic verses relating to purity (*tahara*) are subject to multiple interpretations about the meanings of purity, inclusive of physical, ritual and ethical purity, which are not exclusive of one another, but rather all-encompassing.²

That *tahara* is a pre-eminent element for the validity of prayer is indicated by the priority that the topic is given in classical treatises of Islamic jurisprudence where issues of practices of ritual purification appear as the first subject matter in the section on obligatory acts of devotion to God. As the jurist al-Shafi'i put it, all devotional acts are enabled by *tahara* and can be summarized into two main concepts: cleanliness and worship.³ The pre-eminence of purity in the context of ritual prayer is also reflected in historical and literary narratives, as exemplified by al-Tabari's recourse to the *Sira* to explain the origin of prayer in Islam. There, the need for purity comes as part of an instruction by no less than the Archangel Gabriel.

Purity

Purity is defined as the absence of its counterpart: impurity. Different causes for impurity can lead to a state of minor or major impurity. Muslim jurists posited that certain bodily functions, such as urination, defecation or, for instance, touching a person of the opposite sex, usually result in minor impurity, which can be rectified through a minor ablution (*wudu'*). Other bodily emissions, like semen or menstrual blood, as well as sexual activity, will lead to a state of major impurity which needs to be cleansed through a complete ablution (*ghusl*). While the requirements for purity are gender neutral, two of the causes of major impurity are specific to women: menstruation (*hayd*)⁴ and post-partum bleeding. Neither of these causes, however, imply a notion of substantive impurity or a contagious state.⁵ In legal literature the ritual restrictions for a menstruating or bleeding woman are not confined to prayer (or touching and reciting the Qur'an), but extend to entering a mosque, and other rituals such as fasting and performing a valid *hajj*.⁶

Theologically, purity laws, with reference to prayer, can be interpreted as an expression of the believer's obedience to divine instructions, and as a way of honouring the divine by approaching its message and the rituals it enjoined in a purified state. A socio-anthropological understanding of purity laws focuses on the demarcation of communal identity, specifically among early Muslims vis-à-vis non-Muslims. In attempting to explain the common denominator among Muslim scholars on the causes of impurity, Kevin Reinhart, who examined and adapted Mary Douglas's anthropological approach to purity laws, identified it as loss of bodily control, of which menstruation and bleeding are pertinent examples.⁷ However, cultural anthropologist R. Gauvain counterargues that this would not explain the cases in which, during an extended loss of control caused for example by illness, impurity laws are lifted and the sick person is seen as pure and able to perform a valid prayer. Accordingly, a woman with prolonged bleeding could still perform a valid prayer, enter the mosque and so on.⁸

Most scholars of Islamic ritual laws concur that early Islamic literature does not show an emphasis on substantive impurity, that is, no human being, irrespective of gender, origin or status, is considered as inherently impure. Furthermore, some would argue that, in harmony with the theological understanding of human beings as God's creatures and thus, in principle, partaking the divine covenant, purity laws in early Islam could be understood as 'highly universalistic and egalitarian'.[9] This Islamic position, however, is far from being uncontested, as it varied over time on the basis of doctrinal, political and other considerations. According to several Shi'i Imami scholars, for example, an illegitimate child (*walad zina*) is in a state of physical and moral impurity and, as such, within the ritual context of prayer, cannot lead prayer.[10] As far as gender is concerned, even though, as mentioned above, purity laws are overall gender neutral, a trace of gender-based impurity can be detected in the case of the urine of a baby boy which 'is considered less impure than that of an infant female'.[11] It is open to interpretation whether this example of gender-based substantive impurity is the result of the influence of the so-called *Isra'iliyyat* literature (i.e. narratives derived from other religions) on the development of Islamic legal thought and practice, or an expression of the alignment of Islam with the patriarchal nature of other Near-Eastern religions.

Nevertheless, though the purity laws system is not free from hierarchical stratifications based on socio-cultural and other constructs, it can be stated that, with a few exceptions, the main principles of ritual purity are, as a whole, not explicitly or predominantly gender hierarchical.

Leadership

The same cannot be said of the second element of *salat* which was highlighted in al-Tabari's account of the Prophet and Khadija's first prayer: guidance or instruction on how to pray. It is not clear when this ritual instruction came to be considered as prayer leadership. Al-Tabari also cited other early narratives that show us the Prophet, at particular times, facing the Ka'ba, being joined by a man and by a woman, Khadija, and, as he bows, they bow, as he stands, they stand.[12]

Muslim scholars elaborated upon the occasions in which a prayer leader was required and provided a more defined shape for the figure of the imam. When they did come to specify the prerequisites and characteristics of being an imam, the shift of emphasis was to move decisively towards the social, political, moral and legal spheres. It seems that within this more defined legal context, a gender hierarchical framework gradually comes to the fore. In theory, as shall be seen, there is evidence from the *hadiths* and early legal literature of a selective yet egalitarian principle for the choice of an imam, based on knowledge (of the Qur'an, of prayer rituals) and on personal piety, but this was in time subsumed, with very few exceptions, under an increasingly complex system of requirements which reflect social and other hierarchies.

The definition and understanding of leadership in its various facets have occupied Muslim scholars and scholars of Islam for centuries.[13] The nature of the sources used and specific perspectives in interpreting them may result in reaching different conclusions or emphasizing one feature of leadership over others. For instance, Roy Mottahedeh, in his seminal work on leadership in early Islam based on Sunni and Shi'i sources, has identified different 'strengths' of bonding and loyalty, of which the strongest, he argues, is the leadership of family or tribal bonds based on *nasab* (genealogy) and *hasab* (noble descent, merit), while leadership based on knowledge and piety, though commanding respect, he believes form 'weaker' bonds.[14] Thus, the bases for legitimate ritual leadership in prayer, not unlike political leadership, fluctuated between these weaker and stronger bonds. Scholars like Asma Afsaruddin also identified, during the period immediately following the Prophet's death, contrasting 'traditional' and 'egalitarian' tendencies with reference to the debate on the most excellent leader of the Islamic polity. The introduction of categories of excellence such as piety and knowledge (of the Qur'an) were quite 'subversive' of the pre-Islamic tribal notions of leadership.[15] Subsequent developments, especially during the Umayyad dynasty, however, swung the pendulum towards the deep-rooted tribal and genealogical bonds.

Arabic terms to designate leadership are numerous, neither static nor fixed, and, at times, presuppose categories which are not directly equivalent; for instance, the distinction between authority (*auctoritas*) and power (*potestas*), which has long occupied a number of Western medievalists. Scholars of Islam generally, but somehow artificially, agree that the term *siyada* refers to personal authority, where moral, family/tribal status and charisma play an important role. As far as women are concerned, there are references to individuals being addressed as *sayyida*, they are usually free, or freed, women who may also be in positions of influence, even power. The term *mulk*, on the other hand, is usually associated with political power, one which demands obedience and which is accompanied by command (*amr*). *Mulk* is therefore a term predominatly used to indicate political rule, and, as far as women are concerned, there are various examples of queens and political leaders in Islamic history. Scripturally, the most prominent *malika* (queen) in the Qur'anic narrative is the Queen of Sheba (Qur. 27.23, 'and I found a woman ruling over them (*tamlikuhum*)'). Her power is acknowledged by the leaders of her community, whom she consults before issuing commands, and who state that while they have (military) power, she has the power to command (Qur. 27.33, 'we are endowed with power (*quwwa*) and mighty prowess in war, but the command (*amr*) is yours'). Islamic medieval exegetical tradition did not show much interest in elaborating upon the queen's leadership competence and in making her a paradigmatic figure. This could be either because the Qur'anic narrative focuses on her status prior to her acceptance of Islam or, possibly, because of scripturalist traditions against the political leadership of women.[16]

A more encompassing type of leadership is that expressed by the term *imama*. Some Muslim scholars, past and present, distinguish between the lesser and the greater *imama*: the former (*imama sughra*) refers to ritual prayer leadership, while the latter (*imama kubra*) refers to political leadership as represented by the caliphate. As we will see in the case of a female figure discussed in Chapter 3, though they are quite distinct forms of leadership, prayer and political leadership have more in common than is at first assumed.

In this regard, an example of the link between the two types of *imama* is the well-known narrative found in several *hadiths*, and widely cited in Sunni literature, about Abu Bakr, the first caliph to succeed the Prophet in leading the Muslim community. It is reported that the Prophet, in the course of his fatal illness, delegated

Abu Bakr to lead the people in prayer.[17] This, and other signs of respect shown towards Abu Bakr, for later Sunni Muslims single out Abu Bakr as the intended successor 'chosen' by the Prophet. To extoll the excellence of early Companions may serve, by some parties, to show their legitimacy as community leaders. While Abu Bakr is presented by some as having been the first male to have accepted Islam, for others this priviledge goes to 'Ali b. Abi Talib, the Prophet's cousin and son-in-law. While Abu Bakr was reported as being invested with ritual leadership, during the same year, 'Ali is said to have recited to the pilgrims at Mina the first seven verses of *sura al-Tawba* and, previously, to have been the first man to pray with the Prophet.[18]

The disputes between the Companions over the successorship to the Prophet are therefore expressed on several fronts in terms of political, ritual and eventually genealogical legitimacy, all of which may be interpreted as retrospective claims of their pre-eminence at the time of the Prophet. Such a link between the two *imama*s will continue[19] among the caliphs of some early dynasties who presided over the Friday prayer and/or delivered the sermon (*khutba*). In such cases, leadership of Friday prayer reflected political leadership. Of the two, political leadership is pre-eminent according to the majority of legal scholars, who would regard as valid even the prayer led by a sinful caliph or ruler, and this for the sake of social and communal cohesion as well as political stability.[20] *Hadith* narratives, on the other hand, are concerned with emphasizing personal probity, piety and knowledge as characteristics of the ideal prayer leader.

Because leadership, unlike enforced power, is reciprocal, in the sense that it needs to be recognized as legitimate by the individuals and the community, it is woven into the social, legal and political structure in a given time and place. Hence, as far as female leadership is concerned, its expressions, meanings and understandings are the product of a given context which, in most cases, is formulated through an explicitly and predominantly hierarchical gender discourse. Scholarly, theological and legal discussions on prayer leadership are therefore never fully divorced from political, social and legal norms. As far as the choice of a prayer leader is concerned, and in view of the link between the *imama sughra* and *imama kubra*, there are considerations of political precedence whereby the ruler, the judge and other figures in authority have precedence in ritual leadership. Social considerations are also influential, and are a reflection of a hierarchical social structure that sees free Muslim men being in a position of precedence when compared to, for instance, slaves. Legally, the hierarchical structure is based on legal capacity, both as a theoretical category but also as the capacity of individuals to act; hence, the legal discourse on ritual leadership will take due consideration of categories such as mental sanity, maturity, freedom, and, of course, gender.

Communal prayer: Leadership and the space

Why and when is a prayer leader required? The Qur'an is not explicit about whether the prayer should be led or not, but sanctions group prayer in 'the day of assembly'. Qur'anic exegetes and Muslim scholars agree that communal prayer also became an obligation for Muslims during the first years of the Medinan period. Theologians and historians, including al-Tabari, place the happening of the first collective prayer, led by the Prophet in the presence of his Companions, in Medina, during the first year of the Hijra, and go as far as calling it the first 'Friday prayer'.[21] There are differing accounts about the identity of the first person who led a group in prayer in Medina. On the basis of one report in Ibn Sa'd (d. 845), it was a little-known Companion, a certain Salim Mawla Abi Hudhayfa who, on account of his knowledge of the Qur'an, led the earliest migrants to Medina in prayer, before the Prophet himself reached the city.[22]

From some early narratives, it appears that the minimum number for believers to be considered a congregation and to need an imam to lead them is just two: one who leads and one who is led. Indeed, a *hadith* variously attributed to the Prophet or to one of his prominent descendants, Ja'far al-Sadiq (d. 765), states that two believers constitute a congregation.[23] For all legal authorities, the presence of the imam as a ritual officiant is a necessary requirement for congregational prayer.

In sections on prayer in *hadith* collections, in *fiqh* works and in prayer manuals we can detect a clear distinction between leading prayer in a congregational mosque (*masjid jami'a*), in a private mosque, and at home, or as a visitor in somebody else's house. Of great consequence is also the type of prayer an imam is to lead. That can be one of the five compulsory daily prayers (*fara'id*), which can be performed on one's own or in congregation, the optional communal prayers (*nawafil*), such as the prayers of the two festivals ('*id*), or the compulsory Friday prayer (*jum'a*). The attendance of the latter, normatively in a mosque, was to become a duty for all Muslims, with the exception, according to legal scholars, of women, minors, the sick and slaves. Hence, Friday prayer and its leadership are strictly associated with the body politic, to which the above-mentioned categories of excluded people do not belong. A socio-historical interpretation of the exclusion of these groups considers the early forms of Friday prayer as having been primarily a socio-political event, which free men were compelled to attend as a way of 'showing one's allegiance'.[24]

With the establishment of dynastic powers in the Islamic lands, Friday prayer became more and more linked to polity and, as a consequence, the person leading it needed to exhibit specific characteristics, especially if the prayer took place in mosques. For example, during the 'Abbasid rule, the Iraqi jurist Abu Hasan al-Mawardi (d. 1058) made it sufficiently clear that in the case of a 'government' mosque (*masjid sultani*), its imam needed to meet a set of specifications that were required for the post as *he* was appointed by the sovereign or ruler. The connection to broader governance and relevant regulatory constructs of the body politic therefore affect not only the power balance of who chooses or appoints the imam – namely the ruler rather than the congregation – but also of the shaping of power relations to conform to hierarchically defined gender roles. As will become more evident throughout the course of this chapter, as the mosque as a place of communal prayer becomes increasingly institutionalized, the role that women play in it was to become less visible and more detached from the official and public sphere.

The concept of a 'government mosque' is a historical development and could not be more far removed from the original context of the location of prayer during the time of Muhammad. In the Qur'an, the use of the term *masjid* (lit. a place of prostration) as a place of worship is mainly non-specific; yet, it is also inclusive, as it can apply to pre-Islamic and Islamic, but also non-Islamic, places of worship.[25]

Historically, it has been assumed that the model for all mosques was sanctioned/legally framed on the authority of the *hadith* and portayed in accounts from the *Sira* genre centred upon Muhammad's simple house in Medina and, specifically, its courtyard. As an open space clear of objects, cattle and tombs,[26] such a courtyard was reportedly used for various functions, from religious rituals to mundane communal meetings. In Mecca, Muhammad and his early Companions would have prayed wherever they could, in private houses or, at times, in public areas where passers-by were able to see them.

An illustration of the latter is the account of the Prophet in Mecca praying at dawn facing the Ka'ba with 'Ali on his right and Khadija behind them.[27] Irrespective of its historical authenticity, such an account evokes Prophetic statements reported in several *hadith*s that 'the whole earth has been made for you a *masjid*' so, 'wherever you are when the call of prayer comes, pray there, for that is a *masjid*'.[28]

The traditional understanding of the Prophet's 'house' in Medina as a prototype for future 'mosques' has not gone unchallenged. In recent times historians and art historians have joined forces to revisit the notion of the house of the Prophet being a mosque from their distinctive perspectives. Some contend that the house of the Prophet in Medina, built along the lines of Arabian private dwellings, was no more than a 'private house'. Others consider the Prophet's house to have been built as a place to accommodate religious rituals from the outset even though it could not be strictly identified as a mosque in the later meaning of the term.[29] Drawing mainly on the *hadith* reports and the Qur'an, E. S. Ayyad (2013) critiqued the restrictive 'House of the Prophet' theory. He argued that the Prophet's mosque in Medina did start as a place of worship; and that the non-religious functions, reported to have occurred in it, were consistent with the Prophetic times; while it is only subsequently, over at least a century, that a degree of 'specialization' occurred in the use of the mosque, mainly but not exclusively as a place of religious performance.[30]

In Medina, beside the 'mosque' and multi-functional quarters of the Prophet, built in a land originally owned by the Banu al-Najjar, there are references to places of worship (*masjid*) in the Companions' houses, such as that of Ibn 'Abbas, and also to tribal enclosures such as the mosque of the Banu Salima or the Banu Haritha, or prayer areas (*musalla*) probably in open spaces. There are reports that during the Prophet's time there were nine mosques in Medina, or even as many as the tribes present there.[31] References to the existence of tribal mosques till after the time of the Prophet is evidence of the fluidity of boundaries in late antiquity, and therefore in early Islam between ethnicity and religion. Taking into consideration the broader Near-Eastern milieu, scholars such as Michael Penn argue that religion and ethnicity, specifically during the 7th century, were inextricably linked, or as he puts it 'religious practice was often a primary marker of ethnic identity, and race a primary marker of religion'.[32] That tribal identity was maintained in early Islam finds expression in the building and the permanence of these tribal mosques. This will be relevant in Chapter 3 when discussing the sphere of authority of Umm Waraqa who led in prayer the people of her *dar* (house, tribe).

The earliest sources referring to the mosque of the Prophet and other early mosques are dated to over a hundred years after the time of Muhammad, and retrospectively describe architectural mosque features which in fact developed during the Umayyad dynasty.[33] Among such features, the 9th century historian al-Baladhuri cites an earlier source claiming that two innovations were introduced in the mosque of Basra, Iraq, during the first years of the Umayyads: a rudimentary minaret and an enclosure (*maqsura*) for the imam (or possibly the ruler?).[34] It has been argued that the *masjid* as a place of prayer also became less inclusive, possibly since the late Umayyad or early 'Abbasid times, as a reflection of an increased sense of *haram* (i.e. something sacred to which access is forbidden) not only in terms of exclusion of access to non-Muslims, but also of individuals deemed to be impure, who were therefore not allowed for ritual prayer in a mosque.[35] Attributions and understandings of what consistutes *haram* in relation to a place of worship are problematic and need to be examined on their own individual merit. The risk is to either project back in time and fix what was, in fact, a developing communal identity; to set apart places as being permanently special; or to remove from individual believers the significance they attributed to objects and locations. The quality of 'sacredness' can be contested by opposing groups, but can also be fluid and temporary, as is the case for a prayer area like a *musalla*, or a purpose-built mosque where, outside of prayer times, areas could be used for social and even commercial activities.[36]

Thus, the meaning of the term 'mosque', its physical shape and functions, are open to interpretation. These underwent changes over time which reflected diverse contexts, from an informal and multifunctional place of gathering at specific times of prostration, to the material space which reflected and asserted the ruler's political authority and legitimacy. This is no secondary matter; when for example a 9th century scholar reports that a female companion of the Prophet 'built a mosque' in her house with his permission,[37] it is essential to put this assertion in its appropriate context: was the scholar using the term as understood during his own times or during the times of the Prophet? The same contextual approach should be used in current studies on the importance of collective memory, when applied to the understanding of the past. While these studies are sociologically useful in examining communities and their developing sense of identity, they may risk leaving out altogether a critical and discriminatory approach to sources regarding their historicity, authenticity and the writer's context.

The imam as prayer leader

Imam: What is in a term? Terminology, narratives and contexts

Theoretical positions on the legitimacy of Muslim women leading prayer, as well as narratives about, and cases of, women as imams constitute the main subject of this book. The term imam is deceptively straightforward, with its original meaning of 'the one who is in front (*amama*)'. In fact, the term exhibits diverse, nuanced and polysemic connotations. When referring to women, as will be discussed, it can be both limiting and generic. While there are at present Muslim women leading prayer who are not defined as imams, there are also women performing most, if not all, of the roles of an imam, who are defined, or choose to define themselves, as chaplains, preachers, missionaries, *'alimas* and more. Even though in the course of the book, examples of women in these roles will be mentioned, a full discussion of this category of female leadership will not be included. In addition to the ritual context, the term imam can be used in an ethical-religious sense to refer to an exemplar, somebody to be imitated. Imam, especially within certain minority branches of Islam, particularly Shi'is, is also used to indicate a leader who is considered to be the legitimate spiritual and political guide of the Muslim community. More generally imam is also an honorific term to indicate an authority, especially a legal one, or a knowledgeable person.

In its singular or plural form (*a'imma*), the term 'imam' occurs in the Qur'an a dozen times, ten of which are in the Meccan *suras*, with varying meanings; hence the term is liable to different interpretations and translations. From the sense of being foremost, imam can indicate in the Qur'an a 'guide, model', applicable for example to scripture, such as Moses' book of guidance (Qur. 11.17). More frequently, it refers to a person, a 'leader' in religion and faith, a model, such as the figure of Abraham in Qur. 2.124, 'a leader (*imam*) of humankind'. Only in two Qur'anic verses (28.41 and 9.12) does the term refer to negative leaders, the 'imams of *kufr* (disbelief)'.[38] In half of the Qur'anic passages, the word indicates divinely inspired religious and community leaders, foremost among them the Prophet Abraham, Moses or the Patriarchs among the Israelites (21.73, 32.24). It is no surprise, in view of the commonly agreed Meccan chronology[39] of most of the relevant verses in which the term occurs [and the development of the communal prayer in Medina], that in none of these occurences in the Qur'an does imam specifically indicate a prayer leader.

Muhammad as a model of prayer leadership

According to one story reported in the *Sira* by Ibn Hisham, the first instructor of prayer is the Archangel Gabriel.[40] The angel is described as having joined Muhammad for two days, during which *salat* was divinely prescribed as a religious obligation. The angel also showed the Prophet how to perform ritual ablution before prayer and then prayed with him. In turn, Muhammad performed ablution and prayer in front of his wife Khadija, who imitated his gestures and 'prayed his prayer'.[41] Muhammad is therefore portayed as the first 'human' prayer instructor or guide. This story serves the function of explaining in narrative terms how Muhammad came to perform what would later develop into the 'Islamic ritual of prayer'. If not authoritative in the legal sense, or historically accurate and dependable, nevertheless, the *Sira* genre and the stories in it became culturally relevant as sources of information and inspiration for historians and Muslims in general. Thanks to his access to an angelic instructor, and his status as a divinely chosen prophet, Muhammad's ritual actions thus became the model and guide for all future performances and leadership of prayer.

Not only were Muhammad's gestures and timing of prayer as contained in the *Sira* and *hadith* literature to become normative, his conciseness and light touch in prayer ritual also became exemplary.[42] These accounts of the divine revelatory command to pray, along with the direct or mediated instructions on how to perform prayer have a theologico-doctrinal aim: to present the 'Islamic' form of prayer as original, stemming from the divine and not mediated through, or indebted to, prayer rituals as practised by other religious communities of the time.[43] The existence of 'other' rituals and places of worship is acknowledged both in the Qur'an and the *hadith*s, nevertheless divine revelation conveyed through the Prophet is seen, theologically, as having reaffirmed prayer in its 'original and pristine' form. Historically, the modality of prayer in Islam is often linked to the religious and cultural context of late antiquity along with local Arabian practices.[44]

*Hadith*s and theological texts show the progressive and changing nature and modalities of prayer during the Prophet's lifetime. Indeed a gradual shift can be noted from the Prophet's personal prayer to a more public and eventually communal prayer, the latter evolving in ritual complexity and organization in Medina around the time of the Battle of Badr.[45] It can therefore be assumed that it was during the Medinan period that the specific use of the term *imam* as instructor, perhaps leader of communal prayer among Muslims, began to gain currency.

In Sunni *hadith* collections, from the 9th century onwards, the term imam is used both to refer to a (political) leader, whose main characteristic is that of being a just and virtuous guide[46] for his community (*imam qawmihi*), as well as to a prayer leader. The use of the term imam with the latter meaning is widespread in the *hadith* collections, with hundreds of narratives devoted to the imam's ritual actions and gestures, his physical look, attire, moral characteristics, health, his location in the mosque, in the *musalla*, or other places for prayer or ritual performances, and, above all, his actions before, during and after the performance of the ritual prayer: *salat*.

The figure of the imam in history

It is in relation to political leadership that the term 'imam' came to be primarily used in the first centuries of Islam in a variety of sources. After a series of disputes, the choice of successor after the Prophet to lead the emerging Muslim community fell onto Abu Bakr who, as already mentioned, the Prophet had previously delegated to lead prayer.[47] There is overall consensus in the sources that during the period of the first four caliphs, known as al-Rashidun, and the first Islamic dynasty that followed immediately after them, the Umayyads, the caliph was expected to lead the Friday congregation prayer as imam in the main capital city mosque. During the 'Abbasid dynasty, historical sources indicate that this role was also devolved to regional city governors and other officials. In time, such devolution of ritual leadership went even further, as later testified by the Mamluk historian al-Maqrizi who, with reference to Egypt, identifies the year 856 as the date when the ruler led prayer for the last time.[48] During the 9th century the caliph also gradually stopped delivering the Friday sermon and he was replaced in this capacity by a body of appointed professional preachers or *khatibs*.[49] By the 11th century, the Iraqi jurist al-Mawardi was presenting the nomination of the imam at the central mosques as being a prerogative of the caliph or, in his absence, of high officials such as the vizier or the judge (*qadi*). Over time, in smaller mosques, the community had a decisive role in choosing the imam: the local congregation appointed the imam on the basis of the preference expressed by the majority.[50] The above statements, however, do not account for the variety of the, by now, politically fragmented Islamic world where, for instance, competing leaders did exercise direct ritual authority in their domains, such as the Shi'i Isma'ili Fatimid Imam-caliphs in North Africa and Egypt (909–1171) who are reported to have led prayer on specific occasions.

The office of imam leading Friday prayer in a main congregational mosque thus came to be seen as linked to the ruler of a given time and place.[51] The reasoning behind this link is best expressed by al-Mawardi who, against the backdrop of political instability due to competing Sunni 'Abbasid and Shi'i Buyid and Fatimid dynasties, wrote the treatise that was to become the benchmark text on the Sunni Islamic theory of governance: the *Ordinances of Government*. In it, al-Mawardi presented the caliphate, which he defines as 'the supreme leadership, or imamate', as being the ideal form of Islamic rule to implement Islamic law. As the caliphate is central to the whole political and religious system, al-Mawardi considers all the other offices, including that of prayer leader, as a reflection and an expression of the supreme authority of the caliph himself.

Hence, the imam of the congregational mosque, al-Mawardi argues, is to be appointed by the caliph, whose prerogative it is to officially invest his authority in his deputies.[52] In other words, by having the right to appoint the imams of the government-funded mosques, the caliph could give legitimacy to the holder/s of the office of imam and, in turn, control religious collective worship through their leaders.

The link between political and religious authority had acquired an altogether more encompassing significance among the Shi'is. For them, the term 'imam' (henceforth Imam with a capital 'I') holds the dual connotation of political and spiritual guide of the community of believers. They believe the Imam's leadership to have been spiritually transmitted by appointment, within the same bloodline, on the part of the previous Imam, and conveyed through charisma.

By the 9th century, the doctrine of the infallibility of the Imam developed among Shi'i scholars.[53] Due to his status, the Imam was believed to be ultimately the only rightful leader of congregational prayer. However, only 'Ali, whom the Shi'is consider to be the first Imam, historically held the full political authority and religious leadership. For those Shi'is who came to be known as Twelvers, because of their belief in an uninterrupted line of twelve present and visible Imams, the Imams could nominate a deputy to lead the Friday prayer. However, Twelver Shi'i scholars believe that, in 941, the twelfth Imam went into occultation, thus considering the Imam as still present but no longer visible. As a result, they formulated and expressed contrasting opinions with regards to the status of the Friday prayer itself and the legitimacy of its prayer leader.[54] In contrast, among Sevener Shi'is, particularly the Isma'ilis, religious and visible history converged again during the Fatimid era, when the Fatimid Imam-caliphs did lead congregational prayers or appointed prayer leaders as their representatives.

For other early minority Muslim groups such as the Kharijis, rather than 'prayer leader', the term Imam predominantly referred to an 'elected' guide, whose authority was sealed by an act of allegiance (*imam al-bay'a*). For them the Imam was, concurrently, the military, legal and religious leader of the community. The possible convergence between politico-military *imama* and ritual leadership will be analysed in Chapter 3 in the case of Ghazala, a 7th century Iraqi Kariji woman. It is in the role as prayer leader to a congregation that the term 'imam' will be principally used throughout this book. The function of the imam, however, cannot be restricted to just prayer leader, as it will be shown that the varied roles the imam may have held, and may still hold, are dependent upon historical, social, geographical, theological and political contexts.

Roles of the imam

Some of the roles commonly associated with being an imam can be inferred from statements reported in the *hadiths*, such as 'the imam is appointed so that he may be followed',[55] or more complex ritual-ethical statements like 'the imam is a *junna*[56] (a shield) for the believer', so that each gesture of the imam during prayer is to be copied. More doctrinal-ethical assertions include 'your imam is your mediator/intercessor (*shafi'*) with Allah'; 'do not make a fool or a sinful person (*fasiq*) your intercessor',[57] or similarly 'the imam of the people is the one who ushers them into the presence of Allah'.[58] The above statements imply that given his intermediary role as advocate of the believer in front of Allah, the chosen imam should be the best possible person in the community. In both classical legal and *hadith* literature there are numerous assertions about the imam's main role being that of leading a congregation, however small, in prayer, especially for the five daily *salats*, the Friday midday prayer and the other congregational prayers such as those performed at festivals (*'id*).

There has been disagreement as to whether the same person could act as prayer leader for the five daily prayers and the Friday prayer. For the imam of the *jum'a* and the *'id* prayers, an additional role, especially for smaller mosques with no allocated separate preacher (*khatib*), would be to read the sermon, which carries with it religious-political implications. If the imam of a mosque was also its preacher, in this role he was the representative of the political leaders of the *umma* – their names being mentioned after the sermon as an expression of legitimization of their power – and his main concerns, reflected in his sermon, would be to enhance the sense of identity of the *umma* and work towards its unity.[59] If, on the other hand, the roles of imam and of preacher were to be held by different individuals, then the imam of the mosque was usually responsible for appointing the mosque staff, such as the preacher, the prayer caller or muezzin, the treasurer and the other permanent or temporary staff.

The imam of a mosque should therefore act in a manner which is appropriate to his status as an example to the community, and model his style to that of the

Prophet. An imam who leads the congregation in prayer in the correct manner and at the precise time will reap rewards, as will the people being led. But he alone is responsible for any delays, faults and lacunae in his prayer leading.[60] If the desirable characteristics of knowledge of the Book, of the *sunna* and of *fiqh* were all present in one person, the imam would also have the role of religious/theological and, in some cases, legal expert within the community.[61]

How to choose an imam

The numerous examples referred to earlier show that an imam can be chosen by Prophetic instruction, by appointment, by consensus on the basis of the person's knowledge, by precedence in faith and 'conversion' or because of personal charisma. Appointment and recognition of personal qualities invest the imam with an authority which provides him with the legitimacy to lead. However, this is so only if shared with, and eventually acknowledged by, the community being led. This is indeed a crucial element in the understanding of the relationship between the imam and the congregation. On the one hand there is evidence, in theory and practice, of a hierarchical framework in the appointment of the imam as prayer leader, especially in larger urban mosques. On the other hand, it is the community itself who may decide, by consensus, who their prayer leader should be. This makes the community not a passive recipient of a leadership externally conferred, but rather a group with agency. An example of the importance of communal agreement is provided by the Shi'i scholar al-Muhaqqiq al-Hilli (d. 1277). According to him, if the person who has precedence in being the imam is not available, then the best to lead is 'the one whom the congregation puts forward', or the one on whom the congregation reaches its consensus. Should there be any disagreement among the members of the congregation, the imam should be selected on account of 'qualifications', such as proficiency in Qur'anic recitation, knowledge of *fiqh*, and so on.[62]

Therefore, while on the one hand, ritual leadership in prayer is inextricably linked to broader, more encompassing theories and practices of 'governance', reflective of accepted norms of authority, on the other, there is a fluid relationship between the imam-leader and the community being led. As will be shown in Chapter 4 of this book, today the choice of the imam by community consensus is particularly relevant in mosques in the West. There, in some 'inclusive mosques', imams are chosen through a process that consistently ensures a fair representation of the diversity within the congregation in terms of gender, Islamic denomination and geographical/cultural origins.

The imam's qualities and requirements: Preliminaries

To identify the qualities of the imam as prayer leader is important for two main reasons: to ensure the selection of the best representative of the congregation, and to ensure the validity of the prayer of those being led by the imam. The already mentioned 10th century historian al-Tabari, well into his old age, recollected that by the age of seven he had memorized the whole Qur'an and that, at the age of eight, he led people in prayer for the first time.⁶³ In fact, al-Tabari's assertion could have raised more than an eyebrow among most legal scholars of his time, who considered the prayer led by a minor to be invalid for the people being led.

Muslim legal scholars commonly agreed that majority is attained at the moment of puberty. This brings discernment which is a necessary condition for an individual to fulfil the required religious obligations. Consequently, Islamic schools of law did indicate the attainment of majority as a requirement for being the imam of a group prayer, with shades of interpretation concerning the minimum age (or physical signs) at which such majority was deemed to be reached. For example the Shafi'i school accepted the validity of a prayer led by a *mumayyiz* (a minor of discerning age), a category in which, presumably, an eight-year-old boy like al-Tabari could have been placed. Similarly some Shi'i scholars have no objection to a pre-pubescent boy leading a congregation in prayer or acting as muezzin.

On the basis of *hadith* narratives, the Prophet Muhammad did not consider young age a hindrance to lead prayer. It is reported that he preferred a young man (*shabb*) to lead prayer of his *qawm* (people, but in this case possibly military detachment) over older men on account of his better knowledge of the Qur'an. Reflecting the tribal values of his times on the importance of seniority, an older man is reported on that occasion to have challenged the Prophet's preference for youth over seniority.⁶⁴

If narratives in *hadith*s may testify to variety and flexibility in the choice of leadership criteria, with a recurrent emphasis on religious knowledge and piety, early legal sources, unsurprisingly, seem to focus on more pragmatic considerations. Thus, priority in prayer leadership is to be given to the holders of 'official' authority, and secondly to the people most versed in legal knowledge. So, for example, the jurist al-Shafi'i (d. 820), after indicating the ruler, his deputies or the master of the house as first choice of imam, identifies the preferred imam as the person possessing the best knowledge of the law, followed by the one who is best versed in Qur'anic recitation. Only if the above qualities are equally shared by two people are age and lineage (ideally from the Quraysh, Muhammad's tribe) considered.⁶⁵ Is the order of priorities emerging from these accounts a reflection of two different conceptions surrounding the legitimacy of authority, one upholding piety and religious knowledge, and the other social standing, lineage, and seniority?

In his recollection, al-Tabari does not specify the type of congregational prayer he claims to have led. As a general rule, the qualities and requirements to be an imam are more defined and stringent for obligatory prayers such as the five compulsory daily prayers, performed in congregation, than for optional collective prayers (*nawafil*), such as the prayers of the two 'ids. To a greater extent, requirements are more carefully scrutinized for leadership of the Friday prayer.

The qualities and requirements to lead *salat* prayer also differ according to the location of worship. When, as we saw in al-Mawardi, the location is a governmental mosque, where the prayer leader is appointed by the caliph, there are specific requirements to qualify as the holder of that office. On the other hand, for a privately owned or funded mosque, such as a tribal or a neighbourhood mosque, the choice of an imam, at times by election, rests with the congregation which sets the relevant criteria. As for leading prayer at home or as a visitor in somebody else's house, precedence is given to the owner of the house, who exercises authority over their own domain.⁶⁶ It is around such a type of precedence that women close to the Prophet will come to the fore in the next chapters as landladies leading prayer in their own dwellings.

The variables in the criteria for choosing an imam across legal schools are not only about prioritizing some qualities over others, but about making some of them required qualities for an imam. Lineage is one of these variables. Legitimate birth is a qualification that, for medieval jurists such as the Hanafi Muhammad ibn Ahmad al-Sarakhsi (d. 1096) is a *desideratum*, while for the 13th century Shi'i al-Muhaqqiq al-Hilli it is one of the required characteristics for the leader of congregational prayers.⁶⁷

Even being of a discerning age, which the majority of jurists consider one of the prerequisites for being an imam, particularly of the obligatory prayers, can become a variable under certain circumstances or when other legitimizing criteria are being considered. For example, on the basis of evidence from the *sunna* of the Prophet, the most qualified person to be an imam is the one who has a better knowledge of the Qur'an⁶⁸ in his/her group, irrespective of status, physical condition, age and even, as will be discussed later, gender. After all, there are precedents during the Prophet's lifetime, recorded in the *hadith*s, of knowledgeable imams who, nevertheless, would have been considered by later jurists inappropriate or inadequate to lead prayer. Notable examples are a blind man, 'Itban ibn Malik,⁶⁹ a slave⁷⁰ and, contrary to the jurists' insistence on majority, the case of a child, 'Amr ibn Salama, who led his people in prayer on account of being the most knowledgeable in the Qur'an.⁷¹ And, as we will see in the course of this book, women too.

Despite some notable precedents, for most jurisprudents, majority was agreed as being one of the conditions for being an imam. Unless there are special circumstances, when a person reaches puberty or comes of age (*bulugh*), he/she becomes responsible (*mukallaf*) to fulfil his/her religious duties. The other requirements for being appointed or chosen as imam, in the most widely accepted order of priority, are: being Muslim, being sane, being just and, significant in light of the theme of this book, *being male*. For some jurists, such as al-Mawardi, being male was the first condition pertinent to the office of imam.⁷² However, for scholars such as Al-Muhaqqiq al-Hilli, being male is a precondition only if the congregation being led includes men.⁷³

Even from these preliminary remarks, one can conclude that the legitimacy of leadership in prayer, as well as the validity of the prayer led by a specific imam, are dependent upon a number of conditions and vary according to circumstances and religious-political as well as geographical contexts. First of all, which type of prayer is being led? A minor can be qualified to lead supererogatory prayer, or even, in certain cases, congregational prayer, but not, for most scholars, Friday prayer. Under what circumstances is the prayer being led? Are they ordinary circumstances or are they exceptional, out of necessity? And if, as in the case of the minor 'Amr ibn al-Salama, they are out of necessity, can they be taken as normative precedents?

And how far are some of the instances of 'unusual' prayer leaders narratives of *de facto* occurrences rather than explicit appointments or endorsement in the name of the Prophet himself? The case of the blind 'Itban ibn Malik for example, seems to point to the acknowledgement of a *de facto* leadership. This would be unlike the case of another blind person, Ibn Umm Maktum, whom the Prophet is reported to have chosen as his deputy (*istakhlafa*) to be a prayer leader.[74]

And, also importantly, which congregation is being led? In the case of a congregation of, for instance, people with a speech impediment and fluent speakers, to have an imam with a lisp would invalidate the prayer of the fluent speakers but not that of the other group. Moreover, an intersex/hermaphrodite can lead a congregation of women but not that of men as their prayers would be deemed invalid on account of the gender ambiguity of such a prayer-leader.

The reason for introducing here reports on, and examples of, imams who were minors, blind, slaves, disabled or intersex is that in most sources, from *hadith* collections to *fiqh* manuals, they are grouped together with women in the casuistry of possible prayer leaders. Such cases are not mentioned necessarily to reflect real practises or to display legal competence, but serve a specific purpose: to illustrate the legal, fiscal and ritual necessity to allocate any given individual to a specific group with appropriate legal status, rules and duties.[75] As a result of such a necessity, to address the issue of gender ambiguity, classical Islamic law overall recognizes four main genders: female, male, hermaphrodite and effeminate male. While certain conditions are deemed temporary from a legal point of view, such as minority and bondage, others, such as belonging to one gender, were seen as biologically and legally permanent.[76]

Among the characteristics of being an imam, the absence of which would impinge upon the validity of prayer of the congregation being led, only very few are broadly undisputed: for the imam to be a Muslim, to be sane, to be just and to be male.

There is an overall consensus among the main legal schools about the first two of these prerequisites. As for the extent and the 'content' of the imam's faith, there are different shades of interpretation: an imam who is lacking piety and virtue or has committed a grave error or 'sin', as long as he or she is a Muslim, can still be considered an overall legitimate imam and consequently the prayer the imam leads is valid.[77] Textual evidence for this can be found in a *hadith* stating that even if the imam is an 'apostate', the prayer led is still valid for the congregation.[78]

The third characteristic, which is not necessarily a prerequisite for all scholars or in all circumstances, is the imam's probity or justice. Whether this is a characteristic or a pre-requisite depends on a number of factors, among which are the particular doctrinal backgrounds and perspectives of the legal scholars concerned. Or it could depend on their understanding of the status of the imam with reference to the mosque in which he leads prayer. For example, in the view of scholars such as al-Mawardi, probity or righteousness is the second 'quality' for an imam, after being male. Al-Mawardi held that leadership of the obligatory prayers in a government mosque is an official position, hence an imam who is not just or equitable could still lead prayers, but could not be appointed to a goverment mosque 'because he would be disqualified to hold office'.[79]

The rationale behind the Sunni al-Mawardi and similar arguments, held for instance by Imami Shi'is, is that leadership in prayer is representative or suggestive of a more encompassing leadership (political, religious etc.). Hence a sinful, iniquitous (*fasiq*) imam would not be competent for such a position. In fact for several Imami Shi'i scholars the quality of *'adala* (righteousness) is so essential in a prayer leader for the legality of the prayer he leads, that its absence would make void the prayer of the person being led. This is even more acute in the case of the leader of the *jum'a* prayer, who, in the absence of the Imam, convenes and performs the Friday prayer as his deputy.[80] Thus, for Imami Shi'is, *'adala* becomes a prerequisite for a legitimate prayer leader.

A fourth characteristic for being an imam is being male. This is of paramount importance for the discussions that will follow in this book. Being male is a prerequisite in all cases for the Malikis, while the other schools of Islamic law consider it to be a prerequisite for just a male-only or mixed male and female congregation. In other words, as in the case of intersex or disabled imams, the prayer being led by them is valid on condition that they lead a congregation similar to themselves. So, a mute person can lead mute people and, with gender hierarchical overtones, an intersex can lead a congregation of women or of intersex Muslims.[81] As will be fully explored in Chapter 2, on the basis of the criterion of equivalence between the prayer leader and the congregation, one would expect that a woman could legitimately be the imam of other women. However, as will be seen, the undestanding and the application of this criterion when applied to women have become the subject of much controversy and debate. It goes without saying that while a physical disability is a biological and physical fact (with social accretions), when it comes to gender, physical traits (apparent or not) are viewed and interpreted primarily through the lenses of social construct.[82]

That gender is not viewed as primarily a personal trait but a social conception is consistently revealed by the scholarly and general reasoning, analysed throughout this book, on whether it is permissible or not for a woman to be an imam. The arguments against the permissibility of women to lead prayer are replete with references to socially and culturally accepted gender roles for women, their legal capacity and their status within a hierarchical society. In spite of such apparently insurmountable constructs, the next section is going to show that the application of certain criteria in choosing a prayer leader can lead to unexpected consequences for a few women who were accepted as imams.

Where do women as imams fit? An 'egalitarian' (of a sort) interpretation of leadership criteria

If legal sources share an overall systematic (albeit flexible) approach to the personal characteristics required for the ideal imam, several *hadith* narratives and passages in biographical literature provide examples and cases from which different priorities emerge for the choice of the best possible prayer leader.

One such priority is knowledge (*'ilm*). Variously interpreted as knowledge of the Qur'an, of legal judgments and of Prophetic *hadith*s, it is a commonly cited marker of legitimacy in leadership. In several *hadith*s, being well-versed in the Qur'an is indeed the main prerequisite for being an imam.[83] Knowledge of the Book is usually associated with Qur'anic recitation as, in a ritual context, to know the Qur'an (by heart) is equivalent to being able to recite it. Knowledge of *hadith*s and the legal rules they contain, even down to the number of *hadith*s transmitted and/or memorized, can become an indication of who is most qualified to become a leader. This is what is reported in literature on the excellences of Abu Bakr and ʿAli, the latter having transmitted more *hadith*s than the former (but over a longer period of time).[84]

Knowledge is a very important requirement and several legal schools specify that the best imam is the one who is best learned in *fiqh* or the *sunna*.[85] The already mentioned cases of underage imams, blind imams, slave imams, *khuntha* imams and, as will be seen in Chapters 2 and 3, of women imams, have one feature in common: they are presented as legitimate leaders on account of their greater knowledge of the Qur'an than that of the people they lead. Knowledge, in these cases, does overcome 'discrimination' based on social status, physical abilities, tribal or ethnic background, age or gender. However, this seemingly egalitarian nature that being knowledgeable confers to a person is in turn subverted when, on equal conditions of knowledge, the oldest among two knowledgeable persons is identified as the one who should lead prayers.[86] According to other narratives, the same priority in prayer leadership should be accorded to those Companions of the Prophet who were among the first to emigrate from Mecca to Medina.[87]

Another 'egalitarian' criterion of excellence is proven personal religious piety, which also has a legitimizing function for ritual leadership and is strongly connected to Qur'anic knowledge. Mention of both religious knowledge and piety as qualities for the best possible imam features consistently in *hadith* narratives. In her study based on *manaqib* literature (i.e. praise traditions, a section of the *hadith* corpus) about the excellences of the early Companions of the Prophet, Afsaruddin claims that early Muslim groups, including proto-Shiʿis, shared the view of a just Islamic polity headed by the most morally excellent leader. She identifies two principles underlying the status of moral eminence: precedence (*sabiqa*) and excellence (*fadila*). Precedence refers to temporal priority in submission and service to the cause of Islam; it includes early conversion and early emigration, as well as personal zeal, devotion and loyalty though participation in battles. Expressions of moral excellence are personal piety (*taqwa*), generosity, knowledge of Qur'anic verses and *hadith*s, as well as frequent recitation of the Qur'an.

Afsaruddin argues that the elaboration about the identification of these forms of excellence and precedence of the Companions represent the earliest Islamic discourse on the nature of legitimate political leadership. Her argument further supports the already evidenced link between political and ritual leadership. In the next two chapters, both this nexus and their shared principles of excellence and precedence will be further evidenced, when analysing the qualities attributed to the wives and Companions of the Prophet such as ʿAʾisha, Umm Salama and Umm Waraqa, who represent the earliest known examples of women acting as imams.

Conclusion

Nothwistanding the limitations that the sources used in this chapter present us with when looking at the way they report the past, by contextualizing them we have been able to identify some developments. One of them can be dected in the shift of the semantic use of key terms for ritual leadership such as imam and of terms referring to the place of worship such as mosque. Both terms are polysemic and can be understood generally or specifically, depending on the context. Developments have also been noted on how the link between religious-political leadership and governance could be seen as being projected onto the mosque and its personnel. This led to an institutionalization of the mosque and its staff, primarly the imam, who became the holder of formal office. In turn this impacted upon the requirements and prerequisites for being an imam, and significantly that of being male.

Looking beyond this gender-based prerequisite, the next two chapters will deal with reported episodes of women who led prayer on account of their personal status as loyal Companions and wives of the Prophet. The qualities ascribed to these women to further legitimize their leadership focus on their personal piety, commitment to the faith and knowledge of the Qur'an and *hadith*s. It was their status as the Prophet's wives and Companions that granted them a place of prominence in Prophetic narratives. But while their knowledge and piety were consistently recorded and acknowledged in those sources, their role as prayer leaders was conveyed in a marginal and incidental way. In time, their reported roles in the performance of prayer came to be generally understood as limited to the specific circumstances of their lifetime and thus not applicable beyond that timeframe. In some instances, reports on their leadership role became deliberately sidelined, doctored or ignored in the course of changing discourses on gender and leadership in general and in prayer in particular.

Be that as it may, Part 1 of this book seeks to reinscribe the leading role that these and other women played in the performance of prayer through the male voices who spoke in favour of or against such practice. In Part 2, women imams will speak for themselves.

Notes

1 al-Tabari, Abu Ja'far Muhammad ibn Jarir. *Ta'rikh al-Rusul wa'l-Muluk [The History of al-Tabari]* (Vol. 6). Translated by W. Montgomery Watt and M. V. McDonald. Albany: SUNY Press, 1988. Al-Tabari states that *salat* is the first duty after the statement on Allah's oneness and the rejection of 'idols' and 'false gods'. Note that al-Tabari uses various recensions of Ibn Ishaq's *Sira* in addition to Ibn Hisham's; for this passage al-Tabari uses the earlier recension of Salama b. al-Fadl (d. 807), transmitted to him by Ibn Humayd (d.862). It is of interest to note that the expression used here for leading in prayer is *salla bi-* followed by a noun or pronoun indicating a person or people meaning 'to lead that person in prayer', rather than *amma bi-* or *amma* meaning 'to precede, to lead (in prayer)' which is commonly used in the *hadith*s. Could this be an indication of the later use of *amma* as a technical term for prayer leadership?

2 For physical and ritual purity as expressions of a moral purity according to Muslim exegetes, see Naguib, Shuruq. 'And Your Garments Purify: Tahara in the Light of Tafsir'. *Journal of Qur'anic Studies* 9, 1 (2007): 59–77.
3 For al-Shafi'i's statements as cited by al-Juwayni see Reinhart, A. Kevin. 'Ritual Action and Practical Action'. In *Islamic Law in Theory*, edited by Kevin A. Reinhart and Robert Gleave. Leiden, Boston: Brill, 2014, 89.
4 The Qur'an (2.222) refers to menstruation as a disability (*adha*) which causes temporary impurity; once the bleeding ceases and women have purified themselves, they can resume sexual activity. In fact, there is no direct, nor explicit, link in the Qur'an between menstruation and ritual impurity. The other major cause of impurity, the emission of semen, could also be seen as gender specific with reference to men.
5 This is convincingly argued by Katz, Marion Holmes. *Body of Text: The Emergence of Sunni Law of Ritual Purity*. New York: SUNY Press, 2002, 201, especially when compared with Jewish ritual laws relating to menstruation; already in 1914, Wensinck had noted that, contrary to Jewish law, a menstruating woman according to *hadith*s and in *fiqh* literature does not contaminate or transfer her impurity to the people who touch her, see Wensinck, Arent Jan. 'The Origin of the Muslim Laws of Ritual Purity'. In *The Development of Islamic Ritual*, edited by Gerald Hawting, 75–94. Aldershot: Ashgate, 2006.
6 For these and other restrictions for women in a state of major impurity see Ibn Rushd, Abu al-Walid Muhammad. *Bidayat al-Mujtahid [The Distinguished Jurist's Primer]*. Translated by Imran Ahsan Khan Nyazee. Reading: Garnet, 1994, 41–3, 62–3, 331.
7 Reinhart, A. Kevin. 'Impurity/No Danger'. *History of Religions* 30, 1 (1990): 1–24.
8 See Ibn Rushd, *Bidayat al-Mujtahid*, 66, quoted in Gauvain, Richard. 'Ritual Rewards: A Consideration of Three Recent Approaches to Sunni Purity Law'. *Islamic Law and Society* 12, 3 (2005): 347.
9 Katz, *Body of Text*, 208; this statement, however, needs to be understood within more complex tensions between universalistic tendencies and exclusivist/community-defining roles of purity laws; for Katz's fuller argument on substantive impurity see pp. 145–206.
10 Kohlberg, Etan. 'The Position of the Walad Zina in Imami Shi'ism'. In *Belief and Law in Imami Shi'ism*, edited by Etan Kohlberg. Aldershot: Ashgate, 1991, xi, 237–66. For a *walad zina* not being permitted to be an imam, see al-Tusi, Muhammad ibn al-Hasan, Shaykh al-Ta'ifa. *Al-Mabsut fi Fiqh al-Imamiyya*. Edited by Al-Sayyid Muhammad al-Kashfi. Tehran: al-Matba'a al-Haydariyya, 1958, 155; and for a non Twelver Shi'i see al-Qadi al-Nu'man, Ibn Hayyun Ibn Muhammad (Abu Hanifa). *Da'a'im al-Islam* (3rd edn). Cairo: Dar al-Ma'arif, 1969, 156.
11 Ibn Rushd, *Bidaya al-Mujtahid*, 91–2 as quoted in Gauvain, 'Ritual Rewards', 386. This difference in urine impurity between baby boys and girls is maintained to this day in intepretations of *najasa* on the evidence of a *hadith* found in Abu Dawud, al-Tirmidhi, Ibn Maja that 'The urine of a baby boy should have water sprinkled upon it. The urine of a baby girl is to be washed off'. Ibn Maja, Muhammad ibn Yazid. *Sunan al-Hafiz Abi 'Abdallah* (Vol. 1). Edited by Muhammad Fu'ad 'Abd al-Baqi. Cairo: Dar Ihya' al-Kutub al-'Arabiyya, 1953, 1, *hadith* 522, under Tahara.

Note the differences between Islam and Judaism regarding purity laws with reference to gender, compare Ibn Rushd's statement with Leviticus, 12.2 'A woman who becomes pregnant and gives birth to a son will be ceremonially unclean for seven days . . .', and Lev. 12.5 'But if she bears a female child, then she shall be unclean two weeks . . .'.
12 Qur'anic exegetes came to interpret Qur. 17.1, the Mi'raj verse of the Prophet's ascent to the heavens and his encounter with the ealier Prophets, as an occasion to show

Muhammad's precendence over them, one expression of which was the narrative about Muhammad leading Abraham, Moses and Jesus in prayer.

13 For scholary sources on early and medieval understandings of leadership, authority and power in Islam, see, among others, Makdisi, George, Dominique Sourdel et al. (eds.). *La Notion d'Autorité au Moyen Age: Islam, Byzance, Occident*. Paris: Presses Universitaires de France, 1982; Mottahedeh, Roy P. *Loyalty and Leadership in an Early Islamic Society*. London, New York: IB Tauris, 2001; and Krämer and Schmidke, *Speaking for Islam*, 1–14.

14 Mottahedeh, R, *Loyalty and Leadership in an Early Islamic Society*, esp. 123–56.

15 Afsaruddin, Asma, *Excellence and Precedence: Medieval Islamic Discourse on Legitimate Leadership*. Leiden: Brill, 2002, 35.

16 As argued by Stowasser, Barbara F. *Women in the Qur'an: Traditions and Interpretation*. New York, Oxford: OUP, 1994, 62–66, see in particular her reference (p. 65) to a 'faint echo' of female political role in relation to the queen of Sheba in Ibn Kathir's *Qisas*.

17 al-Bukhari, Muhammad. *Sahih al-Bukhari*. Translated by Muhammad Muhsin Khan. Beirut: Dar al-Fikr, n.d.,1, 6, *hadith* 646, 3.

18 For competing claims about who was the first man to believe in the Messenger's mission and to accept Islam see al-Tabari, *The History of al-Tabari* (Vol. 6), 80–7. Similar contrasting claims are also made regarding the first *adhan* whereby, according to al-Kulayni, *al-Kafi*, it was during the Prophet's ascent to heaven that Gabriel taught the Prophet the *adhan*, who in turn gave instruction to 'Ali to teach it to Bilal; cited in Howard, I. K. A. 'The Development of the *Adhan* and *Iqama* of the *Salat* in Early Islam'. In *The Development of Islamic Ritual*, edited by Gerald Hawting. Aldershot: Ashgate, 2006, 102.

19 The link between the imam and the ruler/caliph is also expressed through debates concerning the legitimacy of the 'personal' *adhan* to the ruler; see for instance al-Shafi'i's position in his *Umm* in Howard, 'The Development of the *Adhan* and *Iqama* of the *Salat* in Early Islam', 101. For Howard, on the basis of some early formulae, there is some scope in considering the *adhan* as a call to the Prophet, and later the caliph, to lead the prayer (ibid., p. 100).

20 Marion Holmes Katz, in *Prayer in Islamic Thought and Practice*. Cambridge: CUP, 2013, 139–48, argues that, overall, for pre-modern Sunni legal scholars, in the context of Friday prayer, concerns on the occurrence of its performance, social stability and obedience to political authority were more important than considerations about the probity and purity of the prayer leader.

21 al-Tabari, Abu Ja'far Muhammad ibn Jarir. *Ta'rikh al-Rusul wa'l-Muluk [The History of al-Tabari]* (Vol. 7). Translated by W. Montgomery Watt and M. V. Mcdonald. Albany: SUNY Press, 1988, 1–2: no number of Companions is specified here; in Tabari's account the Prophet in his 'first Friday prayer' delivered a sermon, on the basis of the *Sira* which al-Tabari quotes (2–4). For the Qur'anic injunction for Muslims ('those who have attained to faith') to pray when they hear the call to prayer on the day of assembly, see *Sura* 62.9–10, which scholars date as an early Medinan *sura*. However, there is agreement between legal scholars that Friday prayer in congregation in a mosque is not mandatory for women or children, but is for free adult males.

22 Ibn Sa'd's *Tabaqat*, cited by Afsaruddin, *Excellence and Precedence*, 38; alternatively, Ibn Sa'd indicates the names of the Medinan Companion As'ad or the Meccan Mus'ab as the first to lead communal prayer in Medina before the Prophet's arrival, see Becker, 'On the History of Muslim Worship', 53–4.

23 Ibn Babawayh, Abu Ja'far Muhammad ibn 'Ali. *Man la Yahdaruhu al-Faqih*. Tehran: Dar al-Kutub al-Islamiyya, 1970, 1, 245–6; also Muhaqqiq al-Hilli, Ja'far ibn al-Hasan, Abu'l-Qasim. *Shara'i' al-Islam fi Masa'il al-Halal wa'l-Haram*. Edited by Muhammad 'Ali 'Abd al-Husayn. Tehran: Manshurat al-A'lami, 1969, 1, 122, where al-Hilli specifies that the minimum number for a *jama'a* is two persons, with one of them being the imam. Unlike in some Sunni narratives, women are counted in the *quorum*, see *hadith* 5 on the authority of Ja'far al-Sadiq, asked about the *quorum*: 'a man and a woman and even if nobody turns up in the mosque, a believer is a congregation because when he calls the *adhan* or the *iqama* behind him two rows of angels pray' Ibn Babawayh, *Man la Yahdaruhu al-Faqih*, 1, bab 56, *hadith*s 4 and 5, 246. In time the *quorum* was raised according to legal authorities, especially in the case when the congregational prayer is the Friday prayer (5 for some Hanafis, 12 for the Malikis or 40 for some Shafi'is).
24 Goitein, Shelomo Dov. 'The Origin and Nature of the Muslim Friday Worship'. In *Studies in Islamic History and Institutions*, edited by Shelomo Dov Goitein. Leiden: Brill, 1966, 112–22.
25 See, for instance, Qur. 18.21 with reference to the legend of the Men in the Cave; for an overview of the development of the term and the area/place of worship see Pedersen, Johannes. 'Masdjid'. In *EI2* (Vol. 6), edited by Peri J. Bearman, Th. Bianquis et al. Leiden: Brill, 1991, 644–5; and Bloom, Jonathan. 'Mosque'. In *EQ* (Vol. 3), edited by Jane Dammen McAuliffe. Leiden: Brill, 2003, 426–7.
26 See al-Tabari, *The History of al-Tabari* (Vol. 7), 5, where it is stated that, during the first year of the Hijra, the Prophet cleared the chosen area for his first house and mosque: he ordered the palm trees to be cut, the land to be leveled and the existing graves to be dug up.
27 *Sira* in Ibn Ishaq, Muhammad. *Sirat Rasul Allah [The Life of Muhammad]*. Translated by Alfred Guillaume. Karachi: OUP, 1978, 113; and al-Tabari, *The History of al-Tabari* (Vol. 6), 81. There are three versions of the narrative in al-Tabari, the first is included in the the text above, the second has Khadija praying with Muhammad, followed by 'Ali, without indication of positions in prayer; the last is set at Mina where the Prophet performs the ritual ablution before praying, followed in his ablution and prayer by Khadija and then by 'Ali (82). All three narratives are placed within the context of who was the first male believer after Muhammad, hence the sequence of prayer gestures and positions reflects the intended pre-eminence of 'Ali who, in the first and third narrative, is made to pray next to the Prophet (while, stated explicitly only in the first narrative, Khadija is behind them).
28 Muslim, ibn al-Hajjaj. *Jam' Jawami' al-Ahadith wa'l-Asanid wa Maknaz al-Silah wa'l-Sunan wa'l-Masanid* (Vol. 4). Vaduz: Thesaurus Islamicus Foundation, 2000, *kitab al-masajid, bab* 1, *hadith* 1190 and ff, 210. See also Al-Tabari, *The History of al-Tabari* (Vol. 7), 5, where with reference to the Meccan period, it is stated the Prophet used to pray wherever he was during prayer time, even in heep enclosures (hence, possibly, in what later scholars would have considered unclean areas).
29 For contrasting interpretations about the house of the Prophet in Medina see, on the one hand, Grabar, Oleg (ed.). *The Formation of Islamic Art*. New Haven, CT: Yale University Press, 1987, 104; and on the other, Pedersen, 'Masdjid', 644–707, and Hillenbrand, Robert. *Islamic Architecture: Form, Function and Meaning*. New York: Columbia University Press, 1994.
30 Ayyad, Essam S. 'The "House of the Prophet" or the "Mosque of the Prophet"?' *Journal of Islamic Studies* 24, 3 (2013): 273–334; he uses additional sources to *hadith*s and *Sira*, like *Diwan* by Hasan ibn Thabit (d. 674) which he presents as the earliest reference to

the 'Prophet's mosque'. See also Ayyad's more nuanced 'An Historiographical Analysis of the Arabic Accounts of Early Mosques: With Special Reference to those at Madina, Baṣra and Kūfa'. *Journal of Islamic Studies* 30, 1 (2019): 1–33, where he understands the *maqsura* as the enclosure for the imam.

31 For the tribal mosques see references from Bukhari, Ibn Sa'd, Ibn al-Najjar's *Durra* etc. cited in Ayyad, 'The "House of the Prophet" or the "Mosque of the Prophet"?'; and some examples in Pedersen, 'Masdjid'.

32 Penn, Michael Philip. *Envisioning Islam: Syriac Christians and the Early Muslim World*. Philadelphia, PA: University of Pennsylvania Press, 2015, 57. On the basis of evidence from 6th–9th century Syriac texts Penn argues that the strong link between religion and ethnicity in early Islam was greatly affected by 'Umar II's policy of Islamization and his change in the taxation system, whereby taxes were to be assessed no longer on the basis of lineage but on the basis of religion (pp. 63–4). See also Bulliet, Richard W. *Conversion to Islam in the Medieval Period*. Cambridge, MA: Harvard University Press, 1979 and Hawting, Gerald R. *The First Dynasty of Islam*. London, New York: Routledge, 2000, 4–5.

33 See for example the *qibla* wall, which scholars now agree to have been a feature since 706 at the Umayyad mosque of Damascus; among the earliest sources describing mosque features see Ma'mar b. Rashid (d.770), al-Khalil b. Ahmad al-Farahidi (d. 791), Malik b. Anas and Ibn Zabala (d. after 814).

34 al-Baladhuri, *Futuh*, 485 cited in Ayyad, 'An Historiographical Analysis of the Arabic Accounts of Early Mosques', note 92.

35 Pedersen, 'Masdjid', 654.

36 Gaffney, Patrick D. *The Prophet's Pulpit: Islamic Preaching in Contemporary Egypt*. Berkeley: University of California Press, 1994, 19–21; Lowry, Joseph E. 'Ritual Purity'. In *EQ* (Vol. 4), edited by Jane Dammen McAuliffe. Leiden: Brill, 2004, 506–7; Katz, *Women in the Mosque*, 5 and passim.

37 See later on in Chapter 3 of this book the assertion by traditionalist Abu Bakr al-Shaybani (d.900) with reference to Umm Waraqa.

38 Imam is also used in the Qur'an to refer to a book of guidance (11.17 the Book of Moses, an imam), or a book of records (36.12). For a detailed analysis of the Qur'anic uses of the term see Yusuf, Imtiyaz. 'Imam'. In *EQ* (Vol. 2), edited by Jane Dammen McAuliffe. Leiden: Brill, 2002, 502–4.

39 The chronology of *sura*s has traditionally been based on extra-Qur'anic sources, particularly from *hadith*s and passages of the *Sira* where the occasions and circumstances of the Qur'anic revelation of specific verses are explained. Such collected material is known as *asbab al-nuzul* (occasions of revelation) which exegetes used as a key to interpreting the Qur'anic text. Intra-Qur'anic methods to establish Qur'anic chronology were also devised on the basis of the theory of abrogation. The division of *sura*s into Meccan and Medinan, though referring back to a list attributed to Ibn 'Abbas (d. 688), became fixed only during the 14th century. Since the 19th century such classification has been subject to extensive debate among Western scholars such as T. Noeldeke and R. Bell, and more recently J. Burton and A. Neuwirth with differing outcomes.

40 The two passages (and two versions) about how *salat* came about are in Ibn Hisham's narrative; on Gabriel and his stay with Muhammad, see Ibn Ishaq, *The Life of Muhammad*, 112–14; for the account of Muhammad's *isra'* and *mi'raj*, his encounter with Moses and his negotiating how many prayers Muslims should pray, see *The Life of Muhammad*, 186–7.

41 Ibn Hisham, 'Abd al-Malik. *Al-Sira al-Nabawiyya*. Edited by Suhayl Zakkar. Beirut: Dar al-Fikr, 1992, 1, 167; and the Engl. transl, in Ibn Ishaq, *The Life of Muhammad*, 112. In al-Tabari's variants to the text, on the basis of the *riwaya* of Yunus b. Bukayr, one significant Prophetic performance of prayer is witnessed by passers-by (p. 113).

42 There are several *hadiths* referring to Muhammad's accommodating approach to prayer (upon hearing a child cry, the Prophet would shorten his prayer to avoid distress on the mother), his brevity and light touch in leading the elderly and the weak but also, practically, those who needed to go back to their own occupations. See Muslim, 'Sahih Muslim', 2000, 1, *salat*, bab 37, 193–4. For Muhammad as role model in prayer see specifically id. *hadith* 1081, 194.

43 For an equivalent example of directly revealed prayer, this time with new contents specific to a developing new Christian community, arising from a Jewish religious context, see Gospel of Luke 11.1–4: when Jesus was asked to teach his disciples to pray, Jesus replies 'When you pray, say: "Father, hallowed be your name . . .'"; compare with Matthew 6.9–13.

44 For scholarly arguments on the Qur'anic revelation as an expression of Late Antiquity and its interplay with Arabian customs, see Reynolds, Gabriel Said (ed.). *The Qur'an in its Historical Context*. London: Routledge, 2008; and Neuwirth, Angelika. *Scripture, Poetry and the Making of a Community: Reading the Qur'an as a Literary Text*. Oxford: OUP, 2014.

45 See the first Qur'anic reference to congregational prayer in the Medinan *sura* 62, esp. vv. 9–10. The identification of *sura* 62 as Medinan follows the traditional and widely adopted order by Ibn 'Abbas (d. 688), but some contest this dating. For scholarly arguments about the gradual development from personal to communal prayer see Bowering, Gerald. 'Prayer'. In *EQ* (Vol. 4), edited by Jane Dammen McAuliffe, 215–31. Leiden: Brill, 2004, 215–31

46 There are a few *hadiths* where 'the imams of unbelief and of evil/darkness' are also referred to, in various *hadith* collections including al-Tirmidhi, Muslim and Abu Dawud.

47 On the polemical nature of contrasting Sunni and Imami Shi'i views on the link between Abu Bakr's prayer leadership and his political leadership, see Afsaruddin, *Excellence and Precedence*, 152–68, 179–82; for an Isma'ili view refuting the link, see al-Qadi al-Nu'man, Ibn Hayyun Ibn Muhammad (Abu Hanifa). *Da'a'im al-Islam [The Pillars of Islam]*, Vol 1. Translated by Asaf Ali Asghar Fyzee. Oxford: OUP, 2002, 49–50. For a summary of the dissent among Arabian tribes during Abu Bakr's caliphate, see Watt, Montgomery W. 'Abu Bakr'. In *EI2* (Vol. 1), edited by Peri J. Bearman, Th. Bianquis et al. Leiden: Brill, 1960, 109–11.

48 Quoting al-Maqrizi's *Khitat*, see Becker, 'On the History of Muslim Worship', 73, note 118.

49 Talmon-Heller, *Islamic Piety in Medieval Syria*, 88–90.

50 Citing historical, legal and documentary sources for the appointments and developing professionalization of the office of imam and *khatib* see Talmon-Heller, *Islamic Piety in Medieval Syria*, 108–114. For an overview of the role of the imam with special reference to Friday prayer, see Pedersen, 'Masdjid', 674–7.

51 For a discussion on the political link between Friday prayer and government as elaborated by some medieval Muslim jurists, see Calder, Norman 'Friday Prayer and the Juristic Theory of Government: Sarakhsi, Shirazi, Mawardi'. In *Norman Calder: Interpretation and Jurisprudence in Medieval Islam*, edited by J. Mojaddedi and A. Rippin. Aldershot: Ashgate Variorum, 2006, xiii, 35–47.

52 al-Mawardi, Abu al-Hasan ʿAli ibn Muhammad. *Al-Ahkam al-Sultaniyya [The Ordinances of Government]*. Translated by Wafa H. Wahba. Reading: Garnet, 1996, 112–20.
53 For a study on the Sunni response by al-Ghazali to the Shiʿi doctrine of the infallibility of the Imam (*ʿiṣma*), see Laoust, Henri. *La Politique de Ġazali*. Alger: Société Nationale d'Édition et de Diffusion, 1971, 75–82, 252–5.
54 For an overview of the Friday prayer in Shiʿism, inclusive of modern developments, see Algar, Hamid. 'Emam-e Jomʿa'. *Encyclopaedia Iranica* (Vol. 8), edited by Ehsan Yarshater. Costa Mesa: Mazda, 1998, 386–391. For a discussion of the differing legal positions among Shiʿis on the performance of *jumʿa* prayer during the period of occultation and when Shiʿis have to practise *taqiyya*, i.e. dissimulation, see Sachedina, Abdulaziz Abdulhussein. *The Just Ruler in Shiʿite Islam: The Comprehensive Authority of the Jurist in Imamite Jurisprudence*. New York: OUP, 1988, 181–204.
55 Muslim, 'Sahih Muslim', 2000, 1, *salat*, bab 19, 173–4.
56 ibid., *hadith* 961, 175.
57 Ibn Babawayh, *Man la Yahdaruhu al-Faqih*, 1, 247.
58 al-Qadi al-Nuʿman, *The Pillars of Islam* (Vol. 1), 'Ibadat, 190, on the authority of Jaʿfar al-Sadiq, from the Prophet.
59 For an overview of the different types of preachers in early Islam see Antoun, R. T. *Muslim Preacher in the Modern World: A Jordanian Case Study in Comparative Perspective*. Princeton, NJ: PUP, 1989, 67–70.
60 Abu Dawud, Sulayman ibn al-Ashʿath. *Sunan Abi Dawud*. Translated by Ahmad Hasan. New Delhi: al-Madina Publications, 1985, 1, *hadith* 580, 52–3.
61 For the advisory role of the imam on ritual matters and Qurʾan recitation see a reference to 14th century al-Subki's work on professions in Syria cited in Talmon-Heller, *Islamic Piety in Medieval Syria*, 109.
62 'Fa man qaddamahu al-muʾminuna fa huwa awwal', i.e 'and the one who is put forward by the congregation [of people being led], that is the foremost', in Muhaqqiq al-Hilli, *Sharaʾiʿ al-Islam fi Masaʾil al-Halal waʾl-Haram*, 1, 125.
63 Al-Tabari's statement is reported by the great biographer Yaqut ibn ʿAbd Allāh al-Ḥamawi al-Rumi in his *Kitab Irshad al-Arib ila Maʿrifat al-Adib al-Maʿruf bi-Muʿjam al-Udabaʾ, aw, Ṭabaqat al-Udabaʾ* (Vol. 6). Edited by David Samuel Margoliouth, Leiden: Brill, 1913, 429–30: 'sallaytu biʾl-nas wa ana ibn thamani sinnin', the expression *salla biʾl-nas* meaning 'to lead prayer' is often found in the *hadith*s, see for example when the Prophet asked Abu Bakr to lead prayer: al-Bukhari, *Sahih al-Bukhari*, n.d., 1, Ch 6, *hadith* 646, 365. See also Franz Rosenthal's introduction in al-Tabari, *Taʾrikh al-Rusul waʾl-Muluk [The History of al-Tabari]* (Vol. 1). Translated and annotated by Franz Rosenthal. Albany: SUNY Press, 1989, 15.
64 Abu Hurayra's *hadith* on the young man leading prayer from al-Razi's *Fadaʾil al-Qurʾan* is cited by Afsaruddin, *Excellence and Precedence*, 134–5 within her broader argument that knowledge of the Qurʾan and piety are 'egalitarian' and 'revolutionary' leadership criteria which challenge old ones based on age and lineage (276–8). The reliability of Abu Hurayra as a *hadith* transmitter has been long challenged by both Muslim and Western scholars (Goldziher, F. Mernissi, Abu Rayya, Juynboll etc.) with some responses in his defense ('Izzi, Shalabi, U. Ghani).
65 al-Shafiʿi, Muhammad ibn Idris. *Kitab al-Umm* (Vol. 1). Beirut: Dar al-Maʿrifa liʾl-Tibaʿa wa-al-Nashr, [1400-/1980s], 157–8.
66 See Abu Dawud, Sulayman ibn al-Ashʿath. *Sunan Abi Dawud*. Edited by ʿAziz ʿAbd al-Raʾas. Hums: Muhammad ʿAli al-Sayyid, 1969, *kitab al-salat*, *hadith* 596, 1, 399;

Muslim, 'Sahih Muslim', 2000, 1, *salat*, bab 54, *hadith* 1564, 266; for Shi'i authorities see al-Tusi, Muhammad ibn al-Hasan, Shaykh al-Ta'ifa. *Tahdhib al-Ahkam fi Sharh al-Muqni'a li'l-Shaykh al-Mufid* (Vol. 3). Edited by Hasan al-Musawi Kharsan. Najaf: Dar al-Kutub al-Islamiyya, bab 3, 32; Al-Mawardi, *The Ordinances of Government*, 115; for additional reasons not to lead prayer in somebody else's house see Calder, 'Friday Prayer and the Juristic Theory of Government', 42.

67 For Sarakhsi, see Calder, 'Friday Prayer and the Juristic Theory of Government', 42. For al-Muhaqqiq al-Hilli, see Muhaqqiq al-Hilli, *Shara'i' al-Islam fi Masa'il al-Halal wa'l-Haram*, 1, Fasl 3, on the congregational prayer (*jama'a*), 124.

68 See al-Bukhari, *Sahih al-Bukhari*, n.d., 1, 54, *hadith* 661, 375 where prayer is led by a slave, and heading to Ch 54 where the statement is made that it is permissible for a minor (or a slave, or an illegitimate child) to lead prayer on the basis of the Prophet's statement that the imam is the one who knows the Qur'an better. See also Abu Dawud, *Sunan Abi Dawud*, 1969, *kitab al-salat*, *hadith* 582, 1, 390 'the one who is most versed in the Book of Allah ... is the one who [should] lead the people in prayer'.

69 al-Bukhari, *Sahih al-Bukhari*, n.d., *adhan*, Ch 40, *hadith* 636, 1, 360, and Ch 72, *hadith* 801, 444–5.

70 For Dhakwan, the slave of 'A'isha leading her in prayer, and Salim, the slave of Abu Hudhayfa, see al-Bukhari, *Sahih al-Bukhari*, n.d., *adhan*, Ch 54 and *hadith* 661, 1, 374–5. For Salim see also Abu Dawud, *Sunan Abi Dawud*, 1969, *kitab al-salat*, *hadith*, 588, 1, 395.

71 For 'Amr ibn Salama, see Abu Dawud, *Sunan Abi Dawud*, 1969, *kitab al-salat*, *hadith*s 585 and 587, 1,393–5. As in the previous example of the slave, the boy was a *hafiz* (who memorised the Qur'an) and hence the one who, among his people/tribe, knew the Qur'an better. Scholars, such as Ahmad ibn Hanbal, have cast some doubts on the reliability of this *hadith* on account of the reputedly weak testimony of 'Amr ibn Salama. To also be considered is the issue of necessity, which can overrule specific requirements. See, al-Bukhari, *Sahih al-Bukhari*, n.d., *salat*, Ch 56, 1, 376: 'Al-Zuhri said: "we think that one should not pray behind an effeminate (intersex: *mukhannath*) unless this is out of necessity (*illa min darura la budda minha*)"'. In the event of necessity see al-Mawardi who cites 'Amr ibn Maslama (read Salama) as a case of an imam who, *de facto*, may lead prayer without having the qualities of the legitimate state-appointed office of imam; Al-Mawardi, *The Ordinances of Government*, 114.

72 Al-Mawardi, *The Ordinances of Government*, 114. For al-Mawardi, being male is the first prerequisite condition for the office of judge ('women ... are not qualified to hold major government positions'; 72); a woman cannot be a minister either, for 'it [the ministry] calls for more soundness of opinion and firmness of purpose than women are capable of, and involves public performance of duty in a manner denied [to] them', 29.

73 Al-Muhaqqiq al-Hilli, *Shara'i' al-Islam fi Masa'il al-Halal wa'l-Haram*, 1, 124.

74 For Ibn Umm Maktum, see Abu Dawud, *Sunan Abi Dawud*, 1969, *kitab al-salat*, *hadith* 595, 1, 398.

75 In addition to the ambivalent status of a *mukhannath* in leading a congregation in prayer, see also the necessity to establish their sex with reference to paying or not paying tributes and taxes such as the *jizya* and the *kharaj*, some of which women were excluded from paying; al-Mawardi, *The Ordinances of Government*, 160. For a discussion on the different meanings of *mukhannath* and the terms used in classical Islamic literature to refer to gender-ambiguous individuals see Kugle, Scott Siraj al-Haqq. *Homosexuality in Islam: Critical Reflection on Gay, Lesbian and Transgender*

Muslims. Oxford: Oneworld, 2010, 238–43. For some examples of the anomalous legal status of hermaphrodites in medieval Islam and issues of social boundaries, see Sanders, Paula. 'Gendering the Ungendered Body: Hermaphrodites in Medieval Islamic Law'. In *Women in Middle Eastern History*, edited by Nikki Keddie and Beth Baron. New Haven, CT: Yale University Press, 1991, 74–95.

76 The 'permanent status' of any of these four genders is at present called into question, with gender reassignment debates between Sunnis and Shi'is in Haneef, Sayed Sikandar Shah. 'Sex Reassignment in Islamic Law: The Dilemma of Transsexuals'. *International Journal of Business, Humanities and Technology*, 1, 1 (2011): 1–10; and Alipour, Mehrdad. 'Transgender Identity, The Sex-Reassignment Surgery Fatwas and Islamic Theology of a Third Gender', *Religion and Gender* 7, 2 (2017): 164–179.

77 Abu Dawud, *Sunan Abu Dawud*, 1969, *salat*, *hadith* 594, 1, 398; scholars have raised doubts about the authenticity of this *hadith* due to weak transmitters.

78 See al-Bukhari, *Sahih al-Bukhari*, n.d., *salat*, Ch 56, 1, 376 from al-Zuhri about praying behind an imam who is a heretic (*mubtadi'*): the sin of heresy is against him, not against those who pray behind him.

79 Al-Mawardi, *The Ordinances of Government*, 112.

80 Sachedina, *The Just Ruler in Shi'ite Islam*, 177–180; about the list of qualifications of the *imam al-jama'a* see al-Tusi, Shaykh al Ta'ifa, *Al-Mabsut fi Fiqh al-Imamiyya*, 1, 157.

81 al-Mawardi, *The Ordinances of Government*, 112.

82 As Paula Sanders successfully demonstrated in the case of hermaphrodites in the medieval period, their 'ungendered body was unsocialized' causing scholars and jurists to use 'strategies' to socialize the body in order to keep social order and define communal and ritual boundaries, Sanders 'Gendering the Ungendered Body', 89.

83 See al-Bukhari, *Sahih al-Bukhari*, n.d., 1, 54, *hadith* 661, 375; Abu Dawud, *Sunan Abi Dawud*, 1969, *kitab al-salat*, *hadith* 582, 1, 390; Muslim, 'Sahih Muslim', 2000, 1, *salat*, bab 54, *hadith* 1564, 266. Most *hadith*s merge together the best recitation and best knowledge of the Qur'an; some authorities and narratives, however, distinguish between the two. For an explanation of the translation of *aqra'uhum li-kitab Allah* as 'the one who is best versed in the Book of Allah', see Muslim, ibn al-Hajjaj. *Sahih Muslim*. Translated by 'Abdul Hamid Siddiqi. Lahore: Muhammad Ashraf, 1976, 1, note 206.

84 Afsaruddin, *Excellence and Precedence*, 113–17, 131.

85 See Abu Dawud, *Sunan Abu Dawud*, 1985, 1, *hadith* 584 on the authority of Abu Mas'ud: 'If they are equally versed in recitation, then the one who has most knowledge of the *sunna*', 154.

86 Bukhari, *Sahih al-Bukhari*, n.d., 1, bab 49, *hadith* 653, 369–70; 'wa la ya'ummakum akbarukum'.

87 Muslim, 'Sahih Muslim', 2000, 1, *hadith* 1566, 266, from Ibn Mas'ud: 'the one who leads the congregation (*qawm*) is the best versed in the Book of Allah and the best in reciting it, if recitation is equal, then the earliest to have emigrated.'

Chapter 2

CONGREGATIONAL PRAYERS: WOMEN LEADING WOMEN

Setting the narrative context: Umm Salama

In the *Book of Guidance* (*Kitab al-Umm*) by al-Shafi'i (d. 820), on the authority of a woman, Hujayra, who said that: 'Umm Salama led them [i.e. the women] in prayer (*ammathunna*) and she stood in the middle'.[1]

In the *Great Book of the Classes* (*Tabaqat*) by Ibn Sa'd (d. 845), the same woman, Hujayra said: 'Umm Salama led us [women] (*ammatna*) in the afternoon prayer and stood in our midst (*wasatina*)'.[2]

Quoted from the *Books* by Muhammad Ibn Sallam (d. 850) from Zayd on the authority of 'Ali ibn Abi Talib: 'Together with the Prophet, I entered the quarters of Umm Salama while the women, in a part of the house (*bayt*) were performing prayer. The Prophet asked: "O Umm Salama: which prayer are they praying?" She replied: "Oh Prophet of Allah, the prescribed prayer (*maktuba*)". He asked: "why have you not led them?" (*a fala ammaytihinna*). She replied "Oh Prophet of God, is this permissible?" He answered: "yes, it is, but do not let them be in front of you nor behind you, [but rather] on your right and on your left"'.[3]

The passages above are by three very different, yet almost contemporary authorities: Abu 'Abdallah Muhammad ibn Idris al-Shafi'i, the famous jurisprudent and eponym of the Shafi'i school of law, Muhammad Ibn Sa'd the Iraqi traditionist, and Abu 'Abdallah Muhammad ibn Sallam, the Shi'i Zaydi theologian. The narratives retrospectively project back to the time of the Prophet the ritual practices and categorization of prayer which by their time had become normative.

They all report that one of the Prophet's wives, Umm Salama, led a congregation of women in prayer and that, instead of leading from the front, she led them from the middle. However, each narrator reports the same event with added nuances which reflect his respective standpoint. While in the first passage Hujayra is presented as a reporter of such an event, in the second she is given a more prominent role as a witness to it on the basis of being a participant. The third author, a Shi'i, instead brings in 'Ali as the principal informant and witness. As for the content, each narrative sheds light on different aspects of the event. For example, the second passage adds to the first that the prayer that Umm Salama led was the afternoon prayer. This last report adds that she was in her own quarters, that the prayer was the prescribed ritual prayer, and not, for instance, a supererogatory one, and that it was the Prophet himself who invited her to lead on condition that she led from the middle, by doing so legitimising a woman to lead other women in prayer. The verb used for such a leadership is, in all three reports, *amma*, which is from the same root as the noun 'imam'. Another 9th century scholar, the Iraqi traditionist Abu Bakr Ibn Abi Shayba (d. 849) also describes, in almost identical words, Umm Salama's prayer leadership of women in two separate *hadith*s, with distinct chains of transmission, one of which also includes Hujayra. He does so in his work *al-Musannaf* where he dedicates a section to *hadith*s on female prayer leadership.[4]

More numerous are the narratives related to another of the Prophet's wives, 'A'isha, leading women in prayer while standing among them in the same row. The *hadith*s describing Umm Salama and 'A'isha leading women in prayer were to be cited as precedents by several subsequent scholars of note, including Abu'l-Hasan 'Ali al-Daraqutni (d. 995), Abu Bakr al-Bayhaqi (d.1066) and Ibn Hajar al-'Asqalani (d. 1445), as part of the discussion on the legitmacy of women leading prayer.

This chapter will analyse the above narratives on Umm Salama leading prayer and contextualize them within the times in which they were written down and included in compilations. The aim is to identify underlying discourses, be they legal, theological or 'sectarian', which would account for differences in narratives and their use. Among such discourses are the use of *hadith*s in legal literature, the requirements for ritual leadership, and the expectations of women's behaviour and role in the performance of prayer. Focusing on Umm Salama, a frequently cited but as yet not extensively studied wife and Companion of the Prophet, it will compare her represented role with that of 'A'isha to identify any constructed templates of behaviour for Muslim women. It will scrutinize not only the narrative context, but also some of the constituent sections of the relevant *hadith*s, specifically their *isnad*. This will extend the analysis to the role of a few female Successors (i.e. the generation of Muslims after the Companions) in the transmission of *hadith*. Asma Sayeed has carried out extensive research on women participation in *hadith* transmission, which has led her to suggest a periodization for their involvement. This chapter will engage with her argument and test her findings.

The *hadith*s linked to Umm Salama's role in prayer will be the starting point to delving into a spectrum of Sunni and Shi'i legal positions on the issue of female prayer leadership of women. An assessment will be made of the scriptural and legal arguments and methods used to justify such positions and an attempt will be made to identify periodization through internal developments within legal schools and beyond. It will be argued that scriptural and legal evidence alone are not sufficient to explain the changed positions on female prayer leadership unless they are seen through the lenses of developments in broader social and cultural attitudes towards female roles. When it comes to the uses of the past, which is the thread throughout this book, this chapter will identify the various methods and aims of using the past as a means to legitimize or explain the varied and changing scholarly opinions on female ritual leadership.

It is noteworthy that both 'A'isha and Umm Salama, who are reported to be well-known authorities of *hadith* transmission ('A'isha as the most prolific female transmitter and Umm Salama as second only to 'A'isha in number of *hadith*s), are credited with ritual leadership. They are not the only named women reported to have led prayer: Umm Waraqa, a Companion of the Prophet, also led prayer on instruction of the Prophet himself (more about her is to be explained and analysed in Chapter 3). Another female Companion, Sa'da bint Qamama, is also reported to have led women in prayer.[5] Over the first centuries following the Prophet's death, few more instances of women leading prayer are recorded. The 11th century Andalusian Sunni scholar Ibn Hazm narrates that 'Abdullah Ibn 'Umar (d. 693), a highly influential son of the second caliph and prolific *hadith* transmitter, appointed an unnamed woman to lead in prayer a female congregation during Ramadan. Both al-Shafi'i and the 9th century Shafi'i jurist al-Muzani cite that a *jariya* (slave girl) of 'Ali ibn al-Husayn acted as prayer leader. He is most likely the same as the fourth Imam of the Imami Shi'is Zayn al-'Abidin (d. 713), who was hailed as the 'exemplary worshipper'.[6] This is the last known woman linked to the family or progeny of the Prophet reported to have led prayer.[7] That women led women in prayer after the Prophet's times is also evidenced by the reference in al-Shafi'i's *Al-Umm* to the well-known *hadith* transmitter 'Amra (d. 716 or 724), who is reported as instructing a woman to lead women in prayer and, as will be analysed in Chapter 3, by the *hadith*s on Umm Waraqa.

All the sources cited above use the verb *amma* (to lead) to indicate the action of individual women leading prayer, a verb that is also employed for men. The cited women are not referred to as imam *per se*, but the verb indicates they were acting as one. The noun '*imama*', in the feminine form, to indicate a female prayer leader, has not been found in any of the sources consulted. A linguistic explanation provided in the renowned 18th dictionary of the Arabic language *Taj al-'Arus*, which quotes classical sources, is that 'imam' is a noun, not an adjective, and therefore the correct expression would be, for example, that a woman is the 'imam of other women'.[8] When reporting on the Prophet or his Companions leading prayer, *hadith*s more frequently use the verb *salla bi*. It is unclear whether the two verbs *amma* and *salla bi* are synonyms or whether they indicate different degrees of technical linguistic or semantic usage.

For pre-modern Muslim jurists and theologians the *hadith*s cited above address, and in theory answer, the question of the permissibility of women leading other women, during and after the Prophet's times. They also indicate the modality of the positioning of the female leader, and which prayers women are reported to have led. For Muslim scholars of *hadith*s, they provide evidence of the reliability and authoritativeness of one transmitter, Umm Salama, on matters of ritual, as she was personally entrusted by the Prophet with ritual leadership. These *hadith*s also validate the authority of those who, like Hujayra, witnessed or participated in the prayer and then reported it. For historians, these traditions – explicitly or implicitly – evoke the milieu of the period in which *hadith* collectors were operating, their different uses of *isnad*, their religious group affiliation and their understanding of the bases of authority and leadership.

Their exhalted status as 'mothers of the believers' made the Prophet's wives the most excellent exemplars of female prayer performers for the faithful to follow. But why, among all the Prophet's wives, have the sources singled out Umm Salama and 'A'isha as prayer leaders? What do they have in common? The contents, implications and legacy of the above narratives, with a focus on Umm Salama, will in this chapter be presented and analysed within the wider framework of the categories used in legal and other literature as part of the Islamic discourse on the nature of legitimate leadership. Among such categories, those of excellence and precedence, as already highlighted in Chapter 1, emerge as being predominant. The *hadith* narratives themselves will be used in the second part of this chapter, in the (mainly legal) arguments in favour of and against the permissibility of women leading other women in prayer.

It has been argued that representations of the women closest to the Prophet were constructed in accordance with Islamic discourses on political legitimacy.[9] Indeed, this will also be shown to be the case for the narrations of prayer leadership by 'A'isha and Umm Salama. Such representations were mainly based on reports that were recorded and crafted not by the women themselves, but by others around them or those who lived after their time. In the case of Umm Salama and 'A'isha, their two personas were often used to articulate subsequent conflicts and debates between Muslim groups, particularly between Sunnis and Shi'is.

Who was Umm Salama? Some considerations on her ritual leadership

Chroniclers and hagiographers report that Umm Salama Hind bint Abi Umayya belonged to the influential Makhzum clan of the Quraysh tribe in Mecca. She was first married to Abu Salama, also from a powerful Qurayshi clan. He was one of the first 'converts' to Islam and, as a supporter of the Prophet, and thus fearing persecution by his own tribe, he migrated with his wife to Abyssinia. After returning to Mecca, he migrated again to Medina, with Umm Salama joining him only after a series of harrowing events. In Medina, Abu Salama fought on the Prophet's side in several battles, was injured and, as a result, died. Hagiographers add that just before his death Abu Salama made his wife promise him that she would remarry and assured her that her new husband would be a better man than himself. Distraught for her loss and pregnant with her fourth child, Umm Salama married the Prophet in year 4 of the Hijra / 626 CE. She lived a long life and became the longest surviving wife of the Prophet, her death occurring between 679 and 680.[10]

Details gathered from the *hadith*s by or about Umm Salama, from *Sira* accounts, biographical and *tafsir* works present an image of a woman of high standing, literate,[11] wise and attentive to detail. They portray a woman with a voice, not afraid of expressing her opinion, even when it challenged that of powerful men, such as when she rebuked 'Umar ibn al-Khattab for interfering in the private affairs of Muhammad and his wives.[12] According to some Qur'anic exegetes, her remark to the Prophet that the Qur'an seemingly addressed only men, prompted – or was linked to – the revelation of the Qur'anic verse 33.35 'for Muslim men and Muslim women, believing men and believing women ...', in which women are indeed explicitly addressed alongside men.[13] We will see in Chapter 4 that this trait, attributed to Umm Salama, will acquire heightened relevance in modern debates.

A number of the *hadith*s on her authority also narrate that Umm Salama was consulted about issues relating to female ritual purity and the correct performance of prayer, from the type of clothes a praying woman should wear to the timing of the prostration cycles (*rak'a*) during the supererogatory (*nawafil*) prayer.[14] Her knowledge on prayer ritual could be seen as linked to her role as prayer leader, the former informing and justifying the latter.

Like the Prophet's wives 'A'isha and Hafsa, Umm Salama is reported to have possessed her own copy of the Qur'an. Moreover, Shi'i authorities refer to other 'secret' books which were passed on from Muhammad to 'Ali and eventually to the Imams after him. For the transmission of one of these books, which reportedly contained 'new knowledge' (i.e. additional to Qur'anic knowledge), Umm Salama plays a pivotal role. In fact Shi'i traditions claim that the Prophet himself gave her a book for safekeeping for the future legitimate leader, who would later claim it. Among the Rashidun caliphs, 'Ali alone asked her for the book.[15] Here Shi'i writers portray Umm Salama as the *trait d'union* between the Prophet and 'Ali, hence legitimizing, on the authority of the Prophet himself, the leadership of 'Ali above the caliphs who preceded him.

Another *trait* of the portrayal of Umm Salama is her active commitment to the Prophetic mission: Umm Salama asked the Prophet permission to join him in battle to tend to the wounded. Even though his reply was that women were not required to carry out *jihad*, it is reported that she did accompany him in at least seven battles. Her presence in the battlefield, at times in the company of other co-wives, is qualified in terms of a supportive role for her husband, as counsellor or advisor, as a guide for other women present, as well as a spokesperson or intermediary in negotiations.[16] These reported roles are certainly not those of a fighter, but it might be of some relevance that the narratives about her note that she belonged to the Banu Makhzum clan, the same clan associated with the 'first female martyr' of Islam: Sumayya bint Khattab.[17] By being present on the battlefield, Umm Salama was in a position to transmit *hadiths* about events relating to specific military actions. Overall, these narratives on her standing and public persona point to the representation of a person fit for leadership.

In view of legal debates that seem to have developed, particularly from the 9th century onwards, about the best qualified individuals to lead prayer, Umm Salama's narratives on her prayer leadership indeed fit many of the legal 'requirements' indicated earlier in Chapter 1 of this book. As one of the most prominent 'mothers of the believers', Umm Salama commanded respect and authority; she had first-hand knowledge of the Prophetic *sunna*, i.e. the lived Prophetic guidance by example. As an authority often consulted by individuals outside her family and clientage circles[18] about details in ritual and other issues of conduct, Umm Salama was indeed presented as knowledgeable about the Prophetic example, but also of the relevant sections of the Qur'anic revelation. Moreover, as an early convert and emigrant, Umm Salama had showed her loyalty and committment to the Prophetic mission before most. Her individual commitment to the faith continued after the migration, as is shown by her willingness, and indeed her resolve, to go to battle along with the Prophet. Additionally, on the basis of the narrative by Ibn Sallam, Umm Salama was in her own household quarters and, as the mistress of the house, she had priority in leading in prayer the people of her own household, those residing there or those visiting. Above all, as the Prophet's wife and belonging to a prominent Meccan family, Umm Salama no doubt qualified to be ascribed the nobility and dignity (*sharf*) to be a prayer leader.

Like Umm Salama, 'A'isha too is reported to have led women in the prescribed prayer.[19] These two wives have several traits in common: they are both from influential backgrounds which gave them additional prestige, and they are presented as outspoken and linked to specific occasions of revelation. Beyond that, they are the most prolific among the Prophet's wives and female companions in their recollection and transmission of *hadiths*,[20] and hence reliable and trusted authorities. There is also a political dimension attached to both.

Already in the *Musnad* by the celebrated Muslim theologian and jurisprudent Ibn Hanbal (d. 855), Umm Salama and 'A'isha are portrayed as figureheads, among the Prophet's co-wives, of two camps. From personal antagonism and competition in influence, these two camps became, after the Prophet's demise, filled with political connotations. While 'A'isha is reported as having actively taken on a leadership role in the Battle of the Camel (656) and allied with Talha and al-Zubayr against 'Ali, Umm Salama is portrayed as being opposed to 'A'isha's decision to take on a public role exemplified by her partaking in that battle. Umm Salama justified her opposition by reminding 'A'isha of the proper behaviour for the Prophet's wives, who, as indicated in the Qur'anic verse 33.33 were expected to remain in their own houses. Not surprisingly, Umm Salama is shown as expressing her support for 'Ali's claims.

Along sectarian lines, Sunni and Shi'i authors would identify, respectively, 'A'isha or Umm Salama as the Prophet's 'favourite' wife after Khadija. It has been noted that what can be considered as a trope about the 'rivalry' between 'A'isha and Umm Salama gradually escalated in the accounts of the Battle of the Camel. Such accounts were retrospectively reported by 9th century Shi'i writers such as al-Ya'qubi as well as 10th century Sunni authors like al-Tabari and Ibn 'Abd Rabbihi.[21] In time, it was Umm Salama's argument of wifely obedience and refrain from female political involvement which would serve as a 'borrowed' voice of both Sunni and Shi'i scholars to express their own views on female participation in politics and more generally in the public sphere.[22]

Basing her research on the *hadiths* transmitted or attributed to 'A'isha and Umm Salama, as well as narratives about them in biographical literature, Asma Sayeed argues that reports of Umm Salama have often been used to counteract those of 'A'isha's. Umm Salama appears to have been consulted for advice on a more selective basis, and her network of transmitters to be less broad than 'A'isha's. This would account for the difference in number of *hadiths* in which each wife was reported as the first authority: over 1500 for 'A'isha compared to around 175 for Umm Salama.[23]

The reports on women as prayer leaders and their sources

In order to locate the above-mentioned narratives on Umm Salama's prayer leadership within a broader context, it is useful to briefly analyse the sources from which those passages were quoted; all of them were compiled at least two hundred years after the death of the Prophet. There is little doubt that the *Kitab al-Umm*, together with other works associated with al-Shafi'i, is among the earliest texts which display an articulated technique for the use of *hadith*s as legal sources as well as the arguments to support the accommodation of the law to such sources. However, both the attribution of the *Umm* to al-Shafi'i and its dating are contested. For Norman Calder the *Kitab al-Umm* is the end-product of a long process of school discussions that emerged after the death of al-Shafi'i, which would date it between 80 to 100 years after 820.[24] Joseph Lowry, on the other hand, defends al-Shafi'i's authorship. The broader subtext of these scholarly discussions is the relation between *hadith*s and the law, as the latter was being developed and systematized.

Indeed the actions of the Prophet's wives can be seen as fitting examples to be used as precedents for subsequent (re)formulations of ritual practice. But to what extent is ritual performance derived from or based on these *hadith*s? Or is the emergence of *hadith*s a response to, and legitimization of, existing ritual practices and customs? In view of the aforementioned *hadith*s on Umm Salama: is her example to be seen as a precedent for what would become legal arguments in favour of or against women leading other women in prayer? Or are these *hadith*s an outcome, perhaps an apt narrative selection, to support legal positions on the permissibility of women leading women in prayer?

The second source cited at the start of this chapter, Ibn Sa'd's *Book of Classes*, belongs to the category of biographical literary genre; the *hadith* on Umm Salama is included in the last volume, which is dedicated to the women who met the Prophet. There are sections on individual women, such as the Prophet's wives. Umm Salama has her own entry which includes her biography and a selection of *hadith*s that she transmitted or *hadith*s about her, which all help to illustrate important periods of her life, such as her husband's death or her marriage to Muhammad. However, the *hadith* on her *imama* is included in another section of the book under the entry for the female transmitter Hujayra bint Husayn, about whom Ibn Sa'd provides no further details; no other *hadith*s are known to have been transmitted in her name.

The *Book of Classes* is a narrative that retrospectively focuses on prominent individuals, in our case, women from Muhammad's time, based on oral and written sources, with a clear emphasis on the *hadith*s linked to specific individuals, which are usually introduced by a chain of transmitters. Ibn Sa'd's portrayal of Umm Salama, not unlike other women in the Prophet's household, reflects the interest he and his contemporaries had for the life of the Prophet's wives and Companions as moral and religious models as well as precedents for developing juridic norms. Such a depiction is clearly idealized and enriched with hagiographical details which, in the case of Umm Salama, serve to pass on moral messages about female 'virtues' of patience, strength, endurance and resignation in harshness, poverty and sorrow, alongside female frugality and modesty, while showing the Prophet to be a just, caring and wise husband.[25]

The third source is by the Zaydi scholar from Kufa, 'Abd Allah Muhammad ibn Sallam ibn Sayyar, who is thought to have lived during the second half of the 9th century.[26] His main informant is the renowned collector of Zaydi *hadith*s, the Kufan Muhammad ibn Mansur al-Muradi (d. 902).[27] A *hadith* with almost identical wording to his is found in the *hadith* collection controversially attributed to Zayd Ibn 'Ali (d. 740), the great-grandson of 'Ali ibn Abi Talib and the eponym of the Zaydi branch of Shi'i Islam. Irrespective of its ascription, such a collection is commonly considered to belong to the early Kufan tradition.

Even though little is known about Ibn Sallam, he is mentioned in several Zaydi works and by the well-respected and influential Twelver Shi'i 12th century theologian and jurist Abu 'Abdallah Ibn Shahrashub. The text of this *hadith* represents one of the rare instances in which direct dialogue between the Prophet and a woman on female prayer leadership is cited. In this verbal exchange the Prophet interrogates Umm Salama who provides well-informed competent answers. The narrative also presents a woman who takes the initiative to ask the Prophet about the permissibility of female leadership in prayer, thus giving her agency. The reference to 'Ali in the narrative as being present in the company of the Prophet betrays a politico-sectarian sub-narrative on the part of the Shi'i author.

The *hadith*s found in Ibn Sallam's works are well-known and often quoted by subsequent Zaydi, Imami Shi'i and Isma'ili authorities, such as al-Qadi al-Nu'man (d. 974), who is widely recognized as the 'founder' of Isma'ili jurisprudence. Al-Qadi al-Nu'man includes this *hadith* in the section on prayer in his *Kitab al-idah*, which was most likely written soon after 926, as one of the sources to support his argument in favour of the *imama* of a woman, providing she leads other women from the middle. Al-Qadi al-Nu'man, who was one of the sources on early Fatimid propaganda, consistently mentioned the participation of women in religious learning and doctrinal sessions. To have selected a *hadith* about female leadership of prayer on the basis of the precedent of Umma Salama, rather than that of 'A'isha, beside possibly betraying negative Shi'i attitudes towards 'A'isha, is revealing about the place Umm Salama holds among Shi'i writers of all groups, from Twelvers, Seveners to Fivers like the Zaydis. Such popularity among Shi'i writers, however, did not diminish her high status among Sunni scholars.[28] The *isnad* in this *hadith* is substantially different from that in the Sunni sources, the transmitter being their eponym, the Imam Zayd ibn 'Ali Zayn al-'Abidin, who transmits from his forebears (*aba'ihi*), and they from 'Ali ibn Abi Talib. Therefore, this transmission stems directly from the authority of the Imams back to 'Ali, who witnessed the event in person.

Ibn Abi Shayba quotes two *hadith*s on Umm Salama's prayer leadership. Unlike those reported by the above mentioned scholars, the second of his *hadith*s exhibits a different *isnad* where the oldest authority is Umm al-Hasan, likely to be the mother of the famous mystic scholar al-Hasan al-Basri (d. 728). All that is known about her is that she was a contemporary of Umm Salama, possibly her maid, and that, according to Ibn Sa'd, she transmitted another *hadith* about prayer on the authority of Umm Salama and was (ambigiously) reported as being a 'narrator' to the people.[29] Some authorities consider her a reliable transmitter while, for others, she is just acceptable.

Al-Shafi'i, Ibn Sa'd and Ibn Abi Shayba transmit the *hadith* about Umm Salama's prayer from Sufyan ibn 'Uyayna (d. 814), who was a young pupil of the leading Medinan scholar and jurisprudent Ibn Shihab al-Zuhri (d. 742).[30] The three *isnad*s are identical, with Sufyan transmitting from 'Ammar al-Duhni (d. 750–1),[31] who transmitted from Hujayra. In the language of *hadith* studies, these *isnad*s occurring in the three sources are made of the same single strand of transmitters, with Sufyan ibn 'Uyayna as the last transmitter. Notwithstanding questions concerning Sufyan's chronology and some suspicion of *tadlis* (tampering with *isnad*s), he is widely cited by classical authorities and considered to be a reliable transmitter; similarly, irrespective of his supposed Shi'i leanings, Sunni authors regard 'Ammar as a reliable source. The text of these *hadith*s is only slightly different, with the noticeable addition, in Ibn Sa'd's case, of the afternoon prayer as that which was being led.[32]

Upon closer analysis of the above *hadith*s, it can be noted that they all exhibit single strand *isnad*s, with some of the transmitters such as Sufyan and Umm al-Hasan seeming to be 'unnaturally old' in order to fit chronological credibility. For *hadith* scholars such as Juynboll this type of *hadith* would accordingly be deemed highly suspicious.[33] However, his negative evaluation of single-strand *hadith*s as being mainly fictitious has been contested by scholars such as Motzki.[34]

Another possible flaw in the authenticity of the shared *isnad* is that its oldest transmitters are little-known female Successors such as Hujayra and Umm al-Hasan. They are among a number of women of the second generation of Muslims to whom one *hadith* is ascribed, under a specific circumstance in which they witnessed one event involving a wife of the Prophet. The details of these women's chronology are unknown, but, for instance for Hujayra, they are credible yet possibly 'elongated', with a gap of 70 years between the death of Umm Salama (d. ca 680) and that of al-Duhni (d. 750–1), who transmitted from Hujayra. To provide a plausible chain of narrators, with a female Successor as the oldest direct witness, was a means to ensure the validity of the transmission and of the *hadith* itself at a time of increased professionalization of the narrators of *hadith*s.

Both Hujayra and Umm al-Hasan are minor *hadith* transmitters who are representative of the period immediately preceding 'the demise of women's participation in *hadith* transmission', a demise that Asma Sayeed has identified as having occurred between the late 8th to the mid 9th century. Both Hujayra and Umm al-Hasan share with other better-known early female transmitters the handing down of *hadith*s from one Companion only and, as in earlier cases of 'A'isha and Umma Salama, they pass down their narrative to male as well as female authorities.[35]

While some scholars have cast doubt on the reliability of these *hadith*s, the majority would rate them as *hasan* (fair), if not *sahih* (sound).[36] This is firstly on account of the extant biographical details of the 'more recent' transmitters; secondly of a reasonable, though not fully clear, degree of overlap between any two consecutive transmitters; and, finally, of a generally recognized and agreed-upon text, known also through strands with alternative Companions or Successors (Umm Salama and Umm al-Hasan). In addition, the *hadith*s in question are cited, with the same *isnad*, by a number of well-known early collectors, as well as by a variety of subsequent authorities, who did not query their authenticity. All these elements concur to an overall claim that these *hadith*s were, and to a large degree still are, *perceived* as being narratives reported by reliable witnesses.[37] Finally, *hadith*s from independent *isnad*s (from Umm al-Hasan and from Hujayra) theoretically corroborate each other.

Yet, if the *hadith*s on Umm Salama's prayer leadership as reported by al-Shafi'i, Ibn Sa'd, 'Ali ibn Abi Shayba and similar ones by other scholars are considered to be reliable, should there not be a consensus among legal Sunni schools about there being scriptural precedents for the permissibility of women leading other women in prayer? This direct causality would assume that textual sources are the only starting point for jurists and that they have been and always will be binding. What also needs to be considered is the alternative theory that laws and customs themselves are the starting point, and that legal arguments are developed to reconcile the laws with the textual sources. Moreover, social and historical circumstances do change, and with them attitudes towards women, making this a factor – for some scholars the main factor – that contributes to the apparent hiatus between scriptural evidence and legal norms. Thus, flexibility is needed to interpret those texts to evidence or enable 'change'. Scholars adopted several means to neutralize or limit those binding texts: they disqualified them as time-bound and hence not to be acted upon, they stated they had been abrogated, they doubted their authenticity, and more. In fact, only the more recent Shafi'i and Hanbali legal schools used the above-mentioned *hadith*s as legal precedents to warrant their positions in favour of women leading women in prayer. Malikis rejected such a position, while Hanafis held various opinions, as will be analysed later on in this chapter.

Are there any other ways of analysing these *hadith*s in order to gather further insights? One notable aspect to consider is that with the exception of al-Shafi'i, all the collectors of the above-mentioned narratives originated from 'Abbasid Iraq. They all include in their chain of transmission the *hadith* scholar Sufyan ibn 'Uyayna. He transmitted from Medinan scholars but, more significantly, also from the Kufan 'Ammar al-Duhni, who in turn transmitted from the Medinan Hujayra, with whom he claimed to have shared the same ancestry.

Both Medina and Iraq, the two main hubs of *hadith* transmission, are represented in this *isnad*. But it is the Iraqi centres of Basra and Kufa that feature prominently in the *isnad*s of the majority of *hadith*s on the *imama* of Umm Salama, A'isha and, as we will see in Chapter 3, Umm Waraqa. Though much more nuanced and contested, this geographical pattern would support the long-held assumption of the conflict between Kufan and Medinese regional 'schools'. It would also endorse the identification of Kufa as a legal centre for the use of *ra'y* (independent legal reasoning) as the main basis for arriving at legal opinions, as contrasted to Medina's reliance on *hadith*. These two regional legal traditions were believed to have survived into later, distinct legal schools: the legal tradition of Kufa surviving in the Hanafi school while that of Medina in the Maliki school.[38]

In view of the above, could there also be any significant regional patterns in the spread of viewpoints about female leadership in prayer? Is the *hadith* shared by the three sources a case of what Benham Sadeghi would term a 'travelling *hadith*'? Indeed, as will be shortly discussed in the case of the Maliki opposition to female leadership, there appear to be two general tendencies, which in time became consolidated. One is linked to Medinan scholars opposing female *imama* of any kind, the other to Iraqi scholars with more varied and nuanced positions. This is evidenced by the geographical origin or association of the known *hadith* transmitters. For instance, when in his *Musannaf* Ibn Abi Shayba organizes his *hadith*s on female prayer leadership into two sections, one including reports in support of and the other section reports against the permissiblity of a female ritual leadership, one can notice that the majority of the transmsitters in the support section are from Kufa and Basra, while those against are associated with Medina.[39] Such a geographical tendency has been noted by both classical and modern scholars, as has the existence of some individual exceptions to these predominant local trends.[40]

Benham Sadeghi also studied *hadith*s about female prayer leadership with *isnad*s which are geographically mixed. Arguing that each city has a distinctive linguistic and legal profile, through analyses of their *isnad*, their wording and contents, Sadeghi concluded that not only can a geographical pattern be identified, but also a temporal development within some locales. Thus, while the majority of *hadith*s with *isnad*s from Mecca and Iraq permit female prayer leadership, those from Medina disallow it, so making Sadeghi conclude that Medina was 'probably the birthplace of categorical opposition to women leading women in prayer'.[41] However, Sadeghi identified a temporal shift in Medina between the 7th century and 8th century, where, though the majority position remained one of opposition, due to increased interaction between cities during the 8th century, there is evidence of individuals importing and adopting positions from other localities and therefore expressing a more 'permissive' stance. One of these authorities with a 'permissive' stance is Safwan ibn Sulaym (d. 750) who is cited by al-Shafi'i and al-Muzani.

What Sadeghi's thorough analysis of *hadith*s shows is how porous the boundaries were during the first two centuries of Islam among the 'nascent' and developing legal schools. Other scholars also argue that not only were the boundaries between legal positions, and eventually between legal schools, much more fluid during this period, but also their association with specific geographical locations might be reconsidered. In this respect, Melchert contends that the competing legal positions in favour of *ra'y* in Iraq and *hadith* in Hijaz were in fact not clearly in place until the 9th century.[42] The in-depth analysis conducted so far, centred around the *hadith*s on Umm Salama's leadership, validates Sadeghi's argument.

What is the extent of the accuracy to which we can reconstruct the position of not only a legal school but also of its individual authorities? A case in point that will be shown is Malik ibn Anas, the eponym of the Maliki school which is associated with disallowing female leadership in prayer under any circumstances.

Hadiths *on female prayer leadership and Sunni jurisprudence*

The following overview of legal positions is not presented in strict chronological order, but rather on the basis of individuals' and schools' positions from the least permissive of women acting as imams to the overall more permissive. This serves to gradually show how the *hadiths* reporting the leadership of Umm Salama, 'A'isha and Umm Waraqa have been used to support specific positions.

The Maliki position on female leadership and the Medinan practice

In the *Kitab al-Muwatta'*, the only extant work by Malik Ibn Anas (d. 795),[43] there is no reference to women leading prayer. There are other references to women in connection with prayer, for instance women attending *salat* in congregation and attracting attention by clapping their hands, as well as sections on female ritual impurity, and also a touching report on the Prophet performing prayer in the company of his little grand-daughter. It is in the works of Malik's later commentators and pupils that we find citations about his reported opinions[44] on women leading prayer. Whether these were indeed Malik's views or the prevailing Maliki position during the specific writer's time is, however, open to question.

Contrasting opinions among Maliki scholars about the permissibility of female leadership of prayer were still occuring in medieval al-Andalus. This region of the Iberian Peninsula had been a province of the Umayyad caliphate since the early decades of the 8th century and, though its rulers were Sunni in doctrine, they were in political opposition to the 'Abbasid caliphs of Baghdad. The Andalusian Maliki theologian Sulayman ibn Khalaf al-Baji (d. 1081) reports that one of Malik's pupils, Ibn Ayman, had claimed that Malik was, in fact, in favour of women acting as imams for other women. This, however, remained an isolated statement but still reflective of a regional and juridical-cultural context of heightened attention to the role of women in ritual.[45]

All other scholars, whose works are still extant, report that Malik rejected the leadership of a woman in all cases, whether for obligatory or supererogatory prayers.[46] Evidence of this stance is found already in the *Mudawwana* by Sahnun ibn Sa'id (d. 854), a Maliki jurist who cites the replies of a pupil of Malik, Ibn Qasim (d. 807), who in turn quotes his legal master's opinions. In the *Mudawwana*, Malik's reply to a question about a woman leading prayer is direct and concise: 'the woman does not lead in prayer' (*la ta'ummu al-mar'a*).[47] In the same passage, Malik is reported to have stated that a child cannot lead in voluntary prayer either men or women, which implies that he could, in theory at least, lead other children. This is not the case for a woman; there is no specification of her potential congregation. One can therefore assume that she cannot lead at all! Later on in the text, this lack of permissibility is repeated with the qualification, not by Malik himself, that she cannot lead in the required prayer. The argument is followed by providing the example of a child who cannot lead because of his lack of attainment of sexual maturity.

Already discussed in Chapter 1 of this book, the issue of maturity is here shown to have become conflated into the discourse against female prayer leadership.

Against those who looked at the narratives on 'A'isha having led in prayer as precedent for female leadership, it is reported that the Medinan Hisham ibn 'Urwa, one of Malik's teachers, could not find a better way to respond than stating the obvious: that 'A'isha was herself led in prayer.[48] It is worth noting, however, that in the case of a man finding himself praying behind a woman, according to the *Mudawwana*, both his and her prayer are nevertheless considered valid.[49]

The theologian al-Baji in his *Kitab al-muntaqa*, which is a commentary on Malik's *Muwatta'*, further expands on Malik's position about women leading prayer by explaining the reasoning behind disallowing a woman from acting as an imam. Reflecting current elaborations on the qualities of a leader, including a prayer leader, al-Baji states that, as the issue of ritual leadership is one of excellence and perfection to which individuals aspire, there should be no deficiencies attached to an imam. However, in the case of a woman, on the basis of a much debated and contested yet widely circulated *hadith*, two types of deficiencies or imperfections (*naqs*) are identified: one in religion (*din*) and one in intellect (*'aql*).[50] Hence, a woman cannot be a leader and, contrary to the assertion in the *Mudawwana*, al-Baji states that whoever prays behind her needs to repeat the prayer.[51] He makes his argument even more unequivocal by reporting the statement, attributed to Malik, that the three conditions that render prayer leadership invalid are: being female, being a minor – hence with no legal capacity (*'adam taklif*) – and deficiency in religion (*din*). To summarize, for al-Baji, unlike a child who is permitted at least to lead voluntary prayers during Ramadan,[52] a woman cannot lead at all; she can lead neither men nor women in the prescribed or the voluntary prayer.

Notwithstanding early variations of opinion, and even allowing for some uncertainty about Malik's own stance on women leading women in prayer, it therefore appears that by the late 9th and early 10th century, the legal positions of the Maliki school on female prayer leadership were presented as having reached an overall consensus: women could not lead prayers under any circumstances. The justifications adduced include scriptural evidence from the *hadiths*, among which is the *hadith* that the best row for women is the last, which would prevent women from leading. Moreover, in terms of a woman's ritual capacity, she has a limitation in that it is not desirable, nor permitted, for her to call the *adhan* and the *iqama*; by analogy, she is not to perform *imama* either. Strictly related to this is another reason provided by Maliki jurisprudents, which is linked to the concept of *'awra* (something to be concealed, private parts): women ought not to expose their bodies, and even their voice should not be heard as, for them, the female voice is also *'awra*.[53] In this regard, al-Baji's argument echoes the ongoing association among jurists between *'awra* and *fitna*, as will be shown later in this chapter.

It also appears from the various statements from Malik and his pupils that group prayers were understood to be of mixed genders and that the option was not envisaged for women to pray the ritual prayer in an all-female congregation. This could also explain one of the bases for the impermissibility of female prayer leadership *tout court*, without the further option of women leading women, which, instead, was considered and discussed by the other Sunni and Shi'i legal schools.

One interpretative key to the Maliki position on women leading prayer is to consider the frequent reliance by Malik, and his school after him, on what they identified as the practice (*'amal*) of the people of Medina – that is, what they believed to be the uninterrupted orally transmitted practice from the Prophet's era down to Malik's own time. For Malik, as explained by his pupils, this practice can be more authoritative than *hadith*s, especially single strand *hadith*s. In his *Muwatta'* there are numerous examples, in cases where two sources are at variance, of Malik's preference for Medinan *'amal* over isolated *hadith*s. This approach also applies to *salat* performance. We saw that in his *Mudawwana*, Sahnun quotes Malik stating that a woman cannot be a prayer leader.[54] In the same section, a number of reports are provided to support this stance by various authorities, some contemporary with Malik, such as the Medinan Ibn Abi Dhi'b, or Malik's transmitters such as Ibn Wahb, others from early authoritative transmitters such as the Kufan *faqih* Ibrahim al-Nakha'i (d. 715).

Of importance in this section of the *Mudawwana* is the (not-so-) implicit refutation of the numerous *hadith*s attesting to occasions of female prayer leadership. In the case of 'A'isha, for example, an alternative tradition on her having a male *imam* for her prayers is related by no less than the Medinan authority Hisham ibn 'Urwa (d. 763), whose transmission from 'A'isha is well-known and extensively used by later scholars such as al-Bukhari and al-Tabari.[55] It is in al-Baji's commentary on the *Muwatta'* that the Maliki writer voices his definitive dismissal of *hadith*s on female prayer leadership, asserting that they cannot be depended on or acted upon; in other words, they are null and void.[56]

What is at stake here is the pre-eminence of the alleged Medinan practice over textual evidence alone. As Yasin Dutton stated in his fine analysis of al-Malik's *Muwatta'*, 'sometimes ... he [Malik] relates a *hadith* which is not in accord with *'amal* precisely in order to make it clear that, although known, it is not acted upon'.[57] For Malik and his followers, the continuity of the Medinan practice is evidenced by the number of authorities who transmitted a particular report as well as by the practice being transmitted down to the writer's time. If Malik or one of his pupils personally heard a report by one transmitter, this would be more authoritative for them than any number of single strand *hadith*s which, they contend, are subject to possible errors and to being later abrogated. This is the case, for example, for one such narrative that states 'the woman does not lead in prayer', which was transmitted by a Medinan authority contemporary with Malik, Muhammad Ibn Abi Dhi'b (d. 776), and cited in the *Mudawwana*.[58] This narrative would be preferred to single-strand *hadith*s like the ones on Umm Salama acting as an imam, which would be regarded as not (or no longer) conforming to the Medinan practice.

One can legitimately wonder which Medina is the one reflected in such a 'Medinan practice'. Is it the Medina during the time of the Prophet, with its diversity of attitudes towards women and their status, as exemplified by the contrasting positions reported in numerous *hadith*s between Muhammad and his Companion 'Umar ibn al-Khattab? Is it the Medina in which the likes of Umm Salama and 'A'isha and a few others lived and are reported to have led prayers? Or rather is it the portrayal, or even the construct, of a Medina as 'imagined' in later times by scholars who were living during the early centuries of the 'Abbasid caliphate? This was a time of economic, urban, military and cultural change which substantially affected the status of Muslim women in general. In light of such changes, did the scholars find in their recourse to the 'Medinan practice' the rationale for the continuity of their own social attitudes?[59] By not limiting the approach here to one of historical accuracy as against scholarly agendas, one could identify and interpret both the concept and the use of the 'Medinan practice' as one instance of what Talal Asad termed 'discursive tradition'. Consequently, this 'Medinan practice' can be considered as the outcome of an interpretative relationship with sources, such as the *hadith*, and one which underpins the reshaping of past models by scholars in light of the times in which they lived.

If Maliki scholars dismissed the *hadiths* reporting examples of female ritual leadership as not-to-be-acted-upon in light of their understanding of the 'Medinan practice', a number of jurists of the Hanafi *madhhab* found other ways to cite those same *hadiths* while disregarding their applicability to their own times.

Hanafi positions on female imama: *Elaboration, selectivity and the theory of abrogation*

Christopher Melchert, in his short yet rich survey of medieval Islamic legal positions on women's access to mosques, warns that 'it is risky to rely on any one authority for the position of a whole school, since there was usually disagreement within schools'.[60] This could not be more accurate than in the case of the Hanafi *madhhab* in respect of women-only prayer groups and women leading other women in prayer. The two issues are linked, though not necessarily consequential to one another. While an all-female group prayer might be disallowed or discouraged, jurists had to consider, in the event of an all-female prayer group actually performing *salat*, whether it was permissible for one woman to be their imam. If so, were there conditions for the prayer of the female leader and that of her female congregation to be valid?

In the course of this section, it will be argued that Hanafi scholars opposing female *imama* exhibited and developed a more nuanced system of justification for such an opposition than their Maliki colleagues. In their arguments, Hanafi scholars did indeed refer to the *hadiths* about 'A'isha, Umm Salama and Umm Waraqa, but many of them selected or reported them in different versions, which fitted better with their own viewpoints about women leading other women in prayer.

Not unlike the case of Malik, the opinions of the Kufa-born theologian and jurist Abu Hanifa (d. 767) are reported in writing not by the master himself, but by his pupils. This has raised doubts among modern scholars about the accuracy of attribution of those statements to the master as the single person from whom such opinions are claimed to have originated. Rather, they argue, the master served as a focal reference, whose opinions were seemingly arranged and explained by his immediate pupils and followers. Moreover, though it has been long assumed that the formation of the 'personal' (i.e. Maliki, Hanafi) legal schools derived from earlier regional schools (i.e Medinese and Kufan), this assumption has in fact been contested by some scholars. For example, in the case of Abu Hanifa and his school, Melchert argues that the geographical association of Hanafi jurisprudence with earlier Kufan legal practices in fact emerged no earlier than the 9th century.

On the basis of the *Kitab al-Athar* compiled by Muhammad al-Shaybani (d. 805), one of the most famous among Abu Hanifa's pupils – in fact for many scholars the one who systematized, and hence modified or adjusted, his master's doctrine – the issue of female prayer leadership is presented by quoting an appropriate *hadith*, followed by al-Shaybani's own assessment. The latter assessment, though, is given full authority by al-Shaybani's claim that it coincides with Abu Hanifa's own opinion. The *hadith* chosen is transmitted through a fully Kufan *isnad*: from Abu Hanifa, who was informed by his own teacher Hammad ibn Abi Sulayman (d. 737) who transmitted from the jurist Ibrahim ibn Yazid al-Nakha'i. The *matn* is that "'A'isha, the mother of the believers... used to lead the women during the month of Ramadan and she stood in the middle".[61] This is followed by al-Shaybani's statement, 'it is not to our liking (*la yu'jibuna*) that a woman should lead in prayer, but if she does, she should stand in the middle of the row, with the women, as 'A'isha did. This is what Abu Hanifa stated.'[62]

Of all the *hadith*s about 'A'isha leading prayer, it is noteworthy here that al-Shaybani, in order to make his case, selects the one in which it is specified that the prayer she led was during the month of Ramadan. This detail was not mentioned in the *hadith*s on 'A'isha's cited by authorities such as Ibn Sa'd or Ibn Abi Shayba, who either assumed or explicitly stated that the prayer she led was a prescribed one (*maktuba*).[63] Instead, al-Shaybani's choice of *hadith* may imply that the prayer led during Ramadan might have been a voluntary one such as the *tarawih* night prayers. This is a type of prayer which, though meritorious, does not require as accomplished and qualified a leader as the obligatory one. In fact, for some scholars, night group prayers during Ramadan do not require an imam at all!

When, as mentioned earlier, the Medinan al-Malik or his pupils opposed the leadership of a woman under any circumstances, they contrasted the case of a woman with that of 'unusual or anomalous' imams, such as a slave or a blind male person, who could lead the voluntary prayers.[64] Instead, the Kufan Hanafi al-Shaybani, while allowing female leadership, limits it to the voluntary prayers and provides an apt *hadith* on 'A'isha's precedent confirming his position. The second part of the narrative is to further explain that female leadership, though permitted and legitimate in the case of voluntary prayers, is nevertheless neither favoured nor desirable.

A century later, the Egyptian Hanafi Ahmad al-Tahawi (d. 933) would make his position on women leading prayer even clearer: it would be better (*afdal*) for women to perform individual prayers rather than to pray in group where a woman leads. As Sadeghi explains, the term *afdal* 'in legal contexts usually implies the permissibility of the less preferred act',[65] so, on the basis of this clarification, one would assume that for al-Tahawi female leadership is still allowed. A number of later Hanafi scholars upheld the same position of disliked permissibility and continued to quote reports about 'A'isha and Umm Salama leading prayers from the middle, adding that these represented a practice of the early period of Islam.

On the basis of the above examples, what seems to be taking place is an attempt to reconcile textual evidence from the *hadith* with increasingly diverging attitudes towards women and their status. In these specific cases, textual evidence indicates the permissibility of women leadership, and the changing attitudes lead the scholars to express dislike, rather than prohibition, of it. They do so by gradually limiting the occasion in which a woman can lead prayer. Such a narrowing of opportunities is evidenced in al-Shaybani's selection of 'A'isha leadership of voluntary rather than canonical prayer and in al-Tahawi's preference for women's individual prayers over group prayers.

Further, some Hanafi scholars such as the Central Asian 11th century Muhammad b. Ahmad al-Sarakhsi and 12th century 'Ala' al-Din al-Kasani refer to the practice of women's prayers, and consequently of female leadership of such groups, as having been abrogated (*mansukha*). In Islam, the legal concept of abrogation (*naskh*) is in itself complex and controversial and, in the case of the above-mentioned scholars, applies to some rulings contained in the *sunna* of the Prophet, who, as mediator of the revealed law, should alone have the prerogative to change such rulings. In other words, abrogation could have only occurred before the Prophet's death. However, this has not been the case as is shown by a number of *hadith*s, including those relevant to prayers led by women. Moreover, the concept of abrogation and its modes, which are believed to have been legally systematized by the 4th century H (ca 900–1000 CE) were not accepted by all jurists, expecially those who held the Qur'an as the only source necessary for the formulation of the law.[66]

As Sadeghi notes in his analysis of the development of Hanafi positions about women's group prayers, neither al-Sarakhsi nor al-Kasani clearly pinpoint the time and circumstances for such an abrogation to have taken place. Both state that abrogation was introduced because of *fitna*, a term typically understood to mean sedition and social chaos but which, when applied to women, refers to the temptation they cause, which in turns leads to social chaos.

For these scholars, therefore, female gatherings including female group prayers could lead to *fitna*. They supported their argument by selecting and interpreting specific scriptural passages to support their position against women's prayers led by women. From the Qur'an they took the injunction to the Prophet's wives to remain in their homes (Qur. 33.33).[67] From the *hadith*s they selected those that spell out that the best prayer for women is the one in the most secluded area of their house. By doing so, they ignored the contextualization of the cited Qur'anic passage which states that the injunction was only intended for Muhammad's consorts. As for the *hadith*s, they overlooked the reference to group prayers as taking place in the women's homes. It is precisely the inside of the 'home' of one of these women, Umm Waraqa, that we will go into in Chapter 3.

Thus, what was to become a commonly held Hanafi position was that practices such as women leading prayer, though carried out in the early days of Islam, had subsequently been abrogated.[68] The issue here is to define what 'the early days of Islam' meant. Much later, the 14th century Hanafi Syrian scholar Akmal al-Babarti, in trying to determine what this period was, could not find any better solution than to state that it was 'the period before the abrogation'.[69] In this way al-Babarti found a convenient formula to overcome the hiatus between legal position and textual *hadith* evidence. Had he been more specific about the exact time of this abrogation to make it coincide, for instance, with the Prophet's death, it would have been highly problematic. This is because there is evidence from a number of sources, including *hadith*s, as we will see in Chapter 3, that the practice of women leading prayer continued after the Prophet.

And even if some statements found in *hadith*s could indeed be interpreted as evidence for abrogation, what exactly was being abrogated? Women group prayers, female leadership in prayer or the desirability of women group prayers and female leadership? These questions found their voice in Egyptian Hanafi jurist Ibn al-Humam (d. 1457), who provides two responses, one about the abrogation of desirability of the practice, the other of the practice itself. However, he does not explicitly side with either.[70] Unlike him, the majority of later Hanafis opted instead for equating non-desirability with prohibition of female leadership itself.

Irrespective of this, when it came to a woman-led prayer, it continued to be considered valid. An interesting legal position is that concerning group funerary prayers where theoretically not only could a woman lead women, but even men.[71] This position can be explained on the basis of funerary prayers being regarded as collective, rather than individual, obligations and being more informal than canonical prayers.

While Hanafi scholars were not unanimous in their interpretation of the implications of non-desirability, one of them in particular stood out by disagreeing with the others that the practice was undesirable at all. He supported his stance by quoting the very same *hadith*s about the prayer leadership of 'A'isha, Umm Salama and Umm Waraqa! He was indeed a thorough and knowledgeable *hadith* scholar, whom Sadeghi calls a 'maverick'! He was the Syrian Badr al-din al-'Ayni (d. 1451). On the basis of the *hadith*s he quotes, he argues that women can pray and lead women groups and that they can do so also for obligatory prayers. As for the issue of abrogation, he doubts that this ever took place, as the *hadith*s he cites show that female leadership was not confined to the early years of Islam.[72] Al-'Ayni's well-respected commentary of the most famous *hadith* collection, known as the *Sahih by Muhmmad al-Bukhari* (d. 870), informed a wider debate and exchange with the author of an even better-known commentary of the *Sahih*, the Shafi'i Ibn Hajar al-'Asqalani (d. 1449).

Al-'Ayni's 'independence of thought' within the Hanafi context might be summed up in the precedence he gave to textual evidence from Prophetic and Companions' traditions over legal opinions of jurisprudents and legal school precedents. His was a position and a methodology that the legal school of al-Shafi'i was credited with having laid the foundation for since the 9th century.

Al-Shafi'i, his school and the pre-eminence of hadiths *by the Prophet and his Companions*

According to those scholars who argue in favour of a development from regional to personal legal schools, if the Maliki school represented a continuation of the

Hijazi-Medinan legal practice, the Shafi'i school exemplified the Iraqi one. It is therefore not surprising that the Shafi'i scholars' overall opinions concerning female leadership of prayer vary from those of the Maliki school. Moreover, an important factor in the development of legal opinions is the methodology used for legal reasoning. Al-Shafi'i's metholodogy of anchoring Islamic legal arguments in the textual evidence of the Qur'an and the Prophetic *hadiths* has been hailed as a turning point for the development of early Islamic jurisprudence. Nevertheless, in recent times, scholars have started to reconsider long-held assumptions about the centrality of al-Shafi'i himself in such a development, in favour of a more nuanced and complex methodological process which became relevant almost a century after al-Shafi'i's death in 820.[73]

Al-Shafi'i's legal arguments about women's congregational prayers and female leadership are clearly centred on the evidence provided by relevant *hadiths*. The Umm Salama report included at the inset of this chapter is the first example of textual evidence referred to by al-Shafi'i in the section on the *imama* of a woman of his *Kitab al-Umm*. It is followed by a *hadith* on the authority of 'A'isha leading afternoon prayer. He then reports on other authorities that it is part of the *sunna* for a woman who leads other women to stand in the middle of the row. Finally, his third instance of female prayer leadership is that of a *jariya* (young girl, female slave) of 'Ali ibn al-Husayn (d. 713), whom he ordered to lead his people (i.e. his household) during Ramadan.

Here al-Shafi'i significantly adds the reported voice of a woman, 'Amra, who, he states, used to instruct a woman [leader] during the month of Ramadan to position herself in the middle of the women, and the woman would lead the women in the obligatory and voluntary prayers. 'Amra ordered her to stand in the middle of the row and, in case the women were too numerous, to make a second row behind the first. This 'Amra has been identified with 'Amra bint 'Abd al-Rahman (d. 716 or 724), a prominent Companion, niece and a pupil of 'A'isha from whom she transmitted numerous *hadiths*. She was considered a learned woman and thus consulted in matters of legal import.[74] Her status, blood link to 'A'isha and the acquisition of knowledge from her, made 'Amra an authoritative instructor on the modality of female prayer leadership and warranted her a place in al-Shafi'i's *al-Umm* as one of the authorities on female prayer leadership.

After his references to *hadiths* and to legal authorities comes al-Shafi'i's own opinion in the form of a statement: a woman may lead women in the obligatory prayer but is advised to stand in the middle. In the event of a woman leading from the front, both her prayer and that of those behind her are, nevertheless, valid. Finally, al-Shafi'i states that his personal preference would be for a woman acting as an imam to be a freeborn woman because of her being veiled while praying.[75] Nevertheless, even if she or the women she leads are unveiled, their prayer is still valid because 'prayer is an obligatory act for each one of them'.[76]

If today one might be tempted to marvel at al-Shafi'i's seemingly 'permissive' attitude toward female leadership, reading the last sentence of the relevant section on female prayer leadership reveals an attitude typical of his period. He states that prayer leadership by a male leader (*qa'id*) has a higher value than that of a female leader, and this value is extended to the congregation he leads. The section in the *Kitab al-Umm* on female leadership of a congregation of women highlights three main concerns pertaining to the most appropriate ritual norms for the mandatory prayer. The first is that the woman leads from the middle; the second is that she abides by the norms of modesty of dress and *'awra* specific to a free woman; the third is that the compulsory nature of prayer overrules less-than-ideal situations in its performance, such as, for example, a woman leading from the front or an unveiled woman leader. Thus, as prayer is a legal obligation (*fard*), this overrides other minor shortcomings in the performance of its leadership.

Al-Shafi'i refers to another issue that is only partly related to the leadership of prayer but is significant for the overall ritual performance. As the Qur'an had sanctioned, obligatory prayers are enjoined for men as well as women. Does this apply also to the congregational Friday prayer? Al-Shafi'i states that it is 'better to pray in congregation than alone',[77] but then clarifies that, in the case of a man praying at home with his family, it would be preferable for him, if he is able, to attend the congregational prayer in the mosque. So, as it is widely reported in *hadith*s, location plays a role in maximizing the value and merit of congregational prayer for men. For women, attendance of the Friday congregational prayer (at the mosque) is not obligatory, as it is not for slaves, travellers and those who have not attained legal maturity. However, al-Shafi'i deems it desirable (*wa uhibbu*) for slaves and old women (*al-'aja'iz*) to attend, provided they are given permission.[78] Later Shafi'i scholars would elaborate on the implicit set of different rules or preferences for old and young women and, eventually, even for unattractive and attractive females.

Moreover, in the section of the *Kitab al-Umm* on the prayer of the eclipse (*salat al-kusuf*), al-Shafi'i reveals two more details concerning the performance of women group prayers. The first is that if with the women there is a male who is *mahram* (hence unmarriageable for them) he can act as their imam, but if he is not *mahram*, then this would be undesirable; nevertheless, if he leads them, it is still acceptable, that is, their prayer is valid. The second detail is that in a female group prayer, it is not appropriate for a woman (*laysa min sha'n al-nisa'*) to proclaim the sermon (*khutba*), but it is good (*hasan*) if she makes reference about it to the other women.[79] This could be interpreted to mean that even though a formal fully fledged *khutba* is not appropriate for a woman to deliver, an informal summary or citation is acceptable.

Al-Shafi'i's pupil Isma'il b. Yahya al-Muzani (d. 878), in his digest (*Mukhtasar*) of his master's opinions, tersly summarizes the section in *al-Umm* on the *imama* of a woman. He does so by keeping only the most relevant *hadith*s such as those on 'A'isha and Umm Salama, and removing al-Shafi'i's own statements on his preferences and additional details of prayer performance.[80] Among the narratives evidencing the practice of female prayer leadership after the Prophet, al-Muzani cites the same case that al-Shafi'i had included in his *al-Umm* of the slave girl of 'Ali ibn al-Husayn. This way the *hadith*s themselves become a self-explanatory way of attesting both the practice of female leadership of prayer during and after the Prophet's lifetime and the opinion of al-Shafi'i in favour of the permissibility and validity of female *imama*.

The last sentence in the *Kitab al-Umm* section on female *imama* about preferring a male imam to a female is further explained and elaborated by one of the most higly reputed Shafi'i jurists, Muhyi al-din al-Nawawi (d. 1277). Al-Nawawi's argument is gradually developed in his *Kitab al-Majmu'*. There he reasserts that the *imama* of a man is better than that of a woman on account of his better knowledge of prayer and his uttering the recitation under any circumstances. This assertion of his can imply that a man is more knowledgeable about prayer than a woman on account of his greater acquaintance with the positions of prayer, given that he performs it more often than a woman, who on regular occasions can be restricted by issues of purity. Or this could be because a man performs prayer in the formal congregation of the mosque where his ritual practices can be corrected by observing other learned men. Additionally, his better quality of recitation could be the result of the above and the fact that a woman's voice in a female-only congregation cannot be as loud and clear as a man's would be for any congregation.

As for a woman leading women in prayer, al-Nawawi reiterates the affirmative opinion of the Shafi'i school, which, he states, is well-supported by the evidence of the *hadith* about Umm Waraqa, a report he qualifies as being reliable, as well as of those about 'A'isha and Umm Salama leading prayer.[81] These *hadith*s prove that a woman can lead women and that women prayers are legitimate; according to the Shafi'i *madhhab*, women group prayers are indeed desirable.

However, most *hadith*s do not specify where these prayers took place. Al-Nawawi quotes the well-known report that it is better for women to perform the obligatory prayers at home rather than in the mosque. He adds, in this case, tellingly with no textual support, that performance of prayer in the mosque is not objectionable (*la yakrahu*) but only for those women who are old and no longer attractive.[82] Therefore, the argument about the legitimacy of a woman leading other women in prayer becomes intertwined with that on the status of the congregational prayers for men and for women. Are congregational prayers an individual obligation (*fard 'ayn*), a collective duty (*fard kifaya*) or a highly recommended action (*sunna*)? For the Shafi'i scholar and commentator Abu'l-Qasim al-Rafi'i (d. 1226), congregational prayers are not strict obligations but recommended actions (*istihbab*) for both men and women. But, he adds, for the majority of scholars of his time, while these prayers are confirmed *sunna* (*sunna mu'akkada*) for men, which is undesirable and reprehensible to miss, they are not so for women.[83] Moreover, for men, congregational prayers are better performed in the mosque, where their value increases, compared to individual prayers and proportionally to the size of the mosque. For women, instead, they are better performed at home and better still in secluded places within the home.[84] Similarly to al-Nawawi, young women's attendance of congregational prayer in the mosque is disliked (*kariha*) because, al-Rafi'i explains, of the fear of *fitna*.

All in all, it becomes evident that, like men, women cannot be categorized as one single group, due to their different social, legal, and hence ritual roles. An example of this is the case cited by al-Shafi'i of the diverse ritual requirments for freeborn or slave women. Unlike men, however, because of more extensive application of *'awra*, women are further subdivided according to age (young, childbearing age, old) and level of attractiveness (in men's eyes). The reference to *'awra* that in al-Shafi'i was expressedly made in terms of preference for a freeborn veiled female imam, in al-Nawawi becomes a qualification based on relevant *hadith*s for women performing group prayers, and prayer in general, at home rather than in a mosque. In time, the association of *fitna* to young attractive women gives way to a more general association with all women, irrespective of looks and age.

Ibn Hanbal and his school: Hadiths *and Prophetic norm, validity of prayer, proper female behaviour and* fitna

Chronologically this is the most recent of the four main Sunni legal schools, named after Iraqi traditionist-jurist Ahmad Ibn Hanbal (d. 855), who reportedly discouraged his pupils from committing his opinions to writing. The Hanbali school of law holds positions concerning the validity of female prayer leadership which are not only varied, but also linked to opinions and reasoning of previous legal schools and their authorities. Ibn Hanbal was a pupil of al-Shafi'i, studied under Sufyan ibn 'Uyayna, who was the foremost Meccan traditionist of his time, and became himself a great collector of *hadith*s, which he assembled in his *Musnad*. It is on *hadith*s that Ibn Hanbal based his legal arguments. If he could not find reliable *hadith*s to provide as evidence, he would refrain from answering a legal question. His *Musnad* features the two *hadith*s on Umm Waraqa, which future Hanbali scholars would extensively cite when dealing with women prayers and female leadership.

Around Ibn Hanbal's time there were two main legal and intellectual trends competing around the method to arrive at legal decisions, one was that of those supporting the use of *hadith*s as evidence and the other of those like the Hanafis supporting individual rational discretion (*ra'y*). Reflecting these debates, the sections on women's prayers by many Hanbali writers do contain direct statements of reliance on *hadith*s, rather than on personal opinions, in order to reach legal decisions. It is on the basis of the *hadith*s on Umm Waraqa, Umm Salama and 'A'isha that Hanbali scholars overall argue in favour of the permissibility of female prayer groups and for a woman to lead women in prayer. The qualification of such permissibility is, nevertheless, more complex to gauge.

It is unclear whether Ibn Hanbal himself considered women's prayer groups and a woman leading them as just permissible or as desirable. Ahmad Ibn Hanbal's son 'Abdullah (d. 903), the first transmitter and compiler of his father's main *fiqh* work, titled the *Masa'il*, reportedly queried him about such a permissibility. Ahmad's reply was indeed positive, adding that a woman acting as imam of women should be located in their midst.[85] Hence, on evidence from the *Musnad* and the *Masa'il*, one could argue that Ibn Hanbal considered it legally permissible, perhaps even desirable on the basis of past precendents, for a woman to lead other women in prayer.[86]

With a few exceptions, most Hanbali scholars did consider it desirable for a woman to lead women in prayer. Even the likes of the influential Baghdadi Ibn al-Jawzi (d. 1200/1), with his heightened concern for the respectability of women when in public and their proper behaviour when praying in congregation, concedes that women group prayers for the obligatory prayers, and female leadership of them, are desirable acts.[87] Some Hanbali jurists cited as evidence for this desirability the *hadith*s on Umm Salama, 'A'isha and Umm Waraqa. The highly esteemed Hanbali jurisprudent Ibn Qudama (d. 1223) indicates that the Umm Waraqa *hadith* points to the leadership having occurred for a compulsory prayer, this clarification being in response to those jurists who held the view that women can lead other women only in voluntary prayers.[88] Ibn Qudama includes two provisos to the desirability of a woman leading other women: that no woman calls the *adhan* and that the one who leads positions herself in the middle of the group. He claims that there is unanimity about this positioning across those jurists who permit female *imama*. Both provisos he justifies on the basis of conforming to the propriety of female behaviour, which entails being concealed (*tasattur*) and lack of exposure. He further explains that to be in the middle of other women hides and protects a woman from being exposed and, similarly, she should not call the *adhan* because her voice should not be loud and conspicuous.[89]

Reflecting on Ibn Qudama's position one can detect a paradigmatic link being made between being female, prayer and the notion of public display. By the 11th century, as already shown in the case of the Maliki and Hanafi scholars, the fear of *fitna* had become a 'central category of legal analysis'.[90] In fact already in his *Masa'il*, Ibn Hanbal had used the term *fitna* in the context of his discussion on whether women could go out to pray for the two main religious festivals, the *'id al-fitr* and *'id al-adha'*. Ibn Hanbal was not pleased with this female public 'exposure' occurring during his lifetime because, he states, women 'are *fitna* (temptation)'.[91] Much later, during the 12th century, Ibn al-Jawzi pushes further this association between *fitna* and women praying outside of their houses. Although quoting and therefore acknowledging the Prophetic *hadith* that women should not be prevented from going out to pray in the mosque, Ibn al-Jawzi nevertheless progressively lays emphasis on the last section of one specific version of the same *hadith*, the one that states that it is best for women to pray in their own houses.[92] Therefore, even though it is legally permissible, or neutral (*mubah*), for a woman to go out to the mosque, Ibn al-Jawzi states that if there is fear that this can lead to *fitna* then she should remain at home!

Hanbali jurists, unlike their Hanafi counterparts, do not explicitly refer to the abrogation of *hadith*s concerning women leading other women in prayer. Instead, many of them justify their position against women attending congregational prayers in the mosque by calling upon the changed conditions of the times. They show that different rules applied in the time of the Prophet, because the women and men of the past were different from those of their own times.[93] In other words, the ideal past, as detailed in the Prophetic *hadith*s, is still normative in principle and in theory, but the changed times require more caution in practice, for the fear of *fitna*. This fragile balance between the normative past and the present, and the way in which the two can be reconciled, is resolved in favour of the normativity of the past by Ibn Qudama's grandson, Ibn Taymiyya (d. 1328). Confirming the

Hanbali reliance on the authority of *hadith*s, Ibn Taymiyya considers women group prayers and their female leadership as legitimate, even meritorious. However, because of the fear of *fitna*, he states that it is advisable for women to pray at home, except for the main festivals, as indicated in the Prophetic *hadith*s.⁹⁴ The shift is not concerned with the principle that women are permitted to lead prayer *per se*, but with their visibility and location: women can lead other women in prayer, as long as these prayers occur in a domestic, non-public arena.

In line with positions of jurists from other schools, here too the fear of *fitna* is directly linked to the issue of a woman's *awra*. For Ibn al-Jawzi, it is imperative that a girl as young as seven is taught about concealing her private parts, which she cannot show even to her mother or sister. Going out of her house, even for prayers in the mosque, would increase for women the chance of exposure of their 'awra, hence leading to *fitna*. The logical conclusion is therefore expressed by an allegedly Prophetic *hadith* transmitted on the authority of a *mawla* of Umm Salama, that for women the best places of worship (*masajid*) are their own houses.⁹⁵ Even within an all-female group prayer, proper concealing of 'awra is a condition for the prayer to be valid. Thus, a specific understanding of what constitutes 'awra is an indication of changed perceptions. For Ibn al-Jawzi concealing 'private parts' for a free woman means covering the whole body, except her face. He therefore goes into great detail in indicating the three types of coverings which are desirable for a woman to pray in: a *khimar* for the head, a loose outer garment and an all-enveloping *jilbab* for the rest of the body.⁹⁶ Moreover, if she leads in prayer, she is spatially covered and 'enveloped' by the women around her. Ibn al-Jawzi's understanding of the requirement for women to lead other women from the middle highlights one of its possible interpretations: that the female leader is sheltered and protected from exposure to the male gaze not only by her elaborate veiling and dress code, but also by the women who surround her. Another interpretation, by the Shi'i jurisprudent al-Qadi al-Nu'man, with more legal connotations of equality in female status or legal capacity will be discussed later on in this chapter.

The four Sunni legal schools on women leading women in prayer:
A collective overview

In this section we will consider opinions, approaches, methodologies and the uses of the past shared by all the four Sunni legal schools. The focus is on two main questions with reference to female prayer leadership. The first concerns the boundaries between schools in methodology and justifications, the second is about their uses of the past, its definition and the extent to which they consider the past as normative, and whether such a normativity is to be understood theoretically, i.e. in principle, in practice, or both.

With reference to female leadership of other women, how rigid were the boundaries between legal schools in terms of their positions and the methodologies they used to justify them? If one was to limit one's answer to the comparison between, for instance, early 9th century Maliki and Shafi'i legal schools, one would find clear differences in opinions (a female imam is not permissible for Malikis while it is permissible and desirable for Shafi'is) and methodology to justify such opinions (the Malikis emphasize the authority of local Medinan custom while the Shafi'is use the authority of Prophetic *hadiths*).

However, differences become more blurred over time, especially when considering developments within schools and across schools. For instance, as Benham Sadeghi has convincingly shown in the case of the Hanafi school with regards to women's groups and their female leader, there was an internal development in their reasoning. This started from a position of disapproved permission, found in sources up to the 10th century, to the theory of abrogation evidenced in 12th century texts, and on to a more uncompromising position of prohibition for a woman to lead women in prayer during the 13th and 14th centuries.

As for developments across schools, scholars who relied on the use of *ra'y* to reach legal decisions, such as Abu Hanifa, were increasingly challenged by the proponents of the rival jurisprudential method of grounding the law in the *hadiths*. By 9th and 10th century all Sunni legal schools had adopted the use of *hadiths* as the main evidence for their legal decisions, thus sharing a common methodological tool.

Such a tool was used to validate legal positions, even as they were starting to shift. In the case of female prayer leadership and of female group prayers, as they both came to be considered no longer desirable or even permissible ritual practices, well-known *hadiths* showing the practice being carried out during the Prophet's time, still continued to be quoted or cited. However, these *hadiths* were presented as being no longer applicable due to either having been later abrogated (Hanafis), not to be acted upon (Malikis) or as being unsound. Nevertheless, the very citation of these 'obsolete' *hadiths* meant that they were still preserved and so was the memory of the scholars and schools of law which used them as evidence of their own divergent legal positions on the matter.

From a wider perspective, it seems that, as stressed particularly in texts from the 11th to 12th century onwards, all Sunni jurists and, as will be shown later, Shi'i scholars too, with different degrees of emphasis, came to share common views about female modesty, the necessity for women to conceal their *'awra*, and, above all, the association of women with *fitna*, which provides the justification for preferring women to pray at home while stressing that female attendance of congregational prayers was not, in any case, compulsory. According to these arguments, then, there is no contradiction between issues of modesty and propriety, such as those which fall within the *mu'amalat* or social interaction category of Islamic jurisprudence, and the divinely sanctioned obligation of worship (*'ibadat*), irrespective of gender. *'Ibadat* can be 'safely' carried out by women at home, alone or with family members.

Referring to the Hanafi legal tradition, Sadeghi's observation that 'the role of the methods of interpretations . . . is not to generate the laws, but rather to reconcile them with the textual sources'[97] is applicable to the other legal schools. But beyond legal argument and textual evidence as factors on which to base legal rulings on female prayer leadership, another factor gradually comes to the fore as being of even greater import: the social attitudes towards women, their visibility and their leadership status. As shown, especially by Hanbali scholars, the relationship between these factors is complex: while the textual evidence of precedents of women leading prayer is accepted as sound and the legal position is, in theory, that of overall permissibility of female leadership of prayer, nevertheless social attitudes towards women and the increasingly common association between women and *fitna* led to provisos and restrictions. By the 13th century, these attitudes resulted in a shared consensus across legal schools that women should pray at home where, theoretically and presumably in practice, they could lead prayer of other women in a domestic or non-formal environment. If they did, this occurrence was beyond the male gaze and so the sphere of interest of historians, jurists and biographers, with the consequence that no record (thus far) has come down to us.[98]

As for the uses of the past, amid the varied geographical, historical and methodological backgrounds of the main Sunni legal schools, recourse to the authority of the past has been a constant tool to validate specific opinions, rules and customs. This authority was embodied above all, but not exclusively, in the textual tradition of *hadith*s. Whether, diachronically, this recourse to the past has seen developments from the oldest schools such as the Malikis to the more recent ones such as the Hanbali, this summary will take a more synchronic stance to focus on the reasons provided to support specific opinions, and in particular the interplay between the past and the concerns of their present.

Shafi'i scholars justified the permissiblility and desirability of group women prayers led by a female imam on the basis of the Prophetic *hadith*s (Umm Waraqa) and those of the close Companions of the Prophet (Umm Salama, 'A'isha). These narratives showed what they considered to be the correct practice during, and soon after, the Prophet's times. For most Hanbalis, such permissibility was, however, not unqualified. Despite an all-female environment, women's modesty was to be maintained in prayer through proper attire, and for the female prayer leader, through lack of exposure of her voice, body and position in the congregation (Ibn Qudama). Each of these conditions was also evidenced though the selection of *ad hoc hadith* narratives.

Among many Hanafis, concerns for the present seem to become more explicit and predominant to the extent that they resulted in making the practice still theoretically permissible, but no longer desirable. *Hadith*s continued to be adduced to show permissibility; however, as in the case of al-Shaybani, some were selected to show progressive specifications on female group prayers. Hence, it was clarified that women could only lead voluntary prayers and that the *hadith*s evidencing female leadership were appropriate for the times of the normative 'golden' past, but had subsequently been abrogated (see al-Sarakhshi, al-Kasani, al-Babarti).

Some scholars argued that *hadith*s such as those on Umm Waraqa were in fact not fully reliable. For a woman to lead could still be permissible for some, but overall became discouraged. The main reason for such a disliked permissibility, justified on *ad hoc* scriptural passages, was that women's exposure was a cause of temptation. The ideal developed into women praying in the most secluded area of their home and, if indeed still leading, women could only lead from the middle or from the back.

The oldest extant Sunni school of the Malikis relied on what they considered as the 'uninterrupted' practice of Medina, which was, eventually, to be supported by *hadith*s of the Companions or Successors. The main justification for the withdrawal of permissibility of women leading prayer is that it was not, or no longer was, a comprehensive Medinan practice. Even if the *hadith*s on the likes of Umm Waraqa were reliable, they were specific to that person at that time; in other words, they were no longer relevant for the present and for women other than the Prophet's wives or his close female Companions. Unsurprisingly, for all the above-cited scholars, it appears that the past is normative, but in selected ways, with relevant *hadith*s, or versions of them, chosen to support their vision of the past.

Shi'i positions on female imama of women: Identity, shared issues and esoteric interpretations

As with Sunni Islam, Shi'ism also developed, over the course of time, a diverse set of legal schools, some with internal variations. The school covered in this section is the Ja'fari *madhhab*, which is the main school now shared by Twelver and Sevener Shi'is. It is named after Ja'far al-Sadiq (d. 765), a direct descendent of the Prophet Muhammad and considered by both Twelver and Seveners to be one of the Imams after 'Ali Ibn Abi Talib. Unlike the Sunnis, the Shi'is consider as authoritative the records of the sayings and deeds of the Imams, in addition to the Prophetic *hadith*s and those of the Companions. In this respect, for the Shi'is, not only was Ja'far al-Sadiq himself a source of authority for the law, but also a trusted reporter of the traditions of his predecessors. As will be seen in the course of this chapter, Ja'fari jurisprudence differs from Sunni jurisprudence, among other ways, by the importance it accords to the rational mode of legal reasoning in finding a solution to a legal question. This method of reasoned argumentation was to be expressed from the 12th century onwards with the term *ijtihad*. For Twelver Shi'is, since the occultation of the last Imam, the practice of *ijtihad* by Shi'i jurists aims to uncover the knowledge of what the Imams' response would have been in addressing particular legal situations.

By the mid 10th century when the best-known Shi'i traditionists such as al-Kulayni and Ibn Babawayh had compiled their extensive collections of *hadith*s, Shi'ism was a force in ascent. The Sunni majorities had to reckon first with the political stance of the Shi'is, but eventually they were confronted by Shi'ism as a politico-religious movement and its doctrinal elaborations. Competing Shi'i groups had asserted themselves in disparate geographical areas and had succeeded in establishing their rule or affirming political power. Shi'i dynasties included the Hamdanids in northern Iraq and, later, northern Syria (ca 904–1003), the Buyids in Iraq and Iran (945–1055), the Fatimids in Ifriqya and subsequently in Egypt and, partly, in the Yemen (909–1171), as well as the Zaydis who, since the late 9th century, had been ruling regions in northern Iran and the Yemen. The original theological affiliations of some of these Shi'i dynasties, as in the case of the Hamdanids, are still far from certain and, also on the basis of the biographies of early Shi'i scholars, it appears that a degree of fluidity was indeed prevalent. During this time, internal doctrinal developments were affecting most Shi'i groups, noticeably Twelver and Sevener Shi'is. The doctrine of the imamate, with its belief in the necessity of a living Imam at all times, had already been expressed by Ja'far al-Sadiq and was shared among Shi'i groups. However, since the early 10th century, it was the belief in the occultation (*ghayba*) of the 12th Imam in its two phases of the 'lesser occulation' (873–4) and the 'greater occultation' (941) which came to delineate the developing identity and political stance of Twelver Shi'is.

The disappearance of the Imam as the spiritual and political leader, who as such was the ultimate ideal prayer leader, impacted upon the Shi'i understanding of the figure, roles and characteristics of the imam as the officiant of the prayer. The *ghayba* belief that the Imam, though living, was in fact not physically present, also affected debates about the Friday congregational prayer, its obligation and who should lead it. Shifts have been identified from an earlier more fluid position among scholars such as al-Kulayni about the obligatory attendance of the group prayer alongside alternative provisions to perform it individually, to later requirements to attend prayer in congregation. Linked to the development of the doctrine of the *ghayba* from a temporary absence of the Imam to a long-term occultation, the prayer leader's role and authority increased in scope and, with it, the qualifications required for the appointment of an imam.[99] Discussions on prayer leadership, including female prayer leadership, appear to be mainly located within a post-*ghayba* period.

As far as doctrinal and theoretical positions regarding female prayer leadership of women, Shi'i scholars present an overwhelmingly positive stance. The justifications adduced are comparable to those of some earlier or contemporary Sunni scholars, informed, as they are, by similar conceptions and uses of textual evidence. Nevertheless, some issues, approaches or – at times – differences in emphasis can be identified as being more pronounced among Shi'i scholars, possibly as a reflection of their theological debates and communal identity.

One of the characteristics of this Shi'i identity is the widespread reliance upon the sayings of the Shi'i Imams as one of the main sources of textual authority. Reflecting the Shi'i doctrine of *'isma* (sinlessness, infallibility) of the Imams, whose knowledge is praised as being the same as that of the Prophet, statements by them are used as supportive evidence for legal and ritual positions and specifically for the legitimacy of women leading women in prayer. In this respect, among the Shi'i Imams, the one most often quoted is Ja'far al-Sadiq.[100]

When commenting upon *hadith*s, or elaborating on whether it is permissible for a woman to lead other women, most Shi'i scholars emphasize the distinction between leading from the front and leading from the middle. As a result, even *hadith*s or assertions about women not being permitted to 'lead' are further interpreted to refer to leadership from the front, rather than leadership *per se*. The verb *amma* (to lead) is therefore used both as a generic expression for leading prayer, as well as a specific one of leading from the front. To further clarify the latter type of leadership Shi'i scholars use the verb *taqaddama* to refer to the front position of the leader.[101]

Of relevance are also the statements that there are occasions in which women can lead other women in prayer from the front: specifically for the prayer recited over the dead and for the supererogatory prayers.¹⁰² It would be desirable to research further whether any connection can be proven between this position among Shi'i scholars from Iran and Iraq and the early Sunni traditions located outside Medina (especially in Kufa), which allowed female group prayers and female leadership for these prayers.¹⁰³ That these prayers are associated with more informal ritual settings might be a possible reason for women being permitted to lead them from the front.

In a more formal setting, the issue of Friday prayer, the attendance of which for Shi'is and Sunnis alike is not an obligation for women, can reflect typically Shi'i debates about the legitimacy and qualities of its leader. As mentioned above, positions ranged from those who held that, during the occultation of the Imam, Friday prayer was in fact prohibited as the Imam was its only legitimate leader, to those who believed that it was advisable or compulsory and that its leader was to be a representative of the hidden Imam.¹⁰⁴ On the basis of such a deputyship, most Shi'i scholars shared the view that the qualities of the rightful prayer leader were linked to those associated with the Shi'i supreme human leader: the Imam. Consequently, as will be seen in more detail in the next chapter, for Shi'i scholars the leader of the Friday prayer could only be male.

As for women-only group prayers, similarly to the favourable position among the classical Hanbalis and Shafi'i schools, most Shi'i scholars agree on their permissibility both in the compulsory (*fara'id*) and the *nawafil* prayers. Moreover, one of most influential Shi'i authorities of the 11th century, Muhammad ibn al-Hasan al-Tusi, also known as Shaykh al-Ta'ifa, states that it is desirable (*yastahibbu*) for a woman to lead women.¹⁰⁵ Along with a few scholars such as al-Qadi al-Nu'man, Shaykh al-Ta'ifa refers not only to the possibility of women leading other women, but also to women uttering the call to prayer.¹⁰⁶ In his *Mabsut*, Shaykh al-Ta'ifa writes that if the woman calls the *adhan* for the men, they can accept the call and get ready for prayer as there is no prohibition against it. However, three centuries after the great Shaykh, another influential Shi'i scholar, Jamal al-din al-Hasan, al-'Allama al-Hilli (d. 1325), partially refutes this statement by arguing that, firstly, the call for prayer by women is not desirable (*laysa mustahabb*) and, secondly, that the female voice is *'awra*, and therefore prohibition is necessary to avoid corruption. But, in defense of the reputation and the authority of the great Shaykh, al-Hilli opines that the master might have meant the case of the woman uttering the *adhan* to her male close relatives, in which case it would be permissible for them to hear her voice!¹⁰⁷ The length to which al-Hilli goes to reconcile the differences between al-Shaykh's permissiblilty of female *adhan* to a male audience and the prevalent opinion of his times about its prohibition shows the degree of variation of viewpoints among Shi'i authorities and a likely development in time within Shi'ism towards positions of lesser permissibility. Such a development does show parallels with that of earlier and contemporary Sunni scholars using concepts of *'awra* and *fitna* as legal categories to justify women's limitations in the public ritual sphere.

In fact, even within a female-only environment, most scholars from al-Qummi and al-Babawayh onwards make reference to the necessity of preserving the principle of modesty so that either in the call to prayer or during its recitation, the female prayer leader is to keep her voice low, yet audible to her congregation, and her demeanor and ritual gestures proper and confined.[108] As with Sunni jurists, Shi'i scholars also hold that modesty is not an absolute concept, but rather, a qualified and relative one which is expressed differently according to the woman's status. Linked to this is also the very identification of 'awra according to a person's status, to the extent that for some scholars even gender is no longer the only marker. Shaykh al-Ta'ifa, in his *Kitab al-Khilaf*, reports that some scholars state that in the case of a slave girl (*ama*), the areas of the body that need to be covered in prayer are those between her navel and her knees, just like for men. On the other hand, the 'awra of a free woman and, for some, of an *umm al-walad*, is her whole body, except for the face, the palm of her hands and the back of her feet.[109]

Alongside ritual scenarios of women praying in groups, and references to the presence of women in mixed congregations located behind the imam, there are also several *hadiths* included in the most authoritative Shi'i collections indicating the home as the preferred place for a woman to perform her obligatory prayers. Significantly, Shaykh al-Ta'ifa mentions the lack of compulsion for women, whether old or young, to attend Friday prayer just before his advice for them to pray at home.[110] In the section on mosques, however, al-Tusi states that the best location to perform compulsory prayers is the mosque while for supererogatory prayers, especially the night ones, the home is best.[111] One could be justified in inferring that for al-Tusi the mosque as the preferred location for prayer is not applicable for those, like women, whose attendance of congregational prayers in mosques is not obligatory.

Moreover, Shaykh al-Ta'ifa's reference to women's age is reminiscent of earlier, yet still ongoing, discussions among Sunnis about the association between women and *fitna*, which is considered more prominent in young women due to their desirability. The well-known *hadith*, often found in Sunni collections, that for a woman to pray in her house is better than to pray in the mosque had indeed been quoted a few decades earlier by Ibn Babawayh without the support of any authorities, perhaps as the *hadith* was too well-known to need an *isnad*.[112] Ibn Babawayh quotes in the same passage, on the authority of the Imam Ja'far al-Sadiq, the notoriously more restrictive advice that a woman's bedchamber or closet (*mikhda'uha*) is a better place for her to pray than the rest of the house.[113] Even if the *isnad* of these *hadiths*, when included, was different in Sunni and Shi'i works, their content was either very similar or the same.

Despite all the provisos mentioned above, which are the most common justifications offered by Shi'i scholars in favour of women leading other women in prayer? As in the case of Sunni scholars, they are predominatly textual, based mainly on *hadiths*, but with traits which are peculiarly Shi'i. Some of the *hadiths* are the same ones used by Sunni scholars, others are transmitted on the authority of the Imams. So, in addition to a few Prophetic *hadiths*, Shi'i scholars use narratives on the authority or on the precedent of the people in Muhammad's household, with examples among his wives predominantly from Umm Salama rather than 'A'isha.[114] Nevertheless, more often quoted as evidence are statements by the Imams, especially Musa al-Kazim and Ja'far al-Sadiq.

Moreover, there might be shifts of emphasis on the interpretation of such *hadith*s resulting from ongoing general tendencies between a 'traditionist' and 'rationalist' approach within Shi'i, particularly Imami, thought. Partially reflecting ongoing debates regarding *ijtihad* and the authority of legal scholars, further textual evidence is provided on the strength of the authority of opinions by Shi'i jurists such as Sharif al-Murtada (d. 1044), or additionally arguments in support of female leadership of other women are used on the strength of logical deduction and reasoning.

The arguments and evidence that Shaykh al-Ta'ifa provides in some of his works regarding female leadership of prayer, are a telling example of such a plurality in legal argumentative methods. In his book on comparative law, the *Kitab al-Khilaf*, containing the different opinions held by mainly Sunni scholars, his evidence in favour of a female imam of women is a mixture of opinions by renowned scholars such as al-Shafi'i, Ahmad Ibn Hanbal and Abu Hanifa. To these, he adds the arguments of lesser-known or in some cases anonymous Companions.[115] The latter *hadith*s could indeed be qualified as *ahad*, of the kind that later Shi'i scholars would criticize the Shaykh for having relied upon. In his authoritative *hadith* compilation, the *Tahdhib al-Ahkam*, Shaykh al-Ta'ifa lists a number of narratives which evidence the permissibility of female leadership of women on the authority of the Imams and other Shi'i authorities. But he also includes reasoned argument when, for example, he augments the case in favour of female leadership of women by adding other *hadith*s on the required qualities of the prayer leader which are gender neutral: evidence of discernment, being the most appropriate person and the one who is best at reciting the Qur'an.[116]

Two centuries later, al-'Allama al-Hilli refined Shaykh al-Ta'ifa's legal methodology. Along with his moderation between 'rationalist' and 'traditionist' positions, al-Hilli combined the methods and arguments of his predecessors. Al-Hilli argues in favour of female leadership of women on the basis of a *hadith*, not by the Imams but by the Prophet himself, stating that the prayer leader is the most knowledgeable person among the congregation. This, he clarifies, is with reference to both males and females.[117] Moreover, to specific arguments that women are only allowed to lead supererogatory prayers, al-Hilli pointedly counter-argues that the Prophetic *hadith* affirms a general rule (*shar' 'amm*) that applies to both male and female. It is only when feminine and masculine are together that the masculine becomes predominant. From linguistic considerations, al-Hilli shifts to a ritual sphere. He provides a variety of scholarly positions with nuances in terms of leadership from the front and from the middle as well as the type of prayer being led. Al-Hilli cites 'rationalist' jurists such as the 12th century Abu 'Abdullah Muhammad Ibn Idris, who by quoting al-Sayyid al-Murtada argue against the female prayer leadership of compulsory prayers, but he also cites other authorities who, on the strength of Prophetic *hadith*s, support the position in favour of leadership of both obligatory and voluntary prayers. After presenting contrasting arguments, al-Hilli reaffirms the superiority of the general rule over the specific one, along with the interpretation of the Prophetic *hadith* allowing the permissibility for a woman to lead women in both types of prayers.[118] In the footsteps of Shaykh al-Ta'ifa, al-Hilli attempted to balance the validity of the traditions with the use of the analytical and rational method of legal reasoning. It is significant that al-Hilli was to be singled out by subsequent Shi'i traditionists, the so-called Akhbaris, as having embedded into Shi'i legal thought the theory of *ijtihad*, and hence the need for the jurists' interpretation of scripture in order to provide legal knowledge.[119]

In addition to justifications for the permissibility of women leading women, based on the precedents of the wives and Companions of the Prophet, on the words of the Imams, on scholarly interpretations and logical reasoning, Shi'i scholars also provide more specifically legal reasons. This appears to be more noticeable among non-Twelver Shi'is such as the Zaydis and the Isma'ilis. A case in point is the recourse to the association between the legal capacity of women and their ritual status. The already mentioned 9th century Kufan Zaydi scholar Muhammad Ibn al-Sallam quotes Imam 'Ali, who states: a 'woman does not call the *adhan*, does not contract marriage and does not lead people in prayer [from the front] (*la ta'ummu*)'.[120] What underlies such legal and ritual limitations is the lack of women's full legal capacity to act, as proven by the need for a guardian to conduct legal transactions for them such as a marriage contract.

The 10th century Isma'ili jurist al-Qadi al-Nu'man provides an allegorical intepretation of *salat* and its ritual leadership to disclose its inner esoteric meaning. In doing so he equates female ritual positioning in leading prayer with a pupil's status in the Isma'ili teaching hierarchy. In other words, just like the pupil who is the receiver of knowledge cannot summon the teacher, a woman cannot lead men and cannot lead women from the front. Hence a woman's ritual leadership from the middle, rather than from the front, is an indication of her not being in a position of precedence in respect to the female congregation, as she shares with them a state of equality 'in status and in rank'.[121] Beyond allegory and metaphorical language, one could ask whether a woman can ever advance the hierarchy of knowledge and reach the status of teacher. Though not free from underlying genealogical motivations, a case in Shi'i Isma'ili history to evidence such a high status for a woman, is nevertheless presented and discussed by Isma'ili scholar and poet al-Sultan al-Khattab (d. 1138). This woman was the Sulayhi Queen of Yemen Sayyida Arwa (d.1138), leader of the Isma'ili *da'wa* (mission or propaganda activity) in Yemen and holder of the status of *hujja* in the Isma'ili religious hierarchy.[122] As a holder of both political and spiritual authority, Queen Arwa is not, however, associated with ritual performance of prayer, nor prayer leadership.

At the heart of Shi'ism lies the female figure of Fatima. As the daughter of the Prophet and wife of his cousin 'Ali, Shi'is place her as the ultimate *trait d'union* between the Prophet and the Imams. In Shi'ism, Fatima is the 'mother of the Imams' (*umm al-a'imma*), matrix and source of the legitimacy of the imamate. She is the fountainhead of the spiritual and political authority that recognizes the Imam, among other virtues, as the ideal prayer leader.

Given her exalted status, it is surpising that there is little mention of Fatima as prayer performer, and there is no known reference to associate her with prayer leadership. In terms of prayer itself, Fatima is mentioned by Qur'anic exegetes with reference to Qur. 3.61 and the so-called 'Mubahala episode', traditionally dated

631, on the dispute between the Prophet Muhammad and a deputation of Christians of Najran about the nature of Jesus. It is narrated that the Prophet proposed a trial by prayer (*mubahala*) and 'offered' his family, including Fatima, as guarantors and witnesses.[123] Shi'i narratives elaborate on this further by recounting that the Prophet asked 'Ali to follow him and for Fatima to follow 'Ali, instructed them to recite 'Amen' after his supplication and then spread a mantle (*kisa*) for himself and the family. This sequence of those following the Prophet is reminiscent of the already quoted performance of prayer of the Prophet with Khadija and 'Ali. Shi'is take this narrative as proof of the excellence of Fatima over all the women of the Prophet's family, including his wives.

An association of Fatima with prayer practice can be found in al-Qadi al-Nu'man who mentions the '*tasbih* Fatima', a rosary-like prayer consisting of three sections of thirty-three blessing formulae, which, added to the *shahada*, invoke the name of God one hundred times, for which Allah will grant benefits equivalent to 1,000 good deeds.[124] For some of today's Isma'ilis, *tasbih* Fatima is associated as being a means of support in times of difficulty. In popular and devotional literature, Fatima is an exemplar of piety, expressed by her intense and prolonged praying which is believed to have earned her the soubriquet of al-Zahra' (the resplendent), for the luminous light emanating from her while she was praying.

Conclusion

We started this chapter with narratives showing Umm Salama leading women in prayer and ended with another member of the Prophet's family, his daughter Fatima, a female figure whose paramount role in Shi'ism might have indirectly influenced their jurists' overall positive attitudes towards women leading women in prayer. In the process we looked at how scholars from the four Sunni schools of law elaborated on *hadith*s concerning Umm Salama and 'A'isha's leadership to reach diverging conclusions as to whether a woman could lead women in prayer. Many of these *hadith*s, especially those on Umm Salama, were also examined by Shi'i jurists, whose interpretations were influenced by their understanding of the spiritual and political authority of the Imam as the ultimate ideal prayer leader. When these legal schools reached different conclusions we identifed the major role played by the adoption of different methodologies when appraising the same *hadith*s. The exploration of a selection of *hadith*s about women leading women in prayer, with a focus on those about the ritual leadership of Umm Salama, has resulted in new insights. These have added to previously unexplored aspects in current scholarship on women prayer leadership.

The analysis of the way in which *hadith*s on women leading women in prayer intersect with legal and doctrinal literature by both Sunni and Shi'i scholars has never been done before. We began with a thorough application of intertextual analysis to the narratives, a process that brought to light important nuances in the descriptions of Umm Salama's prayer performance. In turn, we noted these differences to be dependent upon the subjectivities of the scholars, who selected and reported them on the basis of their respective backgrounds and contexts. These *hadith*s have continued to be cited by scholars and jurists for centuries right up to the present.

The figures portrayed as the most authoritative female prayer leaders are the wives of the Prophet, especially 'A'isha and Umm Salama. Notwithstanding differences in reported personality, political allegiance and extent of their contribution to *hadith* knowledge, both are shown as authorities in their own right, sought after and consulted by their contemporaries. They are sources of *hadith* transmission with their own authorial voice, who directly addressed the Prophet. Their respective network of people to whom they transmitted is wide and varied, overriding kinship and gender boundaries, and with 'A'isha showing a much greater accessibility than Umm Salama.

Female Companions or family relatives feature as prayer leaders, some as little-known contemporaries to the Prophet such as Sa'da bint Qamama, others, such as the higher profile Umm Waraqa, who stretched her leadership beyond the Prophet's lifespan during the time of the caliph 'Umar. 'A'isha's sister Asma (d. 692) is also reported to be the prayer leader of the *janaza* prayer for her own son. It is much rarer to find prayer leaders among the female Successors, with the possible exception of the *jariya* of 'Ali ibn al-Husayn.

If not actors in the performance of prayer, we saw how women played an important role as transmitters – either as witnesses or narrators – of those ritual actions linked to one of the Prophet's wives or Companions. We encountered Hujayra, who transmitted one *hadith* from Umm Salama to a male (d. 735) of her own extended family, but also Umm al-Hasan (late 7th century) who was better known as a 'narrator' to a broader audience. The details we found about them confirm Sayeed's argument that women's contribution to *hadith* knowledge diminished in quantity and quality over the course of the 7th century. They show characteristcs of other minor transmitters, whose contribution is limited to one *hadith*, whose chain of narrators is restricted to family members (Hujayra) or other networks (Umm al-Hasan), and whose role is merely that of preserver, if not of 'narrator or story-teller' (Umm al-Hasan).

The act of leading prayer in these narratives is variously witnessed by the Prophet, by his male Companions or the women who prayed with their female leader. However, unlike the fluctuating importance of the contribution of female *hadith* transmitters, which according to Sayeed's argument waned and later revived from the mid 10th century, we can assert that on the basis of the extant evidence, for female prayer leadership, no such positive development has taken place. After the above-mentioned *jariya* and the female leadership of women instructed by 'Amra, no more reports have been found of pre-modern women leading prayer. Nevertheless, if the trail of women acting as imams, which started with some of the Prophet's wives and Companions, seems to come to an end with this little-known *jariya*, they were preserved in the 'collective' memory and references to them continued for centuries to come, down to the present day, in legal, biographical and other literature.

A variety of factors contributed to the reduction of attested cases of women leading prayer after the time of the Prophet and, since the mid-8th century, to a lack of any mention at all. We noted the interplay between a shift of attitudes towards women in public places of ritual and doctrinal as well as legal elaborations on the concept of *fitna*. We also noted interrelated political and doctrinal developments in the status of the *imam* in urban mosques. A lack of mention does not necessary imply that women stopped leading a group in prayer, but that they were beyond the gaze and focus of the chroniclers or reporters of their time.

From the point of view of the impact and purposes of these narratives, the mention of such occurrences during and soon after the Prophet's time served the purpose of providing a detailed picture of the practices which were carried out by the Prophet himself and directly or indirectly validated by him or his immediate family and entourage. Because of their connection to the Prophet, these were considered as legitimizing and normative precedents for the developing Muslim community.

We saw that the earliest sources which report such details date from the late 8th century, though some of them are compilations of earlier material. But the majority of narratives are included in sources dating from the early 9th century (Shafi'i and Ibn Sa'd) to the mid and late 9th century, a time when both legal and *hadith* seminal works flourished. With the increasing recourse to *hadith*s to support legal opinions, narratives on every aspect of communal life during the time of the Prophet were essential to develop and validate practices. Ritual details, particularly prayer, were paramount in addressing such a need.

We reported variations of opinions on the permissibility of female prayer leadership among scholars and later Sunni schools which have been linked (possibly retrospectively) to local practices, as in the case of the Medinan and Kufan/Iraqi centres. However, as evidenced for each of the Sunni legal schools, in reporting the opinions by the early jurists, their pupils, editors and followers provided contradicting interpretations which reflected a development of increased limitation in the cases in which it was theoretically permissible for women to lead prayer.

Thus, from the early and mid 10th century with the Hanafi Shaybani and the Maliki Ibn Sa'id, the tendency of asserting a more defined opinion of dislike or lack of permission for women to lead prayer had already started. By the 11th and 12th century it seems that most Maliki and Hanafi scholars agreed that not only was female leadership not (or no longer) permissible, but the prayer of those behind her was invalid. With the consolidation among jurists of the association of *fitna* or temptation with the presence of women in the public space, by the 13th century even Shafi'i and Hanbali scholars had come to consider prayer leadership either as undersirable for women or restricted to the domestic space.

Was this change in legal opinions reflective of broader attitudes resulting from internal developments within Arab Islamic society? A possible antecedent for these developments could be seen in the reported attitudes of 'Umar ibn al-Khattab disagreeing with the Prophet about the veiling and movements of women. More specifically, during his own caliphate (634–44) there are narratives about 'Umar being responsible for ensuring that prayers in the mosque were segregated by gender, taking place in different areas of the mosque, with a separate imam for each group, and for ordering a male, Sulayman b. Abi Hathma, to be the imam for the congregation of women.¹²⁵ A related clue to a broader change of attitudes towards women's attendance of mosque-based prayers is a *hadith* attributed to 'A'isha in which she deplores that, had the Prophet known what women were up to (in the mosque), he would not have allowed them to go.¹²⁶ Are these reports mirroring attitudes during and soon after the Prophet's lifetime? Or are they projecting back to that period the concerns of the times of their compilers or editors?

A number of modern scholars have attempted to look beyond legal theory and theological positions by asserting that, compared to the situation during the 7th century, women's actual mobility and participation in the public arena from the 8th century onwards had suffered an irreversible setback. They attribute this to the response to the expansion of Islam and its contact with the Byzantine and Sasanian empires steeped in patriarchal and hierarchical structures.¹²⁷ Increased urbanization during the Umayyad and the first centuries of the 'Abbasid era could also have contributed to a gradual restriction of the public space of women. The spread across legal opinions and beyond of the association of women with *fitna* could accordingly be seen as a response to such a change and an alignment to gender discourses in neighbouring countries.

We showed that, at the interface between theory and practice, factors to be considered in changes of attitudes and opinions about female leadership are the institutionalization of the mosque, particularly urban mosques, and the formalization of the office of imam as prayer leader. In large urban mosques, the imam was appointed by the caliph and acted as the ruler's representative. This resulted in more stringent requirements for the role of imam. When the discourse on ritual leadership is linked to that of political leadership or governance, the issue of gender becomes a prime concern. We identified in the sources that we used two overall tendencies in viewing prayer leadership: one broadly 'egalitarian' and one more 'hierarchical'. The first was based especially on those *hadith*s where the best prayer leader is the most pious and knowledgeable in the community, irrespective of status, ethnicity and gender. The second was predominant in legal sources, especially those with political overtones, where a number of prerequisites were specified for being an imam, including that of gender, exemplified by al-Mawardi for whom being male was the first condition for being an imam.

However, textual evidence commonly dated to the Prophet's times was at odds with this second position. We have identified in this chapter a number of means through which scholars from various Sunni and Shi'i legal schools attempted to reconcile textual evidence with changing legal, political and social attitudes towards women's presence and influence in the public sphere and their roles, including ritual roles. In order to analyse their different arguments, we linked the jurists' opinions to their methodologies, sources of influence and doctrinal-intellectual perspectives.

We provided evidence that pre-modern scholars, not unlike today's scholars, made use of the past selectively, as a legitimizing tool for their varied arguments. Some elaborated upon the extent to which the past was normative for all times. Others juxtaposed the ideal past with contemporary changed circumstances, which warranted some adaptations of past practices by introducing restrictions upon women's attendance of mosques, and conditions of ritual performance and ritual leadership justified on the basis of the association of women with *fitna*.

In the case of female leadership of mixed congregations, most scholars cited no, or very few, examples, as the past was increasingly bereft of precedents, but for one possible exception: Umm Waraqa. Her prayer leadership, legitimized by the Prophet, and the issues of its location and the participants in the prayer will be introduced and discussed in the next chapter as a bridge between past and current debates, the latter to be eventually developed in Chapter 4.

Notes

1 Al-Shafi'i, Muhammad ibn Idris, *Kitab al-*Umm (Vol. 1). Edited by Muhammad Zahra al-Najjar. Beirut: Dar al-Ma'rifa li'l-Tiba'a wa-al-Nashr, [1400-/1980s], 164. The title *Kitab al-Umm* can also be translated as *The Exemplar*.
2 Ibn Sa'd, Muhammad. *Kitab al-Tabaqat al-Kabir* (Vol. 10). Edited by 'Ali Muhammad 'Umar. Cairo: Maktabat al-Khaniji, 2001, 448; also Engl. transl. by Bewley: Ibn Sa'd, Muhammad. *Kitab al-Tabaqat al-Kabir [The Women of Madina]* (Vol. 8). Translated by Aisha Bewley. London: Ta-Ha, 1995, 312 where, however, the translation has a generic 'prayer' rather than 'afternoon prayer'. Compare with Ibn Sa'd, Muhammad. *Kitab al-Tabaqat al-Kabir [Ibn Saad: Biographien: Band 8, Biographien der Frauen]* (Vol. 8). Edited by Carl Brockleman and Eduard Sachau. Leiden: Brill, 1904, Arabic, 356 under the entry on Hujayra.
3 This passage from the *Kutub* by Ibn Sallam is quoted by al-Qadi al-Nu'man in *Kitab al-Idah*. Edited by Muhammad Kazim Rahmati. Beirut: Mu'assasat al-A'lami lil-Matbu'at, 2007, 119; compare with al-Qadi al-Nu'man, Ibn Hayyun Ibn Muhammad (Abu Hanifa). *Kitab al-Idah*. Tübingen University Library, MS Ma vi 322, n.d.. A very similar passage is in the *Majmu' al-Fiqh* attributed to Zayd ibn 'Ali in *Musnad al-Imam Zayd (Majmu' al-Fiqh)*. Translated by Eugenio Griffini. Milano: Hoepli, 1919, 22 (Arabic text). Though the latter attribution is disputed, the *Majmu'* is considered to belong to the early Kufan tradition. The Arabic verb *dakhala 'ala*, lit. 'to drop by, to enter somebody's house, to call on somebody' has been translated here as 'to enter the quarters of . . .'.
4 Ibn Abi Shayba, 'Abdallah ibn Muhammad. *Al-Musannaf* (Vol. 3). Edited by Muhammad 'Awwama. Jidda: Sharika Dar al-Qiblah, 2006, 569 (*hadiths* 4988 on the authority of Hujayra and 4989 on the authority of Umm al-Hasan).
5 For Sa'da bint Qamama see al-Safadi, Khalil ibn Aybak. *Kitab al-Wafi bi'l-Wafayat* (Vol. 15). Edited by Bernd Radtke. Wiesbaden/Beirut: Franz Steiner Gerlach, 1979, 182, entry 254 (al-sahabiyya); see also a reference to another primary source in Afzalur, Rahman (ed.). *Encyclopaedia of Seerah* (Vol. 5). London: Seerah Foundation / Muslim Schools Trust, 1987, 487.
6 On 'Ali ibn al-Husayn, i.e. Zayn al-'Abidin, see Madelung, Wilferd. "Ali b. al-Hosayn". In *Encyclopaedia Iranica* (Vol. 1), edited by Ehsan Yarshater. Costa Mesa: Mazda, 1983, 849–50, where reference is made to his *jariya* who became the mother of his son Zayd; it is unclear, but is likely given her status as *umm walad*, whether this is the same *jariya* who led women in prayer.
7 For the *jariya* of 'Ali ibn al-Husayn see al-Muzani, Isma'il ibn Yahya. *Mukhtasar al-Muzani*. Edited by Muhammad 'Abd al-Qadir Shahin. Beirut: Dar al-Kutub

al-'Ilmiyya, 1993, 28; for the appointed unnamed woman, Ibn Hazm, 'Ali b. Ahmad. *Al-Muhalla bi'l-Athar.* Beirut: Dar Ihya Turath al-Arabi, 2003, 3, 136–7. For Ibn 'Umar see Gorke, Andreas. "Abdallah b 'Umar b. al-Khattab". In *EI3 Online*, edited by Kate Fleet, Gudrun Krämer, et al. Leiden: Brill online. http://dx.doi.org/10.1163/1573-3912_ei3_COM_32433 (accessed 11 February 2019).

8   al-Murtada al-Zabidi. *Taj al-'Arus min Jawahir al-Qamus.* Beirut: Manshurat Dar Maktabat al-Hay'a, 1888, 8, 194.

9   Spellberg, Denise A. *Politics, Gender and the Islamic Past: The Legacy of 'A'isha bint Abi Bakr.* New York: Columbia University Press, 1994.

10 There is uncertainty about Umm Salama's date of death; Sayeed *Women and the Transmission of Religious Knowledge in Islam*, 25 follows the dating given by Ibn Sa'd in his *Tabaqat* as 59 H/679 CE, other sources opt for later dates. The fullest and most detailed account of Umm Salama in English is Amin, Yasmin. *Umm Salama and her Hadith.* MA thesis, American University in Cairo, 2011, esp. 51–71; see also by the same author 'Wives of the Prophet'. In *OEIW* (Vol. 2), edited by Natana J. Delong-Bas. Oxford: OUP, 2013, 426–30; Roded, Ruth. 'Umm Salama Hind'. In *EI2* (Vol. 10), edited by Peri J. Bearman, Th. Bianquis et al. Leiden: Brill, 2000, 856. For Umm Salama's biography see also al-Tabari, *The History of al-Tabari* (Vol. 39). Translated by Ella Landau-Tasseron. Albany: SUNY Press, 1998, 175–7. 'A'isha's death is traditionally given on Ramadan 58 H / 678 CE.

11 For some sources Umm Salama was literate, for others she could read but not write, see Amin, *Umm Salama and her Hadith*, 82.

12 ibid., 88.

13 There is disagreement among Muslim scholars as to the identity of the woman, whose query about the absence of divine messages addressed to women prompted the revelation of 33.35: for Ibn Kathir, on the authority of Ibn Hanbal, she was Umm Salama; for Ibn 'Abbas both Umm Salama and Nusayba bint Ka'b; for al-Wahidi in his *Asbab* she was Asma' bint 'Umays.

14 Ibn Abi Shayba, *Al-Musannaf*, 4, 331; also Amin, *Umm Salama and her Hadith*, 94.

15 Newman, Andrew J. *The Formative Period of Twelver Shi'ism: Hadith as Discourse between Qum and Baghdad.* Richmond: Curzon, 2000, 74, citing a *hadith* from *Basa'ir al-darajat* by the Shi'i Muhammad al-Saffar al-Qummi (d. 902–3). In it, it is transmitted that the Prophet gave a book 'he had written himself' to Umm Salama. Chronology plays an important role here as Umm Salama, unlike Fatima who died soon after the Prophet, was alive during 'Ali's caliphate (Umm Salama died ca 679–80). For other references to Umm Salama having been entrusted with esoteric books, this time by 'Ali, see Amin, *Umm Salama and her Hadith*, 74. During the short time between the Prophet's death and Fatima's, some Shi'i *hadiths* narrate that the Archangel Gabriel revealed a book to her which she then dictated to 'Ali, see Newman, *The Formative Period of Twelver Shi'ism*, 74, 124.

16 Amin, *Umm Salama and her Hadith*, 94–8.

17 On Sumayya, a slave belonging to a member of the Makhzum clan, who died as a result of torture at the hands of a man also of the Makhzum clan, see ibn Sa'd, *The Women of Madina*, 8, 185–6.

18 Sayeed in her *Women and the Transmission of Religious Knowledge in Islam*, 42, notes that the majority of the 80 men identified by al-Mizzi to have narrated from Umm Salama are not related to her – not *mahram* – showing, as was also the case for 'A'isha, a broad network of individuals seeking her advice. Instead, the narrators from the other wives of the Prophet are usually their family members. For Sayeed this is another

instance of the prominence of Umm Salama and ʿAʾisha among the other wives of the Prophet.

19 Among early sources on ʿAʾisha leading prayer, see Ibn Saʿd, *Ibn Saad: Biographien: Band 8, Biographien der Frauen*, Ar., 355–6, where ʿAʾisha is said to lead women in *salat* while standing among them; and Ibn Abi Shayba, *Al-Musannaf* (Vol. 3), 569.
20 For an explanation of the discrepancies in number of *hadiths* attributed to ʿAʾisha and Umm Salama, see Sayeed, *Women and the Transmission of Religious Knowledge in Islam*, 25, note 21.
21 For a more detailed argument see Spellberg, *Politics, Gender and the Islamic Past*, 132–8.
22 ibid., 137.
23 Sayeed, *Women and the Transmission of Religious Knowledge in Islam*, 26–38, where she argues that a different understanding of the strictures of seclusion between ʿAʾisha and Umm Salama, notably ʿAʾisha's positive position on *ridaʾ al-kabir* (transfer of breast milk to an adult male to make him *mahram*) may be the basis of ʿAʾisha's wider network of males who transmitted from her.
24 Calder, Norman. *Studies in Early Muslim Jurisprudence*. Oxford: Clarendon Press, 1993, 67–85 on *Kitab al-Umm*; for an overview of arguments about the book see Musa, Aisha Y. 'Al-Shafiʿi, the Ḥadith, and the Concept of the Duality of Revelation'. *Islamic Studies* 46, 2 (2007): 163–197.
25 For some considerations on the Prophet's wives as paragons of virtue in *hadith* literature, see Stowasser, *Women in the Qurʾan*, 113–18; specifically in Ibn Saʿd see Roded, Ruth. *Women in Islamic Biographical Collections*. Boulder, London: Lynn Rienner, 1994, 11–13.
26 For these and further details about Ibn Sallam see Madelung, Wilferd. 'The Sources of Ismaʿili Law'. *Journal of Near Eastern Studies* 35, 1 (1976): 31, 35.
27 For al-Muradi's dates see Versteegh, Kees. 'Zayd Ibn ʿAlī's Commentary on the Qurʾān'. In *Arabic Grammar and Linguistics*, edited by Yasir Suleiman. Abingdon: Routledge, 1999, 15; see also Madelung, 'The Sources of Ismaʿili Law', 35, where it is stated that al-Muradi was still teaching in 866.
28 That both Sunni and Shiʿi scholars held Umm Salama in high regard is shown by the number of *hadiths* by her or on her authority that they record and refer to in their works, though the various sources portayed certain characteristics and narratives of Umm Salama in their distinct ways to suit their own agendas and aims. See Amin, *Umm Salama and her Hadith*.
29 The second *hadith* is in Ibn Abi Shayba, *Al-Musannaf* (Vol. 3), 569, note 4989: 'narrated to us ʿAli ibn Mushir [d.795, Kufa] who transmits from Saʿid [ibn Abi ʿAruba, Basra, d.772], who transmits from Qatada [ibn Diʿama?, from Basra d. 735] and he from Umm al-Hasan, who saw Umm Salama ... leading women in prayer and she was standing with them in their rows'. In Ibn Saʿd's *Kitab al-Ṭabaqat al-Kabir*, it is stated on the authority of Usama ibn Zayd that he saw Umm al-Hasan recounting or telling stories to people. Whether this means that Umm al-Hasan was a reliable storyteller or a popular narrator of unreliable 'stories' is open to interpretation: see Sayeed, *Women and the Transmission of Religious Knowledge in Islam*, 87–8. If the identity of the transmitters is correct, there is some suspicion about the overlap between Qatada and Umm al-Hasan, as there seems to be a gap of at least 57 years between the two; Umm al-Hasan must have died a very old woman! On Umm al-Hasan as possible maid of Umm Salama see Mourad, Suleiman Ali. 'al-Ḥasan al-Baṣrī'. In *EI3 Online*, edited by Kate Fleet, Gudrun Krämer, et al. Leiden: Brill online. http://dx.doi.org/10.1163/1573-3912_ei3_COM_32433 (accessed 6 December 2019).

30 On controversies about Ibn 'Uyayna's chronology see Juynboll, G. H. A. *Encyclopedia of Canonical Hadith*. Leiden: Brill, 2007, 568–621; as al-Zuhri's pupil, see Motzki, Harald. *Analysing Muslim Traditions: Studies in Legal, Exegetical and Maghazi Ḥadith*. Leiden: Brill, 2010, 24; other references to Ibn 'Uyayna, in al-Tabari, *The History of al-Tabari* (Vol. 11). Translated by Khalid Yahya. Albany: SUNY Press, 1993, 134, note 727, where the translator identifies Ibn 'Uyayna as a Kufan traditionist 'of excellent reputation' who had moved to Mecca in 780. In contrast, Juynboll, while considering Ibn 'Uyayna one of the most prolific Common Links, cites him as an example of those who devised specific methods of authentication for their *isnad*s: in his case, Ibn 'Uyayna stretched his own year of birth as far back as possible to make his contact with Zuhri a credible one (Juynboll, *Encyclopedia of Canonical Hadith*, xxix).

31 'Ammar ibn Mu'awiya al-Duhni, also known as Abu Mu'awiya al-Bajali (d. 750–1) is cited as a transmitter from Kufa in al-Tabari, *The History of al-Tabari* (Vol. 16). Translated by Adrian Brockett. Albany: SUNY Press, 1997, 129, 16 under year 36; (Vol. 17), Translated by I. K. A. Howard, 1990, note 79. Al-Tabari reports that Ibn Hajar accused 'Ammar of leaning towards Shi'ism; some Shi'i scholars did claim him as one of theirs.

32 In Ibn Sa'd, *Kitab al-Ṭabaqat al-Kabir* (Vol. 10), 2001, 448: *ammatna Umm Salama fi salat al-'asr fa-qamat wasatina*; al-Shafi'i, *Kitab al-Umm* (Vol. 1), [1980s], 164: *Umm Salama ammathunna fa-qamat wasatan*; Ibn Abi Shayba, *Al-Musannaf* (Vol. 3), 569, hadith 4988: *ammatna Umm Salama qa'imat wasat al-nisa'*.

33 Juynboll, *Encyclopedia of Canonical Hadith*, xx.

34 Motzki, *Analysing Muslim Traditions*, 75 ff with a specific example to illustrate both Juynboll's argument and Motzki's counterargument.

35 See Sayeed, *Women and the Transmission of Religious Knowledge in Islam*, 63–76.

36 For *hadith* scholars an *isnad* is *sahih* when it exhibits the highest degree of accuracy, followed by *hasan* and *da'if* (weak). According to most past and modern scholars the *isnad* of the above-mentioned *hadiths* on Umm Salama are considered *sahih*.

37 A near consensus of scholarly opinions is in itself not a guarantee of a *hadith*'s reliability or historicity; see the well-known case of Abu Bakra's *hadith* on women's political leadership examined by Mernissi in *The Veil and the Male Elite: A Feminist Interpretation of Women's Rights in Islam*. Cambridge: Perseus Books, 1991, 49–61.

38 For an overview and a critique of the assumptions surrounding the 'controversy' between Kufan and Medinan local customs, ostensibly surviving in later legal schools see Melchert, Christopher. 'How Hanafism Came to Originate in Kufa and Traditionalism in Medina'. *Islamic Law and Society* 6, 3 (1999): 318–47; also Hallaq, Wael B. *The Origins and Evolution of Islamic Law*. Cambridge: CUP, 2005.

39 Ibn Abi Shayba, *Al-Musannaf*, 3: *hadiths* in support of female *imama*: transmitters 'Ammar al-Duhni (d. 750 Kufa) *hadith* n. 4988; Qatada ibn Di'ama (d. 735, Basra) n. 4989; Ibn Abi Layla, Kufa, ns. 4990, 4991; against female *imama*: Ibn Abi Dhi'b (d. 776, Medina) n. 4994; Nafi'(d. 735, Medina) n. 4995. Note that the highly esteemd 13th century Shafi'i jurist al-Nawawi includes in the group of scholars against the *imama* of a woman under all circumstances – along with Malik – the Medinan Sulayman ibn Yasar (d. ca 718, one of the 7 *fuqaha* of Medina) and the Basran *faqih* (born in Medina) al-Hasan a-Basri (d. 728) see al-Nawawi, Muhyi al-din. *Kitab al-Majmu'*. Edited by Muhammad Najib al-Muti'i. Beirut: Dar Ihya al-Turath al-'Arabi, 2001, 4, 68–9.

40 Sadeghi, Benham. 'The Traveling Tradition Test: A Method for Dating Traditions'. *Der Islam* 85, 1 (2010): 203–42, for the exceptions see 228–30.

41 ibid., 228.

42 Melchert, 'How Hanafism Came to Originate in Kufa and Traditionalism in Medina', 32–41.
43 While most scholars believe the *Muwatta'* was authored by Malik, others, like Norman Calder believed the text to have been composed in Cordoba during the second part of the 3rd century H; for the traditional attribution see Dutton, Yasin. *The Origins of Islamic Law: The Qur'an, the Muwatta' and Madinan 'Amal*. Abingdon: Routledge Curzon, 2002, 26.
44 According to Dutton (ibid., 31), the aim of the *Muwatta'* was not to report Malik's opinion, but, rather the agreed practice of Medina; in the *Mudawwana* and other works, in contrast, Malik's own opinions are given more prominence. On Malik's opinion, see also the quote in Dutton (ibid., 33–4) attributed to Malik himself.
45 al-Baji, Sulayman ibn Khalaf. *Kitab al-Muntaqa Sharh Muwatta'* (Vol. 1). Edited by M. Shaqrun. Cairo: Matba'a al-Sa'ada bi Jawar Muhafiza Misr, 1912–13, 235; for the context and broader tensions between Zahiris ('in favour' of female ritual leadership) and Malikis in al-Andalus with specific reference to Ibn Hazm, see Arnaldez, Roger. 'Ibn Hazm'. In *EI2* (Vol. 3), edited by Bernard Lewis, Victor Louis Ménage, Charles Pellat and Joseph Schacht, 795. Leiden: Brill, 1986. Ibn al-'Arabi's favourable position on female *imama* is discussed in Chapter 3.
46 Among others, see Ibn Rushd, *The Distinguished Jurist's Primer*, 1, 161.
47 Sahnun Ibn Sa'id, al-Tanukhi. *Al-Mudawwana al-Kubra li'l-Imam Malik ibn Anas* (Vol. 1). Beirut: Dar al-Kutub al-'Ilmiyya, [1994], 177: 'la ta'ummu al-mar'a'.
48 ibid., 178. This seems to be a rather weak argument as men, not only women, are bound to be led during their lifetime. The Prophet, as shown in the *Sira* narrative, was himself led to be shown how to pray!
49 ibid., 195.
50 For the Prophetic *hadith* on women's 'deficiencies', see Muslim, ibn al-Hajjaj. *Sahih Muslim* (Vol. 1). Translated by Nasiruddin al-Khattab. Riyad: Dar al-Salam, 2007, 168–9, n. 241; and al-Bukhari, Muhammad. *Sahih al-Bukhari* (Vol. 1). Translated by Muhammad Muhsin Khan. Riyadh: Dar al-Salam, 1997, 210, 477. The narrators are diverse, in Muslim (n. 241) the transmitter from the Prophet is the notorious Abu Hurayra, in others the prolific Companion Abu Sa'id al-Khudri (d. 693). This *hadith* is frequently cited by subsequent Sunni and Shi'i scholars. In Bukhari the Prophet is reported to explain that a woman's deficiency in intellect is linked to being an incomplete witness and the deficiency in her religion due to her state of impurity through menstruation, which prevents her from regular prayers. For some applications of this *hadith* in legal discourse, see Katz, *Prayer in Islamic Thought and Practice*, 177–8; and Bauer, Karen. 'Debates on Women's Status as Judges and Witnesses in Post-Formative Islamic Law'. *Journal of the American Oriental Society* 130, 1 (2010): 1–21.
51 Al-Baji, *Kitab al-Muntaqa Sharh Muwatta'* (Vol. 1), 235.
52 ibid., 235–236.
53 The issue of a woman's voice being part of *'awra* is disputed; see for example the influential Egyptian Maliki Ibn Qasim (d. 806) who considered it permissible for women to utter the *tasbih*. However, a possible basis for considering the female voice as *'awra* could be implied in Maliki's statement in the *Muwatta'* (61) that while a man can attract attention during prayer by uttering the *tasbih*, a woman, rather than using her voice, should clap her hands.
54 For the whole section of Malik's opinion, supported by other authorities, on female prayer leadership, see Sahnun Ibn Sa'id, *Al-Mudawwana al-Kubra li'l-Imam Malik ibn Anas* (Vol. 1), 177–8.

55 Both Hisham ibn 'Urwa and his father, 'Urwa, are transmitters from 'A'isha, see Dutton, *The Origins of Islamic Law*, 127; Juynboll, *Encyclopedia of Canonical Hadith*, 184–205.
56 al-Baji, *Kitab al-Muntaqa Sharh Muwatta'* (Vol. 1), 235.
57 Dutton, *The Origins of Islamic Law*, 20, 44 for the report on Malik's opinion as reported by the 12th century Andalusian Maliki scholar 'Iyad ibn Musa (d. 1149).
58 Sahnun Ibn Sa'id, *Al-Mudawwana al-Kubra li'l-Imam Malik ibn Anas* (Vol. 1), 178.
59 For an impassioned, though in places historically arguable, assessment of Medina during the Prophet's time, see Mernissi, Fatima. *Women and Islam: An Historical and Theological Enquiry*. Oxford: Blackwell, 1991, 180–95.
60 Melchert, Christopher. 'Whether to Keep Women out of the Mosque: A Survey of Medieval Islamic Law'. In *Authority, Privacy and Public Order in Islam*, edited by Barbara Michalak-Pikulska and A Pikulski. Leuven: Peeters, 2006, 67.
61 Al-Shaybani, Muhammad ibn al-Hasan. *Kitab al-Athar*. Translated by Hafiz Riyad. London: Turath, 2006, 125, section on *salat*, *hadith* 217.
62 ibid., 125.
63 Ibn Sa'd, *Kitab al-Tabaqat al-Kabir [Ibn Saad: Biographien: Band 8, Biographien der Frauen]* (Vol. 8). Ibn Abi Shayba, *Al-Musannaf* (Vol. 3), 569, where it is specified, on the authority of Waki' who transmitted from Ibn Abi Layla (d. 638, Kufa) that 'A'isha led women in the obligatory (*farida*) prayer. Note that in Ibn Abi Shayba, *Al-Musannaf* (Vol. 3), 570, the *hadith* specifying that women can lead prayers during Ramadan is narrated on the authority of another Kufan *faqih*, al-Sha'bi (d. 721).
64 Sahnun Ibn Sa'id, *Al-Mudawwana al-Kubra li'l-Imam Malik ibn Anas* (Vol. 1), 178.
65 From al-Tahawi's *Mukhtasar*, as cited in Sadeghi, Benham. *The Logic of Law Making in Islam: Women and Prayer in the Legal Tradition*. Cambridge: CUP, 2013, 78.
66 For the edition and English commentary of the work on the theories of abrogation in the Qur'an and the *sunna* by Abu 'Ubayd (d. 838), see Ibn Sallam, Abu 'Ubayd al-Qasim. *Kitab al-Nasikh wa-l-Mansukh (MS Istanbul, Topkapi, Ahmet III A 143)*. Edited by John Burton. Cambridge: Gibb Memorial Trust Arabic Studies, 1987; for a critical overview of the concept of abrogation see Fatoohi, Louay. *Abrogation in the Qur'an and Islamic Law*. Abingdon, New York: Routledge, 2013.
67 For full references of this and the following examples see Sadeghi, *The Logic of Law Making in Islam*, 81–7.
68 Sadeghi identifies, among others, the following Hanafi scholars as holding the abrogation position: al-Sarakhsi (d. 1106), al-Marghinani (d. 1197), al-Kasani (d. 1189), al-Atrazi (d. 1357), al-Zayla'i (d. 1361), al-Babarti (d. 1384). For some of those what was abrogated was the desirability, rather than the permissiblility of the practice.
69 Al-Babarti's passage is quoted by Sadeghi, ibid., 86 note 21.
70 But see ibn al-Humam's statement that a female leading prayer is an act to be discouraged 'to the point of forbidding', see Melchert's translation of *Karahat al-Tahrim* in Melchert, 'Whether to Keep Women out of the Mosque', 64. Ibn al-Humam reports the two contrasting opinions without explicitly stating his own stance. See Sadeghi, *The Logic of Law Making in Islam*, 290–2.
71 See note 83 of Chapter 3 of this book referring to Nafisa Bint al-Hasan leading the funeral prayer of al-Shafi'i. In contrast, see the numerous references to rules prohibiting women from even attending funerals in Halevi, Leor. 'Wailing for the Dead: The Role of Women in Early Islamic Funerals'. *Past & Present*, 183 (2004): 3–39.
72 For al-'Ayni's full argument see Sadeghi, *The Logic of Law Making in Islam*, 87–91.

73 Hallaq, Wael B. 'Was al-Shafi'i the Master Architect of Islamic Jurisprudence?' In *Islamic Law*, edited by G. Picken. New York: Routledge, 2011, 2, 105–26; this article was originally published in 1993. For an alternative hypothesis about the dating of al-Shafi'i's reputation as a major jurist to as early as the third/ninth century, see Lowry, Joseph E. 'Ibn Qutayba: The Earliest Witness to al-Shafi'i and his Legal Doctrines'. In *Islamic Law*, edited by G. Picken, 2. New York: Routledge, 2011, 2, 150–65.

74 On 'Amra bint 'Abd al-Rahman see Sayeed, *Women and the Transmission of Religious Knowledge in Islam*, 66–9, 104–6; and Sadeghi, 'The Traveling Tradition Test', 52, 75.

75 For a number of legal scholars (not Malik), the *'awra* of a slave woman is equivalent to that of a man, i.e. it is limited to the area between the navel and the knees. However, unlike al-Shafi'i, numerous legal scholars would consider invalid the prayer perfomed by unveiled women on the basis of a *hadith* on the authority of 'A'isha that 'Allah will not accept the prayer of a child-bearing age woman unless she is wearing a head scarf', see references in Juynboll , *Encyclopedia of Canonical Hadith*, under Hammad b. Salama, 65.

76 al-Shafi'i, *Kitab al-Umm* (Vol. 1), 164.

77 ibid., 154–5.

78 ibid., 189.

79 ibid., 246.

80 al-Muzani, Isma'il ibn Yahya. *Mukhtasar al-Muzani*. Edited by Muhammad 'Abd al-Qadir Shahin. Beirut: Dar al-Kutub al-'Ilmiyya, 1998, 28.

81 al-Nawawi, *Kitab al-Majmu'*, 4, 69.

82 ibid.,4, 67–8.

83 al-Rafi'i, 'Abd al-Karim, al-Qazwini Abu'l-Qasim. *Al-'Aziz, Sharh al-Wajiz*, known as *al-Sharh al-Kabir*. Edited by 'Ali Mu'awwad and 'Adil 'Abd al-Mawjud. Beirut: Dar al-Kutub al-'Ilmiyya, 1997, 2, 142.

84 ibid., 2, 143. For a short overview of differing legal schools' positions about the value of congregational prayers see Katz, *Prayer in Islamic Thought and Practice*, 128–30.

85 Ibn Hanbal, Ahmad. *Masa'il al-Imam Ahmad ibn Hanbal*. Edited by Shawish Zuhayr. Beirut: al-Maktab al-Islami, 1981, 114. It is also relevant to note that to the question of whether the *jum'a* prayer is compulsory for all Muslims, Ahmad Ibn Hanbal replied that it was, implying that it is so for women too (ibid., 126).

86 A contrasting opinion on Ibn Hanbal's position on female prayer leadership is provided by Ibn Qudama who states in his *Mughni* that Ahmad is reported to have considered it 'undesirable' (*ghayr mustahabb*). In fact, even if this was indeed Ahmad's opinion, it still means that he held it as legally permissible; Ibn Qudama, Muwaffaq al-Din. *Al-Mughni* (Vol. 2). Beirut: Dar al-Kitab al-'Arabi, 1972, 35.

87 Ibn al-Jawzi, 'Abd al-Rahman. *Ahkam al-Nisa'*. Beirut: Dar al-Kutub al-'Ilmiyya, 1985, 25.

88 Ibn Qudama, *Al-Mughni* (Vol. 2), 35. Among the jurists holding this opinion he lists early authorities, the first two from Kufa, the last from Basra: al-Sha'bi, al-Nakha'i (d. 715) and Qatada b. Di'ama.

89 Nevertheless, while praying, a woman can proclaim in a clear voice among men, only if they are *maharim*. Ibn Qudama, *Al-Mughni* (Vol. 2), 35.

90 Katz, *Women in the Mosque*, 103–4.

91 Ibn Hanbal, *Masa'il al-Imam Ahmad ibn Hanbal*, 130, 'sami'tu Abi su'ila 'an al-nisa' yakhrujna ila al-'idayn. Qala: la yu'jibuni fi zamanina hadha li'annahunna *fitna*', among other *hadith* collections, in the *Sahih*s by al-Bukhari and Muslim.

92 Ibn al-Jawzi, *Ahkam al-Nisa'*, 30, where the *hadith* with the section on 'but their houses are best for them' is reported on the authority of Ibn 'Umar, from the Prophet.

93 ibid., 32, statement attributed to the author of *Al-Musannaf*.

94 Ibn Taymiyya, Ahmad. *Majmuʿ al-Fatawa* (Vol. 14). Edited by Mustafa ʿAbd al-Qadir ʿAta. Beirut: Dar al-Kutub al-ʿIlmiyya, 2000, 82–4. For a more extensive discussion on Ibn Taymiyya's position about women's prayers, see Katz, *Women in the Mosque*, 93–98.

95 Ibn al-Jawzi, *Ahkam al-Nisaʾ*, 33.

96 ibid., 24. The use of terms such as *khimar* and *jilbab* by Ibn al-Jawzi seem to directly refer to those mentioned in the Qurʾan in connection with Muslim women's modest dress, with no further indication of the actual meaning either in the Qurʾan itself or during Ibn al-Jawzi's time.

97 Sadeghi, *The Logic of Law Making in Islam*, xii.

98 There are a few references to women delivering a *khutba*, for a 12th century example, see Melchert, 'Whether to Keep Women out of the Mosque', 68, quoting Ibn ʿAsakir; or the 14th century Fatima bint ʿAbbas ʿUmm Zaynab al-Baghdadiyya, a contemporary of Ibn Taymiyya, who is reported as having preached to women from the *minbar*, see al-Safadi, Khalil ibn Aybak. *Aʿyan al-ʿAsr wa Aʿwan al-Nasr* (Vol. 3). Edited by Falih Ahmad Bakkur. Beirut: Dar al-Fikr, 1998 / 1394. Are we to assume that, especially in a women-only gathering, a prayer leadership might have occurred too?

99 See Newman, *The Formative Period of Twelver Shiʿism*, 168–70.

100 See for instance al-Kulayni, Abu Jaʿfar Muhammad al-Razi. *Al-Furuʿ min al-Kafi* (Vol. 3). Edited by ʿAli Akbar Ghaffari. Beirut: Dar Saʿb – Dar al-Taʿaruf, 1980–1, *kitab al-salat, bab al-rajul yaʾummu al-nisaʾ*, hadith 2, 376; or Ibn Babawayh, *Man la Yahdaruhu al-Faqih* (Vol. 1), *salat, bab* 56, *hadith* 86, 259 about female leadership of women from the middle.

101 For the use of *taqaddama* see Ibn Babawayh, *Man la Yahdaruhu al-Faqih*, 1, 259; al-Qadi al-Nuʿman, Ibn Hayyun Ibn Muhammad (Abu Hanifa). *Taʾwil al-Daʿaʾim* (Vol. 1). Edited by al-Aʿzami. Cairo: Dar al-Maʿarif, [1969], 153; al-Tusi, *Tahdhib al-Ahkam fi Sharh al-Muqniʿa liʾl-Shaykh al-Mufid* (Vol. 3), 32; for the use of *amma* as a generic 'to lead' see al-Tusi, *Al-Mabsut fi Fiqh al-Imamiyya*, 157, 'it is permissible for a woman to lead (*taʾummu*) women in the *faraʾid* and the *nawafil* prayers and she is located in their midsts . . .'.

102 For the prayer of the dead see Ibn Babawayh, *Man la Yahdaruhu al-Faqih*, 1, 259; al-Hilli, Hasan ibn Yusuf Ibn al-Mutahhar al-ʿAllama. *Mukhtalif al-Shiʿa fi Ahkam al-Shariʿa* (Vol. 2). Qum: Islamic Sciences Research Center/Markaz al-Abhath waʾl-Dirasat al-Islamiyya, 1371/ , 487; instead, for al-Kulayni a woman cannot lead from the front in either obligatory or supererogatory prayer, see al-Kulayni, *Al-Furuʿ min al-Kafi* (Vol. 3), 376.

103 See Sadeghi's argument about regional *isnad* in 'The Traveling Tradition Test', 227–8, 237.

104 For some of the jurists' opinions about Friday prayer during the Safavids see Stewart, Devin J. 'Polemics and Patronage in Safavid Iran: The Debate on Friday Prayer During the Reign of Shah Tahmasb'. *Bulletin of the School of Oriental and African Studies* 72, 3 (2009): 425–57.

105 al-Tusi, Muhammad ibn al-Hasan, Shaykh al-Taʾifa. *Kitab al-Khilaf* (Vol. 1). Qum: Dar al-Kutub al-ʿAliya, n.d., 198. *Kitab al-Khilaf*, written after 1024, is one of the best known Shiʿi books in comparative jurisprudence.

106 Al-Qadi al-Nuʿman, *The Pillars of Islam* (Vol. 1), 2002, 184

107 al-Hilli, *Mukhtalif al-Shiʿa fi Ahkam al-Shariʿa* (Vol. 2), *salat*, 139.

108 On women reciting in a low yet audible voice see Ibn Babawayh, *Man la Yahdaruhu al-Faqih*, 1, 266, 263. On uttering the call to prayer see al-Qadi al-Nuʿman, *The Pillars*

of Islam (Vol. 1), 2002, 184; Muhaqqiq al-Hilli, *Shara'i' al-Islam fi Masa'il al-Halal wa'l-Haram*, 1, 74; on the modest positions and attire for women in prayer see Ibn Babawayh, *Man la Yahdaruhu al-Faqih*, 1, 243.
109 al-Tusi, *Kitab al-Khilaf* (Vol. 1), 127–9.
110 al-Tusi, *Al-Mabsut fi Fiqh al-Imamiyya*, 146.
111 ibid., 162.
112 Ibn Babawayh, *Man la Yahdaruhu al-Faqih*, 1, *salat*, hadith 8, 245.
113 ibid., *hadith* 88, 259. Note the degree of spatial restriction: better the bedchamber than the house (*bayt*), better the house than the larger dwelling (*dar*, often with courtyard). For a general explanation of the difference between *bayt* and *dar* see Marçais, George. 'Dar'. In *EI2* (Vol. 1), edited by Peri J. Bearman, Th. Bianquis et al. Leiden: Brill, 1965, 113–15; in some *hadith*s, however, the two terms are interchangeable.
114 For Umm Salama leading prayer, in addition to the quote by Ibn Sallam at the beginning of this chapter, see also al-Tusi Shaykh al-Ta'ifa's evidence in favour of women leading prayer from both 'A'isha and Umm Salama in *Kitab al-Khilaf* (Vol. 1), 199.
115 ibid., 198–9.
116 al-Tusi, *Tahdhib al-Ahkam fi Sharh al-Muqni'a li'l-Shaykh al-Mufid* (Vol. 3), 31.
117 al-Hilli, *Mukhtalif al-Shi'a fi Ahkam al-Shari'a* (Vol. 2), 486.
118 ibid., 486–88.
119 For varied scholarly interpretations of the dating and nature of legal disputes between Akhbaris and Usulis in Imami Shi'i thought see Stewart, Devin J. *Islamic Legal Orthodoxy: Twelver Shiite Responses to the Sunni Legal System*. Salt Lake City, UT: The University of Utah Press, 1998; and Gleave, Robert. *Inevitable Doubt: Two Theories of Shi'i Jurisprudence*. Leiden: Brill, 2000.
120 Quoted by al-Qadi al-Nu'man in his collection of Shi'i *hadith*s, *Kitab al-Idah*, 83–4. For a fuller explanation of female legal capacity see Calderini, Simonetta. '"Leading from the Middle": Qadi al-Nu'man on Female Prayer Leadership'. In *The Fatimid Caliphate: Diversity of Traditions*, edited by Farhad Daftary and Shainool Jiwa. London: IB Tauris, 2018, 94–117, esp. 101–2.
121 al-Qadi al-Nu'man, *Ta'wil al-Da'a'im*, (Vol. 1) 245.
122 Cortese, Delia and Simonetta Calderini. *Women and the Fatimids in the World of Islam*. Edinburgh: Edinburgh University Press, 2006, 127–38.
123 Massignon, Louis. 'La Mubahala de Medine et l'Hyperdulie de Fatima'. In *Opera Minora: Textes Recueillis, Classés et Présentés avec une Bibliographie* (Vol. 1), edited by Youakim Moubarac. Paris: Presses Universitaire de France, 1969, 550–72; see also Plate I of a 17th century miniature illustration of the episode inclusive of Fatima. Massignon reports the spatial position of 'Ali on the right hand side of Muhammad, the two grandchildren in front and Fatima on the back (ibid., 557).
124 Cortese and Calderini, *Women and the Fatimids in the World of Islam*, 9; for today's practice of *tasbih* Fatima see https://ismailimail.blog/2016/05/07/the-prophet-prescribed-his-daughter-fatima-a-prayer-to-recite-in-times-of-difficulty/ (accessed 8 February 2019).
125 Ibn Sa'd, *Kitab al-Tabaqat al-Kabir*, (Vol. 7), 2001, 30, n. 1436 (under Sulayman ibn Abi Hathma). It is noticeable that in one of the reports the separate groups of men and women with their respective imams are located in the house of the Prophet. Ahmed Leila, in *Women and Gender in Islam: Historical Roots of a Modern Debate*. New Haven, CT: Yale University Press, 1992, 61, states that 'Umar's ruling about the male imam for women's groups was revoked by his successor 'Uthman.

126 al-Bukhari, Muhammad. *Sahih al-Bukhari*. Translated by Muhammad Muhsin. Riyadh: Dar al-Salam, 1984, 1, 458, *hadith* 828. In this version, 'A'isha does not explicitly mention women's mosque attendance but compares what the Prophet would have done with what she believes the Israelites had already done, i.e. to forbid women from visiting the place of worship. In fact, Jewish women could normally attend both the temple and, later, the synagogue, but their access was denied when they were in their period or post-partum bleeding. During the late Stammaic post-Talmudic period (ca 5–6th century CE) rabbis discussed 1st century texts restricting women's access to the main areas of the temple in order to avoid 'the devil's inclinations' (note parallelism with the concept of *fitna* discussed in this chapter). These arguments would later serve to justify gender separation in synagogues. See Grossman, Susan. 'Women and the Jerusalem Temple'. In *Daughters of the King: Women and the Synagogue*, edited by Susan Grossman and Rivka Haut. Philadelphia, PA: The Jewish Publication Society, 1992, 25–9.

127 Ahmed, *Women and Gender in Islam*, esp. Ch 5.

Chapter 3

CONGREGATIONAL PRAYERS: WOMEN LEADING MEN

Setting the context

If the previous chapter evidenced scholarly controversies surrounding the role of women as prayer leaders of women, here we address an even more contentious question: can women lead men in prayer? We start with a close examination of narratives pertaining to two female figures, one of whom, Ghazala, has been the subject of hardly any scholarly investigation. We then look at contrasting legal debates between those arguing against women leading men and those who were 'not against' the practice. The unique position of Sufism will serve as a form of philosophical reconciliation between the two positions. During the process, for the first time forgotten legal voices will be heard again to show how – whether as a response to practical needs or not – the topic of women leading men occupied a significant space in debates. There is no doubt that the hypothetical case of women leading men entered these debates by default, the core question ultimately revolving around permissibility of prayer leadership as a whole.

Unlike the previous chapters, the key figures here will be two women who were not members of the Prophet's close family. One, Umm Waraqa, was a notable Companion of the Prophet, and the other, Ghazala al-Haruriyya, a Khariji woman presented as holding a prominent position in her own community. The relation between these women and their ritual performances was sidelined, partially censored and almost forgotten. When it was reported, I argue that it was done in a way so as to serve as a warning to other women not to overstep male bounds. It might be no coincidence that Umm Waraqa and Ghazala were both reported to have met a violent death.

In Chapter 1 debates were explored that brought to the fore a link between politico-military leadership, identified as the greater *imama*, and prayer leadership as the smaller *imama*. Here, for the first time we can see how this link can be used as an interpretative key to evaluate the actions of these two women and the status that each acquired from them. We can see such a link between these two types of leadership played out in the home, in the mosque or on the battlefield, and we see their deeds contextualized by the perceptions of social gender boundaries, the relation between women and mosques, a woman's role in battle and, lastly, types of female martyrdom.

This chapter analyses *hadith* narratives and other accounts about Umm Waraqa mainly found in the biographical work of the already mentioned Ibn Sa'd and in a number of *hadith* collections. These works are mainly dated from the 9th century, and I argue that the way in which the narratives about Umm Waraqa's prayer leadership are presented may reflect an underlying discourse on the development of ritual identity for the community of Muslims projected back to the period during – or soon after – the Prophet's lifetime. From the 10th century onwards, scholars cite the same narratives centred about Umm Waraqa's prayer leadership but with different wording than those of earlier versions. By doing so, these scholars might be seen to reflect widespread changes in perceptions about the status and ritual role of women, thus echoing the socio-cultural and legal concerns of their times.[1]

Unlike Umm Waraqa, our knowledge of the events surrounding the Khariji 'rebel' Ghazala and her association with the mosque of Kufa is based exclusively on historical sources. They consist of Sunni works containing anti-Khariji polemics and thus they reflect more the writers' positions towards, and judgment of, the Kharijis and their women than they do on Ghazala herself.

In both cases, neither woman narrated her own story; rather the accounts about them were crafted by others to present them as examples or figureheads serving specific purposes. Thus, although an attempt is made to learn about these women as historical figures, this chapter is more concerned with the construction, by scholars or narrators, of the personas of these two women as exemplified by their reported lives and selected deeds, as well as their positive or negative legacies, which result from such a construction. As examples of the past, they are part of a discursive tradition which continues to shape debates about Muslim women's roles and the extent of female authority.

Building upon the debates about Umm Waraqa and Ghazala, this chapter will then provide an overview of legal and doctrinal arguments about women leading men in prayer by selected Sunni and Shi'i scholars spanning the 9th to the 12th century. For the first time, it will showcase the counter-arguments of lesser-known 9th century jurists who did not reject the permissibility of a woman leading a man in prayer. Three frameworks will be evaluated to assess their views: firstly, the broader context of the *ahl al-hadith* versus *ahl al-ra'y* debates, a tension that we have already observed in Chapter 2; secondly, the formulation of the concept of the pre-eminence of the *Sahaba*; and thirdly, the legal discussions on the principles pertaining to the validity of prayer.

The obscurity of some of these exegetes is contrasted to the fame of Ibn al-'Arabi, one the greatest mystical philosophers, who also engaged with the debates on female leadership of men with surprising insights. In the final section of the chapter the focus moves onto the issue of the extent to which such legal discussions reflected legal theory rather than the actual practice of the community.

Women as prayer leaders of men: Umm Waraqa and Ghazala

Umm Waraqa: From prayer leader to martyr

Umm Waraqa bint Nawfal (d. ca 641) was a Companion of the Prophet, a respected early Ansari from the Banu Najjar, a clan of the prominent Khazraj tribe in Medina. Ibn Sa'd reports that the Prophet used to regularly visit Umm Waraqa in her own house and that she had memorized the Qur'an. Upon her request to the Prophet to allow her to accompany him to the Battle of Badr (624) so that she might become a *shahida* (witness, martyr), the Prophet assured her that Allah would grant her *shahada* (martyrdom). He used to call her '*the shahida*'.[2]

Ibn Sa'd also reports, on the basis of a line of witnesses that ultimately goes back to Umma Waraqa, that she stated that 'the Prophet had ordered her (*qad amaraha*) to act as imam for the people of her household (*ahl dariha*), that she had a muezzin, and that she used to lead [in prayer] (*ta'ummu*) the people of her household (*dar*)'.[3] At around the year 20 H / 640–1 CE,[4] he adds that she died a violent death at the hands of her two male and female servants, who might have tried to steal from her. Ibn Sa'd concludes his narrative by noting that the second caliph 'Umar ordered the killers to be crucified and that this was the first time in Islamic history that such a penalty was inflicted.

Ibn Sa'd's *hadith* provides further details about this notable woman, whose desire to become a martyr is acknowledged by the Prophet. His reassurance that her desire would be fulfilled is one of the instances of reported Prophetic foreknowledge and, in the absence of any explicit denial to her request to join him in battle, this narrative leaves the possibility open that she might have done so at Badr. The reference to Badr situates this exchange during a period of heightened vulnerability for the nascent Muslim community and its individual members. Badr was to become a decisive battle of an unprecedented scale for the early Muslims. It marked a turning point of securing the success of Muhammad's supporters against the Meccan Qurayshi opponents. At this time to conduct the ritual of Muslim prayer could still be considered in itself an act of bravery.

The type of martyrdom Umm Waraqa is reported to have eventually met was not as a result of death in battle; such a person in the language of later jurists-theologians would be considered as a martyr 'in this world and the next'. Instead, she can be viewed either as a martyr 'in the next world', reserved only for those who fight against robbers, or a category said to have been introduced after the period of the early conquests of those Muslims who die a violent death or are murdered while in the service of God. This included men as well as women. The first reported female martyr in Islam, the already mentioned Sumayya bint al-Khattab (d. 615), would, accordingly, belong to the latter category of martyrs.[5]

With reference to commitment to the cause of Allah and martyrdom, the *hadith* in Ibn Sa'd depicts Umm Waraqa as an example of a believer who epitomizes both, without confining martyrdom to the battlefield. This *hadith* could therefore also be read as evidence of competing views on what martyrdom is and who could be termed as a martyr. Such views were part of a wider debate taking place just before and during Ibn Sa'd's time, about which activities, in the path of God, display more merit: devotional-ritual, such as prayer and *hajj*, or combative acts such as *jihad*.⁶

One could also read Ibn Sa'd's account of Umm Waraqa through the lens of the early Islamic debates on the characteristics of the ideal leader of the community and, by extension, the ideal prayer leader. Umm Waraqa displays the main requirements to be a leader: she is a notable early Companion, whose loyalty to the cause of Islam is demonstrated by her willingness to go to battle, and she is pious and has knowledge of what had been revealed of the Qur'an until that time. Her precedence and excellence are undisputed here. On the basis of the narrative, the Prophet personally acknowledges her commitment, visits her on a regular basis and orders her to lead prayer.

A contemporary of Ibn Sa'd, Ahmad ibn Hanbal, the traditionist and eponym of the Hanbali school of law, includes in his *Musnad* two separate *hadiths* on Umm Waraqa. The first begins with a mention of the Prophet's weekly visits to her house, during one of which she asked to go with him to Badr, told him how she desired to become a martyr, and, significantly, adds how the Prophet told her to 'remain (*qirri*)' and that Allah would grant her martyrdom. It concludes with her eventual murder, as already narrated by Ibn Sa'd. The second *hadith* in Ibn Hanbal on her prayer leadership is identical to Ibn Sa'd's.⁷

When read together, the first of Ibn Hanbal's *hadiths* sets out the historical, ethnic-tribal and social background to Umm Waraqa, while the second focuses on her religious and ritual status. As for the *hadith* on her prayer leadership, both Ibn Sa'd and Ibn Hanbal indicate as the first direct transmitter from Umm Waraqa an unnamed woman, who then transmits the narrative to her grandson al-Walid ibn 'Abdallah ibn Jumay'i. The latter is considered overall to be a trustworthy witness and *hadith* transmitter.⁸

Subsequent *hadith* collectors started to introduce further details and variants which reflect their different interpretations of Umm Waraqa's leadership and how the Prophet legitimized it. The slight changes in content (*matn*) of such reports are usually linked to variations in their *isnad*, an occurrence that *hadith* scholars have frequently noted as applicable to numerous *hadiths*.

For example, Abu Dawud in his *Sunan* enriches the narrative by Ibn Hanbal about Umm Waraqa's desire to join the Prophet in battle by adding to the direct speech of the Prophet's reply: 'remain in your house (*qirri fi baytiki*), Allah will surely bestow martyrdom upon you.'⁹ This reply with the addition of 'your house' has been selectively used as evidence up to the present to discourage women from any involvement in warfare, and to support interpretations about women's domestic roles. The sentence 'stay in your house' is also found in a Qur'anic injunction, which under different circumstances was specifically and exclusively addressed to the Prophet's wives (Qur. 33.33). This *sura* is typically dated to the Hijri year 5, three years after the Battle of Badr, the battle Umm Waraqa is reported to have asked to join. This shows that in his report, Abu Dawud may have anachronistically attributed words to the Prophet, echoing a Qur'anic revelation, that had not yet taken place. For many scholars on the evidence of reports of the Prophet's wives' activities, this Qur'anic injunction should not be understood literally. Others interpret it by the letter and even extend it, by association, to all Muslim women. We will see in Chapter 4 of this book the consequences resulting from the variant interpretations of this *hadith* with reference to modern debates on women's mosque attendance.

To the above, Abu Dawud adds, on the authority of a male transmitter, 'Abd al-Rahman ibn Khallad al-Ansari, that the Prophet had put in place for Umm Waraqa a muezzin to call prayer for her and that 'Abd al-Rahman himself had seen her muezzin, who, he states, was 'an old man'.[10] This transmitter, who presents himself as witness to the identity of the muezzin, does not appear in the *isnad* of the earlier *hadiths* on Umm Waraqa's prayer leadership. The inclusion of this direct male transmitter can be seen as a device to reinforce the credibility of the *hadith* as a whole, including its additional statement about the muezzin. This was now a narrative that would rely not only on the direct witness of a woman, Umm Waraqa, but also of a male contemporary of hers, and, like her, an Ansari.[11] Though 'Abd al-Rahman's biography is mostly unknown, he will be included again in subsequent reports of Umm Waraqa's *hadiths*. In fact, 'Abd al-Rahman's witnessing the event may be put into question by other reports indicating that he did not transmsit directly from Umm Waraqa, but through his own father. The clarification that the muezzin was an old man seems indeed to be a form of literary crafting serving as a response to possible concerns of female modesty and propriety due to the presence in Umm Waraqa's house of an unrelated man!

More significant and consequential variants, perhaps even modifications, emerge in the reporting of the text of these *hadiths* by the Iraqi traditionist Abu Bakr al-Shaybani (aka Ibn Abi Asim, d. 900). He belonged to the Zahiri school of law that will be discussed in greater detail later on in this chapter. In his collection of single strand *hadiths* (*ahad*), the version he uses in relaying the vicissitudes of Umm Waraqa, which is based on an all Iraqi *isnad*,[12] includes one new detail and an important omission. The detail is a reference to a *masjid*, or place of worship, which Umm Waraqa asked the Prophet permission to establish (*bana'*) in her own *dar* (house, residence, area). The narration continues to state that the Prophet did permit her to establish a place for her to pray in. The omission is Umm Waraqa's ritual leadership, implying that her place of worship was for her to pray in, not to lead anyone else in prayer. Nevertheless, al-Shaybani's version sheds light on another form of agency attributed to Umm Waraqa, that of being the instigator for the building of a place of worship, a 'mosque', and receiving approval from the Prophet to do so.

Such an omission was not to remain an isolated case and, in time, a number of other scholars no longer mentioned Umm Waraqa's ritual leadership in some of the entries of their biographical collections.[13]

With the Shafi'i scholar Ibn Khuzayma al-Nisaburi (d. 924) we see a turning point in the way in which the dynamics of the relationship between the Prophet and Umm Waraqa are described. In his text the element of 'permission' from the Prophet, with regards Umm Waraqa's desire to join him in battle, is extended to Umm Waraqa's prayer leadership. Here 'the Prophet gave her permission (*adhana laha*) to have the call of prayer recited for her and for her to lead the people of her *dar* in the prescribed prayer'.[14] To use here the term 'permission' to lead prayer, instead of a command to lead it, as indicated in earlier *hadith*s, still reflects endorsement by Prophetic authority of Umm Waraqa's leadership. However, it hints at a different reception by al-Nisaburi of the degree of authority that Umm Waraqa's leadership held: no longer a Prophetic order to lead but permission to do so.

Iraqi Shafi'i scholar 'Ali b. 'Umar al-Daraqutni (d. 995) in his *Sunan*, cites more than one *hadith* about Umm Waraqa. In all he perpetuates the report on the Prophet's permissibility (rather than command) for this woman to lead prayer. However, in one of the versions he reports we find a significant addition. About the type of congregation Umm Waraqa led, he states: 'the Prophet allowed her to have the *adhan* and the *iqama* [called] for her; and to lead in prayer *the women* [of her household] (*wa-ta'ummu nisa'aha*; lit. her women)'.[15] This specific clarification can be interpreted as a reflection of the already discussed progressive change in legal and broader attitudes towards women's roles on the basis of the concept of *fitna*. The insertion of the word 'women' to define her congregation can be considered as an interpolation or a seemingly more legitimate 'transmission by sense'. Irrespectively, the majority of scholars down the ages selected this over all of al-Daraqutni's versions on Umm Waraqa's leadership *hadith*s. This is so that, if Umm Waraqa was ever to be considered a precedent for female ritual leadership, it would only be for an all-female congregation. When, as we will see in the following sections of this chapter, some scholars, most of whom were Shafi'is like al-Daraqutni, held positions 'not against' women leading men in prayer, they resorted to legal and philosophical discussions rather than referring to the Umm Waraqa *hadith* as a precedent. One possible explanation is that the all-female version by al-Daraqutni was the one they were familiar with. This scholarly trajectory will have profound consequences that we will discuss further in Chapter 4.

Subsequent references to Umm Waraqa can be found in biographical collections as well as legal literature exhibiting varied interpretations of her leadership (when mentioned), variations which are, again, matched to different *isnad*s.[16] Today, those who advocate the right of women to lead men alongside women in prayer invoke Umm Waraqa's *hadith* in the Ibn Sa'd version.

Because of the current relevance that this *hadith* has been having in informing attitudes toward female prayer leadership of mixed congregations, it has been the object of scrutiny more than other *hadith*s. However, while studies have considered this *hadith* on its own merits, this book for the first time examines it within a wider context of narratives and debates on prayer leadership as well as multiple interpretative keys, which open up a varied range of understanding and appraisal of its uses.

Wishing to argue in favour of women leading men in prayer and introduce the Umm Waraqa *hadith* as textual evidence for this assertion, Nevid Reda (2005) elaborates on the meaning of the term *dar* found in Ibn Sa'd's *hadith*. Rather than using the more common meaning of 'house, household', Reda points to another attested semantic use of the term *dar* to refer to an 'area, locality'. She justifies her choice mainly by linking it to the number of people mentioned in the *hadith* as being in her *dar*, i.e. the muezzin and the two servants who eventually killed her.

Reda thus argues that *dar* meant more than her home as she would not need a muezzin to call only three people to prayer.

Her main argument about Umm Waraqa as imam of her 'area' is that the Prophet had entrusted her with a far more encompassing leadership role to be an imam. Reda stretches her exegesis of Ibn Saʿd's use of vocabulary when she equates the term *dar* with mosque, not as a generic place of worship, but as one with a wide-ranging social and communal importance – in her words, a 'second mosque' after the one established by Muhammad in his own house. Accordingly, Reda states that when 'the need for a second mosque arose, the Prophet chose a woman to act as the imam'.[17] In pre-empting a possible objection to her understanding of Umm Waraqa's *dar* as a mosque, she explains that during the time of the Prophet, the place of prayer was not a separate building, but an area, a section in a home, as in the case of the Prophet's house where its courtyard functioned as the place of prayer. In short, the implications that derive from Reda's reasoning are that the *dar* coincides with a physical location of prayer which is large enough to accommodate a large number of people, both men and women, so as to warrant the presence of a muezzin, people for whom the Prophet had ordered Umm Waraqa to lead in prayer.

The conclusion that one draws about the various aspects of Umm Waraqa's leadership is dependant, as shown in the sample of narratives above, upon the scholar's choice of *hadith*s, the version of the *hadith* transmittted, the interpretation of the terms used in its text and the context that frames the intended use of it. For example, if we were to rely on one source alone, such as Abu Bakr al-Shaybani, we can observe that both the terms *masjid* and *dar* are indeed present in his narrative, where he states that the *masjid* was established in Umm Waraqa's *dar*. However, he also specifies in his narrative that this place of prayer was 'for her to pray in' – that is, for her private use. Moreover, nowhere in his narrative does he include the figure of the muezzin, and, more importantly, in al-Shaybani's account there is no mention of any prayer leadership at all.

It is thus clear that the *hadith*s on Umm Waraqa can be interpreted from different perspectives. Synchronically, she is presented as a respected member of the prominent Banu Najjar clan in Medina, possibly related to the Prophet through his mother's side. Umm Waraqa's high standing can be inferred by the Prophet's regular visits to her. Her keenness to show her support to the Prophet is expressed through her desire to join him at the Battle of Badr. This could reflect, or serve as a recognition of, her tribe's wider support for the Prophet. Significantly, her association with a place of worship in her *dar* recalls the role played by the Banu Najjar, on whose land it is reported that Muhammad established the first mosque (*masjid*) and his living quarters (*masakinahu*).[18]

To reinforce the claim that Umm Waraqa led men and women in prayer, it would be more fitting to interpret the term *dar* not as a physical place as Reda does, but rather, as evidenced in some sources, as a collective of people. The use is attested in a number of early texts of *dar* meaning tribe, as in the Prophetic *hadith* quoted in al-Bukhari where the Prophet praises the Banu Najjar, the very same tribe of Umm Waraqa, as the best tribe (*khayr dar*) among the Ansar.[19] This use of *dar* would give a different spin on the understanding of her 'leading the people of her *dar* (tribe)'. The link between specific places of worship in Medina during the time of the Prophet and tribal identity has already been discussed in Chapter 1 of this book.

Irrespective of whether the various *hadith* narratives on Umm Waraqa are to be considered as accurate historical records of the Medinan period they refer to (just before the Battle of Badr), or rather as the product of literary crafting by subsequent generations of scholars, the figure of Umm Waraqa enjoyed varied receptions from the different audiences which over time became familiar with her vicissitudes. For some, Umm Waraqa becomes an exemplar of support for the Prophet's cause and a means of honouring her tribe and the early Ansar as a whole.

Diachronically, her multiple associations with prayer (place of worship, modality, ritual leadership) point to a number of ritual statements and changes occurring at that time which shaped the identity of the nascent Islamic community. Paramount among these ritual statements is what Gerhard Böwering called the 'institution of ritual prayer', which resulted in the clarification of ritual practices associated with *salat*, such as the change of the direction of prayer (*qibla*), traditionally dated to the same year as the Battle of Badr (624),[20] the timed nature of prayers (Qur. 4.103), their number, and their prescriptive nature for men as well as for women (Qur. 33.33).[21] Of particular relevance for the ritual understanding of the Umm Waraqa narrative is the reference to the muezzin as an expression of the gradual formalization of the public call to prayer. Thus, the elements of Umm Waraqa's narrative, i.e. her eagerness to go to the Battle of Badr, the Prophet's permitting her to have a muezzin and ordering her to lead the prayer, can all be seen as pointers to the recording of, or reporting about, a period when the developing *umma* was defining itself in terms of political allegiance to the Prophet and, theologically, in terms of its religious identity through a distinct set of rituals associated with prayer, the performance of which had been prescribed for men as well as for women.

Irrespective of the variance in the text of the narratives on Umm Waraqa and the reliability of some of their transmitters, the *hadiths* on her *imama* kept on being quoted in their different wording and adduced for various purposes, particularly to substantiate pre-modern legal positions on ritual performance and leadership. Towards the end of the 12th century the great Andalusian philosopher, theologian and jurist Ibn Rushd in his *Bidayat al-Mujtahid (The Distinguished Jurist's Primer)* reported the differing opinions concerning the *imama* of a woman. He stated that while the majority of jurists 'maintained that she cannot lead men, they disagreed about her leading women'.[22] Ibn Rushd adds that there were exceptions to that majority and that those who permitted her unrestricted *imama* quoted as evidence the Umm Waraqa *hadith*, as reported by Abu Dawud. Ibn Rushd stands out as one of the few great scholars of his time who gives credibility to the understanding of Umm Waraqa's *hadith* as showing that she led men in prayer. Only a scholar of his calibre could not fail to recognize the importance of Umm Waraqa as a legal precedent. As we will see in the final chapter of this book, Umm Waraqa's narrative witnessed a revival during the early 21st century as a result of debates on female leadership in prayer and gender social and ritual equality in Islam.

In Chapter 2 we analysed Umm Salama's reports on her prayer leadership, and through a number of interpretative keys we identified the salient characteristics of her reported persona and roles. Though not enjoying the elevated status of mother of believers that Umm Salama did as the Prophet's wife, Umm Waraqa was also a woman of high standing and, like Umm Salama, belonged to a prominent tribe. Both are portrayed as pious and knowledgeable women who knew the Qur'an, were loyal to the Prophet and were committed to his mission to the point of asking to join him in battle, with Umm Salama reported as having joined him in a number of them. Both are depicted as women who were fit for leadership. Both had agency. However, there are details about them which betray different contexts for the use of that agency. Their chronology points to Umm Salama having married the Prophet in 626, two years after the Battle of Badr, by which time Umm Waraqa had already been ordered by the Prophet to lead the people of her *dar* in prayer, had been assigned a muezzin, and more importantly one might infer that she led a congregation made of a diverse constituency. As for Umm Salama's leadership, it is consistently reported that she led women in her own house. On the basis of some accounts, the Prophet is shown as inviting her to lead almost incidentally, having noticed, upon visiting her, that some women were already praying in a corner of her house. Furthermore, the way in which the respective *hadiths* are handed down points to an added agency that Umm Waraqa is ascribed by being the first source of transmission of her own leadership and the immediate circumstances relevant to it.

This brief comparison between the narrated circumstances and activities of two women contemporary to each other highlights differences in the recounted performance of prayer and the role these women played in it that might be seen as capturing a transitional phase in the 'institution of ritual prayer' discussed earlier in this chapter. Envisaging a 'before' and 'after' scenario, the watershed moment for the shift in the reported events could be identified with the Battle of Badr. As noted earlier, Badr was an important victory for the early Muslims, which must have given them added confidence in their mission. In the process of the changes to the ritual of prayer that took place around the time of the battle, female leadership might have also been impacted in a way that influenced subsequent attitudes on the position of a woman holding that role.

Beyond the 'chronological time' of Badr, a different interpretation to its mention in these narratives is what al-Azmeh would describe as the transposition from its context, as one of the local raids in Arabia, into Islamic salvation history, or into 'the perspective of eternity', where Badr would 'textually read' as *jihad* and martyrdom.[23] In light of al-Azmeh's interpretation of the reading of Badr, Umm Waraqa's narrative acquires a new nuance when, in her zeal, she asks to join the Prophet at (a paradigmatic) Badr in the hope of gaining martyrdom.

A very different narrative context and reading is that of (a post-Badr) Umm Salama who asks to join the Prophet in (unspecified) battles to tend the wounded. The two narrative personas here reflect not only different motivations to accompany the Prophet in battle, but also two very different contexts of female agency.

When taken at face value both narratives relating to Umm Salama and Umm Waraqa's prayer leadership equally meet the criteria that qualify *hadith*s to be used as precedents in legal terms to inform practices for Muslims to follow on the basis of the Prophetic *sunna*. However, the destiny of their uses as precedents would develop in different directions, with Umm Salama's being uncontroversially used across Islamic legal schools, while Umm Waraqa's were, as a whole, sidelined or obscured.

Ghazala al-Haruriyya: Political and ritual leadership?

In Chapter 1 we explored the theoretical link between *al-imama al-kubra* (politico-military leadership) and *al-imama al-sughra* (prayer leadership) with practical examples of such a link involving male leaders. In Chapters 2 and 3 we saw from the narratives on Umm Salama and Umm Waraqa, who performed ritual leadership, their association with the participation in battle. In this section we are going to test that link against the activites as reported in historical accounts of a Khariji woman named Ghazala (d. 77 H / 695–6 CE), who actively participated in battles, was referred to as an *imam*, and who very publicly performed prayer in front of men in the mosque of Kufa.

Given that she lived after the lifetime of the Prophet, that she belonged to a religio-political dissenting rebel group, and that her deeds are known through historiographical works alone, the narratives around her carry no weight as far as the formulation of Islamic law is concerned. Despite – and in spite of – the above, the fact that in recent times she has become, not unlike Umm Waraqa, quite a protagonist in current arguments in favour of women imams of mixed congregations warrants her the right to be included in this book on female leadership. Ghazala has witnessed a 21st century revival as either a positive role model of female leadership or a reviled female rebel. As in past historical accounts, today she continues to inspire polarized views, being variously defined as 'a battle commander who led her troops in prayer' or 'an insane female "Khariji"'.[24]

Our knowledge of the Kharijis is shaped by the reports in historical and adversarial sources which portray them as the quintessential 'heretics' of the first centuries of Islamic history. They are additionally reported as holding an 'egalitarian' view of leadership whereby the essential prerequisites for a leader, whom they call *Imam*, are piety and justice, irrespective of the person's status, tribal origin and, possibly, gender. Most of them were also believed to have included *jihad* as of one the pillars of belief and for it to be a religious duty for both men and women. They justified women's involvement in battle as legitimate based on the precedent of women warriors during the time of the Prophet.[25] In fact, modern scholars are very cautious about the use of the term Khariji by pre-modern Muslim writers, to the extent of questioning whether the Khariji theological content was in fact a 'theological construct' aimed at discrediting them.[26]

The Kharijis emerged as a schismatic movement in the course of a conflict between the fourth caliph, 'Ali, and the governor of Syria, Mu'awiya, that took place in 657 at Siffin. The origin of the dispute lay in Mu'awiya's resentment of 'Ali's inability to punish the murderers of the third caliph, hence Muʿawiya's refusal to pledge allegiance to ʿAli. Given their belief that an unjust or sinful leader must be deposed, the Kharijis 'pulled out' by opposing both sides and considering both ʿAli and Muʿawiya to be illegitimate rulers.

Khariji warriors, depicted as fierce fighters and rebels, were heaviliy defeated by the caliph ʿAli, and eventually they retaliated by carrying out his murder in the mosque of Kufa in 661. They continued to oppose the Umayyad caliphs through 'guerrilla warfare' in the eastern parts of the Islamic empire, especially around Basra and Kufa where Umayyad governors eventually faced them in battle. One of these revolts, possibly the last and one of the most dangerous, was led by the Khariji commander Shabib al-Shaybani.

His wife, Ghazala al-Haruriyya is referred to by a number of historical sources which provide slightly contradictory narratives about her. Admired for her horsemanship and courage, Ghazala belongs to those few female warriors who are reported to have directly participated in battle after the advent of Islam. She is associated with praying in the city mosque of Kufa in 695 when her husband entered the city, which was under the governship of the competent but highly unpopular Umayyad commander al-Hajjaj. Ghazala's presence in the mosque and her ascending the pulpit (*minbar*) and praying there are mentioned in a number of sources.

Only a selection of those will be mentioned here, namely the 9th century chronicler Khalifa Ibn Khayyat, the great historian al-Tabari, the 10th century historian al-Masʿudi and the heresiographer al-Baghdadi. The aim of the analysis of the narratives on her is to evaluate the diverse accounts of her presence in the Kufa mosque, what she is reported to have done there as well as the significance and politico-sectarian uses and agendas the narratives on her character served.

Ghazala's context
The events surrounding Ghazala and her husband Shabib ibn Yazid al-Shaybani al-Haruri can be best understood within the political context of the rebellions and discontent directed towards the Umayyads. These stemmed from the Umayyads' presence in Iraq, their general military and fiscal policies and their rule backed by the Syrian tribal army. The role of Syrian troops in the Umayyad army in Iraq led to widespread resentment among Iraqi tribal leaders and soldiers directed against the privileges accorded to the Syrians.

The Umayyad caliph ʿAbd al-Malik had been in power since 685 ruling from the capital Damascus. His governor in Kufa was the experienced commander al-Hajjaj, whose principal aim during the first years of his governorship was to suppress various rebellions in Mosul and Kufa by tribal chiefs who resented the strict governmental control over their territories. Some of these tribal chiefs united forces with Khariji commanders such as Shabib. The extent to which Shabib's rebellion had sectarian or theological contents is unclear; though Shabib is defined as being a Khariji, sources do not provide specific details about his 'Khariji' identity. All they report about him are some relevant Qurʾanic verses he supposedly recited and a few typical 'slogans' attributed to the Kharijis, such as their famous watchword '*la hukma illa li-llah*' ('there is no judgment but God's')[27] which historians commonly used with reference to the Khariji rejection of 'Ali's arbitration with Mu'awiya. In line with Khariji interpretation of political leadership, al-Tabari reports that Shabib's followers held that the best leader is to be chosen on the basis of piety and virtue and not by genealogical descent from the family of the Prophet.[28]

From Mosul, Shabib was able to threaten the Umayyad rule in central and southern Iraq and succeeded in entering Kufa twice, in 76 and 77 of the Islamic calendar, with a much smaller force than that deployed by the Umayyad governor al-Hajjaj, who resided in the city palace on the south end of the main mosque of the city.

After some remarkable victories in the early months of the year 77, Shabib was confronted by additional Syrian troops that al-Hajjaj had requested the caliph to send to Iraq. Thus, under pressure, Shabib moved to Iran, where he was killed while crossing the Dujail river. Other Khariji rebellions against the Umayyads and, later, the 'Abbasids, continued after his death, some perhaps led by Shabib's own son.

The sources about Ghazala

Information about Ghazala's origins is scarce. According to the famous 'Abbasid Iraqi writer al-Jahiz (d. 868–9), she was married to the Khariji commander Salih ibn Musarrih and, when he died, Shabib, who succeeded him, 'inherited' her from him (*khalafaha 'alayhi shabib*) and Shabib married her.[29] Is this a reference to the pre-Islamic custom of inheriting (against their will) the wives of the deceased, a practice expressedly condemned in the Qur'an (Qur. 4.19)? Is al-Jahiz here associating Kharijis with un-Islamic practices? On the other hand, as argued by Carolyne Baugh in her study on Khariji women, al-Jahiz's emphasis when reporting on Ghazala and other Khariji women is on their piety and eloquence, along with their courage and revolutionary zeal.[30]

From 9th century onwards, writers reporting on Shabib's anti-Umayyad rebellion, particularly in Kufa, consistently include details on Ghazala in their narratives. As with Umm Waraqa and others, in time, narratives on Ghazala were progressively enriched with more detail. The Basran chronicler and traditionist Khalifa Ibn Khayyat al-'Usfuri (d. 854–5) in his *History* situates her in the mosque of Kufa within the context of Shabib's entry to the city in 76 H (Hijri) as evidence of his successes against the governor al-Hajjaj and his forces. Al-'Usfuri does not specify Ghazala's relationship with Shabib. He reports that she entered the mosque of Kufa where she recited *wird* – that is a set private supererogatory prayer which concentrates on the recitation of the Qur'an. She also ascended the pulpit, and all this as a fulfilment of a vow she had previously made. Al-'Usfuri includes a quote from a poem where Ghazala's vow is shown as being in itself praiseworthy and her skills in horsemanship acknowledged. In the same poem al-Hajjaj is instead scolded for letting Ghazala overcome him in military action and, afterwards, for letting her 'disappear into thin air'.[31] Therefore, al-'Usfuri's description of her in relation to al-Hajjaj can be seen as using her as a foil to serve the purpose of belittling him as a man that even a woman could defeat! Al-'Usfuri's final reference to Ghazala is a terse mention of her being killed during one of al-Hajjaj's counter-offensive actions in the following year.[32]

Al-'Usfuri's short account of Ghazala contrasts with that of al-Tabari's much more detailed and lengthy narrative of Shabib's military exploits and zeal. Al-Tabari, who uses different sources to present various perspectives on the unfolding of events, starts his narrative with Shabib's entry into Kufa in the year 76 H, accompanied by Ghazala who is introduced as his wife.[33] A year later, Shabib enters the city again with her, but no further details are added.

Drawing from the later historian Abu Zayd 'Umar ibn Shabbah (d. 877), al-Tabari reports that, on entering the city for the second time (hence in 77 H, unlike in al-'Usfuri), Ghazala performed two *rak'a*, or ritual prostrations, in the mosque of Kufa and recited two of the longest Qur'anic *sura*s – the Cow and the Family of 'Imran – to fulfil a vow she had made.[34] In al-Tabari's account, Ghazala did not survive Shabib, but was killed in the latter part of 77 H. Al-Tabari includes two further stories relevant to Ghazala's fate: one is the gory detail of an enemy horseman decapitating her and taking her head to Hajjaj as a trophy.[35] However, her head was recovered by Shabib who, having performed the customary funerary rituals, buried it while extolling Ghazala's virtues in front of his supporters.[36] Al-Tabari provides a sort of narrative closure whereby al-Hajjaj, after Shabib's defeat, enters Kufa, goes to the mosque, ascends its pulpit and ridicules Shabib by informing the congregation how he had fled the camp and left his wife unprotected,[37] a sure sign, for the audience of the time, of cowardice on his part.

In al-Tabari's long and detailed narrative of Shabib's rebellion, Ghazala plays a corollary role to her husband's exploits. Rather than being expressly presented as a leader in her own right, she is depicted as a skilled, determined and defiant fighter, whose actions only reinforce her husband's. The real leaders in al-Tabari's account are Shabib and al-Hajjaj, for whom military command and ritual leadership go hand in hand. In fact, as well as leading prayer for their own troops in existing or make-shift mosques, both commanders are reported to incite their soldiers by means of sermons. The pulpit of the mosque of Kufa is the location from where al-Hajjaj orders the men of Kufa to go and fight Shabib; similarly, in al-Mada'in (a city in Iraq near the ancient Ctesiphon), Shabib leads the noon, afternoon and sunset prayers and, on each occasion, incites his troops to fight and to focus their thoughts on the afterlife.[38]

Given the centrality placed in the narrative of prayer leadership in the Kufa mosque, taken as the occasion for military incitement by rival parties, the location of Ghazala's defiant act of prayer in it acquires special significance. Well-known for being one of the oldest in the Islamic world, the *jami'a* (large congregational, Friday mosque) mosque of Kufa, originally built around 638 and frequently rebuilt thereafter, had assumed its 'definite' form less than three decades before Ghazala's visit to Kufa. Al-Tabari associates the great mosque of Kufa with the presence in 661 of another Khariji woman, Qatam ibna al-Shijna, who was performing a monthly retreat there. She was said to have been involved in the plot that led to 'Ali's assassination at the hands of three Khariji men at the mosque that same year.[39] Together with the governor's palace (*dar al-imara*), the *jami'a* constituted the centre of the city; significantly, the *dar al-imara* was adjoined to the mosque on the south.

Hence, for al-Shabib and Ghazala to be able to enter the mosque was highly symbolic in terms of the extent of their hold on the city and a direct provocation towards the Umayyad governor al-Hajjaj who was residing in the building next door. No wonder Ghazala had made the vow that, were the Kharijis to be successful in entering Kufa again, she would pray in its main mosque and recite the *suras al-Baqara* and *Al al-'Imran* there. This was to be no hurried gesture on her part! It normally takes at least one and a half hours to complete the recitation of these two *suras*. The reference to Ghazala's performance therefore served to affirm, both spatially and temporally, the Khariji success in the city. Like for Umm Waraqa before her, the narrative on Ghazala shows one important trait of authoritativeness associated with the ideal leader: knowledge and memorization of the Qur'an!

Almost a century after al-Tabari, the renowned historian al-Mas'udi (d. 956) provides further details about Ghazala in the city mosque. His emphasis is on the vow that she had made about entering the mosque and performing two *rak'as* as she recited the two *suras*.[40] Al-Mas'udi adds that, as she was in the mosque, 70 men entered to perform the *ghada* prayer. When she completed the Qur'anic recitation, Ghazala left the mosque, thus fulfilling her vow. The passage ends with a statement about her courage and skills in battle. Al-Mas'udi does not mention her ascending the pulpit, nor does he give any further explanation of the 70 men, though one can assume they were part of her guards or warriors and the reference to the *ghada* prayer indicates a voluntary prayer, which would not require the presence of an imam.[41]

Could this mention of the men present in the mosque be a strong enough basis for the claim made by modern scholars and feminist activists that Ghazala led men in prayer?[42] In respect of these unidentified men, some historical sources covering Shabib's rebellion do mention 70 or 75 men as being his core supporters. The number is presumably notional if contrasted to the more numerous soldiers in al-Hallaj's army, which the sources indicate as being in the thousands.

As for Ghazala's vow to pray in the mosque, this was not an uncommon practice among women. The vow itself could be interpreted as a supererogatory act of piety which the chronicler Khalifa ibn Khayyat had reported as being laudable. The reference to this vow and its uses is open to interpretation. It could be seen as an act of piety and devotion to God, specifically a gesture of thanks-giving for having entered Kufa for the second time, an act that Ghazala duly fulfilled, and by which she could have acquired merit. Additionally, Ghazala's conditioned vow and its fulfilment could have been made to incite others, and her prayer performance in the mosque a means to strengthen both her status and her husband's military credentials.[43] In both cases, this was an act of political defiance directed against the city governor.

The last interpretative key tallies with the narrative found in the next source. The Anatolian Shafi'i jurist and heresiographer Abu'l-Husayn Muhammad al-Malati (d. 987), in his entry on the Khariji groups, provides some telling new details and developments about Ghazala in the Kufa mosque. He reports that when Shabib entred Kufa, his (unnamed) wife ascended the pulpit of the city mosque and delivered a sermon in which she cursed al-Hajjaj and his people. She did so to fulfil a vow she had made.[44] In al-Malati's narrative there is no mention of the recitation of the two Qur'anic suras.

One can speculate that for a reader, al-Malati's narrative about Ghazala's action makes her even more daring: the voice of a woman resounding in a mosque from the pulpit, which is traditionally seen as a location linked to religious and political authority, in a city like Kufa renowned for its scholars' critical attitude towards a woman's overstated visibility in the mosque, loudly delivering a sermon from its pulpit. Al-Malati was a heresiographer who, in a passage of the same book, states that Khariji women fight on horses just as their men do.[45] Could al-Malati's reference to the sermon, unparalleled in previous sources and only repeated in a later, also heresiographical, work be therefore a mere polemical device to evidence the Khariji's extreme and heretical ideas and practices? With no mention of any recitation of *suras*, al-Malati's narrative emphasis is mainly political, an instance of Ghazala and her husband's rebellion and opposition to the Umayyads and the governor of Kufa. This political content is developed even further in the next source.

Focusing on Ghazala's presence in the mosque and her skills in battle, the Ash'arite writer on sectarian Islamic groups Abu Mansur Ibn Tahir al-Baghdadi (d. 1037) presents in his work *Al-Farq Bayna al-Firaq* a different take on the mosque episode. Even before introducing Ghazala, al-Baghdadi, in a passage on the Khariji group known as Shabibiyya, states that its eponym Shabib and his supporters were at variance with the previous Khariji commander Salih by allowing the imamate of a woman among them (*ajazu imamat al-mar'a minhum*), a woman who, still unnamed, 'took charge of their affairs and fought (in battle) against their opponents'.[46]

Only after this clarification does al-Baghdadi mention Ghazala, whom he introduces, at variance with other sources, as being Shabib's mother. Al-Baghdadi informs us that, after the death of her son Shabib, a group of Kharijis claimed that Ghazala held the 'imamate'. He adds that the Kharijis provided as evidence for their claimed status for her the fact that when Shabib entered Kufa 'he installed his mother on the pulpit'[47] and that she delivered the sermon. Al-Baghdadi goes on to report that upon entering the city, Shabib was accompanied by a thousand Kharijis, among whom were his mother Ghazala, his wife Jahziya and 'two hundred Khariji women armed with lances and girded with swords'.[48]

Furthermore, al-Baghdadi states that Shabib led his companions in prayer in the mosque and, for the morning prayer, it was he who recited the two *suras* of the Cow and the Family of 'Imran. Eventually, after Shabib was killed, his followers gave allegiance to his mother Ghazala.[49] In stating this, al-Baghdadi not only presents us with an act sealing and further legitimizing Ghazala's leadership (*imama*), but describing it in the way he does, he evokes the way a caliph of his time received a pledge of allegiance (*bay'a*) from the members of his community!

At the end of the narrative, the aims of al-Baghdadi's account of Ghazala become clear, as does the relevance of some details he provides about her. He links the story of the Khariji commander and his mother's 'imamate' to the battle of the Camel and the leadership role of 'A'isha. Al-Baghdadi shows the inconsistency of the Kharijis' opposition to 'A'isha's 'imamate' and their double standards. He claims that they had accused 'A'isha of having become a heretic because she contravened the Qur'anic injunction to the Prophet's wives to remain in their houses. Therefore, he reports that the Kharijis claim of her leadership was not permissible. Nevertheless, al-Baghdadi continues, they allow the 'imamate' of Ghazala and the Khariji women's involvement in fighting in battle. Al-Baghdadi concludes by invoking Allah's protection against heresy.

For al-Baghdadi, the Kharijis are one of the 72 heretical sects within Islam, all of which, he believes, will be damned. One instance of their deviant nature is that they disregard the Prophetic saying that the imamate, meaning here the political leadership of the Muslim community, legitimately pertains to males of Quraysh descent. Thus, the imamate of Shabib al-Shaybani, who was not a Qurayshi, would be deemed, according to Baghdadi and with him most Sunni scholars, as illegitimate. Furthermore, al-Baghdadi states that all Kharijis share their condemnation for 'Ali and the opposing camp, the so called 'followers of the Camel'. Significantly, al-Baghdadi exonerates 'A'isha from any responsibility in the divisive events associated with the Battle of the Camel as, he claims, she 'was aiming to set affairs right between the two parties [but the Banu Dabba and al-Azd overruled her opinion] and fought against 'Ali without her permission'.[50]

Thus, one interpretative key for his passage about the Shabibiyya and his narrative of Ghazala is that it provides al-Baghdadi with further evidence of the heretical beliefs and practices held by one of the Khariji subgroups. The Shabibiyya, for him, accepted the imamate of a woman, meaning that they allowed a woman to hold political and military leadership 'when she took a prominent place in their affairs'.[51] By al-Baghdadi's time female involvement in military and political action was considered illegitimate, being perceived as contrary to the Prophetic *sunna*.[52] In this context, al-Baghdadi's use of *imama* is to be understood to refer to military and community leadership; like all the other sources examined here, al-Baghdadi does not explicitly mention female prayer leadership.

Nevertheless, Shabib's instalment of Ghazala on the pulpit to preach is seen as a proof that the Kharijis themselves use to justify the status and future legitimacy of Ghazala's political and military leadership. The sermon would be addressed, presumably, to the Khariji supporters who entered the mosque with Shabib. In al-Baghdadi's narrative, prayer leadership is reserved for Shabib; he is the one who leads his supporters in prayer in the mosque. Only here are the two types of *imama* embodied in one person: the commander and prayer-leader Shabib. With all the heretical traits and unlawful practices that heresiographers like al-Baghdadi attributed to the Kharijis, nevertheless they do not go so far as to openly accuse them of having a woman leading men in prayer!

Which imama *for Ghazala?*
As already mentioned, al-Mawardi, a contemporary of al-Baghdadi, discussed the link between the two types of leadership, the politico-military and the ritual within the context of the Islamic theory of governance. Such a link is explained by several writers on the basis of the well-known precedent of Abu Bakr, whom the Prophet had chosen to lead prayer when he was ill. In al-Baghdadi's narrative on Ghazala, the Khariji followers of Shabib reportedly make a similar claim when they justify Ghazala's leadership after Shabib's death based on his previous act of installing her on the pulpit.

The narrative of Ghazala's vow and her prayer in the mosque of Kufa was reported by a few subsequent writers, with some variations. Biographer Ibn al-'Imad

(d. 1679) perpetuates the double account of Ghazala's military skills, which surpassed the skills of men: 'she fought in these battles a fight which all the men were incapable of',[53] and the account of her Qur'anic recitation in the Kufa mosque. True to the genre of biographical literature, in Ibn al-'Imad's narrative, Ghazala is the main protagonist, the fighter who goes to battle and enters the mosque with the 70 men and, in it, fulfils her vow. As with previous scholars, al-'Imad makes no reference to Ghazala leading prayer.

Syrian historian 'Umar Rida Kahhalah (d. 1987), in his biographical dictionary on prominent women in the history of Islam, conflates references from several and diverse pre-modern sources to draw a picture of Ghazala as a courageous and skilled fighter, and at the same time a pious and ascetic woman. With other Khariji women, she helps Shabib in the siege of Kufa, heads to the city mosque where Shabib kills the guards and the people inside it, and puts Ghazala on the *minbar* where she gives a sermon. Kahhalah also asserts that upon the death of her husband, his supporters pledged their allegiance to her.[54] This biographical picture, for modern readers, is of a multifaceted female character who is at ease both on the battlefield and in the mosque!

Of note here is that, in line with the Khariji concept of leadership, piety and asceticism are the attributes that are required for a person to be a leader, an Imam. As reported by al-Tabari, Shabib stated that 'the best of people in God's sight are the most pious, and the most deserving of them for the [imamate] is the one who is the most pious and virtuous among them'.[55] Thus, Kharijism can be also viewed as a 'militant ascetic' movement, with an understanding of fighting as a form of piety which might lead to martyrdom. Al-Jahiz's inclusion of Ghazala and other Khariji women in his *Kitab al-Bayan* among the 'pious and ascetic among the people of eloquence' could therefore be explained in light of such an interpretation of Kharijism.

On the basis of the sources outlined above, what kind of leadership is Ghazala attributed to have held? Was it *imama kubra*, politico-military leadership? Ghazala is indeed portrayed as being associated to military activities as a Khariji female fighter, an implicit reference, especially in heresiographical accounts, to the alleged pre-Islamic and un-Islamic practice of fielding women warriors,[56]

To answer the above question, three expressions of her leadership can be highlighted. The first is Ghazala's physical presence in the Kufa mosque as a sign of the Khariji hold on the city, which points to her status as representative of the military commander and, in most accounts, to her active role in embodying, through performance, such leadership. The second is Ghazala being in the pulpit, with the *minbar* representing a seat of power from which the caliph or his representatives typically address the congregation. The third is her uttering the sermon from the pulpit. For al-Malati that sermon serves as a political tool to assert Khariji authority and leadership, of which she acts as spokesperson, while cursing the Umayyad opponents. Al-Baghdadi is the most explicit writer in reporting that a group of Kharijis recognized her as being their Imam after al-Shabib's death, and that they provide as evidence of the legitimacy of her role as leader al-Shabib's act of installing her on the pulpit from which she delivered a sermon.

As for prayer leadership (*imama sughra*), all the above narratives on Ghazala, including those referring to her as the political leader of her community, attribute it exclusively to men. The only ritual element connected with Ghazala is her vow to pray in a mosque and her Qur'anic recitation there. Both acts of piety are attested in connection to women in classical sources.

A link between the two types of *imama* can be identified in the narratives, but only with reference to male leaders. As seen in both al-Tabari and al-Baghdadi, al-Hajjaj and Shabib are shown as being at the same time military commanders and prayer leaders for their troops, to whom they also deliver sermons to incite and prepare them for battle. As for Ghazala, only in Baghdadi's account is there an explicit connection which is reported to have been made between her politico-military *imama* and her being in the Kufa mosque and delivering a sermon. However, as already mentioned, al-Baghdadi explains this link to have been made by her Khariji supporters in order to legitimize her role as their political leader.

Therefore, contrary to some modern claims, Ghazala's *imama* is to be understood as political leadership. The basis of such claims could be a misunderstanding of the type of 'leadership' attributed to her and, in other instances, to a few other Khariji women.[57] Additionally, there could be a few elements which, if put together haphazardly by a rushed or a partial reader who conflates sources, might have led to such allegations: Ghazala's presence in the mosque, her Qur'anic recitation in the presence of men – who are likely to be her Khariji co-fighters – her sermon, and the use that her own husband made of sermons to his troops. These confused conflations in modern narratives, to the discerning, reveal more about the writers' agendas than they do about the sources on Ghazala and even less about the portrayal of Ghazala herself.

Women and war, women at war

We have observed that in the narratives about 'A'isha, Umm Waraqa, Umm Salama and Ghazala, whether on the basis of *hadith*s, biographical works or historical sources, there is a noticeable process of literary adjustment and editing. As noted, while the *hadith*s have a legal weight, historical accounts do not. What all these portrayals have in common is a paradigmatic association between being female, military participation and ritual action.

Despite all the difference between Umm Waraqa and Ghazala, one a positive role model and a high-status female Companion of the Prophet, the other a rebel who ostensibly contravened not only political but also female modesty roles, there are also telling similarities; for example, both met a violent end, being murdered by house servants or in a military context. But while Umm Waraqa is considered a martyr, Ghazala, though she was killed as part of military conflict, is but a sectarian rebel, undeserving of such an honour, except among her own community. The narrators' perspectives make one a heroine and the other a rebel.

Significantly, both Umm Waraqa and Ghazala, as well as 'A'isha and possibly others yet to be discovered who have been linked to performance of ritual prayer and leadership, are indirectly or directly associated with fighting and wars. These were activities that, by the time of the collectors or writers reporting on them, were considered to be male domains. Umm Waraqa's zeal and loyalty to the Prophet made her request the Prophet's permission to let her accompany him to the battlefield to gain martyrdom, while Ghazala was, like other Khariji women, an experienced and courageous fighter in battle who was carrying out what Kharijis believed to be a religious obligation for both men and women.

Instances are not lacking of women in pre-Islamic or early Islamic eras who are reported as having been directly involved in wars and fighting, women who 'went forth in battle'.[58] Some women did go beyond the more commonly accepted supporting roles such as nursing the wounded, or functional roles such as ralliers of disheartened soldiers. From well-known individuals like the Ansari companion Nusayba bint Ka'b, also referred to as Umm 'Umara, or the Prophet's aunt Safiyya bint 'Abd al-Muttalib, to less-known female companions Umm Hakim, Asma bint Yazid or Umm Harith, these women seem to continue a female involvement in war which Muslim sources were to associate with the Jahiliyya period.[59]

Yet, emerging from the Prophetic *sunna* and historical sources, there is ambivalence in opinions and attitudes about the acceptability of women's direct role in war or fighting. On the one hand, on the basis of some *hadith*s, the Prophet does not encourage or, as in the case of Umm Waraqa, does not explicitly permit a woman to follow him in battle. On the authority of one *hadith* from 'A'isha, who was asking him about *jihad*, the Prophet replied 'your (fem. pl.) *jihad* is the *hajj*'.[60] On the other hand, according to *hadith*s, Umm Salama is reported to have been present at seven battles, and the Prophet expresses admiration for Umm 'Umara's fighting to secure, by the sword, his own safety.[61]

After the Prophet's demise, historiographers such as al-Tabari mention that at the battle of Yarmuk (636), which signalled the end of Byzantine rule over Syria, women from the Quraysh fought with swords and were 'competing with men'.[62] Among them was Umm Hakim bint al-Harith, who had been the caliph 'Umar's wife and who had participated in other battles. Another notable woman mentioned by al-Tabari is Abu Sufyan's daughter Juwayriyya who fought at Yarmuk together with her husband and who was wounded.[63] But it is the likes of renowned heroines such as the by-now mature Hind bint 'Utba, who was Abu Sufyan's wife, or Khawla bint al-Azwar, the sister of the commander Zarrar, who were to inspire writers and trigger audiences' imaginations. The presence and courage of Muslim fighting women, especially at Yarmuk, did not escape the attention of Byzantine chroniclers.[64] Military historian David Nicolle in his study of the battle of Yarmuk goes so far as to state that the role of Muslim women is not to be underestimated among the various factors which contributed to the Muslim victory, particularly the morale impact on the Byzantines, who would have been 'deeply shocked'[65] by the Arab women's reputation, and acts, of 'ferocity' in battle.

In Islamic sources, to recount the participation of individuals in battle was proof of commitment to the Prophet, an expression of religious zeal in the hope of martyrdom or of status in the community. In their own way, both Umm Waraqa and Ghazala, on the basis of some narratives, can be credited with religious zeal and martyrdom. But to take part or fight in battle had its material rewards too. One was booty sharing, though with regards to women this seems to have been a contested practice. Moreover, the caliph 'Umar is credited with having instituted, possibly around 636, a *diwan* or register of pensions in which, after the Prophet's wives, precedence was given to Migrants and Supporters who had fought at Badr.[66]

As for narratives on Ghazala's participation in battle, they can be seen to serve specific literary, sectarian and polemical purposes as they fit well with the broader accounts on the Kharijis and their women, but can also reflect a pietist and gender-egalitarian understanding of leadership.[67] The sources on Ghazala are indeed vague and contradictory and, for a general reader with a purpose, Ghazala as a character can be made to serve diverse roles and agendas, depending on the choice of emphasis and selection. She can be a positive determined heroine in her own right, a representative of women's agency for 21st century feminists, or, for traditionists, she can be a gender-role-subversive heretic. The tapestry that modern activists (with a limited sense of historical contextualization) can weave around her is as rich and colourful as they want it to be. To the historians, narratives on her tell more about the writers themselves than they do about Ghazala.

Legal arguments on women leading men in prayer

Legal arguments against women leading men in prayer

A number of pre-modern Muslim jurists present the link between greater *imama* and smaller *imama* as one of the reasons for the interdiction of a woman leading men in prayer. The 12th century Sicilian or Tunisian authoritative Maliki scholar Abu 'Abdallah Al-Maziri, for example, expressedly refers to the analogy between the two types of leadership (*imama*), for both of which a woman is unqualified on account of female deficiencies in intellect and religion. Such deficiencies give a woman a more disadvantageous status than that of, for instance, a male slave, as they are qualities peculiar to – and *essential of* – women, unlike slavery which is understood as an accidental state.[68] For the 13th century Maliki jurist Abu al-Hasan al-Rajraji, prayer leadership, like political leadership, is a 'degree of honour' which can only be exercised by 'someone who is complete in religion and in essence'.[69] Al-Rajraji claims that there is consensus against women holding political leadership and that the majority of jurists prohibit them from being prayer leaders for men because leadership is a position of high status, in which low and deficient individuals (like women) have no share. Al-Rajraji makes this the principal reason for women not being permitted to lead men in prayer, and evidences it through *hadiths* such as the one by Abu Bakra warning that no people who are led by a woman can ever know prosperity.

Several jurists across legal schools and traditions within Islam, whether Sunni, Shi'i, or Zaydi,[70] make use of the same reasoning behind prohibiting ritual female leadership over men on the basis of the claimed lack of legitimacy for women to be in any position of authority. They quote Qur'anic passages and *hadiths* as supposed evidence of a more encompassing principle: that women cannot be leaders of men.

For instance, Qur'an 4.34 is usually cited (*al-rijal qawwamuna 'ala al-nisa'* ...) to prove that men are in charge of, or are managers, supporters of women.[71] More frequently than the Qur'an, scholars quote weak *hadith*s such as the already mentioned narrative by Abu Bakra, or that by Ibn Maja, '... and never ever may a woman lead a man in prayer'.[72] On the evidence of these examples, they argue that women cannot lead men in prayer as, unlike men, they are not endowed with *walaya* (sovereignty, rule) in any sphere, be it political, judicial or ritual.[73]

Though specifically aimed at the case of women leading men, this argument is not dissimilar from that of the scholars who, as seen in the previous chapter, stated that male leadership in prayer has a 'higher value' for the male imam and his congregation than female leadership. This was on the premise that men have better knowledge of prayer ritual and can lead under any circumstances.

If in Chapter 2 we provided a diachronic approach to the arguments against female prayer leadership of women, here the approach will be synchronic to include a short overview of additional justifications for disallowing female leadership of men.

For the overwhelming majority of Muslim jurists and theologians, lack of historical precedence of female imams, during the formative and normative early centuries of Islam, would render cases of female imams of men an innovation (*bid'a*), which consequently should neither be introduced nor accepted.

Secondly, community ritual and social customs are cited whereby, as women pray behind men in the mosque, they cannot possibly lead them. These customs are presented as being sanctioned by selected *hadith*s, the most commonly used being on the authority of Abu Hurayra: 'The Prophet said: the best row for men is the first, and the worst the last, the best row for women is the last and the worst the first'.[74]

Thirdly, given the large (yet not universal!) majority opinion of Muslim jurists on this matter, legal consensus (*ijma'*)[75] is also cited to reject the *imama* of a woman for a mixed congregation.

Fourthly, scholars also argue that women cannot lead men in prayer because of the issues of female modesty and 'shamefulness'. Indeed, for some, exposure of *'awra* can invalidate the prayer of the congregation.

Finally, concepts of female ritual impurity and of female seductiveness are cited to support arguments against female prayer leadership as a whole, including that of men.

Does a woman's impure state due to menstruation or puerperium render the prayer of a man praying behind her invalid? Most jurists would reply positively, but this is not what emerges from a *hadith* on the authority of 'A'isha evidencing that the presence of a menstruating woman does not invalidate prayer.[76] As for seduction, scholars indicate that the visible presence of a woman in prayer, be it on the same row or in front, may cause almost unavoidable lustful thoughts in the man's mind.[77]

Arguments against the permissibility of women leading men may be composite, relying on various sources and applying diverse approaches. This is the case with the Isma'ili jurist al-Qadi al-Nu'man, who bases his opinion against women leading mixed congregations in prayer on legal consensus as well as on esoteric theological considerations. Unlike those scholars, especially Malikis, who see this interdiction as a result of ontology in terms of a woman's 'innate' deficiencies in religion and intellect, al-Qadi al-Nu'man relates it instead to a woman's legal capacity.[78] He establishes a link between the type of female ritual leadership a woman can exercise and her full legal capacity, the one being, according to him, the consequence of the other. So he argues, as already discussed in Chapter 2, that a woman can indeed lead other women in prayer, on the condition that she positions herself in their midst. This is because she is not in a position of priority or excellence towards them, as an imam is expected to be, because a woman acting as an imam, like the women she leads, lacks full legal capacity to act. An example in al-Nu'man's jurisprudence of this legal limitation is that she cannot contract a marriage without a male guardian, irrespective of her age.

In his book *Ta'wil al-Da'a'im*, which aims to disclose to Isma'ili initiates the inner meaning of the legal rulings included in his legal work, al-Nu'man provides an esoteric reading of his legal assertions. The passage on women leading prayer is to be understood symbolically: prayer is symbolic of the Isma'ili mission and the language of gender is used to refer to states of spiritual knowledge in the Isma'ili hierarchy. Therefore, the feminine refers to a recipient of knowledge, while the masculine to a giver of knowledge; accordingly, as a disciple cannot summon the master, a woman cannot lead men.[79] Al-Qadi al-Nu'man's statements on female prayer leadership can thus be read through three interpretative lenses: ritual, legal and esoteric. The ritual and legal perspectives justify the illegitimacy of a woman leading, from the front, other women on account of her lack of legal capacity to act. However, (ostensibly) beyond the social and exoteric realm of legal discourse, in esoteric language a woman as imam of men is symbolic of the state of knowledge proper to a pupil and of the religious hierarchical status of an ordinary initiate, who cannot lead her master or her religious guide.

There are nuances in scholarly opinions about the legitimacy of a woman leading men in voluntary or supererogatory prayers. For instance, it is reported that Ahmad ibn Hanbal considered it permissible for a woman to lead men in *tarawih* prayers provided she stands not in front, but behind them. This opinion was shared by early Hanbalis and was to be accepted by Ibn Taymiyya (d. 1328) who considered it permissible for a woman to lead men in *tarawih* prayers out of necessity, if none of the men was knowledgeable of the Qur'an.[80] More scholars held this opinion, with some specifying that Ibn Hanbal would only permit a woman to lead a man in recitation, not in other aspects of the prayer. However, they added, she could lead in recitation of *tarawih* only if the men are illiterate, in which case they would stand behind her.[81]

As for funeral prayers, it is the opinion of some Hanafi jurisprudents that the prayer of a man is not invalidated by a woman coming in line with him, since funeral prayers are not seen as proper 'communications with God', but as a collective obligation to fulfil the right of the deceased.[82] Despite legal injunctions against women's attendance at funerals and of them leading prayer, there are a few rare references to the actual practice of female leadership, such as to Nafisa Bint al-Hasan who led Imam Shafi'i's funeral prayers.[83]

Legal arguments 'not against' women leading men in prayer

In the case of pre-modern scholars discussing the instance of a Muslim woman leading a mixed gender congregation, it is necessary to rephrase the issue at stake. Rather than dealing with arguments *in favour* of the *imama* of a woman leading men, it will be more appropriate to define their arguments as being *not against her imama*. I will focus on the evidence and the arguments provided in the legal and broader context of the 9th century, mention two noteworthy subsequent scholarly arguments and analyse any possible links between legal theory and ritual practices.[84] As already mentioned, Ibn Rushd stated that while the majority of jurists argued that a woman cannot lead men, there were some exceptions to this rule. He then cites Abu Thawr al-Baghdadi (d. 854) and Muhammad Ibn Jarir al-Tabari (d. 923), who 'deviated [from the majority]'[85] and permitted the *imama* of a woman unrestrictedly (*'ala al-itlaq*), in absolute terms – that is, irrespective of the type of congregation.

Ibn Rushd points out that those who do not allow a woman to lead men justify their argument first on lack of precedent and second on the ritual practice, based on evidence from the *hadith*s, that women pray behind men. On the other hand, those who allow a woman to lead in prayer use as evidence the Umm Waraqa *hadith*, as reported in Abu Dawud, and which Ibn Rushd quotes in its original wording.

Other scholars also cite Abu Thawr and al-Tabari as not objecting to a woman leading men in prayer. The Hanbali jurist Ibn Qudama al-Maqdisi in his legal treatise records that Abu Thawr argued that 'he who prayed behind her does not need to repeat the prayer,'[86] implying that his prayer is valid. In turn, Ibn Qudama introduces another scholar who held the same opinion, the well-known Shafi'i jurist Abu Ibrahim al-Muzani (d. 878). In addition to Abu Thawr, al-Tabari and al-Muzani, more scholars can be identified as not being 'against' the *imama* of a woman of a mixed congregation. Among them, Dawud al-Isfahani al-Zahiri (d. 884) and Muhyi'l-Din Ibn al-'Arabi (d. 1240).

Focusing on Abu Thawr, al-Muzani and al-Zahiri, their reported voices, which had been thus far obscured, are now brought back to light as contributors to the debate on ritual female leadership of men. All three share a chronological context and a legal approach and training. I argue that, being all linked, directly or indirectly, to the scholar or legal 'school' of al-Shafi'i, they primarily based their legal opinions on the *sunna* and specifically on the Prophetic *hadith*s and those of the Prophet's early Companions. Among the scholarly opinions of the time upholding the concept of the pre-eminence of the Companions of the Prophet, to cite the *hadith*s on Umm Waraqa would constitute a normative example of just such a pre-eminence.

All three scholars are considered representatives of a wave of legal opinion that was developing during the 9th century, which was subsequently put under the umbrella term of *ahl al-hadith*. They lived during a formative period of debate between those who, like them, relied mainly on the first two sources of law: the Qur'an and the *sunna* / *hadith* and those, referred to as the *ahl al-ra'y*, who saw wider scope in the use of *ra'y* as well as *qiyas*, that is analogy, which after the Qur'an and the *hadith*s is another recognized authoritative tool for law making in Islam.

Al-Zahiri, in particular, is reported as being a strong supporter of the literal meaning of the Qur'an and the *sunna*, not unlike the traditionist Ibn Hanbal who is said to have rejected *ra'y* and *qiyas*. Whether these were in fact separate groups or, more likely, overlapping ones is still a matter of academic debate.[87]

These three scholars were voicing further legal debates which occupied 9th century *fiqh* specialists. One of them was to do with the principles pertaining to the validity of prayer, in its diverse legal formulations, for instance by the Shafi'is and the Hanafis. Is prayer valid on account of the person who performs it for him/her self, irrespective of whoever leads it as held by the Shafi'i school? Or is it on the basis of the imam's recognized status and the validity of the imam's own prayer? Such contrasting views reflect interpretations of prayer not only in terms of a ritual carried out by an individual but of the impact an individual's ritual has on the ritual of the congregation as a whole. Specifically in our case, the gendered body of the ritual practitioner in a communal setting may be seen as acquiring a social connotation and becoming a social body, which reflects social conventions of gender hierarchy.[88]

Little is known about the first of these three scholars, Abu Thawr, except that he was a respected traditionist and legal expert who met al-Shafi'i' and followed his school. Some writers claim Abu Thawr founded his own legal school, which was reported to be still active at the end of the 10th century, but which later became extinct. They add that he was opposed to the use of *ra'y* in forming legal opinions, while, for others, he supported some positions of the *ahl al-ra'y*. His precise juristic positioning remains thus far a matter of uncertainty. As for female leadership in ritual, it is reported by writers that he approached it from slightly different perspectives, without them clarifying what those perspectives are. It is thus unclear whether his argument about not objecting to a woman leading men in prayer was rooted in the framework of discussions on the validity of a man's prayer, when he is led by a woman, or the permissibility for men and women to follow a woman as imam.[89]

Unlike Abu Thawr, whose works are no longer extant, but are known to us through citations in books by the likes of Al-Mawardi and other jurists, for the second scholar, the Egyptian al-Muzani, his treatises, though incomplete, are still available. In his *Mukhtasar* his discussion on the prayer leadership of a woman is framed within the context of the validity of the prayer led by 'unconventional' imams such as a woman, an effeminate male, or a few others. As for the prayer led by a woman as imam, at variance with his master al-Shafi'i, who stated that such a prayer is not valid and needs to be repeated, al-Muzani justifies its validity by stating that 'each person prays for himself, [hence] his prayer is not invalidated by other than himself'.[90] Al-Muzani's argument echoes debates about ritual impurity and whether or not any woman is intrinsically impure, thus transmitting her impurity to others. Rather than explicitly advocating the permissibility of a woman leading men in prayer, it therefore transpires from this short passage that al-Muzani, by considering as valid the prayer of the man led by her, and implicitly her own prayer, does not reject the legitimacy of a woman leading a man.

The third scholar, Abu Sulayman Dawud al-Zahiri, is considered to have been an important jurist who founded a distinct theologico-legal 'school', the Zahiriyya, which, though influential in legal thought especially under the Almohads of Morocco and al-Andalus (12–13th century), had nevertheless by the 14th century become extinct. Prominent figures associated with the Zahiriyya are al-Shaybani, al-Tabari and the Andalusian Ibn Hazm. Al-Zahiri was a prolific writer; however, of his numerous books, none has survived except in the form of quotations cited by later writers. Like for Abu Thawr, his argumentative framework, not against the permissibility of a woman leading a man in prayer, is hard to pinpoint. The Zahiriyya (i.e. the literalist group) was characterized by a restrictive interpretation of the *usul al-fiqh*. They relied on the literal meaning of the Qur'an and of the *hadith*s, including the single-strand *hadith*s. They rejected the use of *ra'y* and *qiyas*, but applied the legal tool of consensus (*ijma'*) by limiting it to the first generation of Muslims. Only textual evidence was deemed acceptable for them to support any legal arguments. The school that followed al-Zahiri's principles is said to have leaned towards Mu'tazili theological positions, which could account for its eventual demise.[91]

Like most of the aforementioned scholars who did not reject female *imama*, the well-known polymath Abu Ja'far ibn Jarir al-Tabari was also affiliated with the Shafi'i school, though he has been reported as being the 'founder' of the Jaririyya school. This school eventually ceased to exist possibly as it became subsumed under the Shafi'i *madhhab*. He is reported to have studied with the son of al-Zahiri with whom he exchanged legal debates. Beside Ibn Rushd, numerous scholars claimed that al-Tabari permitted female ritual leadership of men, as well as approving that women could act as judges in an unlimited capacity.[92]

But unlike well-known scholars such as al-Tabari, we only know about the opinions of Abu Thawr and al-Zahiri because they were cited by other scholars, who usually held views opposed to theirs. Through citing them as dissenting voices, however, the very reporting of their opinions gave them a continued visibility and secured them a place in legal thought and collective legal memory. Their indirect voices continue to be reported to this day, in some instances to show legal acumen and reaffirm the soundness of traditional consensus, in others, as will be seen in Chapter 4, to provide legal-historical evidence and form the basis of modern arguments in favour of women leading men and women in prayer.

Their positions 'not against' a woman leading men in prayer can be attributed to the application of a specific legal methodology emphasizing literal interpretation of scripture. However, an equally valid assessment of their stance is that they were providing answers to questions emerging from very practical scenarios. When or if circumstances arise whereby a woman (or a blind or intersex person etc.) does lead prayer, perhaps being the most qualified person to do so in a group or community, what takes precedence – the fulfilment of prayer as a religious obligation or the characteristics of its 'ideal' leader? As we saw in Chapter 2, it was al-Shafi'i who had explicitly affirmed that the compulsory nature of prayer overrides particular modalities, even 'shortcomings' of its leadership; this could account for the association of all the above-mentioned scholars with the Shafi'i legal school. Thus, beyond their seemingly positive position towards female prayer leadership, the primary concern of these jurists was not to enhance the status of women or even to pass a comment on that status *per se*. As jurists, their primary concern was to offer solutions to any circumstances that might jeopardize the obligatory performance of prayer.

In his article on classical Islamic legal positions concerning female mosque attendance, Christopher Melchert identified a 'spectrum of permissiveness' whereby Shafi'i and Hanbali legal scholars are shown to represent less restrictive approaches towards female mosque attendance than those found in the other *madhhabs*. Similarly, as far as female leadership of men in prayer is concerned, on the basis of the sources here examined, we found that most of the scholars who were not against such a leadership either belonged to or were associated with the Shafi'i *madhhab*, or – as in the case of the permissibility of women leading men in *tarawih* prayers – they belonged to the Hanbali legal school. Melchert suggests that the position of these two schools could be traced back to their minoritarian status, which led them to be 'less concerned to maintain hierarchy within',[93] thus allowing for a wider range of alternative or minority opinions.

Ibn al-'Arabi and *female* imama

Another dissenting voice of the majority opinion against the permissibility of female *imama* of mixed congregation comes from the Western margins of the Islamic empire: the Andalusian philosopher and mystic Muhyi'l-din Ibn al-'Arabi (d. 1240). His approach and argumentation in favour of women leading men are quite distinct from those of the majority of jurists analysed thus far. He justifies his support for women acting as imams by linking, in gender neutral terms, spiritual attainment and ritual leadership. However, when translated in specific examples of imams as prayer leaders, this spiritually egalitarian approach is found to retain some social hierarchical constructs.

In his voluminous work *al-Futuhat al-Makkiyya* (*The Meccan Revelations*), which represents the *summa* of his Sufi thought, Ibn al-'Arabi states that women share with men all spiritual levels, including that of *Qutb* ('Pole') which in his mystical philosophy represents the supreme spiritual leader of the age. Ibn al-'Arabi argues that, unlike political leadership, which is bestowed by humans, spiritual leadership is granted by God to whomever God wills, whether a man or a woman.[94] On several occasions in his *Futuhat*, he reiterates that the level of spiritual perfection (*kamal*) is not limited to men, as evidenced by Qur'anic verses about the Pharaoh's wife and about Mary the mother of Jesus, both of whom for Ibn al-'Arabi did achieve the status of perfection.[95]

Ibn al-'Arabi opens the section of his *Futuhat* on female leadership of prayer thus: 'Some people allow the imamate of a woman absolutely (*'ala al-itlaq*) before [a congregation of] men and women. I support this view'.[96] He continues by objecting to those who are against female *imama*, stating that there is no real proof, nor text, supporting such a prohibition. With this lack of evidence to the contrary, Ibn al-'Arabi asserts that the basic principle is that of permissibility of female *imama* (*wa'l-asl ijazat imamatiha*).

Ibn al-'Arabi goes on to evidence his argument from an esoteric perspective by linking female *imama* to female achievement of spiritual perfection. He states that the Prophet himself has testified that some women attained this state of perfection, as did some men. Such perfection is embodied in prophethood (*nubuwwa*), which, for him, is [a form of] leadership (*wa'l-nubuwwa imama*).[97]

In a work attributed to Ibn al-'Arabi, the *Tafsir al-Shaykh al-Akbar*, while commenting upon the Qur'anic verse on Mary, the mother of Jesus, we are given an example of a female figure attaining both spiritual perfection and prophethood (*nubuwwa*). Ibn al-'Arabi here presents Mary as the archetypical mystic, whom God elevates above all potentialities and powers of the 'carnal soul'.[98]

Back to his *Futuhat*, in accordance with his mystical cosmology and philosophy, Ibn al-'Arabi establishes a parallel between the (non-gendered) human being (*insan*) and the universe as a microcosm reflecting and embodying the macrocosm. Ritual leadership of a congregation is the outward, exoteric form of the inward, esoteric leadership of the three main leading 'agents' of Intellect, Soul and Desire (*hawa*). Leadership of the Soul, in its position of precedence over Desire, is necessary to keep Desire in check. Thus the *imama* of the Soul is legitimate. Ibn al-'Arabi then draws a parallelism between the *imama* of the Soul and the *imama* of a woman, hence showing the spiritual and metaphysical basis for its legitimacy, and the *imama* of the Intellect with the station/level of the *imama* of a man.

It is at this point in his argument that Ibn al-'Arabi draws a parallel between the cosmic hierarchy of Intellect, Soul and Desire and the human hierarchy of prayer leaders (*imams*), hence revealing the underlying gender, social and legal structure of his own time. Of the three types of *imama*, reflecting the three cosmic 'agents', Ibn al-'Arabi compares the male imam to the state of Intellect. He qualifies the male imam as being Muslim, legally mature, knowledgeable and of legitimate birth. He also qualifies the lowest type of *imama*, that equivalent to the macrocosmic leadership of Desire, which in human terms, he describes as the leadership of the hypocrite, the infidel and the sinful.[99] However, the female imam remains unqualified, except with the implicit reference to the spiritual achievement required for being an imam and its necessity to control the leadership of Desire.

With its premise of an underlying moral and spiritual equality between men and women, Ibn al-'Arabi's argument is indeed remarkable for his time. Some scholars go so far as to see it as an instance of the 'counter narratives of gender that destabilize patriarchal norms'.[100] However, it should also be more accurately understood within the context of 12th–13th century Andalusia, the elaboration on the 'Feminine' in Islamic mysticism and the Sufi understanding of the capacity for moral and spiritual achievements of pious women and men. A personal testimony of this is Ibn al-'Arabi's own biography and his acknowledgement of the influence on his spiritual education and development of two female *shaykhas*: Fatima bint al-Muthanna and Shams Umm al-Fuqara'.[101] Upon closer scrutiny, some of Ibn al-'Arabi's theoretical assertions and practical examples still reflect a hierarchical framework that upholds the gender social hierarchies of his time. Even the purest and highest of women like Mary, while she can attain *kamal* and *nubuwwa*, nevertheless cannot achieve *akmaliyya* (superlative perfection) nor *risala* (messengership), both of which can only be attained by men.[102] As for the female imam, though her leadership in prayer is theoretically legitimate, in practice it is the male imam who is the benchmark for ritual leadership and against whom characteristics and qualities are normatively measured.

Conclusion

At the start of this chapter we saw two cases of women who, on the basis of different sources, are reported to either have led men in prayer or performed ritual from the pulpit in their presence in a mosque.

As the final chapter of this book will detail, these two cases have been brought to the fore in modern debates as legitimizing precedents in connection to 21st century instances of women imams of mixed congregations. Some modern scholars and activists, who have, to some extent, 'appropriated' these two female figures (along with *hadith*s on the Prophet's wives leading women in prayer), cite them as evidence of gender equality during the first years of Islam. Specifically, they hold that the Umm Waraqa *hadith*s might have reflected an early Medinan practice of ritual female leadership and that the gradual modifications to its text could be seen as attempts on the part of the *hadith* compilers and legal scholars to deal with the changed social attitudes towards female leadership of prayer. From one legal perspective, the *hadith* of Umm Waraqa could instead be seen as a precedent, which later developed into a set of legal rules, the specific contents of which rely on the most suitable version of the narrative text which would suppport them.

Alternatively, if it is argued that the starting point for the jurist is not the text but the rule, the Umm Waraqa *hadith* and its 'modifications' in their wording represent efforts to reconcile the text with the rule. Whether such a precedent did historically occur in the way in which it is described in its various versions is not relevant to this discussion; its importance lies in the particular understanding of the development of Islamic law from individual cases to relevant norms, an interpretation that still divides modern scholars.[103] In other words, the purpose of the legal discussions presented above, including those 'not against' female mixed leadership, would be to illustrate legal casuistry rather than advocating social change.

To my knowledge there are no further reported cases in pre-modern Islamic history of female *salat* leadership of a mixed congregation. There are indeed a few pre-modern textual references to females performing rituals to a mixed congregation in mosques or in public places. One is the already mentioned Nafisa Bint al-Hasan leading Imam Shafi'i's funeral prayer. Others are female preachers in mosques, usually for a female audience such as the 14th century Fatima bint 'Abbas 'Umm Zaynab al-Baghdadiyya', a contemporary of Ibn Taymiyya, who is reported to have preached to women from the *minbar*, allegedly with her face uncovered.[104]

In view of such paucity of evidence, is there any alternative to inferring that these references and discussions were purely theoretical cases of legal or theological thought detached from actual ritual practices? One avenue for further analysis is to question assumptions on, approaches to, and selection and types of source used. Pre-modern legal sources reported opinions, arguments and counter-arguments to inform the reader and display competence in legal reasoning and in selecting relevant *hadith* as evidence for those opinions. They also revealed differences in opinions, variations in terms of local customs but also of the subject treated. So for instance, Katz' study on female access to mosques reveals that in legal rulings women did not constitute a legal monolithic category but were distinguished according to age, status, attractiveness, religious learning and personal propriety. Katz' findings also question the extent to which practice during the Prophet's time was consistently deemed normative for all ages. So, for instance, even though women did attend 'mosque' or congregational prayer during the Prophet's lifetime, some jurists considered that times had since changed and, with them, standards of behaviour, which warranted changes such as restricting attractive women from attending mosques.

Though there is some scope in attempting to 'reconstruct' practice, this is hard to achieve and marred with difficulties. The actual reason for specific rulings might not lie in practice at all but, as mentioned above, in perpetuating the law through time and reconciling the law with textual evidence. Some changes in attitude can indeed be detected from the varied emphases on scholarly use of concepts such as that of *fitna* as a basis for some Hanafis prohibiting women from attending prayers in the mosque. However, references to an increased danger of social unrest can be no more than a well-tested rhetorical device.[105]

For a possible reinscribing of social practice, a diverse range of sources would need to be consulted; in the case of historiographical narratives on Ghazala they report and provide evidence of a woman being in a mosque as a result of a vow she had made, a practice carried out by women and men, that is actually mentioned in both historical and legal sources. As for Ghazala, the fulfilment of this practice through Qur'anic recitation and her presence in the mosque are set within a military context, whereby her presence and her prayer are part of a performative act, asserting the authority of the Kharijis who had succeded in entering the city and its mosque. The additional information that some scholars report of her being in the pulpit, though unusual, also tallies with a few cases of historical references to women preaching or teaching from the pulpit. However, when al-Baghdadi includes the detail of her delivering a sermon from the pulpit, the broader argument the writer develops and the highly polemical nature of the source reveals a specific agenda which means the story, while not fully implausible, is divorced from historical reliability.

As for women's participation in communal prayers, studies based on documentary and material sources do yield some results. For instance, on the basis of independent sources such as a collection of *fatwas* and also a traveller's account from 12th century Syria, evidence can be gathered of Nablus' women attending *jum'a* prayer. Acts of endowment can occasionaly reveal the types of rituals carried out in certain premises. One instance is the *khanaqa* that was established for women (*faqirat*, i.e. poor or Sufi women) in Aleppo by Fatima Khatun, the daughter of the Ayyubid sultan Malik al-Kamil (d. 1238), a place where it is reported that the five daily prayers were conducted.[106]

However, with regards to female leadership of congregational prayer, such a reconstruction is thus far made unworkable by the paucity of references in sources and the extent of the historicity of some of them. Scarcity might point to lack of practice, but also to the likelihood that, if women did lead congregational prayers, it might have occurred in smaller and more private locations, like village and neighbourhood mosques, a shrine or a *khanaqa* or, more likely given the legal and social elaborations on female *'awra* and its link to *fitna*, in private homes – locations which are not the main focus of attention for historians or legal theorists.[107] The reference to Umm Waraqa's leadership in her *dar*, whether this meant leading prayer in her home, in her locality or leading her tribe, does put her role in a context where she is able to exercise her authority while keeping her modesty among a familiar group.

We might therefore question whether places other than mosques would be more apt to look for evidence of female ritual leadership. With a much more substantial and diverse range of sources for the modern era, in Chapter 4 we will be able to point to women leading prayer in a variety of spaces beside the mosque.

This chapter has provided examples of various positions regarding female prayer leadership of a mixed congregation. It has applied Talal Asad's 'discursive tradition' as an interpretative relationship with sources, which underpins the reshaping of past models to guide the present, and plan or configure the future. The scholars examined did engage with the past 'creatively' and selectively to reflect or establish the current understandings and social attitudes of their own time. However, they also reported on minority positions, some of them from extinct legal schools, but by doing so, they secured the visibility of and continued ability to witness a much wider range of arguments.

We found that even when these scholarly efforts had the purpose of discrediting minority views as irrelevant and no longer applicable, they nevertheless still preserved a wealth of debates and positions from throughout the long and varied life of Islamic thought. The cases of female prayer leadership they report, whether historically accurate representations, narrative characterizations to confirm stereotypes on heretic groups, or literary foils to pass judgment on opposing characters, nevertheless, similar to Pirandello's *Six Characters in Search of an Author*, they continue with a life of their own. For those modern Muslim women engaged in asserting their understanding of gender as an aspect of a wider principle of social justice, reputable female Companions become heroins and rebel Khariji women, after centuries of theological vilification, can become models of activism and female agency.

We began by highlighting the boundary that exists between the *hadith* as an authoritative source for Islamic jurisprudence and historiographies which do not hold legal authority, thus separating the impact of the examples of Umm Waraqa and Ghazala. In the next chapter we will see that this boundary is blurred, if not removed, when we tap into other sources to find evidence that serves different agendas. In the next chapter we can at last find the voices of some of today's women imams themselves and their own use of that discursive tradition.

Notes

1. For a detailed study on Umm Waraqa, see Calderini, 'Classical Sources on the Permissibility of Female Imams', 53–70.
2. *Shahid* in the Qur'an usually means 'witness', even though in some verses directly related to war (Qur. 3.140), the meaning of martyr can be assumed, as *tafsir* scholars such as 10th century Tabari did. Afsaruddin argues for a semantic development of the term from a non-combative meaning to a combative one, and that by the late 8th century it came to be used to mean 'martyr', in Afsaruddin, Asma. *The First Muslims: History and Memory*. Oxford: Oneworld, 2007, xviii. See also her work *Striving in the Path of God*. Oxford: OUP, 2013, where she delineates a more detailed semantic trajectory for the term. In this chapter the term martyr will be used, with the connotation of both concepts of 'bearing witness' and 'martyrdom'. For the development in Syriac sources from witness to the faith to martyr see Raven Wim. 'Martyrs'. In *EQ* (Vol. 3), edited by Jane Dammen McAuliffe. Leiden: Brill, 2003, 282.
3. Ibn Sa'd, *Ibn Saad: Biographien: Band 8, Biographien der Frauen*, 335; same narrative, with a slight variation in *isnad* in the 9th century Zahiri Ibn Rahwayh. *Musnad Ishaq ibn Rahwayh*. Beirut: Dar al-Kutub al-'Arabi, 2002, 294–5.
4. Caetani, Leone. *Annali dell'Islam* (Vol. 4). Hildesheim, New York: Olms, 1972, 443–4.
5. See Kohlberg, Etan. 'Shahid'. In *EI2* (Vol. 9), edited by Peri J. Bearman, Th. Bianquis et al. Leiden: Brill, 1997, 203–7; Sumayya, the mother of an early battlefield martyr, who was reportedly tortured and killed after she openly embraced Islam, is considered the first martyr in Islam (p. 205). Afsaruddin, *Striving in the Path of God*, argues that the association of martyrdom and battles, or military *jihad*, dates to the Umayyad period, where it emerged to promote Umayyad military engagement and encourage men to join the military effort.
6. See Afsaruddin's analysis of such debates based on *hadith* literarure during the 8th and 9th century, *Striving in the Path of God*, 116–44.
7. Ibn Hanbal, Ahmad. *Musnad al-Imam Ahmad ibn Hanbal* (Vol. 6). Edited by Samir Taha al-Majdhub. Beirut: al-Maktab al-Islami, 1993, 453, *hadith* 2/27273.
8. For evaluations on Walid's trustworthiness as a witness and *hadith* transmittter see Calderini, 'Classical Sources on the Permissibility of Female Imams', 63–4.
9. Abu Dawud. *Sunan Abi Da'ud* (Vol. 1). Edited by Hamd ibn Muhammad Da'as, 'Izzat 'Ubayd Khattabi. Hums: Muhammad 'Ali al-Sayyid, 1969, 396.
10. Abu Dawud, *Sunan Abi Da'ud*, 1969, 1, 397. The specification of the muezzin's age could be seen as a sign of his respectability but also of maintaining the rules of gender boundaries (see Qur. 24.31).
11. On 'Abd al-Rahman see al-Mizzi, Yusuf ibn 'Abd al-Rahman. *Tahdhib al-Kamal fi Asma' al-Rijal*. Edited by 'Awwad Ma'ruf Bashshar. Beirut: Mu'assasat al-Risala, 1992, 17, 82–3; where al-Mizzi also states that it was said that 'Abd al-Rahman reported from his father and his father from Umm Waraqa. Mizzi provides no biographical information about 'Abd al-Rahman, and adds that according to some scholars his whereabouts and status are unknown, by this implicitly raising doubt about his reliability or even his historicity.
12. Al-Shaybani's (Ibn Abi Asim's) *isnad* for this *hadith* starts with Ibn Abi Shayba (Iraq d. 849) through Waki' (Kufa d. 812) back to the authority of al-Walid ibn Jumay' (Kufa) already mentioned by Ibn Sa'd and Ibn Hanbal. For more details on the reliability of some of these transmitters see Calderini, 'Classical Sources on the Permissibility of Female Imams', 63–4.

13 For more details on the scholars omitting Umm Waraqa's prayer leadership see Calderini, ibid., 63.
14 Ibn Khuzayma, al-Sulami al-Nisaburi. *Sahih Ibn Khuzayma*. Edited by Muhammad Mustafa al-A'zami. Beirut: Al-Maktab al-Islami, 1970, 3, 89.
15 al-Daraqutni, 'Ali ibn 'Umar. *Sunan al-Daraqutni*. Edited by Majdi ibn Mansur al-Shura. Beirut: Dar al-Kutub al-'Ilmiyya, 1996, 1, 284, *hadith* 1071, 388 *hadith* 1491.
16 For a detailed analysis of the link between variation in content *(matn)* and the chain of transmitters in Umm Waraqa's *hadith*s, see Calderini, 'Classical Sources on the Permissibility of Female Imams', 53–69.
17 Reda, Nevin. *The Islamic Basis for Female-Led Prayer*. [2005]. www.irfi.org/articles/articles_351_400/islamic_basis_for_femaleled.htm (accessed 27 May 2020)
18 Al-Tabari, *The History of al-Tabari* (Vol. 7), 5. It is reported that the Banu al-Najjar did not accept any payment for the land.
19 *Dar* attested with the meaning of 'tribe' in Lane, Edward William. *An Arabic-English Lexicon* (Vol. 1). Lahore: Suhayl Academy, 2003, 931, referring to *ahl dar* 'the people of the tribe'. For the Banu Najjar as the best tribe / family (*khayr dar*) among the Ansar, see al-Bukhari, Muhammad. *Sahih al-Bukhari [The Translation of the Meanings of Sahih al-Bukhari]* (Vol. 8). Translated by Muhammad Muhsin Khan. Riyadh: Dar al-Salam, 1997, 54.
20 Al-Tabari, *The History of al-Tabari* (Vol. 7), 724; for most commentators the change of *qibla* occurred two months before the Battle of Badr.
21 See Qur. 33.33, traditionally dated as ca. 5 H, or for some 3 or 4 H, where the performance of prayers is enjoined for the Prophet's wives; Bowering, 'Prayer', 215–30.
22 Ibn Rushd, *The Distinguished Jurist's Primer*, 1, 161.
23 Al-Azmeh, *The Times of History*, 32, 73.
24 On Twitter a description of Ghazala, allegedly based on al-Baghdadi and Ibn al-'Imad, evidences her ritual leadership: 'Ghazala ... entrered Kufa in her husband's absence where she preached the sermon and then led the morning prayer (of men)'. Twitter, مأمون السلفي @The Muwahhid, 19 April 2015; also Twitter, مأمون السلفي @The Muwahhid, 14 July 2015.
25 For *jihad* and Kharijism see Robinson, Chase F. 'The Ideological Uses of Early Islam'. *Past & Present* 203, 1 (2009): 205–28; for the legitimacy for Khariji women to partake in war see Ahmed, *Women and Gender in Islam*, 71.
26 For interpretations on the nature of the Khariji rebellions in Iraq, see Morony, Michael G. *Iraq after the Muslim Conquest*. Princeton, NJ: PUP, 1984, 468–77; and Kenney, Jeffrey T. *Muslim Rebels: Kharijites and the Politics of Extremism in Egypt*. Oxford: OUP, 2006.
27 For the uses and meanings of the term Khariji by pre-modern historians, see Kenney, *Muslim Rebels*, 24–50. For Khariji identity/ies and the nature of their rebellions, see contrasting arguments in: Robinson, Chase F. *Empire and Elites after the Muslim Conquest: The Transformation of Northern Mesopotamia*. Cambridge: CUP, 2000, 109–26; and Timani, Hussam S. *Modern Intellectual Readings of the Kharijites*. New York: Lang, 2007.
28 Gaiser, A. R. 'Imamate in Kharijism and Ibadism'. In *EI3 Online*, edited by Kate Fleet, Gudrun Krämer, et al. Leiden: Brill online. Article published 2017. http://dx.doi.org/10.1163/1573-3912_ei3_COM_32433 (accessed 7 November 2019).
29 Al-Jahiz, 'Amr ibn Bahr Abu 'Uthman. *Kitab al-Hayawan*. Beirut: al-Majma' al-'Ilmi al-'Arabi al-Islami, 1969, 5, 590.
30 Baugh, Carolyn. 'Revolting Women? Early Kharijite Women in Islamic Sources'. *Journal of Islamic and Muslim Studies* 2, 1 (2017): 50–1.

31 Ibn Khayyat, Khalifa. *Ta'rikh khalifat ibn Khayyat*. Edited by Akran Diya al-'Umari. Beirut: Mu'assasat al-risala, 1977, 352.
32 ibid., 354.
33 al-Tabari. *Ta'rikh al-Rusul wa'l-Muluk [The History of al-Tabari: The Marwanid Restoration]* (Vol. 22). Translated by Everett K. Rowson. Albany: SUNY Press, 1989, 44. For the reliability of Abu Mikhnaf as a source for the events, see Dixon, 'Abd al-Ameer 'Abd. *The Umayyad Caliphate 65–86 / 684–705: A Political Study*. London: Luzac, 1971, 182.
34 Al-Tabari, *The History of al-Tabari* (Vol. 22), 114.
35 For the symbolism of the severing of the head and parading it, see Mediano, Fernando Rodriguez. 'Justice, Crime and Punishment in 10th / 16th Century Morocco'. In *Public Violence in Islamic Societies: Power, Discipline, and the Construction of the Public Sphere, 7th–19th Centuries CE*, edited by Christian Lange and Maribel Fierro. Edinburgh: Edinburgh University Press, 2009, 190–2. In al-Baghdadi, Shabib's head too was severed to be taken to al-Hajjaj; al-Baghdadi, 'Abd al-Qahir. *Al-Farq Bayna al-Firaq [Moslem Schisms and Sects]*. Translated by K. Chambers Seelye. New York: Ams, 1966, 114.
36 Al-Tabari, *The History of al-Tabari* (Vol. 22), 117–18.
37 ibid., 119 where the account includes how Ghazala was sodomized to spite her husband.
38 ibid., xxii, 100–1, 105; for Shabib 'building' a mosque at al-Sabakha, on the edge of Kufa, see ibid., p. 108. For the political leadership use and symbol of the pulpit among the Umayyads, see Pedersen, Johannes. 'Minbar'. In *EI2* (Vol. 7), edited by Peri J. Bearman, Th. Bianquis et al. Leiden: Brill, 1993, 74–5.
39 Al-Tabari, Abu Ja'far Muhammad ibn Jarir. *Ta'rikh al-Rusul wa'l-Muluk [The History of al-Tabari: The First Civil War]* (Vol. 17). Translated by Gerald Hawting. Albany: SUNY Press, 1996, 214–15. For Qatam bint Shijna and her role in 'Ali's assassination in the Kufa mosque see Baugh, 'Revolting Women?', 40–3.
40 al-Mas'udi, 'Ali ibn al-Husayn. *Muruj al-Dhahab wa Ma'adin al-Jawhar* (Vol. 3). Beirut: Dar al-Kutub al-'Ilmiyya, 2004, 168–9.
41 In fact the *ghada* prayer could be the same as Ghazala's voluntary prayer to fulfil her vow with the 70 men accompanying her to the mosque. Modern Syrian historian Kahhalah states that Ghazala herself prayed the *ghada* prayer, not just the 70 men as in Mas'udi, see Kahhalah, Umar Rida. *A'lam al-Nisa'*. Beirut: Mu'assasat al-Risala, 1977, 4, 7. The *ghada* prayer indicates a morning prayer between the *fajr* and the *zuhr* prayer.
42 Hatoon Awjad al-Fassi's statement that Ghazala in the mosque of Kufa 'preached the sermon and then led the morning prayer' is based on her interpretation of al-Baghdadi and the 17th century al-Ikri al-Hanbali, in al-Fassi, Hatoon Awjad, 'Women in Eastern Arabia, Myth and Representation'. In *Gulf Women*, edited by A. Sonbol and K. Dreher. London: Bloomsbury, 2012, 42.
43 On vows by women which entail visiting the mosque, see Katz, *Women in the Mosque*, 114–16. On types of vows and legal opinions, Pedersen, Johannes. 'Nadhr'. In *EI2* (Vol. 7), edited by Peri J. Bearman, Th. Bianquis et al. Leiden: Brill, 1993, 846–7.
44 Al-Malati, Muhammad ibn Ihmad Abu'l-Husayn. *Al-Tanbih wa'l-Radd 'ala ahl al-Ahwa' wa'l-Bid'a*. Edited by Muhammad Zahid Kawthari. Baghdad: Maktabat al-Muthanna, 1968, 51, 'wa-khatabat wa la'anat al-Hajjaj wa bani marwan 'ala 'l-minbar'.
45 This is with reference to a specific group of Kharijis, the Haruris, from Eastern Iran (Sijistan, Herat and Khurasan) Al-Malati, *Al-Tanbih wa'l-Radd 'ala ahl al-Ahwa'*

wa'l-Bid'a, 53. Note that Malati's attitude towards Khariji groups is not uniform – while he condemns some groups for their brutal warfare tactics, he cannot hide admiration (while still condemning them as heretics) for the courage and skills of others, as in the case of the Haruriyya for their mastery in horsemanship and their courage.

46 al-Baghdadi, 'Abd al-Qahir. *Al-Farq Bayna al-Firaq*. Beirut: Dar al-Ma'rifa, 1970, 110.
47 ibid., Arabic text, 111: *wa za'amu anna ghazala umm shabib kanat al-imam ba'da qatl Shabib*. For Shabib making his mother 'mount the pulpit', al-Baghdadi, *Moslem Schisms and Sects*, 112.
48 al-Baghdadi, *Moslem Schisms and Sects*, 113; Arabic 111–12. Shabib's mother is also known by the name of Jahiza.
49 al-Baghdadi, *Al-Farq Bayna al-Firaq*, Arabic text, 112, Engl., 114.
50 al-Baghdadi, *Moslem Schisms and Sects*, 2, 214–15, Arabic text, *al-farq*, 350–1 (*qasadat al-islah bayna al fariqayn . . . wa qatalu 'Ali duna idhniha*).
51 ibid., Engl transl., Part 2, 89, Arabic, *al-farq*, 110.
52 For one instance of this see al-Isbahani, Abu'l-Faraj (d. 967–8) about Layla bint Taris, the sister of a Khariji leader who accompanied him in battle dressed in full armour, quoted in Kruk, Remke. *The Warrior Women of Islam: Female Empowerment in Arabic Popular Literature*. London: IB Tauris, 2014, 8–9.
53 Ibn al-'Imad al-Hayyi ibn Ahmad al-Ikri al-Hanbali, *Shadharat al-Dhahab* (Vol. 1), Beirut: al-Maktab al-Tijari li'l-Tiba'a wa-al-Nashr wa-al-Tawzi', 1960, 83.
54 Kahhalah, *A'lam al-Nisa'*, 4, 7.
55 Gaiser, 'Imamate in Kharijism and Ibadism'; Morony, *Iraq after the Muslim Conquest*, 475. For Ghazala in Jahiz see Baugh, 'Revolting Women?', 36–55.
56 For a critique of the binary logic of gendering peace and war, see Cooke, Miriam. 'Ungendering Peace Talk'. In *Women and Peace in the Islamic World: Gender, Agency, Influence*, edited by Yasmin Saikia and Chad Haines. London: IB Tauris, 2015, 25–42. Cooke argues that peace is not gender related or conditioned, nor emblematic of gender as 'women [are] not created to be peace loving in utero, they are told they are' (p. 25).
57 For an example of attribution of leadership to a Khariji woman, see Hammada al-Sufiya, mentioned only as a Sufi ascetic by al-Jahiz and Ibn al-Jawzia, while the modern biographer Kahhalah attributed to her leadership (*riyasa*), influence, and prestige (*nufudh*) among her people; Kahhalah, *A'lam al-Nisa'*, 1, 292; also Baugh, 'Revolting Women?', 37.
58 The Arabic expression is *kharaja*, so for instance Umm Waraqa asks the Prophet, with reference to Badr, to 'go forth with you' (*fa akruj ma'aka*), as does the young Umayya bint Qays with reference to Uhud. The Prophet declined the first but allowed the second to join him (see Ibn Sa'd, Muhammad. *Kitab al-Tabaqat al-Kabir* (Vol. 8). Beirut: Dar Sadir, [1968], 293). From these and several other reported cases, one can conclude that women's presence on the battlefield was dependant upon circumstance and the status of the women involved, be they the Prophet's wives, his Supporters or his Companions's wives.
59 Ibn Sa'd, *Kitab al-Tabaqat al-Kabir* (Vol. 8), 1968, 412–16 on Umm 'Umara, 41–3 on Safiya.
60 ibid., 412. There are other versions of this *hadith* on the authority of Umm Salama; in one the Prophet stated that women's *jihad* is to perform *hajj* and *'umra*; in another that *hajj* is the *jihad* of those who are physically weaker; see Amin, *Umm Salama and her Hadith*, 361–2.
61 Ibn Sa'd, *Kitab al-Tabaqat al-Kabir* (Vol. 8), 1968, 412; on Umm 'Umara's presence in seven battles and on her heroic defence of the Prophet, see 413–15.

62 al-Tabari, *The History of al-Tabari* (Vol. 12). Translated by Yohanan Friedmann. Albany: SUNY Press, 1992, 133.
63 al-Tabari, *The History of al-Tabari* (Vol. 11), 99–100. On Juwayriyya see Ibn Sa'd, *Kitab al-Tabaqat al-Kabir* (Vol. 8), 1968, 239.
64 See references in Kaegi, Walter E. *Byzantium and the Early Islamic Conquests*. Cambridge: CUP, 1992, 141.
65 Nicolle, David. *Yarmuk AD 636: The Muslim Conquest of Syria*. London: Osprey, 1994, 89, also *passim*, 69–89. Similarly, Arab chroniclers of the Crusades are intrigued by the presence of armed women in the 'Frankish' army, see quotation in Kruk, *The Warrior Women of Islam*, 19.
66 On the controversial issue of women and booty, see Roded, *Women in Islamic Biographical Collections*, 36; for one instance Ibn Sa'd, *Kitab al-Tabaqat al-Kabir* (Vol. 8), 1968, 293 (Umayya bint Qays); on preference in amount of stipends for those who participated in Badr, see Afsaruddin, *Excellence and Precedence*, 47–8.
67 Ahmed, *Women and Gender in Islam*, 70–1; and Salem, Elie Adib. *The Political Theory and Institutions of the Khawarij*. Baltimore, MD: John Hopkins University Press, 1956, 86–7. For more examples of Khariji women in battle see Layla bint Tarif, cited by Kruk, *The Warrior Women of Islam*, 413–14.
68 Translation of Al-Maziri Abu 'Abdallah, *Sharh al-Talqin* in Jalajel, *Women and Leadership in Islamic Law*, 222, also 148: 'our associates have argued for the categorical prohibition [of women leading prayer] ... by making an analogy on the [ruling of] supreme [political] leadership'. For the distinction between essential and accidental qualities (being female and slavery) see translation of al-Mawardi, *Al-Hawi al-Kabir* in Jalajel, *Women and Leadership in Islamic Law*, 233.
69 Al-Rajraji, Abu al-Hasan (d. before 1281) *Manahij al-tahsil*, Engl transl. in Jalajel, *Women and Leadership in Islamic Law*, 225.
70 For a Zaydi argument against female leadership of men see Ibn al-Murtada, Ahmad ibn Yahya. *Al-Bahr al-Zakhkhar*, quoted and annotated in *Al-Manar fi'l-Mukhtar* (Vol. 1), edited by Maqbali, Salih ibn Mahdi. Beirut: Mu'assasat al-Risala, 1988, 215, with Ibn al-Murtada stating that a man cannot be led in prayer by a woman, irrespective of the type of prayer, and that any statements to the contrary, for instance by al-Tabari, are erroneous.
71 For some translations of this verse, see Asad, Muhammad. *The Message of the Qur'an*. Gibraltar: Dar al-Andalus, 1980, 109; Arberry, Arthur J. *The Koran Interpreted*. London: OUP, 1964, 77; Pickthall, Marmaduke. *The Meaning of the Glorious Koran*. London: Allen & Unwin, 1976, 104; compare with Laleh Bakhtiar's translation in her *The Sublime Quran*. Chicago: Kazi, 2007, 94. Among others, see al-Mawardi's explanation of this verse following al-Shafi'i in his *Al-Hawi al-Kabir* in Jalajel, W*omen and Leadership in Islamic Law*, 232.
72 On the authority of Muhammad b. 'Abdallah b. Numayr, from 'Ali b. Zayd, 'people, turn to Allah in repentance before you die ... and never ever may a woman lead a man in prayer, nor a Bedouin a Muhajir, nor an immoral person lead a believer', in Ibn Maja, *Sunan al-Hafiz Abi 'Abdallah* (Vol. 1), 343, hadith 1081. This *hadith* is used to justify Ibn al-Murtada's position against a woman leading a man in prayer in his *Al-Bahr al-Zakhkhar*, quoted and commented upon in al-Maqbalī, *Al-Manar fi'l-Mukhtar* (Vol. 1), 215.
73 For instance, al-Mawardi attributes to al-Shafi'i the statement that women fall short of *walaya* and *qiyam*, in al-Mawardi, Abu'l-Hasan 'Ali ibn Muhammad. *Al-Hawi al-Kabir fi Fiqh Madhhab al-Imam al-Shafi'i, wa Huwa Sharh Mukhtasar al-Muzani* (Vol. 2).

Edited by 'Abd al-Fattah Khalid Shibl. Beirut: Dar al-Kutub al-'Ilmiyya, 1999, 326. In his *Ahkam*, al-Mawardi claims that al-Tabari permitted women to hold judgeship under all circumstances but dismisses this position by noting that it was unanimously rejected by all scholars; al-Mawardi, *The Ordinances of Government*, 81.

74 Abu Hurayra's *hadith* is reported by Abu Dawud in *Sunan Abi Dawud*, In *Jam' Jawami' al-Ahadith*. *Vaduz*: Thesaurus Islamicus Foundation, 2000, 1, 116–17, as well as by Muslim, al-Tirmidhi, ibn Maja etc., but not by al-Bukhari. This *hadith* is also reported on the authority of 'Ali in al-Qadi al-Nu'man, *The Pillars of Islam* (Vol. 1), 195.

75 Ibn Qudama defines this consensus as being 'universal' (*wa la-khilaf*), in his *Al-Mughni* (Vol. 3), 33.

76 Abu Dawud, *Sunan*, 2000, and others: on the authority of 'A'isha: 'I was between the Prophet and the *qibla* ... and I was menstruating'. Abu Dawud adds that a list of authorities fail to mention 'and I was menstruating', in *Jam' Jawami' al-Ahadith*, *salat*, *hadith* 710, 121. For al-Bukhari, see *Sahih al-Bukhari* (Vol. 1), n.d., 8, 231–2.

77 Al-Sarakhsi in his *Al-Mabsut* – passage translated in Jalajel, *Women and leadership*, 245–6. For a summary of opinions and overall comment on female seduction, ibid., 131–4.

78 For a full analysis of al-Qadi al-Nu'man's argument see Calderini, '"Leading from the Middle"', 94–117.

79 Al-Qadi al-Nu'man, *Ta'wil al-Da'a'im* (Vol. 1), 241, 245.

80 Ibn Taymiyya, Ahmad. *Naqd Maratib al-Ijma'*. Beirut: Dar al-Kutub al-'Ilmiyyah, 1970, 78.

81 Ibn Qudama, *Al-Mughni*, 3, 33; Al-Zarkashi, *Sharh al-Zarkashi*, translated by Jalajel, *Women and Leadership in Islamic Law*, 240–1. Among Hanbali legal positions see also al-Bahuti, Mansur (d. 1641), *Kashshaf al-Qina* in Jalajel, ibid., 243.

82 Al-Sarakhsi (d. 1096), *Al-Mabsut*, in Jalajel, *Women and Leadership in Islamic Law*, 246, and, in more detail, Sadeghi, *The Logic of Law Making in Islam*, 60, 97–104.

83 On Nafisa Bint al-Hasan leading Imam Shafi'i's funeral prayers, see Kahhalah, *A'lam al-Nisa'* (Vol. 5), 188.

84 For a fuller analysis see Calderini, Simonetta. 'Contextualising Arguments about Female Ritual Leadership (Women Imams) in Classical Islamic Sources'. *Comparative Islamic Studies* 5, 1 (2009): 5–32.

85 Ibn Rushd, Abu al-Walid Muhammad. *Sharh Bidayat al-Mujtahid wa Nihayat al-Muqtasid* (3rd edn). Edited by 'Abdallah al-'Abadi. Cairo: Dar al-Salam, 2006, 1, 339, where the Arabic verb *shadhdha* means 'be an exception, stand out, deviate'. The attribution of such an opinion to these scholars, repeated in several other sources, is contested by modern scholar Zaid Shakir; for a response to this, see Jalajel, *Women and Leadership in Islamic Law*, 68–71.

86 Ibn Qudama, *Al-Mughni* (Vol. 3), 33; for an analysis of Ibn Qudama's context and opinion on the topic of female leadership see Calderini, 'Contextualising Arguments about Female Ritual Leadership', 16–18.

87 See Melchert's argument that the two groups were mainly ideal and that individual scholars, rather than being classified with one or the other group, were in fact rather eclectic; Melchert, Christopher. 'Traditionists-Jurisprudents and the Framing of Islamic Law'. *Islamic Law and Society* 38, 3 (2001): 393.

88 For Paula Sanders' analysis of the link between gender and the maintenance of communal and social boundaries see her 'Gendering the Ungendered Body', 80–9.

89 For the first report on Abu Thawr, see al-Mawardi, *Al-Hawi al-Kabir fi Fiqh Madhhab al-Imam al-Shafi'i* (Vol. 2), 326. For more on Abu Thawr, see Judd, Steven C. (2012-), 'Abu Thawr', *EI3 Online* (accessed 3 March 2020).
90 For al-Shafi'i see al-Shafi'i, *Kitab al-Umm* (Vol. 1), 145 where he states that the prayer of men behind a female imam is not valid because Allah made men '*qawwamuna 'ala al-nisa*"; for al-Muzani see al-Muzani, *Mukhtasar al-Muzani*, 37.
91 On biographical reports and some sources on Dawud al-Zahiri, see Adang, C. (2005) 'The Beginnings of the Zahiri Madhhab in al-Andalus'. In *The Islamic School of Law: Evolution, Devolution and Progress*, edited by P. Bearman. Cambridge, MA: Harvard University Press, note 10, 241–2. For an overview, see Melchert, Christopher. 'Dawud b. Khalaf'. In *EI3 Online*, edited by Kate Fleet, Gudrun Krämer, et al. Leiden: Brill online, 2012. http://dx.doi.org/10.1163/1573-3912_ei3_COM_32433 (accessed 2 March 2020).
92 For the claim that al-Tabari permitted a woman to lead a man in prayer see al-Baji, *Kitab al-Muntaqa Sharh Muwatta'* (Vol. 1), 235, and many more after him, including al-Mawardi as already seen.
93 Melchert, 'Whether to Keep Women out of the Mosque', 69.
94 Ibn al-'Arabi, Muhyi al-Din. *Al-Futuhat al-Makkiyya* (Vol. 3). Cairo: Dar al-Kutub al-'Arabiyya, 1911, 97.
95 Ibn al-'Arabi, Muhyi al-Din. *Al-Futuhat al-Makkiyya* (Vol. 8). Edited by 'Uthman Yahya, Ibrahim Madkur. Cairo: al-Hay'a al-Misriyya al-'Amma li'l-Kitab, 1983, 151; and Vol. 7, 1981, 50.
96 Ibn al-'Arabi, *Al-Futuhat al-Makkiyya* (Vol. 6), 1978, 428. As customary in a number of sources, the section on the *imama* of a woman comes immediately after that on the *imama* of a minor and a sinful person, but precedes that of an illegitimate child.
97 ibid.
98 Ibn al-'Arabi, Muhyi al-Din. *Tafsir al-Qur'an al-Karim* (Vol. 1). Edited by Mustafa Ghalib. Beirut: Dar al-Andalus, 1978, 185.
99 Ibn al-'Arabi, *Al-Futuhat al-Makkiyya* (Vol. 6), 1978, 429–30.
100 Winkel, Eric. *Islam and the Living Law: The Ibn al-Arabi Approach*. New York: OUP, 1997, 92.
101 Eccel, A. Chris. 'Female and Feminine in Islamic Mysticism'. *The Muslim World* 78, 3–4 (1988): 209–24.
102 Ibn al-'Arabi, *Al-Futuhat al-Makkiyya* (Vol. 3), 1911, 97.
103 See the differing positions of scholars such as Joseph Schacht, Chafik Chehata or Ya'akov Meron; for a partial re-visitation of the relationship between legal theory and legal practice in favour of a more dialectical link, see Johansen, Baber. 'Casuistry: Between Legal Concept and Social Praxis'. *Islamic Law and Society* 2, 2 (1995): 135–56.
104 Al-Safadi, *A'yan al-'Asr wa A'wan al-Nasr* (Vol. 3), 1394. For female preachers during the Fatimids see Cortese and Calderini, *Women and the Fatimids in the World of Islam*, 33. For a 12th century reference see Melchert, 'Whether to Keep Women out of the Mosque', 68, quoting Ibn 'Asakir; for preachers, mostly for a mixed audience, in biographical collections, see Roded, *Women in Islamic Biographical Collections*, 10.
105 Katz, *Women in the Mosque*, 71–83.
106 For both cases and details of sources, see Talmon-Heller, *Islamic Piety in Medieval Syria*, 59–60.
107 Brink, Judy. 'Lost Rituals: Sunni Muslim Women in Rural Egypt'. In *Mixed Blessings, Gender and Religious Fundamentalism Cross Culturally*, edited by Judy Brink and Joan Mencher. London, New York: Routledge, 1997, 201.

Part II

THE PRESENT

Chapter 4

PRESENT DEBATES AND PRACTICES

Introduction

Having analysed in the previous chapters the legal debates and reported cases of female leadership of prayer during the first centuries of Islam, focusing on the period between the 7th and 12th centuries, this chapter will deal with current debates about, and examples of, today's women imams. It explores the different ways in which modern scholars, activists and the female imams themselves appeal to the classical past to validate their positions and arguments. Prayer leadership will be discussed as a theoretical field concerned with the permissibility of 'being an imam', but also as a concrete, professional activity with relevant roles, community functions and expectations.

This chapter aims to analyse some of the main modern developments in female prayer leadership in terms of expressions and reach, set within specific geographical and cultural contexts. This will involve an analysis of new uses and understandings of the expected roles of a modern imam, particularly, but not exclusively, in countries where Muslims are a minority community. The very term *imam*, which already in the Qur'anic usage had showed multiple meanings, has kept to this day such a polysemic feature. Similarly, the term *mosque* may refer to both a physical site where worship and female leadership are exercised, but also to a 'community of worship'. As a physical place what will be referred to as a 'mosque' may variously indicate a purpose-built edifice, a location adapted to be a place of worship, or a make-shift *ad hoc* place of congregation and prayer where only the core features of cleanliness and suitability for worship are kept.

With reference to women-only mosques, this chapter will address the question of whether, in their different contexts, they can be regarded as examples of women's empowerment and agency, or as a perpetuation of cultural-religious gender separation, or both. Examples of women imams in different geographical contexts are featured, from China to the USA, South Asia, Africa and Europe. Another of its aims is to identify and comment upon the ways in which such contexts have influenced or shaped the imams' status alongside the exercise of their authority as leaders, and how contexts have affected their uses of the past in their arguments to legitimize their own position. It will also address the question of the extent to which today's women imams' articulation of arguments differs from that of the classical scholars examined in the earlier chapters.

Thanks to the development and the abundance of mass media and social media, a performance of female prayer leadership in any one country can reach a much wider audience and lead to realtime responses beyond the more defined religious, theological and legal scholarly circles. As a result, this chapter will employ a variety of sources through which these responses are expressed, so as to analyse the types of reactions that a given performance has received.

As detailed in earlier chapters, on the basis of pre-modern Islamic texts, some of the meanings and uses of the term 'imam', as well as the core pre-requisites for being selected, nominated or appointed as an imam were: being a pious and just Muslim, being sane, knowing the Qur'an and the *sunna*, and, for some schools of law and in certain circumstances, being male. In time, further attributes required for being an imam were indicated, such as personal probity, maturity, legitimate birth, age, specific knowledge of *fiqh*, or, during the period immediately following the Prophet's time, to have performed *hijra*.

The roles of the imam have indeed developed over time. From being predominantly ritual, as leader of the prayers, and ethical, as spiritual guide, the role of imam became more specialized and yet also more wide-ranging, especially since the 9th century increase in the professionalization and specialization of religious personnel in larger urban mosques. There, the imam also assumed the role of mosque administrator and manager who appointed, for example, the *khatib* or sermon preacher for Friday prayer, the muezzin, the treasurer and other mosque staff. If competent not only in Qur'anic recitation, but also in the *sunna* and *fiqh*, the imam could also be the community expert and reference point for theological and legal matters. Especially when appointed by the caliph, the sultan or their representatives, the office of the imam acquired a more political function; however, especially in Sunni Islam, there was not, and still there is not, one universally acknowledged governing body to supervise imams.

Thus, in modern contexts in Islamic and Muslim minority countries, both the criteria for selecting or appointing an imam and the imam's roles, functions and community expectations have expanded, and they continue to be adapted to complex and variable circumstances. Criteria of selection, roles and expectations are strongly interconnected.

In Muslim minority countries, additional issues to do with migration, intergenerational differences in priorities and educational backgrounds have affected understandings and assumptions about the figure of the imam. Interviews with British Muslims, conducted between 2008 and 2010, revealed that divergent expectations from imams emerged between the older and younger generation in terms of their qualifications, language, cultural and identity references. The findings were that the older generation of Muslims preferred their imams to be trained in their own country of origin and to give the sermon in their native language, presumably to reflect what they believed to be a more 'authentic' model to preserve their cultural and religious identity. In contrast, younger British Muslims wished their imams to hold UK educational qualifications, communicate in English and be well-aware of local context, ways of life and the issues young Muslims face.¹

All in all the current core duties of imams exhibit a mix of traditional and modern, while their overall remit has grown in scope. While imams are traditionally expected to lead the daily *salat* and the *jum'a* prayers, oversee life rituals and advise on legal and theological matters, they are now also expected to be teachers and preachers, to be involved in mosque administration and, increasingly in the West, to liaise with local government and services while being community spokespersons over controversial issues such as radicalization, health matters or 'traditional cultural harmful practices'.² Consequently, one can state that the position and status of an imam in Muslim minority countries are perceived as being much more public and prestigious than those of imams in Islamic countries.³

When current female imams in the West are asked to identify the defining roles of an imam, in addition to that of leading prayer, some tend to emphasize the pastoral roles such as spiritual guidance, counselling and community service.⁴ Indeed, the figure of the imam in most Western societies has taken on wider pastoral roles and civil community tasks as a result of Muslim believers' and wider society's expectations and needs.⁵ One of those expectations is that imams should possess recognized qualifications such as that of being an *'alim*, which involves traditional Islamic training in theology, *hadith*, *tafsir*, jurisprudence or, for some, holding Western university degrees in Islamic studies. The progressive 'professionalization' of the role of the imam in Europe along Christian-based priestly models has led Danish sociologist Niels Vinding to talk of a 'churchification of Islam', with the risk that non-Muslim observers of Islam may misunderstand and misrepresent the history and functions of religious leadership and authority in Islam.⁶

As far as the term 'imam' is concerned, in present times it is still used in its generic meaning of guide and specifically prayer leader, but also of Muslim community representative. When applied to women, however, a number of Muslim academics, spokespeople and leaders, including some female imams, prefer the more encompassing and neutral expression of 'faith leader' to reflect religious leadership in Islam in a more accurate and inclusive manner than 'imam'. Moreover, there is also increased awareness among academics of the question of whether the term imam can be meaningfully applied cross-culturally, thus incurring the risk of becoming a decontextualized category. As such, it can be deprived of its own complexity in relation to specific religious communities and local traditions, but also in view of gender dynamics and varied expressions of leadership.

Still, imam is the most common and popular word used, albeit often misperceived as the Muslim equivalent of the figure, functions and pastoral roles of Christian priests, Jewish rabbis or other ministers of faith.⁷ In fact, in a number of instances from non-academic, wide-reaching sources, any references to women 'imams' risk being inaccurate if the meaning of the term imam is not clarified. So, attention-grabbing headlines like 'Female imams in Germany, the call of the muezzin women' or 'Female imams in German mosques get a mixed reception'⁸ reveal content which in fact does not refer to female prayer leaders at all but, instead, to trained preachers or chaplains, who do not lead congregational prayer.

Because of this current expansion in the use and understanding of the term imam, and though the focus of this book is on women as imams, in this chapter we will also make references to other Muslim female faith leadership roles which are not traditionally associated with the term imam, as well as cases of Muslim women in the professional capacity as preachers, chaplains or teachers in educational institutions, who might act, under certain circumstances, as prayer leaders. This is to reflect more accurately not only a changing understanding of the figure of the imam in general, but also varied expressions of religious authority and of 'new faith leaders'. The intention is therefore not to limit our research to cases of self-defined or more broadly acknowledged female 'imams'. When applied to a woman, the term imam itself could be reductive, inadequate, mostly controversial and consequently, in several cases, not used at all.

Some current cases of women imams of women

Similarly to the first part of this book, female prayer leadership is presented in separate sections depending on the type of congregation being led. This is not only to reflect past and present distinct arguments and positions about its permissibility, but also to identify possible differences in the functions played by women-only mosques and gender-mixed places of worship.

Pre-modern legal-theological Muslim opinions about the permissibility of women leading other women in prayer specified, in their arguments, the type of prayer being led, the location and the spatial positioning of the leader among the congregation. These opinions were mostly supported by *hadith*s, some of which recount narratives that could serve as precedents based on the Prophet's wives or Companions, but also by local customs, particularly the Medinan practice. In time, legal schools' positions – whether Sunni or Shi'i – became more uniform in this respect moving towards a preference, a recommendation or even a rule for women to perform *salat*, especially Friday prayer, at home rather than in a public place of worship.

How far the theory was replicated in the practice of women leading other women in prayer is hard to gauge given the scarcity of references in sources on women's performance of ritual prayer in both formal and informal settings. What does transpire, however, is that the mosque was not usually identified as the typical location for females to perform *salat*, particularly *jum'a* prayer. A recent study on the history of legal thought and social practice of Muslim women's presence in the mosque has revealed that this does not mean that mosques in the past were not frequented by women, but rather that the activities they undertook in them and their timings were different to those of the men.[9] In other words, the usage that women made of the mosque was to some extent distinct from that of men. The choice of days other than Friday to attend the mosque, for example, is evidenced by modern ethnographic accounts from Central Asia where, in the mosque of a pilgrimage site, women would perform rituals on other days of the week.[10]

However, there is evidence that even this alternate use of shared ritual space did not encourage the already limited participation of women in congregational rituals in the mosque.¹¹ Instead, alternative spaces were – and still are – used by women: *musalla*s, shrines, make-shift areas in markets, community rooms or private homes. In these spaces, some women gather to perform *salat* together and, more often, non-compulsory prayers such as the *tarawih* prayers during Ramadan. In today's Tajikistan and Kyrgyzstan for example, *tarawih* prayers are led by women in *mahallas* (neighbourhood, district) or in houses, with a female leader who does not stand in front of the female congregation, but prays with them in the first row.¹²

To date, because of a combination of Muslim-wide negative socio-cultural attitudes towards female participation in rituals in the mosque, in reality its praying facilities are for many Muslim women unsatisfactory, limited or non-existent. Media coverage of events of Muslim women leading prayer in public, and the ensuing broader debates around women's presence and roles in mosques, have resulted in the issue of women facilities in the mosque being addressed at different levels within Muslim communities. Actions range from official state-supported campaigns to improve mosque spaces for women – as in the case of Turkey – to the creation of online platforms to gather information about facilities for women in mosques, to Muslim practitioners' research leading to directories highlighting (and exposing) the extent of 'women-friendly mosques' in particular countries.¹³

To respond to the heightened interest in women in the mosque and redress the shortcomings of female mosque facilities, in Saudi Arabia, designated spaces for women referred to as *musalla* (prayer room) are being built outside the mosques. Perhaps a well-meaning initiative, it however risks reinforcing an image of women's marginalization, if not exclusion. In Indonesia, local prayer houses for women have also been established, like the one in Kauman village in Java, where female faith leader Ibu Uswatun leads early morning prayers and delivers the sermon.¹⁴ In 2006, news reached the international media about a 'women's mosque' in the Afghanistan capital Kabul. This was a period when political and religious decisions in the country were often inconsistent and being influenced by fluctuating levels of Taliban and other Islamist groups' dominance. This 'women's mosque' was reported to have been established as a result of a combination of grassroots women activism and state effort via the Ministry of Religious Affairs. In fact, this 'mosque' turned out to be no more than a designated floor for women within an existing mosque.¹⁵

Though controversial in the opinion of some, having specific and separate spaces devoted to women can indeed create a fertile environment for promoting female agency, empowerment and leadership. Whether as prayer rooms, *ad hoc* places of worship or women-only mosques, these gendered spaces can at the very least represent an appropriation of space where women state they 'feel safe' and 'valued' and where they can teach, preach and, in some cases, even lead prayer.

Women-only mosques can be found in different countries; they were established as a result of specific circumstances, but all share a common denominator: they are a response to a slow-paced change in attitudes towards female participation in mosque activities or towards access to a ritual space for them beyond cultural, political or religiously motivated constraints. In such mosques, various forms of female faith leadership are exercised, from scholarship and transmission of knowledge to prayer leadership, counselling, support, being in charge of the mosque's governance, its funding and its activities. Potentially, such activities may result in the acquisition of transferable skills which could be empowering for women outside the mosque context.

Women's mosques

Though diverse in their geographical, historical and political contexts, the examples of women's mosques to be introduced below share some common traits.

One is a combination of 'favourable' circumstances that resulted in the rise of female leadership and an assigned space for it. A second is the strong link between female religious education and female leadership, in some cases education impacting upon or justifying leadership, in others the need for female religious education creating the conditions for gender exclusive environments. Thirdly, there is a shared perception that a women-only space is 'safe',[16] presumably from male interference or judgement, male gaze or, perhaps, male harassment. And fourthly, in order to pre-empt possible accusations of innovation, a common feature among the representatives of these mosques is the perceived necessity to provide textual, theological or historical justifications for the legitimacy of female authority and of the space where it is exercised. In a number of instances, women's mosques are therefore under scrutiny to check that female leaders and attendees conform to the gender paradigm of the observer, such as specific authoritative members of the Muslim community, and to moral and social norms. Adjustments may be required to make the ritual performed by women 'acceptable' to satisfy some conservative views.

Female *imama* of women occurs both in Islamic and Muslim minority countries, thus examples will be provided of both, even though those which feature more prominently in this chapter are of women's mosques in Muslim minority countries. Given the much more controversial situation of women imams of men, only examples in Muslim minority countries can be included for this.

Women's mosques in China

The oldest women's mosques originally intended for the sole use of women – still operational today – are the women's mosques (*nusi*) in the central, north-western and eastern regions of China. They cater for the Chinese-speaking Hui Muslim community, one of the ethnic Muslim groups of that country.[17] In this section no reference is made to other Muslim communities in China, such as the Uyghur, whose position and status in the country is very different from that of the Hui. Ethnographer Maria Jaschok and anthropologist Shui Jingjun, in their joint monograph, detail the history of Chinese women's mosques and discuss the roles and authority of their female faith instructors (*nu ahong*) who are in charge of the mosques' religious affairs.[18]

Though the status and roles of a *nu-ahong* vary in different localities and mosques, Jaschok believes that it is justifiable to refer to her as an 'imam', especially in terms of her 'formal rank and contractual status with respect to a mosque or other Islamic institution'.[19] The *nu ahongs* are now typically employed by mosque management committees, which were originally set up by the Chinese government in the mid-1950s. We will see that in the women's mosques, which are branches of men's mosques, the role of the *ahong* is much more limited than that in autonomous women's mosques. A female *ahong*'s main responsibility is to preside over the activities in the *nusi* mosques, including performance of prayer, preaching, religious education and other community-related services. The existence of these mosques and the roles of their female *ahong* are rooted in the specific historical circumstances of Muslim minorities in China.

During the Ming dynasty (14th–17th century) forced assimilation policies of minorities to Chinese Han culture were put in place. By the 16th century, Hui Muslims – the largest Muslim group in China – responded to the possible risk of losing their religious and cultural identity by initiating a religious educational movement. They spread the knowledge of Islam among their communities through the translation into Chinese of Islamic scriptures and the setting up of Islamic schools, including women's schools. However, socio-cultural-religious traditions of gender separation, shared by Confucianism, Buddhism and Islam, did not sit comfortably with the presence of male teachers in an all-female class. In a complex context of new expressions of Chinese Islam, arising from the influence of diverse Sufi orders known to have been established in China since the 17th century, Hui leaders identified the importance of the role of women in spreading the knowledge of Islam, with the first teachers being the wives of faith educators. By the 18th century the religious schools for women eventually developed into women's mosques, usually adjacent to men's mosques. At first, they were established and supervised by men, but some, later, were run by female *ahong*.

More favourable circumstances for the status of women's mosques came during the early 20th century Chinese state reforms, which targeted women's education as part of an underlying discourse on gender equality. The 1949 victory of Communism and its state ideology demoting the official status of religion meant that the government took over control of the mosques; it carried, nevertheless, a strong message of gender equality in education and work, and brought a vision of the 'new Chinese woman' which had an impact on the perception of the *nu ahong* as an example of female leadership. From the late 1950s to the end of the Cultural Revolution (late 1970s), all organized religions were regulated and controlled with the eventual closure of places of worship. Since 1993, state policies on compulsory registration of places of worship in China have given government-approved recognition and more secure financial status to women's mosques. However, the recent rise in influence of more conservative forms of Islam is posing increased challenges to the perception of the religious permissibility of female *ahongs* and the very existence of independent women's mosques.[20]

Maria Jaschok has traced some developments in the way in which the female *ahongs*' authority and leadership are acquired. The early *ahongs* received knowledge through their own family members. Subsequently, learning became 'institutionalized' in *madrasas* and, then, in their own mosques. Learning has therefore constantly been at the core of their authority. Family status is an additional component, with personal conduct and sacrifice for the cause of Islam as essential traits for a female *ahong*.

Authority and leadership in order to be asserted need to be acknowledged. Given the absence in (Sunni) Islam of the equivalent of the Christian 'ordained' clergy, for Muslim religious leaders, and in this case for the *nu ahong*, religious authority 'rests in a nexus of social relationships'.[21] Thus, authority is a relational product of a constant negotiation between the *ahong* as holder of authority, the female believers and mosque attendees who acknowledge it, and the male *ahong* and Muslim male scholars, who might scrutinize and contest it. The female *ahong*'s authority is therefore reliant upon her reputation based on her qualities as a leader, but also her behaviour and actions and the extent to which they conform to the religious and cultural expectations of her gender roles. So, if the female *ahong* steps outside the boundaries of female segregation, and of her commitment to self-sacrifice towards her congregation and community, her authority might no longer be upheld. This is what happened to Yang Huizhen (d. 1989), a female *ahong* from the Henan province in Central China, who went beyond the remit of the mosque to which she was contracted as *ahong*, by organizing a welfare centre for refugees during the 1945–9 civil war. Because of the perceived transgression of her duties and disobedience to the Islamic authorities, Huizhen's employment was terminated by the manager who had originally appointed her. There were multiple actors in 'the nexus of social relationships' which made it possible, eventually, for her to be reinstated.[22]

The legitimacy of the female *ahong*'s authority continues to be a controversial issue, contested politically by some Muslims because of links with – in fact endorsement by – the watchful state, as well as doctrinally on the basis of it constituting *bid'a* (innovation).[23] The largest, possibly the oldest, Muslim *madhhab* present in China is the Hanafi school. Most Hanafi scholars view female leadership in prayer (from the front) as a *makruh* (disliked) act, with some considering it prohibited altogether; if, however, the female *imam* is located among the congregants, most Hanafis would regard the action as permissible. Moreover, the call to prayer by a woman, as well as her giving a sermon, are also *makruh*. These legal-doctrinal positions had an impact upon the material features of *nusi* mosques: they do not have their own minaret nor does their prayer room include a pulpit.[24]

Chinese Muslim scholars are not alone in raising concerns about the legitimacy of women's mosques and female leaders there. When Ingrid Mattson, Canadian Muslim scholar and the first woman to be elected head of the Islamic Society of North America, visited China and prayed in one of its women's mosques, she too began to question the status and the role of *nu ahong* vis-à-vis the concept of *bid'a*. She resolved that women's mosques could be seen as being a 'laudable' innovation, in that they are a means towards the meritorious or recommended goal of spreading the knowledge of Islam. Still, Mattson felt the need to explain that 'traditional rules of ritual law' are safely adhered to, given that these 'female imams do not conduct Friday congregational prayer and, in accordance with their Hanafi legal tradition, they do not even lead other women in daily congregational prayer'.[25] She described the *nu ahong* as being ritual and Qur'anic instructors, resident moral guides, as counsellors for other women and performers of some funerary rituals on women.

There are of course geographical and individual variations in the way women mosques are administered and the activities carried out by women imams. Jashok gave the example of a women's mosque in Henan province where it is the male imam who recites the Qur'an, because of the consideration of the female voice as Xiuti (the equivalent of *'awra*) and so not to be heard in public.[26] As for the leading of daily congregational prayer, it is reported that elsewhere some *nu ahong* do lead women in prayer by being in the middle of the front row, and that they do give sermons.[27] Even if considered as a 'laudable' or a 'good' innovation arising from a practical necessity, many Muslims would commonly perceive the function of *nu ahong* as lacking precedents.

An example of the way a Chinese female imam responds to the charge of innovation is provided by one single-minded *nu ahong* from the 'most autonomous *nuse* in Henan', whose name is Du Ahong. Du Ahong explains that 'A'isha and Fatima, the most popular female role models among Chinese Muslims, are not only leaders of women in Paradise, but also women who 'provide leadership for women on earth'.[28] From the vantage point of an outspoken educated female leader from a self-managing mosque, Du Ahong could challenge some of the conventional narratives about female figures of the past: the emphasis on family life, the duties of wives and daughters, conformity to modesty and obedience. By linking female leadership in heaven with that on earth, Du Ahong is able to provide a ready-made explanation for the legitimacy of the status of women like herself, whose responsibility is to guide and lead the women of her community.

Elaborating on past female role models for the benefit of contemporary women did not originate from the women themselves. It was in fact an expression of the dominant narrative of the past as recounted by men. During the early 18th century Liu Zhi, the Chinese male scholar and author of the most influential book on Islamic thought in the Chinese language, had already highlighted the great virtues of the Prophet's wives and his female Companions. He qualified Khadija as the first 'convert' to Islam, Sumayya bint Khayyat (d. 615) as the first Muslim female martyr and 'A'isha as the indefatigable facilitator of the spread of knowledge of Islam.[29] The memory of the past, however, is not fixed and passive, but reshaped and adapted to new contexts. In recent times, in line with the use and appropriation of the gender equality discourse by ideological agendas of the Chinese Communist government, the more independent and assertive *nu ahong*s no longer limit female precedents to the women of the Prophet's time. They also include more recent Muslim women such as the female political leaders of Pakistan and Bangladesh, Chinese heroines like the already mentioned Yang Huizhen or even early Communist female activists. This way, they forge their own narrative of a more extended and varied past to better fit the present, thereby expressing their commitment to both the nationalist agenda of the Chinese state and to the tenets of the wider Islamic *umma*.

It would be inaccurate, however, to hail the *nu ahong* and women's mosques as a whole as fitting examples of full female achievement in the modern (mainly

Western) understanding of gender agency, equality and gender justice. These mosques and the status of the *nu ahong* vary according to location and whether they are economically subordinate to, or independent from, the male mosques nearby. To rely on the administrative and financial support of the male mosque has obvious consequences for the female mosque's upkeep, their use of funds and the extent of the activities and functions of their female imams, who would be selected and appointed by the administrator of the men's mosque.[30] In self-administered women mosques female *ahong* are in charge of training the future *ahong* and the female administrators who will select her.

During training, women *ahong* may follow a more limited curriculum than their male colleagues, use different textbooks and learn fewer chapters of the Qur'an, all of which impact upon the extent of their knowledge of Islamic doctrine and practice and, consequently, upon the perception – or recognition – by others of their authoritative status. The *nu ahong*'s responsibilities and tasks are in general similar to the male *ahong*'s with the exception, in specific contexts, of Friday prayers, which women are in any case not compelled to attend, and of leading funeral prayers which is usually the male imam's remit. Additionally, due to the socio-religious values and mores perceived as being pertinent to women, there are greater restrictions for *nu ahong* in their activities, movement and life choices.

With the expansion of Salafi Islamic missionary activity and financial resources in China, along with Chinese imams being trained abroad, the opposition of Chinese Muslim communities to *nu ahong* and women mosques is likely to grow. Another cause for concern about the future of female imams and their mosques is expressed by third-generation imam Sun Chenying who, in 2010, stated that 'women don't want to be imams anymore, because the salaries in the mosques are too low. No one is willing to do it'.[31]

Women's mosques in China face a number of challenges including the spread of more traditional interpretations, according to which women's mosques and their female imams are considered as religious innovations. Their status can be undermined by the higher standing of male scholars with more prestigious qualifications obtained in Islamic countries where they are able to reside and get training for up to six years. Moreover, they can be subject to internal political pressure from the state to conform to national values, as well as pressures due to the limited funding, as voiced by the imam mentioned above. Nevertheless, women's mosques and female *ahong* do continue to be a testament to the beneficial contribution they have made to the community by exercising religious leadership. The leadership status of the women imams at the women's mosques is legitimized by varied and interconnected means. Among these is the appointment of new female *ahongs* by established *ahongs* or by local male Muslim leaders, the acknowledgement of their status by the mosque congregation, and being part of the state registration of mosques, after having undergone the state training required of its leaders. Other means by which the *ahongs*' status is legitimized is by the external acknowledgement of their personal piety and commitment to serving the Muslim community, as well as of their acquisition of religious knowledge and experience. Finally, in their educational sessions and lectures their inclusion of references to historical precedents of female leaders confers legitimacy to their own leadership status.

All in all, women *ahong*s can be seen as an example of the exercise of Muslim women's rights in China and, beyond this, of having a recognized socio-religious place of their own and an 'official' role in society. Their rights specifically include participating in the ritual activities of the mosque and in its management, in some cases attaining self-governance and self-reliance, as well as accessing, shaping and spreading religious education. These are rights that cannot be taken for granted given that many Muslim women are not able to exercise them elsewhere, either in Islamic or non-Islamic countries.

Women's mosques in the USA and Europe

In a number of countries where Muslims are a minority there have been significant developments in women's participation in rituals and leadership positions. In the USA, where according to a 2009 Gallup poll[32] attendance of mosques by Muslim women (but not necessarily for ritual prayers) almost equalled that of men, a women-only 'mosque' was established in 2015 by the Women's Mosque of America organization in Los Angeles. This was the outcome of decades-long Muslim women's discussions and awareness-raising events set against the perpetuation of patriarchal and hierarchical social practices among Muslim communities in the USA. One expression of such practices was the almost universality of male-dominated mosque governance.[33]

The Women's Mosque of America, instead, is women-focused as well as women-led. It is not located in a purpose-built mosque, but is a place of worship reminiscent of the original Arabic meaning of *masjid* as 'place of prostration'. This mosque has a provisional physical space, at first in an interfaith building in Los Angeles, more recently in its Koreatown district where once a month a female congregation gathers for Friday prayer. Prayer rituals are officiated by women; a woman calls the *adhan* (in different recitation styles according to the specific training received), one delivers the *khutba* (or as at times specified, the pre-*khutba* or *bayan*) and leads prayer. Sermons are usually available via virtual streaming and *adhan* can be listened to on Soundcloud or iTunes. It is a welcoming and inclusive communal space and experience, where relevant social, health, legal and other issues are openly discussed after the sermon and prayer by the congregants sitting in a circle with the *khatiba*. The mosque's *khatiba*s and imams come from diverse heritage and ethnic backgrounds; some are academics and educationists, others professional lawyers, doctors, scientists, businesswomen, entrepreneurs as well as social and human rights activists; most of them are in employment and, at the same time, directors, executives or members of NGO organizations, as well as being active in public speaking at interfaith events, peace initiatives, projects against racism and so on. They include born-Muslim and 'reverts' to Islam.

At a *jum'a* prayer I attended in April 2019, the sense of female solidarity was palpable and underlined by the oft-repeated assertion, by the congregants I spoke to, of feeling comfortable and at ease in a 'safe' place where theological and ethical issues were illustrated and explained through examples from personal experience which all the women present could relate to. In some respects, this was more like a combination of a *jum'a* prayer and a spiritual-communal circle. The *jum'a* was performed according to the traditional format, with a sermon which included praise to Allah, invocation, exhortation and recitation of a Qur'anic *sura* followed by the performance of Friday prayer. What followed the *jum'a* was at once an informal study circle and an exchange of personal narratives and experiences which were relevant to the topic covered by the *khatiba* and the Qur'anic *sura* selected.

Inclusivity at this mosque was expressed in various ways: by the *jum'a* being open to Muslim and non-Muslim women, by the shared reading of a Qur'anic passage with each participant in turn reading a verse, by the open dress code, with some women wearing the *hijab* and others choosing not to, and the opportunity to be informed about and become part of specific awareness projects and fund-raising events benefiting people irrespective of their religious identity.

The Women's Mosque of America positively and un-controversially affirms that it 'complements existing mosques, offering opportunities for women to grow, learn, and gain inspiration to spread throughout their respective communities'.[34] Similar to other women's mosques, it is perceived as addressing the need by Muslim women for direct access – and connection – to religious leaders and as responding to the poor state of facilities for women in some American mosques, as well as to Muslim male attitudes towards women's attendance of mosques.

The first *khutba* delivered in English on 30 January 2015 by Bosniak American community spokesperson Edina Lekovic is revealing of the context from which the initiative emerges. Lekovic clarifies that the mosque is a proactive affirmation of Muslim women's ownership of their own faith, not intended to be in competition with, but to supplement, existing mosques. She tellingly emphasizes the legitimacy of a women's mosque: it is not unique, there being other mosques like it in various countries, some of them having been in existence for centuries (i.e. in China). Like other women's mosques, it 'offers the opportunity to gain intellectual ownership of Islamic teaching where women are active and they are asking questions and this is a return to the golden age of Islam'.[35] The reference to the golden age of Islam is to the time of the Prophet. More specific scriptural references in Lekovic's *khutba* point to the role model of Umm Salama, whom, she states, queried the Prophet about divine revelation not being explicitly addressed to women. This is believed to have prompted the revelation of verse 35 (for Muslim men and Muslim women, believing men and believing women . . .) in *sura al-Ahzab* (Qur. 33.35). Harking back to Umm Salama's precedent shows that the reclamation of a woman's voice is nothing new, it is 'not a departure from our tradition as Muslim women, it is a continuation of the proud legacy of Muslim women'.[36]

By repeatedly sanctioning the legitimacy of the Los Angeles based Women's Mosque through references to scripture and the paradigmatic function of Islamic sacred history, Lekovic pre-empts possible counter-arguments of breaking with tradition and the consequent imputations of *bid'a*. Though similar arguments have been used to dismiss the validity of an all-women congregation and female leadership, responses to the Women's Mosque of America have been in fact much more varied and nuanced. They included outright support and a gained sense of female empowerment, critical reflection on possible implications for Muslim women's equal right to spaces of worship, as well as strong politically based allegations of the Women's Mosque feeding into anti-Islam Western narratives.[37]

In Europe, activist and imam Sherin Khankan, founder of the Mariam Mosque, which she established in 2016 in Denmark, has launched a more assertive challenge to the patriarchal layers present in traditional interpretations of Islam. To name the mosque after Mary, the mother of Jesus, whom Khankan calls 'the mother of religions' and whom she sees as a figure who 'unites and protects where there is no hope or light'[38] is significant in several ways. It reflects the inclusive nature of the mosque, the inter-faith dialogue it promotes and the inter-faith marriages which are celebrated there.[39] The figure of Mary, bridging Judaism, Christianity and Islam, has also been seen by some modern scholars analysing Qur'anic narratives which identify Mariam as belonging to the House of 'Imran, as providing a female genealogy alternative to the patrilineal Abrahamic descent.[40] The choice of the name could also echo the association of Mary with prayer, including prayer leadership, which stems from interpretations of Qur'anic passages about Mary.[41] Moreover, it alludes to Khankan's upbringing in a Muslim-Christian household and the bi-cultural identity of growing numbers of children of interfaith marriages in today's Europe as well as Western converts to Islam. The Mariam Mosque celebrates the role that a few Muslim scholars, above all Ibn al-'Arabi, one of Khankan's inspirational masters, give to Mary as a Prophet (*nabi*).

With a Western university education and Syrian qualifications, Khankan, inspired by the writings and activities of the likes of amina wadud and German *shaykha* and *imam* Halima Krausen, supports a feminist interpretation of the Qur'an. Khankan asserts a gender-neutral understanding of ritual leadership by recalling that the original requirement for the role of imam was that of knowledge.[42] The female imams of the Mariam Mosque, which is permanently located in a building block in Copenhagen, need to have completed full bespoke training and have acquired various qualifications from both Western universities and Islamic colleges. They lead prayer from the middle of the congregation. Confident of her own familiarity with Prophetic *hadith*s and Islamic legal arguments in favour of female *imama*, Khankan is able, through scripture, to provide evidence to her community and the general public of the legitimacy of women leading women in prayer. The Mariam Mosque also received support or endorsement from some prominent male imams such as the imam of a *jami'a* mosque in Indonesia and by non-Muslim leaders. In its own dedicated premises, the Mariam Mosque has a women-only access policy during Friday prayer 'not ... to exclude men, rather to avoid unnecessary controversy'.[43]

The aim of the Mariam Mosque is also to provide a platform for dialogue and the promotion of an inclusive vision and spiritual understanding of Islam. As in the case of the Women's Mosque of America, its very existence is explained in terms of being a more conducive space for discussion among women and for a more direct access to the (female) imam. It is also a space of study where the Qur'an is read as being relevant to today's world and where it is possible to challenge its traditional patriarchal interpretations. At the same time, there is a call for a return to the *sunna* of the Prophet. Khankan uses the precedent of Umm Waraqa to illustrate this point: 'If a woman could lead the prayer at the time of the Prophet, she is more than capable of doing it in Denmark in 2016'.[44]

The legitimacy of the Mariam Mosque and the religious authority of Sherin Khankan are contested by some Muslim scholars and leaders who argue that Khankan does not have traditional Islamic qualifications to warrant her claim to be a religious leader. But the strongest opposition to Khankan in Denmark comes from the supporters of far-right movements, as well as some quarters of the media; to have a well-educated Danish woman as a voice of Islam does not conform to the 'Us vs Them' narrative. Nor does it tally with Islamophobic stereotypical identifications of Muslims with terrorists, and Islam with violence, identifications which, some believe, have been further strengthened by international Muslims' reactions against the publication of the Danish cartoons and the ensuing events.[45] On the other hand, media or individuals of different political persuasion critique Khankan's association with foreign heads of state who might use her example of a progressive Muslim European as an endorsement of their own political agendas.[46]

If Khankan's role as imam stems mainly from her academic qualifications and the development of her religious and cultural identities, for Halima Krausen (possibly the first female imam in Germany) it came with knowledge and community experience, as well as her endorsement by Seyed Mehdi Razvi (d. 2013) whom she succeeded. Razvi was Krausen's male teacher and the leader of the Hamburg Muslim community, for whom she had worked for several years and from whom she had obtained an *ijaza* (licence to teach Islamic sciences). Razvi publicly endorsed Krausen, who is addressed as *shaykha* and, officially, she held the position of *imamin* (female imam in German) until 2014. Krausen's tactful approach to the issue of female leadership provides her with a broad consensus among the German-speaking Muslim communities in Germany. She writes *khutba*s, but only proclaims them or leads prayer if the whole congregation agrees. Her authority strongly rests on consensus from her community.[47]

To what extent is the growing presence of women-only mosques a successful example of female religious agency and leadership? Women's mosques can indeed be seen as successful examples when, as in the case of the long-established *nusi* mosques in China, they represent an officially acknowledged location for spiritual education, training and guidance by knowledge and by example. But even such mosques can be defined and shaped by social norms, which limit or stifle the variety of expression and actualization of female religious agency and leadership.

More recent women's mosques in the West are expressions of Muslim women's endeavour to reaffirm the gender egalitarian message of Islam and provide Muslim women with easier and more women-friendly access to religious education and training. When gender segregation is resorted to, with the aim of harmonizing the gender balance of knowledge and debate, it can, nevertheless, create a greater chasm between male and female leaders and their congregations on the basis of not only separate, but diverse, parallel contents, modes and platforms of knowledge and spirituality. Women's mosques or those which are gender-exclusive only for *jum'a* prayer, can indeed be 'empowering and liberating' spaces for Muslim women and, on occasion, for men. The main challenges they face are recognition and legitimacy of authority by the Muslim communities at large and by the representatives of mainstream Islam. For some, they are seen at best as 'temporary solutions' to women's marginalization in mosques.[48] A further challenge is that of political 'manipulation' at the hands of Western media and activists with diverse agendas. Their gender-specific space and programmes also raise the question of whether or not they will eventually lead to greater community integration and to a heightened sense of solidarity and unity within the wider *umma*.

Women's mosques in some Islamic countries and female prayer leadership of women

This section aims to illustrate different configurations of female leadership exercised in contexts which may challenge the traditional identification of the figure and roles of the imam, the bases of her leadership and the link between leadership and space.

There are reports and studies on a number of 'women's mosques' in Islamic or Muslim majority countries that include Indonesia, Malaysia, Senegal, Sudan, Kenya, the Comoro Islands, the Maldives and Somalia.[49] This list might be longer yet. The definition of some of these spaces as women's mosques is somehow ambiguous, as it could refer to places of prayer for women, or where women have access (as contrasted to those attended only by men), or a women's prayer room situated inside or next to a mosque. Women's mosques might therefore be best understood in this section as functional spaces attended by women for ritual and other religious activities, *masjid*s rather than the larger *jami'a*, several of which might have features such as a demarcated *qibla* wall or niche. The two mosques examined here have been chosen because of the greater availability of information regarding the status and roles of their female prayer leaders.

Across the archipelago of the Maldives in the Indian Ocean, where Islam arrived via mainly Sufi sea traders during the 12th century, women's mosques appear as a relatively recent phenomenon. During the late 1970s the state officially recognized them as public spaces and their female leaders, known locally as *mudahim*, became government employees. It is recorded that by 2005 there were over 250 women's mosques in the Maldives. Following natural disasters and national political unrest which led to political change, along with 'religious reform' aligning the Maldives to one interpretative version of the global *umma*, in 2009 the Islamic Affairs Ministry started to close, ostensibly on financial grounds, most women's mosques. By 2018 it appears that female mosques are no longer in existence.[50]

From the modernizing discourse of the 1970s, identifying the government social initiative of constructing women's mosques as a means to let women out of their 'domestic' environment, the official narrative of the early 21st century has changed to affirming that for women the best place to pray is their home.[51] Similarly to the longer acknowledged male colleagues of the Maldivian (male) mosques, the *mudahim* (used to) act as caretakers of the women's mosque, preparing it for prayer and performing the daily prayer; however, unlike their male colleagues in the main mosques, the *mudahim* do not utter the call to prayer. As in the case of the *ahong* of China, there is some ambiguity in the sources about the extent to which the *mudahim* of the Maldives can be primarily viewed as prayer leaders of other women. Empirical research conducted in the late 20th century offers evidence of *mudahim* leading prayer, with some of them associating it to their educational role of instructing other women on how to pray.[52]

Women's mosques in the Maldives have been the object of study by Western scholars, mostly anthropologists. While undertaking their fieldwork, they could observe, participate in and interpret the lived experiences of the *mudahim*. On the basis of her fieldwork in the Maldives, and augmented by historical sources, American cultural anthropologist Jacqueline Fewkes argues against the use of blanket terms such as imam for individuals who live and perform in disparate contexts, as it hides the complexity and the 'heterogeneity of experiences of being an imam'.[53]

In a context such as the Maldives, where Islam is the state religion by constitution (1997, 2008) and the President its highest authority in propagating Islamic doctrine, the mosque and its personnel are inextricably linked to government politics. Both male and female faith leaders or 'imams' of the Maldivian mosques are salaried state employees; neither of them gives the sermon for Friday prayer, as this is the role of the state-appointed *khatib* who reads the weekly *khutba*, the text of which is issued, nationally, by the Islamic Supreme Council, with the stated aim to ensure religious unity across the archipelago. This is one official key to viewing the role of the *mudahim*; however, Fewkes shows another which emerges from the spoken words of her interviewees who talk of the local island context and the community of believers, rather than central government, as the definer of the identity of their mosque and their own status as religious leaders.

Similarly, there are two parallel narratives on the establishment of women's mosques in the Maldives and the authority of their *mudahim*. The state links the existence of the mosques to the 1970s state-endorsed policy of women empowerment through the establishment of local women's committees and, later, women's mosques led by government-appointed *mudahim*. An alternative narrative, propounded especially by older *mudahim*, points to an earlier origin of women's mosques and their female leaders as an expression of the local Maldivian tradition of female social hierarchy and hereditary charismatic leadership. Indeed, some of these older leaders claim that their position of *mudahim* was inherited from their own mothers, who, in turn, were 'leaders' of the local women.[54]

These narratives are an example of contrasting perspectives and agendas and reveal the multiple bases of female leadership: the formal recognition by the state which legitimizes a leadership role as 'custodian' of the place of worship alongside that by the community itself, grounded on local social order and status in addition to personal piety, knowledge and experience. What will happen to the *mudahim* now that the state has closed their mosques and ceased their employment? Will their religious authority continue to be acknowledged by their community? Will the community re-group in alternative locations? Or will they disperse into individuals performing prayer and learning about Islam in the women's sections of the 'other' mosques? Can communities of faith keep their identity irrespective of a physical gathering space, especially in a country where places of worship and their staff are regulated by the state? Or will these communities of faith still exist locally without being defined by official status and recognition? Thus far it is too early to answer these questions given the silence of official sources about the fate of women's mosques and their leaders. The changing fortunes of the women's mosques of the Maldives over the last fifty years show that both the communities of faith and their female leaders have been (are) at the intersection of multiple structures and discourses of identity and authority which developed and adapted to local, national and international contexts.

The fluidity of the relationship between space, identity and leadership can be identified in other instances of women's mosques. One is the women's mosque of Gabiley, in north-west Somalia (now Somaliland).[55] This mosque is another example of the intersection between local and wider contexts impacting upon expressions of gendered ritual space and of religious leadership.

A geographical area which has been exposed to Islam since the 9th century with Muslim traders and preachers settling along its coast, Somalia, with its social clan structure, has long been responsive to the Sufi formulation of Islam and its practices. During the 19th and early 20th century Sufi orders, and the loyalty and authority they commanded, were instrumental in organizing political resistance against successive colonial powers while propounding a message of Islamic revival. Propelled by nationalist ideology, Somalia gained independence in 1960 becoming, under a civilian government, the Republic of Somalia. It was in the aftermath of the 1969 *coup d'etat* by General Siad Barre, who within only a few years was to implement nationalization of industries and widespread literacy programmes, that the building of the women's mosque of Gabiley began.

Female education, specifically religious education, was an important motivational factor for the establishment of the women's mosque in Gabiley. Since independence, negotiations had been conducted between the supporters of the state educational project of massive expansion of secular schools and local religious leaders, who wanted to retain the primacy of Islamic education and maintain gender separation. A compromise was reached in that religious education (only available for boys) was to become a prerequisite for entry into state schools. This meant that girls were left unable to achieve any educational qualifications and hence could not gain access to work and educational opportunities. Moreover, not only were there no religious schools for women to attend, but also the main mosque in the city did not have the facilities to accommodate women's presence for the performance of rituals, for learning the Qur'an or for acquiring religious knowledge. Eventually during the mid-1960s state girls' schools were opened, with Islamic religious education as part of the curriculum, and female teachers of Islam required. One of them, Sheikh Marian, a religiously educated woman originally from the Ethiopia–Somali border area, daughter and wife of *shaykh*s, reached Gabiley, taught Islam at the local elementary girls' school, opened a Qur'anic school for girls and also started teaching Islam to women in the recently created state women's community centres.

In 1970, Sheikh Marian with the local women secured some state funding to build a mosque for women on some land adjacent to the main mosque. It was intended as a separate though contiguous space where women could pray, receive and impart religious education. It was the local women's grassroots response to a lack of religious facilities for them, as well as to the broader reduction over the years of women's social and financial status brought about by urbanization, commercialization and the contradictory legacy of Western colonization. Eventually, some issues relevant to the legal status of women were to be addressed politically, in 1975, with the implementation of a 'progressive' more gender-balanced family law.

It took a relatively long time to build the women's mosque in Gabiley due to scarcity of funds, as local Muslim men would not contribute to the project. In theory the predominant Shafi'i position on women-only congregations would be to prefer group prayer to individual prayer, as well as to consider female prayer leadership of women as legitimate, based on the precedent set by some of the Prophet's wives. Nevertheless, in practice, this position was side-stepped and the reality in Gabiley was that women were not expected to attend the mosque at all but to pray at home.

When the mosque was eventually completed in 1972, with a capacity of 300 congregants, the women asked the imam of the adjacent mosque to allow a door to be opened between the two buildings so that both men and women could pray, separately, while being led by the shared male imam. Upon the imam's refusal, Sheikh Marian was chosen by the women to lead prayers in the women's mosque until such a time as when a door was allowed. She therefore became a prayer leader by community consensus on the basis of her religious knowledge, status and experience. Asserting the right to a space for women's ritual performance and religious education while, at the same time, being willing to comply with religious (and cultural) tradition, Marian made sure that she was positioned slightly behind the male imam next door and performed prayers in unison with the male congregation there. Eventually in 1973 a door was built for access to the adjacent (male) mosque.

The Somali civil war which erupted in the late 1980s damaged both mosques; while the main mosque was rebuilt, the women's mosque was left in a state of disrepair. Despite its current poor state, the women's mosque of Gabiley is still a female religious centre managed by women; it can be hailed, symbolically, as a case of a self-governing women's public space for learning and worship. It is also proof of the extent to which gender space can be contested, and of the need for negotiations to maintain its existence and to have its legitimacy acknowledged. Somali cultural geographer Abdi Samatar, whose publications have brought the case of the Gabiley mosque to the attention of the academic community, reiterates his understanding of the existence of this women's mosque as signalling 'the availability of a progressive Islamic alternative to a Euro-Americacentric view of women's liberation'.[56] Samatar presents Sheikh Marian as prayer leader in two different contexts: the women's centre, where she teaches Islam to local women, and the women's mosque. However, while her leadership at the women's centre is just mentioned in passing, perhaps as he makes the assumption that her prayer leadership was part of her educational activities, her leadership in the mosque, in contrast, he develops into a more detailed narrative, indicating all the steps taken before, during and after its occurrence. The details of these steps seem to serve the aim of presenting the performance at the mosque as neither confrontational towards male leadership in prayer, nor divisive for the community of faith.[57] Indeed, on the basis of Samatar's account, female prayer leadership acquires a heightened social significance, and so potential for contestation, when carried out in the Islamic space *par excellence*: the mosque.

Beyond women's mosques and 'women imams'

As pointed out throughout the previous chapters of this book, the mosque has traditionally served as a multifunctional place, combining, among other things, ritual and educational activities. It is in the context of the latter that we have the reported instance of women who, though not traditionally an 'imam', act as imams under certain circumstances. One example comes from Egypt where, in the mid 1990s, in Cairo's 'Umar mosque, the well-known preacher Hajja Faiza used to give regular religious lessons to women. If the call to prayer was made during teaching, rather than moving to join the male imam, she would complete her sessions and lead the women herself. Additionally, she would regularly lead the *tarawih* prayers in that mosque during Ramadan. When she was criticized by the mosque's male imam for leading prayer, she answered that she was following the majority of legal schools for which it was permissible for women to lead other women in prayer, whereas he was following the minority Maliki position.[58]

Thus, on the basis of her knowledge of legal arguments on female leadership of prayer, she was able not only to articulate an informed response to the imam's remark, but also to turn round his own argument as being a minoritarian one within the fold of Islamic jurisprudence. When knowledge is appropriated, it can indeed become a tool of self-empowerment, in this case used by a woman to justify and assert her Islamic right to lead other women in prayer.

Hajja Faiza is one reported instance of a woman acting as an imam. Within the context of the Egyptian women mosque movement, brought to academic and wider attention by Saba Mahmood, there must be other women who, like Hajja Faiza, act as imam of women during their various religious activities for women at the mosque. Though Hajja Faiza is a respected and well-known preacher, by leading prayer on her own initiative, she was criticized for her actions by an established male imam who questioned the validity of her leadership. By contrast, in another part of the Islamic world, there was an unusual occurrence of women being asked to lead other women in prayer by no less than the state religious authorities.

So, a second example of a woman acting as imam comes from the Twelver Shi'i Islamic Republic of Iran. In August 2000, under the presidency of Muhammad Khatami, there were news reports of a *fatwa* affirming the permissibility of women leading other women in Friday prayer.[59] As far-reaching a ruling as it sounds, nonetheless, the official justification for this *fatwa* was in fact not linked to mosque-based prayers, but to solving the issue of prayers at girls' schools 'to encourage female students to pray and attract them to group prayer'.[60] Hence the women acting as imams would most likely have been the school's female teachers. To my knowledge, there has been no further published evidence about the effectiveness of this *fatwa* and whether it did actually translate into widespread female prayer leadership in girls' schools in Iran or even into a change in women's practices in the mosque.

Women leading other women in prayer is attested in a number of different contexts, including in Islamic educational institutions (*madrasas*, seminaries etc.) where Muslim women attend religious seminaries, such as for example the Indonesian Islamic boarding schools known as Pesantren. As part of their religious training and also while teaching, female seminarists are reported to have led other women in prayer.[61] Other occasions for female leadership of women are the more frequently recorded cases of women acting as imams of women for *tarawih* prayers during the month of Ramadan and in family contexts, all of which are considered legally permissible, as already discussed in this book.

Though outside the thematic boundaries of this book, it is worth adding here a brief reference to other expressions of female religious leadership exercised in Muslim minority countries, particularly in the West. This is because the women in these positions fulfil some of the expectations and roles associated with being an imam, occasionally acting as prayer leaders. In many cases authorization to act as faith leaders is not officially or formally given by the Muslim community, nor by one of its (male) representatives, nor by a specific Islamic institution.

The example provided here is that of Muslim chaplains, who are usually associated with counselling, ritual-religious leadership and doctrinal instruction in conjunction with hospitals, prisons, schools, the armed forces and universities. While the majority of Muslim chaplains today are male, there is an increasing recorded presence of significant numbers of female chaplains, especially working in prisons and universities. In a 2013 overview of Muslim chaplaincy in the UK, Sophie Gilliat-Ray noted that there was a gender difference in training, as well as in some specific roles, between male and female Muslim chaplains. While at the end of the 20th century Muslim women became chaplains through experience gained from previous relevant social or community work, younger chaplains in the 21st century need to have completed some form of chaplaincy training.[62]

Significantly, when referring to Friday prayer, the gender gap widens as, for instance, female prison women chaplains were found not to be much involved in the organization or preparation of *jum'a* prayer, or did not attend it at all, ostensibly because 'according to most interpretations of Islamic law, it is optional for them [i.e. for female Muslims attending *jum'a* in a mosque or public space]'.[63] As one female prison chaplain put it: 'as far as we were taught, women don't have to partake in congregational prayer'.[64] Despite such an assumption of the expected gender roles among several members of Muslim communities in the UK, there are instances of some female prison chaplains having both organized and led *jum'a* prayer for a female congregation.

Female chaplains have become quite creative in circumventing perceived ritual limitations to their role, as is the case with American university chaplain Marwa

Aly, who herself writes the text of the Friday sermon but has it delivered by one of her male students as a way of training and coaching them.[65] One wonders how far this perpetuation of ritual gender roles will go uncontested among her female students!

Being employed by secular or state institutions such as prisons, hospitals and universities that appoint their staff on the basis of qualifications allows qualified Muslim women to gain a religious leadership role as female chaplain. Thus they overcome the authorization that they would have needed to be the 'official' representatives by established Muslim community leaders or community religious institutions.[66] Despite the assumption of restrictive roles for women chaplains in some ritual activities, the role of chaplain appears to open up various opportunities of ritual performance for women, from uttering the *adhan* to a new-born in hospital, to writing a sermon for Friday prayer, or public recitation of the Qur'an.[67] It is indeed the case, as in the words of Gilliat, that 'chaplaincy roles are often empowering for women; they grant them religious authority and recognition that would be otherwise hard to achieve'.[68]

Types and forms of congregational prayer in the multifarious expressions of Islam are not limited to *salat*, i.e. the obligatory prayer performed five times a day by Sunni Muslims and usually three times by Twelver Shi'is. Similarly, as already seen earlier in this chapter, female prayer leaders are not limited to those commonly referred to as 'imams'. As a final example of the various expressions of female prayer leadership of other women and its link to the configuration of ritual space, we move to an Isma'ili *jama'at khana*.

For Nizari Isma'ilis, a community without a state of its own, scattered across continents, the 'prescribed obligatory ritual prayer in Arabic'[69] is the *du'a*, which is recited three times a day in congregation, usually in a community house of worship called *jama'at khana* (lit. 'house of assembly'). For scholar of religion Tazim Kassam, the Isma'ili *du'a* 'occupies a functional status similar to that of the obligatory ritual *salah*'.[70] Because of the esoteric nature of teachings behind ritual practices, there are a number of interpretations that can be provided of the same ritual, thus Isma'ilis might refer to *du'a* also as a *tariqa*-specific supererogatory prayer.

In the *jama'at khana*, male and female leaders, appointed by the Isma'ili Imam as his representatives, preside over the daily ritual prayers for a congregation of men and women seated in distinct but adjacent areas in the same prayer hall, with no physical barrier between them.[71]

The female leaders are referred to as *mukhiani* and *kamadiani* and the male leaders are called *mukhi* and *kamadia*. Traditionally, the *mukhiani* and *kamadiani* were the wives of the *mukhis* and *kamadias*; however, increasingly, their role has developed into acquiring a status in its own right. The *mukhi*, who is considered the first amongst equals and serves as the master of ceremonies, can usually call upon anyone in the congregation, male or female, to lead prayers for the entire congregation. For other rituals performed in *jama'at khana*, women would usually interact with the *mukhiani* and *kamadiani* while men would approach the *mukhi* and *kamadia*.[72]

For the Isma'ili community, to have a woman in ritual and religious positions of leadership is not an innovation but one of the identifiers of religious identity stemming from the guidance of the Isma'ili Imams and recorded in their shared written and oral religious history. From a legal point of view, we saw in Chapter 2 that the most famous Isma'ili jurist, al-Qadi al-Nu'man, had argued in favour of the legitimacy of women leading other women in prayer. It is unclear when this legal position actually translated into female ritual leadership in practice. In the modern era, the 48th Isma'ili Imam, Sultan Mahomed Shah (d. 1957) (Aga Khan III) made use of modernist gender-inclusive discourse, yet still located it within the Islamic context when, addressing Muslim women in Pakistan in 1953, he clearly set priorities for women's fight for their rights. He stated: 'First of all you [i.e. Pakistani women] must win the right to prayers, then win your right to equality in production, industrial service and in office work'.[73] In that same speech he equated the right for women to attend prayer in congregation in 'public' (i.e. in the mosque) with a first step for women to assert their self-respect and self-confidence and as the 'foundation of religious equality' on which to build other forms of equality with men.[74]

For his own community, Sultan Mahomed Shah began a wide-ranging reform programme in the fields of education, jurisprudence and ritual. The latter saw the start of a systematization of ritual practices to be shared by all branches of Isma'ilis across the world as well as of the *du'a*, now fully in Arabic instead of in vernacular languages, with the aim of consolidating a 'pan-Isma'ili identity'.[75] For his educational reform, he encouraged families to prioritize their daughter's education in case of financial hardship.

In the footsteps of his grandfather, the present Imam, Prince Shah Karim al-Husayni (Aga Khan IV) continues to develop for the community a pan-Islamic and pan-Isma'ili identity with gender-inclusive ritual practices and support for female leadership and participation in governance at different community levels. New developments in religious education policies since the 1970s mean that religious training has been open to Isma'ili women at various levels, from religious teacher for school children to a post-graduate level *wa'iza* (religious instructor) trained through the currently named Isma'ili Tariqah and Religious Education Board.[76] For Isma'ili women as well as men, the International Waezeen Training Programme has provided, over the past two decades, a structured 'blended learning' model of formal lectures and research, with fieldwork in communities, youth groups and schools. All this with an emphasis on support work for teachers, pastoral care and translating religious doctrines and practices to present-day contexts.[77] As far as prayer is concerned, in addition to the religious leadership role of *kamadiani* and *mukhiani*, in Nizari communities the public recitation of daily ritual prayers and the *tasbih* are performed by women as well as men.

Though for the majority of legal Islamic schools female prayer leadership of other women is permissible, in legal terms, most scholars would define it as a 'disliked' action. Most of the aforementioned examples of women leading a female congregation have shown, in different guises, how such a 'dislike' is expressed and articulated. This can take the form of theological or textual challenges to the practice on the part of established scholars; a *de facto* reduction in the traditional educational curriculum or training opportunities for female leaders-to-be in comparison with those available for male leaders; a limitation of their permitted rituals and fields of activity; or the lack of recognition of individual competence and religious qualifications. Nevertheless, in various geographical areas and in particular circumstances, female imams, as well as women in a temporary capacity as prayer leader, have been able to rise to the challenge and exercise their leadership by negotiating its extent and form, carving out for themselves a more fluid leadership role and adapting the spatial locus of their activities. What all the above examples of female prayer leaders of women have shown is that female agency is indeed historically, geographically and culturally specific and that its most effective articulation is by adaptation, rather than subversion of the cultural and social norms.

Some current cases of women imams of mixed congregations

When it comes to female imams of mixed congregations of men and women, in view of the majority position of non-permissibility to lead prayer, adaptability becomes the essential tool for them to exercise their agency and gain lasting visibility. The opposition by both scholars and ordinary Muslims to women leading men in prayer has been so widespread, and the tone so fierce, and at times even threatening, that ritual events and individual performers have had to adopt security measures in order for them and their congregants to be protected. The physical landscape where prayer leadership is performed is thus more fluid and varied than for women imams of women, with numerous pop-up 'mosques', only a few of which are used on a weekly basis, and more often temporary and make-shift prayer rooms. The spiritual landscape is inhabited by a good number of female imams, of different ages, levels of religious education, status and origins. Some of them are well-known through the media, in very few cases shaped by it, in others resisting pigeon-holing. There are also female imams who lead prayer but are not defined by this ritual role alone. In fact, rather than imams, many would rather define themselves as Muslim faith leaders, spiritual seekers, religious professionals, scholars, *'alimas*, academics, preachers, and human rights and gender justice activists. Female *imama* can indeed be a charged expression and some prefer to use more neutral terms. These women leaders and the communities they represent, or are part of, are usually labelled as being progressive and inclusive. In the eyes of their detractors, however, they are illegitimate self-appointed imams, inconsequential representatives of fringe groups, or even Western-backed agents of 'secular imperialism'.

A towering figure: amina wadud

Several women have acted as imams of mixed congregations over the last few decades, particularly since the mid-1990s, in countries as varied as South Africa, Canada, the USA, India and in a number of European nations. Some of them are more well-known than others due to media coverage and online presence, such as Ghazala Anwar, Nakia Jackson, Yasmin Shadeer, Raheel Raza, Pamela Taylor and Laury Silvers.[78] Of all of them, the one who has most influenced modern debates about female leadership for mixed *salat*, who has more successfully included her ritual performances within her broader Islamic theological elaboration of gender justice and who has inspired and influenced the activities of gender-inclusive and civil society initiatives and organizations throughout the world, is amina wadud. Her multiple identities as an Afro-American woman, a Muslim convert, an internationally recognized authoritative and critical Islamic Studies university professor, a social and gender justice theorist and activist, a woman and a mother, inform her theological arguments, social engagement and activities.

The two defining events associated with her are the delivery in 1994 of a *khutba* at Cape Town Clermont mosque and her leadership of *salat* to a mixed gender congregation at St John the Divine cathedral in New York City in 2005. The 11 year gap between the two events is significant in that it shows that the public prayer leadership had been long pondered and was the culmination of careful elaboration and dissemination of the underlying principles of theological, legal, social and ritual gender justice. Between 1994 and 2005 amina wadud refined and developed her use and application of Qur'anic hermeneutics from a woman's perspective as first formulated in her book *Quran and Woman* (1992). These she developed in subsequent publications as well as through media engagement. Her formulation of the Islamic scriptural basis for social and gender justice came to a head with the publication in 2006 of her monograph *Inside the Gender Jihad*.

With the insight of decades of experience and scholarly research, amina wadud argues for the egalitarian foundations of Islam by means of what she presents as the '*tawhidic* paradigm'.[79] She explains that '*tawhid* relates to relationships and developments within the social and political realm, emphasizing the unity of all human creatures beneath one Creator'.[80] While Allah is one, unique and transcendent, Allah's creatures are in a mutual relationship of horizontal reciprocity, in a condition of parity with one another. Consequently, she argues, the status of being creatures removes any differences of race, gender or class, the only distinction being that which relates to individual piety or moral consciousness (*taqwa*) (Qur. 49.13). In practice, the *tawhidic* paradigm when applied to everyday life and social interaction would dissolve all gender limitations, including those in the public and ritual spheres.

wadud's reading of the Qur'an does not stop at the literal meaning but seeks to identify the principles informing the words of revelation, the divine wisdom behind the word. Her hermeneutic process is similar to that used in the legal field of the *maqasid al-shari'a*, which move from the level of the written laws and regulations on to identifying the mutual benefit informing those laws, and reach the level which finds the overall principles and basic beliefs underlying those laws and regulations. For wadud, the main principles informing the Qur'anic revelation are those of justice and compassion. It is no accident that, upon conversion, she chose the name wadud, one of the attributes of Allah with the meaning 'loving God of justice' or 'the all-loving'.[81] Her exegesis of Qur'anic verses directly relevant to women such as on marriage and divorce is therefore one of an egalitarian reading based on the principle of gender justice, which denounces the injustice of hierarchical and patriarchal textual interpretations.

In the context of the South African social justice movement, just a few months after Nelson Mandela's election as President in 1994, amina wadud gave a sermon in Cape Town. The content was 'Islam' as surrender, which she explained as being a proactive 'engaged surrender' rather than just a 'submission' and which she illustrated through the experience of pregnancy and childbirth. For the mother, carrying her child for nine months becomes one act of surrender to the will of Allah, as does giving birth with the mother's acceptance, through submitting to the contractions, to 'let go'.[82] In an unprecedented articulation of the meaning of being Muslim, amina takes a woman's experience as normative in the discourse on Islamic identity. To this topic all women listening to the *khutba* could easily relate, as shown by their resulting feeling of self-empowerment. However, in the debates that followed the event, rather than the content of her sermon, what received most attention was her role as *khatiba*, sermon deliverer, for a mixed congregation.

The 2005 prayer performance in New York, during which amina wadud delivered the sermon and led from the front both men and women in Friday prayer, had been preceded by the online publication of Reda's article on women imams and some media coverage. No mosque could be found that would host the prayer event, and because of death threats, the location had to be changed three times before it was finalised as the Synod House of the Episcopal Cathedral Church of St John the Divine in New York City.

The *khutba* for the New York prayer was more extensive and complex, included numerous Qur'anic passages and was delivered mainly in Arabic, followed by English translation. Its main theme was the principle of *tawhid*, the oneness of the Creator and the unity of human beings in their common origin from a single *nafs* ('soul', 'being', Qur. 4.1). The Qur'anic verses amina wadud recited, including 33.35, 'For Muslim men and Muslim women, for believing men and believing women ...' provided evidence for and illustrated the horizontal reciprocity of the *tawhidic* paradigm and its gender symmetry. Another expression of gender symmetry was the use wadud made of both female and male pronouns when referring to Allah, selecting 'She' when dwelling on the divine attributes of Mercy, Love and Forgiveness. As a sign of additional inclusiveness, wadud also used 'It' as a gender neutral pronoun for Allah.[83] Her action of leading prayer in front of a mixed congregation is therefore one visible, performative and public aspect of the affirmation of the equality among creatures, and, within the framework of the *tawhidic* paradigm, any exclusion to ritual leadership on the basis of gender would be seen as, at the very least, arbitrary and unfounded.

The New York prayer was extensively covered by the media, with some journalists present at the event, prompting numerous responses, in print and online, about the issue of female prayer leadership. It had been planned and endorsed by more than one group, including the Progressive Muslim Union, now defunct, an association then representing diverse Muslim voices with the common goal of social justice for Muslim communities. amina wadud consciously refrained from becoming a participating tool in the media frenzy that followed the prayer, and soon distanced herself from the Union while continuing to support other Muslim progressive initiatives, such as the NGO Sisters in Islam.

Another means of implementing the *tawhidic* paradigm has been for wadud to apply it in practice to the field of Islamic law, thus challenging cases of gender injustice and discrimination resulting from patriarchal textual interpretations. In 1988, with six Muslim women, wadud co-founded 'Sisters in Islam', a civil society organization based in Malaysia, with the aim of promoting women's rights on the basis of the principles, enshrined in the Qur'an, of equality, justice, freedom and dignity, and by so doing be able to 'empower women to be advocates for change'. In their online mission statement, Sisters in Islam affirm the need for Muslim women's participation 'as full and equal partners in the *ummah*'s socio-economic development and progress' and they 'conclude that it is imperative that the female experience, thought and voice are included in the interpretation of the Qur'an and in the administration of religion in the Muslim world'. As if to pre-empt any possible accusations of innovation (*bid'a*), they grounded these aims in the precedent of the normative past and state, 'We are inspired by the active participation of women in public life during the time of Prophet Muhammad ... Biographical collections devoted to the Companions (*Sahabat*) of the Prophet included the biographies of over 1,200 female Companions. Among them were transmitters of *hadith*, saints and Sufis, martyrs, liberators of slaves and heroic combatants'.[84] Inevitably, an accusation was made via a 2014 *fatwa* by one of the members of the Malaysian state Islamic Religious Council declaring that Sisters in Islam and other 'liberal' organizations 'deviate from the teachings of Islam'.[85] In 2019, the High Court in Malaysia then dismissed the appeal against the *fatwa* on the grounds that the ruling was not in the jurisdiction of the Civil Court but of the Syariah Court (religious Shari'a court).

wadud subsequently led other mixed congregational prayers, by invitation, in Europe, for instance in Barcelona (2005), in Oxford (2008) and in London (2015). The angry opposition that followed the New York prayer has not abated. Threats continue against her personally and against her supporters. She has had to take security measures and, a full ten years after the New York prayer event, death threats against her were caught on camera by a TV crew. The meanings of *jihad* discussed in Chapter 3 in relation to women ritual leadership acquire a personal, painful contemporary relevance.

wadud's legacy cannot be underestimated; her ritual leadership as well as the content of her academic and broader arguments within the framework of social and gender justice gave rise to debates, still-ongoing, on the permissibility, extent and significance of female leadership and female authority in Islam. Such debates took shape in the form of online discussions and publications, scholarly works and specialist studies. For the general public, her gestures and interviews raised awareness of the variety of voices within Islam and greatly contributed to general public discourse about Islam and gender. amina wadud's engagement with Muslim communities and with small- or large-scale organizations in various parts of the world gave endorsement to numerous projects and community events. Directly or indirectly, her arguments and actions became a significant precedent to take inspiration from for Muslim individuals and groups to further their own goals and activities. Her stature as a modern Muslim female religious leader will be hard to replicate.

Female imama *as inclusive ritual leadership*

Inclusivity in ritual prayer leadership is one of the main expressions of the founding ethos of a number of gender integrated prayer spaces – mosques in a wider sense of the term – throughout the USA, Canada, the UK, South Africa and other countries. There, women can lead the Friday mixed congregation from the front, as well as calling to prayer and delivering the sermon. Two such mosques are the Canada-based El-Tawhid Juma Circle and the London-based Inclusive Mosque Initiative (IMI); for both, inclusivity goes beyond gender binaries: acknowledgement of and support for shades of gender identities is explicit in their mission statement, and gender fluidity is welcome at both leadership and participant level.

In a country with a relatively small percentage of Muslims (ca 3.5% of population), many of whom migrated from South Asia, East Africa, the Arab world, Iran and other countries where they were facing political or religious persecution, Muslim Canadian female voices are a reflection of ever-changing communities with mixed conservative and progressive voices. An example of the latter, El-Tawhid Juma Circle was founded in 2009 by Islamic studies academic Laury Silvers and human and gay rights activists El-Farouk Khaki and Troy Jackson as 'a gender-equal, LGBTQI2S affirming mosque, that is welcoming of everyone regardless of sexual orientation, gender, sexual identity, or faith background'.[86] The *tawhidic* paradigm as elaborated by amina wadud is here translated into a prayer space where 'diversity and inclusivity are celebrated'. The El-Tawhid Juma Circle is a faith community travelling mosque with no dedicated permanent location.

Similarly, the Inclusive Mosque Initiative (IMI), established in 2012 in London, UK, by two young Muslim women, welcomes people 'regardless of their religious belief, their race, gender, impairments, sexuality or immigration status'.[87] Its fortnightly *jum'a* prayers, held in a multi-faith space in central London, are attended by predominantly young Muslims in their 20s and 30s, of diverse denominations, and non-Muslims alike; prayer performance alternates between Sunni and Shi'i rituals and imams and *khatib*s reflect gender diversity and include women. A member of the mosque management team, after consultation, draws up a rota of imams on the basis of availability, but also to reflect balance in gender and denominational representation.

Prayer leadership is not only about performance itself but can also become performative, that is, it can change perceptions and effect change for an individual or a group. On the IMI website, a blog features a telling emotional testimony about attending *salat* led by a female imam as a 'life-affirming' experience. From a male point of view, prayer in gender-integrated rows may also become a liberating experience as it can remove the perception of 'impurity' from sitting next to a woman. amina wadud is an undeniably inspirational figure for IMI members and participants. She features as principal speaker in activities and annual lectures co-organized by IMI, her Qur'anic interpretation is regularly mentioned in some of the *khutba*s delivered during *jum'a* prayer and her understanding of the *tawhidic* principle of horizontal reciprocity of all human beings transpires in the understanding of leadership as not being 'about authority or greatness but about being mirrors of one another'.[88]

One of the IMI founding members explained the need for an inclusive prayer space on the basis of her experience of marginalization or rejection in the mosques she had previously attended. The historical precedent she provides for this Islamically validated inclusivity is the Prophet's mosque in Medina, at the very heart of the early Muslim community. It is seen as featuring the normality of a family context, with the Prophet's grandchildren moving around while the adults were praying and where, on the basis of scholarly interpretation, there appears to have been no gender segregation.[89] The mosque in Medina is thus given as the reference point for the actualization of a 21st century 'mosque' initiative in the heart of London.

The *jum'a* prayers I observed during 2018–20 were attended by mainly Muslim students and some young professionals.[90] They were local or coming especially for the prayer, from other cities in the UK or from Europe, as well as visitors from India, the Emirates, Pakistan, Turkey, Iran and other Islamic countries. Participants and observers from other faiths or of no faith were also a regular presence at the *jum'a* prayers. The calls to prayer were also delivered in British sign language. *Khutba*s were varied in their contents and format, and always included exegesis of Qur'anic passages, whether by past (Ibn al-'Arabi) or present scholars (wadud, Asma Barlas), or individually argued on the basis of personal experience and with examples from current news and debates. Qur'anic recitation was often delivered in Arabic and followed by English translation. *Hadith*s were also referred to and used as evidence in the *khutba*, with some *khatib*s showing critical awareness of debates about their historicity or reliability. The variety of Islamic *fiqh* was also the topic of a *khutba* to illustrate the diverse positions regarding, for instance, ritual practices. The choice of topic here was made not only to illustrate diversity within Islamic jurisprudence but also to celebrate the legitimacy of diversity (and inclusivity) within Islam. It is an implicit critique to the literalism and absolutism of some modern expressions of political Islam. Other *khutba*s featured personal experiences by the *khatib* / *khatiba*, including examples of gender, racial, or other forms of discrimination, as well as inspiring recollections of individual spiritual journeys of identity and reconciliation. At an online *jum'a* during the Covid-19 lockdown, the topic of the *khutba* was solitude and retreat, and was illustrated by relevant narratives about the Prophet and about female figures in the Qur'an.

Some of the female imams at IMI have been featured in the British media, with frank, well-informed and non-confrontational statements, yet with a firm stance on addressing and fighting social and gender injustice. In the words of *imama* Asma Bhol, to lead Friday prayers felt natural but also made her feel empowered in a role which was the expression of consensus among her community.[91]

A more radical stance against conservative understandings of Islam is that of Seyran Ateş a lawyer, human rights activist of Turkish-Kurdish descent and female imam, who founded in 2017 in Berlin a mosque named – significantly – the Ibn Rushd-Goethe mosque.[92] Though living six centuries apart, Ateş presents Ibn Rushd and Goethe as exemplars of free thinking, as deeply spiritual and yet critical minds through whom philosophy met theology, and who, through their works and ideas, represent a bridge between East and West.[93] The mosque has a dedicated location in a part of the building of the Sankt Johannes Protestant Church, and is inclusive, welcoming Muslims of various denominations and non-Muslims.

A picture of its inaugural Friday prayer in June 2017 appeared on a number of news sites showing a male and a female imam leading prayer in front of a congregation of men and unveiled women side by side in the same rows. It provoked strong online reactions, including an 'indictment' by the Egyptian Dar al-Ifta' (a government centre for legal research, charged with issuing legal opinions) which asserted the invalidity of prayer of women and men in the same row, denied the legitimacy of female leadership of men and concluded with the full rejection of 'liberal mosques' (*al-masajid al-libraliyya*).[94] The use of such a neologism to indicate this type of mosque betrays the Egyptian jurists' deliberate effort to present it as an expression of discontinuity with the Islamic past. The public statement by the Dar al-Ifta' against female prayer leadership of a mixed congregation is no surprise. As we will see later on in this chapter, a few months later, as a response to a query about the permissibility of a woman leading women in prayer, the Dar al-Ifta' posted a *fatwa* on its official website stating that while it is permissible for a woman to lead other women in prayer, provided she does not lead from the front, it is not permissible for women to lead men. Moreover, to have a prayer row of mixed gender is 'scandalous' and a cause of corruption.[95]

Politics, both national and international, play a strong role in the criticism of the Ibn Rushd-Goethe mosque. Some Turkish newspapers ridiculed the location of the mosque and launched a scathing personal attack on Ateş, accusing her of being a Kurdish supporter of the Gulen movement. While some Muslim spokespersons acknowledge that this gender inclusive mosque represents a need for reform within Islam, especially in terms of gender equality, they question Ateş' claim to authority and warn against the use that Western politicians and media make to press their agendas of supporting a form of 'liberal Islam' which more closely reflect their own values.[96]

Contemporary arguments and debates on female imams of men

Since 2005, when amina wadud led the New York mixed prayer, debates on women leading prayer have extended from specialized scholarly and academic circles into broader spheres. Only a sample can be surveyed here which is deemed representative of some of the main perspectives adopted in these responses. In a number of instances, academic, theological, political or human rights approaches overlap. In a fast-moving world where the news is constantly updated and events announced and analysed even before they take place, amina wadud's prayer leadership in New York on 18 March 2005 had been preceded by an article written by a then

PhD candidate, Nevin Reda and published on 10 March 2005 on the website 'Muslims Wakeup!' Beside the build-up to the event, staged by the Progressive American Union and other groups, Reda with her article helped to pave the way to build a scholarly basis leading to a potential congregation to consent to wadud's leadership. The reaching out to create a platform for the event was further asserted by journalist Mona Eltahawy, who announced and covered the event in the *Washington Post* on the same day it was due to take place.[97]

Nevin Reda's argument in support of women leading mixed prayer had already appeared online in January 2005 and was then uploaded again on another site just before amina wadud's prayer.[98] In it, Reda uses textual and contextual hermeneutics of the *hadith*s already analysed in the present book to argue that there is no explicit prohibition of women leading prayer, either in the Qur'an or in reliable *hadith*s, hence dismissing *hadith*s such as Abu Bakra's. She focuses on the Umm Waraqa *hadith*s, interpreting the congregation she led as being mixed, inclusive not only of the muezzin and the male servants of the household, but enlarging her understanding of the term *dar* (Umm Waraqa led the people of her *dar*) to mean 'locality, area'. As already mentioned, Reda thus argues that Umm Waraqa was appointed by the Prophet as the imam of a new mosque, in addition to that in the Prophet's home, a 'second mosque' with her as imam of her area. To provide a legal basis to this female prayer leadership, Reda focuses on the arguments of the (now extinct) early Sunni schools which permitted women to lead prayer unrestrictedly and concludes, questionably, that 'in medieval Islam, many men supported the leadership of women'.[99]

Reda also responds to a series of objections and statements by contemporary Muslims against female imams, such as accusations of being influenced by Western feminist values, lack of education or training in Islamic sciences, issues of innovation (*bid'a*) leading to *fitna* and issues of female ritual impurity. Reda concludes the article by appealing to a return to Allah as source of wisdom and by rejecting what she considers to be a blind and uncritical imitation of past scholars and ancestors. Despite some naïve and out-of-context assertions, Reda's article does present a multifaceted argument, which was to become influential even when it was the object of criticism.

Arguments against a woman leading men in prayer

Less than a month after the New York prayer on 5 April 2005, a collection of *fatwas* and legal opinions on the topic of women leading prayer was published online claiming to 'represent a consensus amongst contemporary Islamic and Muslim legal scholars on this specific issue' and with the aim of 'guiding Muslims to the right path'.[100] The use of the consensus (*ijma'*) tool is meant to reflect the authoritative status of these opinions. All the contributors are Sunni Muslims, all arguing, on slightly different grounds, against the female leadership of mixed congregation in *salat*. Contributors include *shaykh*s and *mufti*s from prestigious Islamic universities such as al-Azhar, as well as scholars with both Western and Islamic university qualifications.

The only female contributor is academic and *fiqh* specialist Hina Azam, University of Texas at Austin, who critiques Nevin Reda's argument on the basis of what Azam sees as a flawed methodology in her legal argument. For Azam, Reda's interpretation of the texts leading to her assertion that women could lead men in Friday prayer violates not only several authoritative and authentic sources, but also well-established interpretative principles. Azam contends that the textual sources used by Reda cannot be interpreted as supporting the permissibility of a woman leading Friday prayer, but only of leading men in two very specific circumstances: first, for a woman (like Umm Waraqa) to lead her own male kin in her own house, if she is the most knowledgeable among them; and second, for a woman to lead men in non-obligatory prayers in the absence of a man who knows the Qur'an (as allowed by some legal schools). Therefore, female leadership of men is only limited to these two cases and cannot be extended beyond them.

Azam thus asserts that leading prayer falls under matters of worship (*'ibadat*) and cannot be modified, but instead must be carried out 'as the Prophet did'. Though acknowledging the alienation Muslim women may feel as a result of substandard provisions for women in mosques, Azam concludes that this cannot lead to a violation of 'the sanctity of our *ibadat*'.[101] Azam's critique goes into further detail and it is included here as an example from a female Muslim scholar specializing in Islamic jurisprudence with special reference to legal cases specific to women.

A number of scholars have analysed the arguments presented in the above-mentioned *Collection of Fatwas*, and among them I have selected those of Elewa and Silvers.[102] Elewa and Silvers grouped the critical positions in the collection into three main categories: those based on legal consensus whereby the majority of classical scholars agreed against the legitimacy of women-led mixed prayer; those based on modesty issues, repeatedly voiced by Egyptian Qatar-based scholar and media religious expert Yusuf al-Qaradawi, according to whom a woman imam would arouse men's instincts; and those based on what they term as 'default state', that is the assumption-premise that female leadership is not permissible.

Elewa and Silvers, who are themselves in favour of unrestricted female leadership, respond to each of those positions with the support of classical or contemporary scholarly arguments or examples of practices. On women's modesty, they provide alternative textual interpretations of the *hadith* on the best rows for women and suggest that modesty can be maintained by keeping gender separation in rows and by having the female imam leading from the front located out of the direct sight line of the men. About legal consensus, they question the equation of majority position with consensus. Unanimity for them is out of the question given the examples of dissenting classical scholars such as al-Muzani, al-Tabari and Abu Thawr, even if their schools are now extinct. Finally, Elewa and Silvers indicate that the default position is in fact that ritual obligations are inclusive of women, unless stated otherwise, and quote Ibn al-'Arabi's *Futuhat* to support the legitimacy of unrestricted female prayer leadership. In a conciliatory move towards those who reject the legitimacy of female leadership, Elewa and Silvers acknowledge their underlying concerns for the preservation of unity and the well-being of the *umma* as a whole.

With reference to *hadith*s, most contributors to the *Collection of Fatwas* would concur that the Umm Waraqa *hadith*s are weak, and that even if they were not, they would not be used as precedents for Muslim women at large because they are time-bound and circumstantial rather than normative. However, al-Qaradawi differs from this shared opinion, based on Ibn Qudama, that the Prophetic order for her to lead prayer would have been peculiar to Umm Waraqa alone. Al-Qaradawi argues that, if some conditions are met (a woman's knowledge of the Qur'an), women could indeed be prayer leaders of women and men for *salat* or *tarawih* prayers, but only if within the domestic sphere and not leading from the front so that their modesty would be maintained.[103] By contrast, other scholars in the *Collection*, for instance Shakir, understand that Umm Waraqa led a women-only congregation.

The issue of gender justice, though not fully elaborated, is not lost to some scholars, as seen before with reference to Hina Azam's argument. The overarching consideration, however, is not to aim at individual or gender liberation, but rather to achieve spiritual goals which, as Shakir puts it, would avoid confrontation, and people would 'come to embody the spirit of mutual love ... encouraged by our Prophet'.[104]

Fear of divisions within the *umma* resulting from the woman-led prayer event is indeed a concern shared by several scholars writing in the *Collection of Fatwas*. Among them, with regard to wadud's leadership, al-Qaradawi appeals to American Muslims to stand united against 'conspiracies' and states: 'I also advise my Muslim brothers and sisters in the United States not to answer this stirring call and to stand as one in front of these trials and conspiracies woven around them'. Zaid Shakir is rather more outspoken when he states that 'non Muslims ... seek to exploit the situation to create confusion among ... the Muslims as to what Islam is, and who its authoritative voices are'.[105] This last reference to identifying legitimate religious authorities for modern Muslims could be rather ambiguous. On the one hand, it implies that the writers in the *Collection of Fatwas* present themselves as constituting those authoritative voices, varied but still united in their position against unrestricted female leadership of prayer. On the other hand, by Zaid Shakir's own statement that he had structured his paper as a response to the essay in a Progressive Muslim webzine by Nevin Reda, Shakir is in fact indirectly acknowledging Reda with a degree of authority that would have been unthinkable less than two decades earlier, in a pre-web world.[106]

The 2005 New York prayer performance resulted in several *fatwas* on the topic of female prayer leadership throughout the Islamic world. Among them, in Indonesia, the country with the world's largest Muslim population, the Indonesian Scholars' Assembly issued one in 2005 declaring the leadership by a woman of a mixed congregation as being *haram*. The reasons they provided to evidence this opinion were all based on *hadith*s except for one which referred to 'consensus' among the Companions about the lack of precedence of such an occurrence. Significantly, the first *hadith* cited is that of Umm Waraqa, hence a potential contradiction to such a lack of precedence. However, the scholars interpret it to mean that the Prophetic command for her to lead prayer was limited to her family only, and, presumably, that it was also situational and specific to her alone. The

Assembly also decreed that a woman's leadership of a female congregation is permissible.[107]

Arguments in favour of women imams of men

A number of male Muslim scholars, leaders and activists have spoken out in support of women leading men in prayer. Their positions vary from acknowledgement of its permissibility under certain circumstances to unconditional support. Among the latter is Abdennur Prado, activist and Chair of the International Congress of Islamic Feminism. In his immediate response to the New York prayer performance by amina wadud, he stated that prayer led by a woman for a mixed congregation is permissible 'so long as the congregation agrees to it.' To which he added, 'We agree'.[108] For Islamic law and human rights academic Khaled Abou El-Fadl the response came five years after the New York prayer in the form of a *fatwa*. In it, his emphasis is on identifying the imam with the person who possesses greater knowledge, irrespective of gender, thus concluding that 'a female ought not be precluded from leading *jumu'a* (Friday prayers) simply on the grounds of being female'. The condition, however, is that men are not placed behind her, but on her side.[109]

On similar grounds, the controversial Sudanese politician Hassan Turabi (d. 2016) appeals to the primacy of religious knowledge as the basis for prayer leadership. Turabi illustrates this by referring to the precedents of Umm Waraqa, who he said led men and women of her household, and of 'A'isha who was more knowledgeable than most men and who, Turabi states, led prayer at the front.[110] Finally, hailed as one of the most influential Muslim personalities of France, Algerian former Grand Mufti of Marseille Sohaib ben Cheikh has thus far been the most prominent Muslim religious scholar to have joined in 2006, upon his request, a *salat* prayer led by a female imam.[111]

A male Muslim voice, Jamal al-Banna

Of these Muslim male advocates, one stands out as the only one thus far to have actually written a whole book in support of female-led prayer of a mixed congregation. He is the Muslim Egyptian intellectual, activist and trade unionist Jamal al-Banna (1920–2013). The younger brother of Hasan, who was the founder of the Muslim Brotherhood, Jamal wrote within three months of amina's leadership event in New York a monograph titled *The Permissibility of Female Prayer Leadership of Men (Jawaz Imamat al-Mar'a li'l-Rijal)*. In it, he provides an informed, clearly articulated, supportive, heartfelt response, hailing amina as a courageous individual who entered the mosque from the front door and 'shattered the stone of fear',[112] and as a symbol of much-needed reform within Islam. For al-Banna, amina's action is an opportunity to show that Islam can reform itself without following the Western path; he argues that all the negative reactions to her leadership mask the fact that the main issue at stake is not prayer leadership, but that of 'woman'.

Therefore, in his book, Jamal al-Banna examines the issue of female *imama* as an example of the masculine bias pervasive in the Islamic world through its established scholars past and present. Al-Banna states that he wrote the book out of a sense of duty and fairness towards womankind. He envisages an Islam with a 'new *fiqh*' informed by the guidance of the Qur'an to establish 'a society of values of freedom, compassion and strength for all the people'.[113] In that society female leadership of men will no longer be seen as a problem.

Al-Banna (re)introduces an 'original past' freed from patriarchal accretions, which he believes were added by the *various 'ulama'* and *fuqaha'* (jurists) who were reflecting the ideas and practices of their patriarchal society. He provides an even stronger, unequivocal criticism of the modern jurists who deny the validity of female *imama* as being imitators (*muqallidun*)[114] of 'the past' with no personal interpretation, intellectual engagement, or use of God-given reasoning (and use of it through *ijtihad*). He is able to see through the *fuqaha*'s shared argument that female *imama* is a form of innovation, which leads to dissent and the breaking up of the unity of the *umma*. He examines classical, mostly Sunni, writers as well as current religious authorities such as the then Grand Mufti of Egypt 'Ali Jum'a, al-Qaradawi, and Muslim American *fuqaha'*. Of the Grand Imam of al-Azhar, Muhammad 'Ali al-Tantawi (d. 2013), al-Banna quotes an interview which, he believes, shows what he sees as a deeply rooted idea among Muslim scholars past and present: the 'inferiority' of woman. Al-Banna identifies another recurrent opinion: that things, to be acceptable, need to remain as they have been 'since the appearance of Islam'.[115]

For al-Banna, critics of amina and deniers of the permissibility of female leadership of prayer perpetuate a long-established patriarchal misreading of the Qur'anic message. He distinguishes between the Islam of the Qur'an and the Prophet, which affirmed on several occasions the equality of men and women, and what he calls '*salafi fiqh*', or the 'jurisprudence of the ancestors', which expressed and reflected patriarchal values and practices.[116] He contrasts the rigidity of the past, frozen by the imitators who repeat the words of the past with no reference to the present or future needs of society, with the fluidity and inclusivity of the Qur'anic message, which anticipated universal values of justice, gender equality and democracy. Al-Banna refers to the ideal time of the Prophet, when women had rights, could lead prayer and be involved in warfare, but which came to an abrupt end when the 'textualists' (*al-nususiyyun*) started to select some fitting passages and 'lock' others out. The concept of good innovation (*bid'a hasana*) which was present during the Prophet's time was replaced by the dogma that any innovation constituted an error resulting in hellfire.[117] Al-Banna does not reject the past *per se*, but rather the one he sees as an ossified, stagnant and sterile past as re-constructed by the 'imitators'.[118]

With his mixture of idealism, pragmatism and reformist ideas, Jamal al-Banna was both a thinker and activist of his own times. His ideals of progress and reform reflected the intellectual milieu of the Egyptian and Arab intellectuals of the early decades of the 20th century, alongside his rejection of alien (i.e. Western colonial) role models. However, such a rejection seems to be only partial, still imbued with ideas such as the 'backwardness' of Muslim society and patriarchal Arab thought contrasted with the 'egalitarian' American society and reformist 'evangelical'

Christianity which allows female priests. His progressive approach does not appear to have been affected by post-modern critiques of the evolutionary progress of society, of binary categories of gender, or by successive waves of feminist ideas. He does not seem to acknowledge or accept that the concept of gender equality (*musawa*)[119] needs to be qualified and contextualized, and that it is not universally envisaged or supported by Muslim contemporary scholars, whether male or female. But his response is well-evidenced, frank, incisive and passionate. It is an example, as yet little-studied, of stimulating critical argumentation on the subject of female ritual leadership.

Jamal al-Banna was a controversial but well-respected figure during his lifetime, and, since his demise, he is still hailed as a reformist progressive feminist voice of Islam, who supported free speech and opposed the opinions of the religious establishment, who in turn not only condemned his world-view but also banned his books.[120] His numerous books in Arabic remain untranslated into other languages, including his monograph in support of women imams, which consequently had a limited impact beyond the Arabic speaking Islamic world. However, his understanding of the use of *ijtihad*, or individual independent reasoning, to adapt Islamic *fiqh* to the modern times, as well as his 'revivalist humanism' are increasingly studied, particularly in Indonesia. His call for a reform of Islam and his feminist ideas continue to be featured in Western media and be analysed by academics, especially in the USA.[121]

Uses of the past in contemporary debates

While for the first part of this book the sources used to present or infer arguments in favour or against women acting as imams were overwhelmingly scholarly (exegetes, jurisprudents, theologians, historians, and mystic philosophers), for this second part on the modern and post-modern era, i.e. the 'present', sources and arguments are much more varied. They include scholars of different levels of training and qualifications, female imams, experts, state-trained or home-schooled preachers, political activists and reformists, local authorities, government officials, as well as online or media female voices such as i-preachers, who appear to be somehow detached and freed from a physically visible gendered body and space.

As the arguments put forward by Jamal al-Banna have shown, the past is still very much drawn on with the aim of giving evidence to the legitimacy of the various arguments or positions. The past, though presented as fixed and normative, is in fact dynamic, elastic and flexible, and can be used for contrasting arguments. In some cases the past is revived, remembered, selectively forgotten or imagined, yet it is rarely ignored. The actors and authorities involved in this debate overwhelmingly invoke, to different degrees, their 'perfect past' to reform what they believe to be an imperfect present. Depending on their background, experience and level of knowledge, they use the past following one or more of these methods: scriptural exegesis, precedents from tradition / custom and national or local recent history and legal opinions.

Scriptural exegesis remains the most authoritative method to support any appeal to the past. The Qur'an, as the eternally present divine guidance, is cited as *ad hoc* evidence for a practice or argument. A Moroccan *'alima* explains that women cannot lead men in prayer on the basis of Qur. 2.228, 'and men have precedence over them [i.e. wives]'.[122] The context of the passage referring to wives and husbands, rather than generic women and men, is (deliberately) overlooked. Yet, as far as female political leadership is concerned, the Qur'an (27.23–44) does also refer to the Queen of Sheba as a female ruler exercising both authority and power, in consultation with her Council of Elders. And several scholars and preachers concur that nowhere in the Qur'an is there any prohibition for a woman to be a prayer leader.

A second way of recalling the past is made by harking back to precedents, usually taken from *hadith* narratives on the life of the Prophet. The Prophet's wives, or his Companions, become the foremost exemplars of past practice in the case of women leading women or, as for Umm Waraqa, leading, for some, a mixed congregation. However, even agreed-upon notable precedents might not be sufficient evidence in favour of women imams: after all, the Prophet's wives, on the basis of the Qur'an (33.32), are not like any other woman, so their precedent might not be universal. However, the same is made to apply also to the Companion Umma Waraqa, whom the Prophet ordered to lead prayer.

A very popular, and seemingly more 'convincing' resort to the past as a means of argumentative proof is, in fact, a lack of precedents and hence the branding of some practices as innovation. Academically, this method opens up issues of historical memory, of selectivity of sources, context and time span. We examined in this book the modification of narratives, or the assertion that they were no longer relevant or applicable.

The past is not necessarily temporally or geographically fixed, but may become more localized and recent than was traditionally the case, with the aim of resonating to a specific audience. For a religion of universal appeal, missionary impetus and wide geographical spread like Islam, prior examples of female ritual leadership are not exclusively confined to the precedents of the early centuries of Islam in Arabia or the Near East.

In Central Asia, for instance, Islam spread along trade routes thanks to merchant-cum-missionaries who became knowledgeable of, by interacting with and reinterpreting, local traditions. Stories of male and female 'saints' are to this day a very common religious and ethical pedagogical tool. For instance in the fertile Ferghana valley, where Islam has been a significant religion since the 9th century, female faith leaders, known as *otyncha* or *otun*, lead women in *salat* and *tarawih* prayers,[123] and narrate stories of local female saints during special celebrations they lead. On Tuesdays, celebrations take place of the popular (Sufi) saint Bibi Seshanbe (i.e. 'The Lady of Tuesday'). The story is told and re-enacted of a harassed young orphan girl who meets Bibi Seshanbe praying with a group of women in a cave, finds refuge and support with her and eventually marries a prince. As a sign of gratitude, the girl initiates thanksgiving rites on Tuesdays in honour of Bibi Seshanbe.[124] The story of Bibi Seshanbe retold in a female communal prayer, set in a secluded space, is re-enacted in the celebrations with the presence of elderly women and a young girl. It serves not only to glorify the example of a pious and generous female saint, but also to legitimize the female congregation and the role of the communal female Tuesday rituals. It can also be interpreted as validating the role of the *otun*s as religious authorities who organize, lead and perform both ritual and narrative.

Another instance of the use of recent, localized, even 'national' past as evidence to oppose female prayer leadership is that made by the Moroccan Fatwa Council. The Council is reported to have supported a 2006 edict against the permissibility of women leading prayer by specifying that 'it has not been shown either in the history of Morocco, or by Moroccan scholars, that a woman has ever led men or women in prayers in the mosque'.[125] Therefore, one could infer that the time span of 'the past' has shrunk to the existence of Morocco as a nation state and the sources to Moroccan scholars. Significantly, the Council added the location of prayer leadership, a mosque, presumably in the modern accepted meaning as a designated building, hence excluding leadership in the home or non-institutional spaces. The 'national' past reference is also a political statement of the religious authority of the Moroccan Fatwa Council itself. What the Council eventually explained is that female leadership in prayer is historically contrary to the Maliki position, which is the predominant legal school in Morocco and the one the Council itself represents.[126]

This introduces a fourth authoritative resort to the past by means of legal precedents and opinions. This is often presented in terms of consensus, as implicit in the Council statement above, where the expression 'Moroccan scholars' alludes to a consensus of all the Moroccan scholars consulted. In fact, consensus is difficult to achieve in practice, or to historically evidence, as seen in previous chapters of this book. There might be political and theological agendas to invoke consensus as a signifier of cultural specificity, national identity and unity against *fitna*, as in the case of Morocco and its predominant Maliki legal school.[127] However, in different parts of the world, especially as a result of wider access to online *mufti*s, the relevance of allegiance to one *madhhab* over another is dwindling or decreasing, to be replaced by *ad hoc* case by case preferences.

With pressing political or social agendas, the past can be authoritatively retrieved and shaped by a state leader or government apparatus, who thus forge a local-national precedent of a 'recent past'. In 2003, for instance, a seminal year in Morocco for the implementation of a long-awaited gender egalitarian reformist programme in family law and religious instruction, King Muhammad VI invited Dr Raja Naji Mekkaoui, a university female academic in jurisprudence from Rabat University, to deliver the Ramadan lecture at the mosque of the royal palace. In front of Moroccan state officials and international Muslim clerics, she justified the reforms on the basis of Qur'anic evidence of gender equity. Dr Mekkaoui was, shortly afterwards, to become one of the actual implementers of gender equality as part of the Ministry for Islamic Affairs educational programme on female preachers or *murshidat*.[128] The royal endorsement of a female scholar lecturing in front of male authorities became a newly forged precedent for the official acknowledgement of the legitimacy of female authority. In subsequent years more female scholars were invited to deliver similar lectures. Such legitimacy is further heightened by the constitutional status of the king of Morocco as 'Prince of the believers' (*Amir al-Mu'minin*).

Specifically related to female prayer leadership, the New York prayer performed by amina wadud is by far the most cited example of a recent past used as precedent by current female imams to legitimize female ritual leadership. The authority on which this precedent rests is, in this case, embodied in the academic and theological stature of wadud, her ability to engage with Islamic scripture and tradition from a woman's perspective, as well as the reach of her work and activities. This is quite a novel type of religious authoritativeness if compared to the one of established and traditionally trained scholars of institutional bodies such as the Moroccan Fatwa Council or the Dar al-Ifta' of Egypt.

Like individuals, institutions are subject to change due to political, financial and other pressures. They respond and adapt to current debates, and so does their use of the past. We saw earlier in this chapter that, within days of the online release of pictures of the female-led mixed congregational Friday prayer at the Ibn Rushd-Goethe mosque in Berlin in June 2017, the Egyptian Dar al-Ifta' responded with an online 'poster-like' assertion rejecting female leadership of men, gender-mixed prayer rows and 'liberal' mosques. It was a statement for a wide audience that was sending a clear unequivocal message.

A few months later, in response to a query addressed to the Dar al-Ifta' about the permissibility of women leading women in prayer, the *mufti* (jurist issuing *fatwas*) provided a full *fatwa* (legal opinion) that was uploaded on the official site of the Dar al-Ifta'. This is an informed, nuanced, multifaceted response, which, to the discerning, can be open to varied shades of interpretation. The text follows the format of a traditional legal opinion, providing a selection of scriptural references, especially from *hadith*s, interspersed by the jurist's assertions, and then concluding with a statement which reveals the opinion of the jurist.

On the evidence of the *hadith*s provided in this *fatwa*, the names were at last spelt out of those women of the normative past who were reported as having led prayer, names ready to be known and used as precedents. They were those names that we have brought to the fore, analysed, scrutinized, contextualized and interpreted throughout this book! And the same names were emerging from *hadith* versions that other jurists in the past had stopped using. From the *hadith*s cited in the *fatwa*, it emerges that 'A'isha and Umm Salama led women in the obligatory prayer, that Umm Waraqa, by order of the Prophet, led in prayer the men and women (*ta'ummahum*) of her family. There is even a mention of the *jariya* of Ibn 'Umar.

Almost as an implicit response to the by-now exposed patriarchal readings of scripture, the *fatwa* opened with selected Qur'anic verses and *hadith*s. It is then stated that 'there is no gender difference between men and women in terms of the desirability of the congregational prayer and the *imama* of a woman is legal and recommended or desirable ... this shows that women are equal (*mustawiyat*) to men in terms of the preference of the congregational prayer'.[129] Moreover, the *fatwa* asserts that female leadership of women is part of the *sunna*, that it was never abrogated, and that it is legitimate and permissible on the basis of the Prophet having 'ordered' Umm Waraqa to lead prayer.

One can read the *fatwa* as revealing a position of conditioned and limited acceptance even of the legitimacy of a woman leading men in prayer on the basis of the evidence of Umm Waraqa. The 'people of her *dar*' she led included men as well as women. This is a conditioned legitimacy which restricts this mixed congregation to the people of Umm Waraqa's house (*bayt*), which is how the *mufti* understands the *dar* in the *hadith*. But, beyond this case, the general assertion in the *fatwa* is that it is not permissible for a woman to lead a man.

But in this fast-moving world, how many people will have read (in Arabic) the whole *fatwa* with its numerous scriptural references and the variety of possible interpretations? If one simply looks at its last few lines, the answer to the query about female leadership is clear enough: it is legitimate for a woman to lead other women, as long as she leads them from the middle, because it is preferable for her to be concealed, enveloped by them. A woman cannot lead men and the mixing of men and women in the same row is 'scandalous'.[130] So, with all the possible nuances as illustrated by the *hadith*s contained in it, this *fatwa* reveals that its writer, while using language which echoes current concerns with gender justice and while providing a nuanced and moderate response to the legitimacy of female prayer leadership of women, is also keen to maintain gender separation in ritual. It also shows that the engagement with the past is an active one, and that those references, or others, are open to interpretation. Most importantly, it shows the ongoing relevance of debates about women as imams.

Conclusion

This chapter has analysed modern developments in female prayer leadership not only through the theoretical debates about the theologico-legal permissibility for a woman to be an imam, but also through specific living examples of women who are leading prayer and who interpret, justify, negotiate and adapt their own understanding and exercise of such a leadership.

The main developments that have been identified across the diverse examples here presented are centred around the expressions of such a leadership, as well as its reach. We have encountered women who are employed to be imams and whose role is to run a mosque to various degrees of autonomy, be it financial or managerial. The *nu ahong* of China are leaders in their dedicated space, whose roles might be as comprehensive as those of a male imam. They may lead prayer and perform other religious rituals, preach, teach, collect and manage funds and train future leaders. Some other *ahong* might be teachers and performers of some rituals, but not of Friday prayers, and the mosque management might be shared with a male imam.

We also encountered women who act as imams as a result of specific circumstances like Sheikh Marian in Gabiley, Somalia, who started as a religious teacher and who became by female community consensus an imam of women when the local imam refused to acknowledge a female space of prayer. The ways in which female leadership is exercised are therefore contingent upon local contexts, cultural, communal as well as political conditions as we saw in the cases of women's mosques in China and the Maldives where the state confers legitimacy, while, to some extent, also *de facto* acknowledges the religious status already given by the community to some women.

The reach and influence of such female ritual leadership is defined by both space and faith community, the mosque where women are leaders, and the community they represent and lead, but also by their status in the broader male and female Muslim local or national communities, and in wider society. This might be quite localized to an island in the Maldives, a village in Somalia, a school in Tehran. On the other hand, for female imams, whose performance is made public through the media, as in the case of amina wadud in New York, the imams of the Women's Mosque of America or Seyran Ateş in Berlin, the reach and influence is beyond physical borders; such exposure, however, may also lead to more widespread criticism and rejection. In some extreme cases this exposure has resulted in acts and threat of violence against these women because of their determination to reclaim the ownership of their spiritual and physical spaces in performing an act of piety.

As for the reach to Muslim faith communities and individual believers, female leadership, especially in its expressions of inclusive mosques in the West, resonates not only with Muslim women but also with gender-fluid believers. Moreover, it appeals to those with multiple cultural and national identities (Mariam Mosque of Copenhagen) and those adhering to varied formulations and ritual practices of Islam in the same congregation (ritual variety in IMI, London) as it provides a regular sense of belonging to a polychrome *umma*.

The assessment of women-only mosques from the point of view of women's empowerment, gender equality and inclusivity is more complex than was assumed. Indeed women's mosques, whether in countries that sit at opposite ideological, political and cultural spectra, like China and the USA, represent gendered spaces. These spaces are a statement of female agency and empowerment, especially in the face of commonly held assumptions that lead to restrictions for women in accessing mosques and being involved in their governance. For a woman to be on a mosque's board of governors, for example, is still quite a remote prospect in the West, let alone in Islamic countries.[131] At the same time, women's mosques can be seen as perpetuating or validating gender separation and the implicit acceptance of the arguments on the association of women with *fitna*, whereby for a mosque to be a woman-friendly, woman-affirming and a safe 'sanctuary', it has to be gender-exclusive (i.e. to exclude men).

The chapter has also shown, through the various examples of women leading prayer, that geographical, historical, social and political contexts do matter in order to understand the ways in which female imams exercise their leadership and how they justify it. One example, as we have discussed, is that of the Chinese *nu ahong*. Similarly, the context of post-modern Europe with its multi-cultural multi-faith societies shapes the discourse of inclusivity presented by Danish imam Khankan who names her mosque after the 'interfaith' figure of Maryam and appeals to Umm Waraqa to legitimize her status as a female imam. As Khankan succinctly puts it: if the Prophet, recognizing the ability of Umm Waraqa to lead prayer, ordered her to do so, why would this not be applicable to an educated pious 21st century Muslim woman? This leads to a final consideration on the extent to which modern scholarly articulations of arguments, particularly those by women imams themselves, differ from those of past scholars. Both of them seemingly use the same sources, i.e. the Qur'an, *hadith*s, *tafsir* and classical scholars, to support their opinions on the permissibility of women imams. Both select the most apt and relevant verses, *hadith*s and passages to evidence their own opinion.

However, there are at least three main differences between past and present interpreters and their arguments.

The first is about the interpreters themselves: the scholars we analysed in the first part of this book were traditionally trained exponents of an elite class, representing the status and privileges of their own position, they had an extensive knowledge of exegetical tools, of Arabic, and of a variety of classical sources, and most were affiliated to one legal school. Some modern scholars are still trained in famed Islamic religious institutions, which have themselves undergone changes due to historical and political developments. While many of those whose views are included in this book might be very well-known experts, preachers and academics, they might not have the traits or qualifications of a traditional *'alim*, a religious expert. They may not have trained in well-recognized and widely acknowledged Islamic institutions; they might, instead, hold degrees from Western universities or from little known Islamic seminaries and institutions based in the West. Their philological ability to interpret primary sources might be limited. And they might not necessarily identify with one *madhhab*, but have a syncretic approach to Islamic jurisprudence. But the main difference between present interpreters and past scholars are the newcomers to the debate: the women imams themselves.

The second difference is the intellectual, academic and religious-theological milieu in which the arguments are being elaborated. Modern expressions of Qur'anic exegesis, inclusive of neo-conservative, Islamist, humanist and feminist approaches, have affected the articulation of arguments; at times individual scholars or interpreters explicitly uphold and support those approaches. And in the case of women imams, those arguments might be put into practice and expressed through performance of the very prayer leadership being discussed. We saw amina wadud reclaiming the Qur'an as the primary source of authority in Islam, and championing Qur'anic hermeneutics based on the principles of gender and social justice which, in turn, support her activism and prayer leadership. To some extent, wadud and other female imams become part of the very narrative about female prayer leadership, as references or precedents in the wider debate not only on the permissibility of female prayer leadership, but on the basis and justification for its occurrence.

The third difference between past and present arguments is the reach of their audiences and the means to achieve that reach. Scholarly and academic audiences are reached by academic publications and lectures. Local communities of faith are engaged by attending prayer performances and activities. The above can be in electronic or physical form. But news coverage by traditional and social media has reached a far greater audience of global proportion, comprising Muslims as well as non-Muslims. In some cases online publications are clearly targeted to an audience of Muslims living in the West, and there are differences in presentation and content in websites in different languages.

Wider and diverse audiences do not necessarily have sufficient educational, cultural or faith grounding to enable them to position the fragmentarily reported statements in their original contexts. They might not be in a position to engage critically with the material being published or uploaded. This leads to responses and reactions which, behind the screen of anonymity or the use of pseudonyms, contain strong and divisive statements. These real-time emotive responses, by circulating uncontrollably, create pockets of resentment or support which propagate content, giving it a life of its own, and that exacerbate polarization without any chance of finding resolution. The latter is due to a lack of any space – real or virtual – for genuine exchange and objective confrontation of different ideas.

In turn, especially for individuals at the receiving end of criticism, there is an increased awareness of justifying statements, and eventually one's right to hold opposing views. For women imams this leads to repeated statements about their legitimacy. In these cases, appealing to past precedents has become a constant of every event, performance, *khutba*, speech uploaded and streamed.

In this chapter we saw that debates on the legitimacy of female prayer leadership are taking place in diverse and ever-enlarging spaces. They are voiced by scholars, by experts and by persons with varied backgrounds and competence. The position in favour of women leading other women in prayer seems to have gained ground among some Muslim scholars, as expressed by the *fatwa* of the Dar al-Ifta', but to have lost ground among others, as seen by the fate of women's mosques in the Maldives and China. The position in favour of women leading men in prayer is still confined to a minority.

Debates by their very nature never abate, because they capture the ever-changing moods of society without an outright winner or loser, but result in fluctuating and reversible outcomes of 'majority vs minority views'. Whenever a majority tries to prevaricate, minorities have always found ways to respond, defend themselves and even subvert opinions and practices. For good or bad, until recent times these processes were within the control of humans who, notwithstanding all their limitations, were in charge of their own destinies. Today that control is in danger of being increasingly delegated to an algorithm. The more the current debate on female *imama* becomes owned by social media, the more likely it will be an algorithm that decides what constitutes Islamic past, *bid'a*, *fitna* and precedent for social media users. Control of algorithm-based media is what will sway and mobilize Muslims and non-Muslims in favour of or against female *imama*. The exegetes, jurists and historians examined here were the 'algorithms' of their own time in the way in which they shaped opinions but also reacted in consonance to the moods of their contemporaries.

The topsy-turvy history of the debates explored in this chapter and in the book as a whole, with all their contradictions and reversals of fortune, gives us a glimpse of the complexities to come in keeping track of the discussions on female *imama*. It is the ephemeral, fragmentary, and often unsubstantiated nature of the online sources feeding into current and future debates, along with the power of whoever is in control of these sources, that will determine the future of the views on female *imama* and the way in which these views will be recorded.

Notes

1 Scott-Baumann, Alison and Sariya Cheruvallil-Contractor. *Islamic Education in Britain: New Pluralist Paradigms*. London: Bloomsbury, 2015, 63–5, findings of the Muslim Faith Leader Training Review Project.

2 In the Islamic Religious Community in Austria (IRCA) Constitution, the imam is defined as a: prayer leader, preacher, sermon writer, reciter, prison chaplain and being involved in interfaith dialogue and other social and legal issues; IRCA, 1979, §20 cited in Kroissnbrunner, S. 'Turkish Imams in Vienna'. In *Intercultural Relations and Religious Authorities: Muslim in the European Union*, edited by W. Shadid and P. van Koningsveld. Leuven: Peeters, 2002, 204 note 28.

3 See for example in Turkey where in the hierarchy of the Diyanet (state Directorate of Religious Affairs), the status of prayer leader is lower than that of other state religious functionaries like *mufti*s, preachers, and Qur'an teachers. Hassan, Mona. 'Women Preaching for the Secular State: Official Female Preachers (Bayan Vaizler) in Contemporary Turkey'. *International Journal of Middle East Studies* 43, 3 (2011): 456.

4 See for example various interviews with Halima Krausen ('more than anything else the role of imam is about being a counsellor') and Sherin Khankan ('the essential part of being an imam or an imama is to serve the people of the community') in IEMed Barcelona, interview, 2018, www.youtube.com/watch?v=10Ix50yJAzs. Chakanetsa, Kim. 'Women Leading Muslim Communities'. *The Conversation*, BBC World Service online, radio interview with Halima Krausen and Sherin Khankan, 2 April 2018, www.bbc.co.uk/programmes/w3cswp16 (accessed 13 June 2020).

5 Scott-Baumann and Cheruvallil-Contractor, *Islamic Education in Britain*, 66–7. For similar conclusions in the American context, Şenses Ozyurt, Saba. 'Bridge Builders or Boundary Markers? The Role of the Mosque in the Acculturation Process of Immigrant Muslim Women in the United States'. *Journal of Muslim Minority Affairs* 30, 3 (2010): 295–315, esp 298.

6 Vinding, Niels Valdemar. 'Churchification of Islam in Europe'. In *Exploring the Multitude of Muslims in Europe*, edited by Niels Valdemar Vinding, Egdunas Račius and Jörn Thielmann. Leiden: Brill, 2018, 59–64.

7 On the basis of questionnaires I distributed in the UK in 2018 to Muslim and Christian university students, academics, Christian ministers and pastors, Muslim activists and imams, the response to the question 'How would you define/describe what an imam is' for all Muslim participants was 'a prayer leader' while for the majority of Christians was a 'spiritual leader' or a 'religious leader', or even 'an Islamic minister' or 'Islamic priest' thus replicating the role of priest with which the participants were familiar.

8 Respectively: Hummel, Ulrike. *Female Imams in Germany: The Call of the Muezzin Women*. 2008. https://en.qantara.de/content/female-imams-in-germany-the-call-of-

the-muezzin-women (accessed 4 September 2019), article in German, the article states, in passing, that the woman interviewed in fact does not lead prayers as [leading Friday prayers] 'is a task reserved for her male colleagues'; and Halici, Nihat. 'Female Imams in German Mosques Get a Mixed Reception'. *Deutsche Welle*, 7 October 2006. www.dw.com/en/female-imams-in-german-mosques-get-a-mixed-reception/a-2195419 (accessed 13 June 2020).

9 Katz, *Women in the Mosque*, 4–6.
10 Cieślewska, Anna. *Islam with a Female Face: How Women are Changing the Religious Landscape in Tajikistan and Kyrgyzstan*. Krakow: Ksiegarnia Akademicka, 2017, 145–7, where women would gather in the female section of the mosque, only to be eventually refused access by the mosque imam due to his opposition to what he considered to be non-Qur'anic practices performed by women during the celebrations.
11 For the 2009 prohibition for Muslim women to go to mosques in Bukhara, see *Ferghana*. 'Uzbekistan: Women in Bukhara are Prohibited to Go to Mosques'. *Ferghananews.com*, 17 August, 2009. http://enews.ferganews.com/news.php?id=1324 (accessed 13 May 2019).
12 Cieślewska, *Islam with a Female Face*, 122.
13 For Turkey see Kreuter, Kiron. 'Turkey: Women Want Equality in the Mosque'. *Deutsche Welle*, 10 November, 2011. www.dw.com/en/turkey-women-want-equality-in-the-mosque/av-6656710 (accessed 13 June 2019); *Side Entrance: Photos from Mosques around the World, Showcasing Women's Sacred Spaces*. https://sideentrance.tumblr.com/ (accessed 13 June 2019), which invites people to post pictures of women's spaces in mosques; and directories of Women Friendly Mosques such as the 2010 UK based Faith Matters. *Developing Diversity: Meeting the Needs of Muslim Women, A Directory of Mosques in England*. Faith Matters, 2010. www.faith-matters.org/images/stories/publications/Developing_Diversity.pdf (accessed 13 June 2019).
14 For Saudi Arabia, see Le Renard, Amélie. 'From Qur'anic Circles to the Internet: Gender Segregation and the Rise of Female Preachers in Saudi Arabia'. In *Women, Leadership, and Mosques: Changes in Contemporary Islamic Authority*, edited by Masooda Bano and Hilary Kalmbach. Leiden: Brill, 2012, 109–10; for Indonesia, Van Doorn-Harder, Pieternella. *Women Shaping Islam: Reading the Qur'an in Indonesia*. Urbana and Chicago, IL: University of Illinois Press, 2006, 90–1.
15 Ratbil, Shamel. 'First Mosque for Women in Kabul'. *Deutsche Welle (DW)*, 9 February 2006. www.dw.com/de/erstemoschee-f%C3%BCr-frauen-in-kabul/a-1890595 (accessed 2 November 2018); allegedly this was referring to the 'Ali Mosque of Eastern Kabul.
16 Though the term 'safe' for a women-only mosque is often used by attendees or founders, it is not fully articulated. See opening statement of The Women's Mosque of America. https://womensmosque.com/about-2/. (accessed 2 November 2018): 'The Women's Mosque of America will provide a safe space for women to feel welcome, respected, and actively engaged within the Muslim Ummah. It will complement existing mosques, offering opportunities for women to grow, learn, and gain inspiration to spread throughout their respective communities'. For a Prophetic precedent of creating a safe environment for women cited by Edina Lekovic, watch *Stepping Up*. Full video of her first *khutba* at the Women's Mosque of America, 30 January, 2015. http://womensmosque.com/videos/ (accessed 18 April 2018).
17 There are at least ten ethnic Muslim groups in China with diverse attitudes towards women's access to mosques, for examples of some Uyghur communities of western China, which forbid women even to access the mosque grounds, see Jaschok, Maria.

'Sources of Authority: Female Ahong and Qingshen Nusi (Women's Mosques) in China'. In *Women, Leadership, and Mosques: Changes in Contemporary Islamic Authority*, edited by Masooda Bano and Hilary Kalmbach. Leiden: Brill, 2012, 40, note 8. For the architectural differences between Uyghur and Hui mosques see Mawani, Rizwan. *Beyond the Mosque: Diverse Spaces of Muslim Worship*. London: IB Tauris, 2019, 17–26. Speaking a Turkic language, not abiding by the compulsory registration of mosques and in some cases promoting a conservative form of Islam, the Chinese government sees Uyghur communities as 'foreign' (and a threat) to the Chinese values promoted by the state.
18 Jaschok and Shui, *The History of Women's Mosques in Chinese Islam*; Shui is affiliated to the Henan Academy of Social Sciences.
19 Jaschok, 'Sources of Authority', 40.
20 Jaschok and Shui, *The History of Women's Mosques in Chinese Islam*, 69–92, 186–200.
21 Jaschok, 'Sources of Authority', 38.
22 For a more detailed story of Yang Huizhen see Jaschok, 'Sources of Authority', 52–3.
23 See the remarks about a stronger opposition to women mosques in the north-west provinces of China, especially those bordering with Pakistan and Afghanistan, in Lim, Louisa. 'Female Imam Blaze Trail Amid China's Muslims'. *npr.org (National Public Radio USA)*, 21 July 2010. www.npr.org/2010/07/21/128628514/female-imams-blaze-trail-amid-chinas-muslims (accessed 15 April 2019), where Lim also states that, after training inclusive of classes in Arabic, an *ahong* has to take an exam to be able to get a license from the state. *National Public Radio (npr)* is an American non-profit privately and publically funded syndicator to over 700 radio stations in the USA.
24 Jaschok and Shui, *The History of Women's Mosques in Chinese Islam*, 93–4.
25 For Mattson, see Mattson, Ingrid. *Can a Woman be an Imam?* 2005. http://ingridmattson.org/article/can-a-woman-be-an-imam/ (accessed 10 May 2018).
26 Jaschok, Maria and Shui Jingjun. *Women, Religion and Space in China*. New York, London: Routledge, 2011, 189–90.
27 Jaschok includes the delivery of sermons among the duties of *nu ahong* in Jaschok, Maria. 'Nü ahong'. In *OEIW* (Vol. 2), edited by Natana J. Delong-Bas. Oxford: OUP, 2013, 15; Jaschok, 'Sources of Authority', 42, 45. For leading prayer from the middle of the front row, see Jaschok and Shui, *The History of Women's Mosques in Chinese Islam*, 165; for leading Friday prayer, see top image in Allen-Ebrahimian, Bethany. 'China: The Best and the Worst Place to Be a Muslim Woman'. *Foreign Policy*, 17 July 2015. https://foreignpolicy.com/2015/07/17/china-feminism-islam-muslim-women-xinjiang-uighurs/ (accessed 2 November 2018); and participant observation in Henan province in Huey Fern Tay. 'China's Female Imams Carrying on Ancient Islamic Tradition'. *Australia Broadcasting Corporation (ABC)*, 6 March, 2014. www.abc.net.au/news/2014-03-05/an-china-female-imams-feature/5298860 (accessed 2 November 2018); see also Lim, 'Female Imam Blaze Trail Amid China's Muslims', where female imam Yao Baoxia in Henan does lead prayer standing alongside the other women.
28 Quoted in Jaschok and Shui, *The History of Women's Mosques in Chinese Islam*, 201–2.
29 Liu Zhi (d. 1745) as reported in Jaschok and Shui, *The History of Women's Mosques in Chinese Islam*, 52–6. For Sumayya see Chapter 3 of this book.
30 Jaschok and Shui, *History of Women's Mosques in Chinese Islam*, 157.
31 Quoted from interview conducted by Lim, 'Female Imam Blaze Trail Amid China's Muslims'.
32 Gallup American Muslim Report. *Muslim Americans: A National Portrait*, Gallup & Muslim West Facts Project, 2009, at www.themosqueinmorgantown.com/pdfs/GallupAmericanMuslimReport.pdf (accessed 18 May 2018).

33 For studies on Muslim American women see Haddad, Yvonne Yazbeck, Jane I. Smith and Kathleen M. Moore. *Muslim Women in America: The Challenge of Islamic Identity Today*. New York: OUP, 2006; Karim, Jamillah. *American Muslim Women: Negotiating Race, Class, and Gender within the Ummah*. New York: New York University Press, 2009; and Hammer, Juliane. *American Muslim Women, Religious Authority and Activism: More Than a Prayer*. Austin, TX: University of Texas Press, 2012.

34 http://womensmosque.com/about-2/ (18 May 2018).

35 For the Pico Union Project in Los Angeles watch *Reimagining Religion: Stories of Religious Creativity in Los Angeles*. 9 October, 2017. Edited by Elliot Lockwood. USC, Dornsife, Centre of Religion and Civic Culture. www.youtube.com/watch?v=csujYp3cZQE (accessed 18 May 2018). For the full video of the first *khutba* by E. Lekovic at the Women's Mosque of America see Lekovic, Edina. *Stepping Up*. http://womensmosque.com/videos/ (accessed 18 April 2018).

36 Lekovic, *Stepping Up*.

37 For some responses to the Los Angeles women's mosque opening, see Street, Nick. 'First All-Female Mosque Opens in Los Angeles'. *Al-Jazeera America*, 3 February 2015. http://america.aljazeera.com/articles/2015/2/3/first-all-female-mosque-opens-in-los-angeles.html (accessed 8 May 2018); Hammer, Juliane. 'A (Friday) Prayer of Their Own: American Muslim Women, Religious Space, and Equal Rights'. *University of North Carolina, Religious Studies News, American Academy of Religion*, 24 March 2015. http://rsn.aarweb.org/articles/friday-prayer-their-own (accessed 18 May 2018); and the all-modern political accusation of playing in the hands of Western liberalism narrative by Hassan, Mona. 'Women-only Masjid Opens in California'. *The Khilafah*, 4 February 2015. www.khilafah.com/women-only-masjid-opens-in-california/ (accessed 18 May 2018).

38 Khankan, Sherin. *Women are the Future of Islam: A Memoir of Hope*. London: Rider, 2018, 5.

39 On interfaith marriages, see ibid., 179–82, 199–200.

40 Neuwirth, Angelika. 'The House of Abraham and the House of Amram: Genealogy, Patriarchal Authority, and Exegetical Professionalism'. In *The Qur'an in Context*, edited by Angelika Neuwirth. Leiden: Brill, 2010, 499–532.

41 Calderini, Simonetta. 'Mary and Prayer in the Qur'an, *Tafsir* and Interpretation'. *Studi Magrebini*, 13 (2014–15): 129–55.

42 Kim Chakanetsa with Halima Krausen and Sherin Khankan, 'Women Leading Muslim Communities'.

43 *The Copenhagen Post*. 'Danish Mosque Continues to Make History'. *Copenhagen Post Online*, 10 August, 2016. http://cphpost.dk/?p=66605 (accessed 10 November 2018); for the support by the Indonesian 'grand imam' see Khankan, Sherin. *Sherin Khankan on Islam*. Interview by Bart Schols on Belgian TV, 2017. https://mimeticmargins.com/2017/05/31/sherin-khankan-on-islam/ (accessed 10 November 2018).

44 Kim Chakanetsa with Halima Krausen and Sherin Khankan, 'Women Leading Muslim Communities'.

45 For the Danish cartoons, Langer, Lorenz. *Religious Offence and Human Rights: The Implications of Defamation of Religions*. Cambridge: CUP, 2014; Winston, Brian. *A Right to Offend*. London: Bloomsbury, 2012; for a broader context, see Fekete, Liz. *A Suitable Enemy: Racism, Migration and Islamophobia in Europe*. London: Pluto, 2009.

46 For female imams, the media and politics see Petersen, Jesper. 'Media and the Female Imam'. *Religions* 10, 3 (2019), 159. For Khankan's 2018 visit to France's president Emmanuel Macron, see *The New Arab*, 'Danish female imam Sherin Khankan meets with French president to discuss "future Islam"'. *The New Arab*, 27 March 2018. https://

english.alaraby.co.uk/english/news/2018/3/27/macron-sees-new-vision-of-islam-with-female-imam (accessed 13 July 2020).
47 On Halima Krausen's form of authority, see Spielhaus, Riem. 'Making Islam Relevant: Female Authority and Representation of Islam in Germany'. In *Women, Leadership, and Mosques: Changes in Contemporary Islamic Authority*, edited by Masooda Bano and Hilary Kalmbach. Leiden: Brill, 2012, 437–55.
48 Auda, Jasser. *Reclaiming the Mosque: The Role of Women in Islam's House of Worship*. Swansea: Claritas Books, 2017, 15–16.
49 Studies on some of these mosques can be found in Fewkes, Jacqueline H. *Locating Maldivian Women's Mosques in Global Discourses*. Cham: Palgrave Macmillan, 2019; Forbes, A. D. W. 'The Mosque in the Maldive Islands: A Preliminary Historical Survey'. *Archipel* 26 (1983): 43–74; Frisk, Sylva. *Submitting to God: Women and Islam in Urban Malaysia*. Seattle: University of Washington Press, 2009; Lambek, Michael. 'Localizing Islamic Performances in Mayotte'. In *Islamic Prayer across the Indian Ocean: Inside and Outside the Mosque*, edited by David Parkin and Stephen Headley. London: Curzon, 2000, 63–98; Samatar, Abdi Ismail. 'Social Transformation and Islamic Reinterpretation in Northern Somalia: The Women's Mosque in Gabiley'. In *Geographies of Muslim Women: Gender, Religion, and Space*, edited by Ghazi Walid Falah and Caroline Nagel. New York, London: The Guilford Press, 2005, 226–48.
50 Fewkes, *Locating Maldivian Women's Mosques in Global Discourses*, 201–5; for a figure of pre-2008 estimated women's mosques in the Maldives, see Fewkes, Jacqueline H. 'A "Women's Space" at the Indian Ocean Crossroads: Women's Mosques in the Maldives'. In *Gender at the Crossroads: Multi-disciplinary Perspectives*, edited by Nurten Kara. Famagusta: Eastern Mediterranean University Press, 2009, 277. In some documents these women's mosques are in fact described as 'mosques with facilities for women' which could refer to rooms or annexes to existing mosques.
51 Fewkes, *Locating Maldivian Women's Mosques in Global Discourses*, 89, reports a government minister's interpretation of the origins of the women's mosques 'to provide public spaces for women to, as she put it, "get women outside of the home"'. Compare with the 2009 article cited by Ritchie, Megan, Terry Ann Rogers and Lauren Sauer. *Women's Empowerment in Political Processes in the Maldives*. Washington: IFES, 2014. www.ifes.org/publications/womens-empowerment-political-process-maldives (Accessed 26 May 2020), 28, reporting the published statements of a high official of the Islamic Affairs Ministry.
52 Baksi-Lahiri, Sudeshna. *Women's Power and Ritual Politics in the Maldives*. Ithaca, NY: Cornell University, 2004, 147, 152; Fewkes, *Locating Maldivian Women's Mosques in Global Discourses*, 159–61.
53 Fewkes, *Locating Maldivian Women's Mosques in Global Discourses*, 163–4.
54 Fewkes, 'A "Women's Space" at the Indian Ocean Crossroads', 281–2. An example of the official narrative is found in the 1989 report *Status of Women: Maldives*, by the Office for Women's Affairs, Maldives: 'These committees serve a modest but useful purpose in improving life on the islands. Of special benefit to women is their promotion of island cleaning and the construction and maintenance of women's mosques', quoted in Gopalan, Jayalakshmi. *Women in Politics in South Asia* (Background Paper Series Number 1). Chennai: The Prajnya Resource Centre on Women in Politics and Policy, 2012. http://retro.prajnya.in/prcbg1.pdf (accessed 7 July 2020), 37.
55 The town of Gabiley is the capital of the eponymous district in the western region of what is now Somaliland (a de-facto independent state since 1991). During the 1960s, just for a few days, the territory had become independent from the UK as the State of Somaliland.

56 Samatar, 'Social Transformation and Islamic Reinterpretation in Northern Somalia', 228.
57 ibid., 240.
58 In Mahmood, *Politics of Piety*, 86–9.
59 See, on the authority of Iran's official *IRNA* news agency, *BBC News*. 'Iranian Women to Lead Prayers'. *BBC News Online World Middle East*, 1 August, 2000. http://news.bbc.co.uk/1/hi/world/middle_east/861819.stm (accessed 29 March 2018). This was quoted in detail by Kar, Mehrangiz. 'Women's Political Rights after the Islamic Revolution'. In *Religion and Politics in Modern Iran: A Reader*, edited by Lloyd Ridgeon. London: IB Tauris, 2005, 265. For a tongue-in-cheek statement by Iranian female preacher Mrs Omid of the reason why female *imama* was not allowed in Iran during the early 1990s: 'in Iran it is legally forbidden to act as prayer leader (*pishnamaz*) because women are not considered to be just ('*adel*)', yet, she subtly undermines such a statement by her living example as a just woman, see Torab, Azam. 'Piety as Gendered Agency: A Study of Jalaseh Ritual Discourse in an Urban Neighbourhood in Iran'. *The Journal of the Royal Anthropological Institute* 2, 2 (1996): 244–5; and Torab, *Peforming Islam*, 65–6.
60 Kar, 'Women's Political Rights after the Islamic Revolution', 265. For the political context of Khatami's presidency, the discourse of women's rights and statistics on poor mosque attendance in post-revolution Iran, see Osanloo, Arzoo. *The Politics of Women's Rights in Iran*. Princeton, NJ: PUP, 2009, 71–3.
61 Anwar, Etin. 'Sexing the Prayer: The Politics of Ritual and Feminist Activism in Indonesia'. In *Muslima Theology: The Voices of Muslim Women Theologians*, edited by E. Aslan, Marcia Hermansen and E. Medeni. Frankfurt: Lang, 2013, 211–12, see also 210 for women leading *tarawih* prayers.
62 For an example of qualifications, experience and training of an American Muslim prison female chaplain, see Levine, Jihad, S. E. *Out from Darkness . . . into Light: A Grief and Bereavement Booklet for Muslims in Prisons and Jails*. S. E. Jihad Levine and the Pennsylvania Prison Chaplains Association, 2010. http://paprisonchaplains.org/Content/out-from-darkness-into-light.pdf (accessed 22 March 2018); for the Canadian armed forces' first female Muslim chaplain see Demiray, Suleyman, Helms Barbara and Serap Bulsen. 'CAF [Canadian Armed Forces] Welcomes First Muslim Female Chaplain and Chaplain Candidate' *The Maple Leaf*, 12 April, 2018. https://ml-fd.caf-fac.ca/en/2018/04/12195 (accessed 18 June 2018).
63 Gilliat-Ray, Sophie, Mansur Ali and Stephen Pattison. *Understanding Muslim Chaplaincy*. London, New York: Routledge, 2013, 72.
64 ibid.
65 Long, Ibrahim J. 'Muslim Chaplains: Serving in Diversity'. AMC, 2010. https://associationofmuslimchaplains.com/muslim-chaplains-serving-in-diversity (accessed 4 July 2017).
66 For university chaplains, Khoja-Moolji, Shenila S. *An Emerging Model of Muslim Leadership: Chaplaincy on University Campuses*. The Pluralism Project at Harvard University. 2011. http://pluralism.org/wp-content/uploads/2015/08/Khoja_Moolji_Muslim_Chaplaincy_2011.pdf (accessed 20 June 2020).
67 See respectively: *adhan* in Lahaj, Mary. 'Making It Up As I Go Along: The Formation of a Muslim Chaplain'. *Reflective Practice Formation and Supervision in Ministry*, 29 (2009): 148–53; writing the Friday sermon, see Long, 'Muslim Chaplains'; public Qur'an recitation in 2014 by USA university chaplain Tahera Ahmad, in *Northwestern*. 'Associate Chaplain Recognized as Leading Female Muslim: Tahera Ahmad Honored at the White House During Women's History Month'. *Northwestern Now*, 28 March,

2014. https://news.northwestern.edu/stories/2014/03/chaplain-ahmad-white-house-honor/ (accessed 22 March 2018).
68 Gilliat-Ray, Ali and Pattison, *Understanding Muslim Chaplaincy*, 93.
69 For the functions, structure and contents of the *du'a* for modern Isma'ilis, see Kassam, Tazim. 'The Daily Prayer (Du'a) of Shi'a Isma'ili Muslims'. In *Religions of the United States in Practice* (Vol. 2), edited by Colleen McDannell. Princeton, NJ: PUP, 2001, 32–43.
70 Kassam, 'The Daily Prayer', 35.
71 For a description and interpretation of space in the prayer room within an Isma'ili *jama'atkhana*, see Dossa, Parin Aziz. *Ritual and Daily Life: Transmission and Interpretation of the Ismaili Tradition in Vancouver*. PhD thesis, University of British Columbia, 1985, especially Ch 3 and diagrams 7 (87) and 10 (102). In addition to the daily congregational prayers, a *mukhiani* or *kamadiani* may also lead other prayers for special occasions, such as for the *milad al-nabi, imama* day; however, it is not customary for women to lead the two festival prayers ('*id namaz*). This is a current issue of debate among some Isma'ili communities.
72 Dossa, *Ritual and Daily Life*, 88–9.
73 Sultan Muhammad Shah. *Message to the World of Islam*. Karachi: Ismailia Association for Pakistan, 1977, 58–9. For an analysis of Sultan Muhammad Shah's interpretation of the veil see Calderini, Simonetta. 'Female Seclusion and the Veil: Two Issues in Political and Social Discourse. The Reforms of Sultan Muhammad Shah'. In *Islam and the Veil: Theoretical and Regional Contexts*, edited by Theodore Gabriel and Rabiha Hannan. London: Continuum, 2011, 48–62.
74 Sultan Muhammad Shah, *Message to the World of Islam*, 60–1.
75 Asani, Ali. 'From Satpanthi to Ismaili Muslim: The Articulation of Ismaili Khoja Identity in South Asia'. In *A Modern History of the Ismailis: Continuity and Change in a Muslim Community*, edited by Farhad Daftary. London: IB Tauris, 2011, 113–15.
76 For an example of Isma'ili women as religious teachers in Chitral, see Marsden, Magnus. *Living Islam: Muslim Religious Experience in Pakistan's North-West Frontier*. Cambridge: CUP, 2005, 164–5.
77 For a life testimony of a Kenyan-Canadian Isma'ili female preacher and educator, see Nanji, Afroza and Alykhan Nanji. 'Charting a Family's Journey'. *The.Ismaili: United Kingdom*, 6 January, 2008. https://the.ismaili/our-stories/charting-familys-journey (accessed 11 April 2018). As stated by Daftary, the main function of Isma'ili religious teachers and preachers is no longer to proselytize, but rather to instruct their own community about their religious tenets and history, Daftary, Farhad. *The Isma'ilis: Their History and Doctrines*. Cambridge: CUP, 2007, 499.
78 For the background, arguments and activities of some of these women imams see, among others: Bano and Kalmbach, *Women, Leadership, and Mosques*; Hammer, *American Muslim Women, Religious Authority and Activism*; Elewa, Ahmed and Laury Silvers. '"I Am One of the People": A Survey and Analysis of Legal Arguments on Women-led Prayer in Islam'. *Journal of Law and Religion* 26, 1 (2010–11): 141–171.; Safi, O. (ed.). *Progressive Muslims: On Justice, Gender and Pluralism*. Oxford: Oneworld, 2003.
79 wadud, amina. *Inside the Gender Jihad: Women's Reform in Islam*. Oxford: Oneworld, 2006, 24–39.
80 ibid., 28.
81 Compare with Qur. 11.90 and 85.14; for an introduction to the *Maqasid al-shari'a* see Auda, Jasser. *Maqasid Al-Shari'ah: A Beginner's Guide*. London, Washington: The International Institute of Islamic Thought, 2008.

82 For the text of the Cape Town sermon see wadud, *Inside the Gender Jihad*, 158–62. For an analysis of the contents and contexts of her 1994 and 2005 *khutba*s, see Calderini, Simonetta 'Islam and Diversity: Alternative Voices within Contemporary Islam'. *New Blackfriars*, 89, 1021 (2008): 324–32. Note the parallelism between maternity as surrender and the narrative of Mary's acceptance of maternity as obedience to the will of God.
83 wadud, *Inside the Gender Jihad*, 249–52 (English text of the 2005 *khutba*).
84 Sisters in Islam. 2007. www.sistersinislam.org.my/BM/mission.htm (accessed 9 April 2020).
85 Bedi, R. J. 'Sisters in Islam files for judicial review on fatwa', *The Star*, 31 October 2014. www.thestar.com.my/news/nation/2014/10/31/sisters-in-islam-files-for-judicial-review-on-fatwa/ (accessed 20 April 2020); for the 2019 rejection of the appeal see Bernama. 'In Sisters in Islam Case, High Court says Fatwa is Syariah Court's Jurisdiction'. *New Straits Times*, 27 August 2019. www.nst.com.my/news/crime-courts/2019/08/516547/sisters-islam-case-high-court-says-fatwa-syariah-courts (accessed 9 April 2020).
86 El-Tawhid Juma Circle. www.jumacircle.com/ (accessed 5 October 2018)
87 Inclusive Mosque Initiative. *About*. http://inclusivemosqueinitiative.org/about/ (accessed 5 October 2018).
88 Inclusive Mosque Initiative. *IMI Is Not Doing Anything New*. http://inclusivemosqueinitiative.org/imi-isnt-doing-anything-new/ (accessed 5 October 2018).
89 Shannahan, Dervla, S. 'Gender, Sexuality and Inclusivity in UK Mosques'. In *Studying Islam in Practice*, edited by Gabriele Marranci. London and New York: Routledge, 2014, 124–134. For the precedent of the Prophet's mosque see 129–30.
90 I attended as an observer a number of the fortnightly *jum'a* prayers between June 2018 and April 2020. Aware of the limitations of a front-stage–back-stage approach to observation, I have also used published interviews, online webpages and blogs as well as chapters in edited books, included in these notes.
91 See Bhol, Asma. 'I'm a female imam'. *FT.com Magazine*, 14 May 2016. www.ft.com/content/2ccda9ea-17c7-11e6-bb7d-ee563a5a1cc1 (accessed 12 May 2018); and Iqbal, Nosheen. 'Raise Your Gaze: "Islamic Feminism is Overlooked in the Mainstream"'. *The Observer*, 16 September 2018. www.theguardian.com/world/2018/sep/16/new-radicals-2018-raise-your-gaze-muslim-feminists-mosque (accessed 10 November 2019).
92 Seyran Ateş authored a number of books, including *Selam, Frau Imamin: Wie ich in Berlin eine Liberale Moschee Gründete (Salam, Mrs Imam: How I Founded a Liberal Mosque in Berlin)*. Berlin: Ullstein, 2017.
93 ibid., 278–81. For Goethe, see Goethe, Johan, Wolfgang von. *West-Östlicher Divan*. Translated by Martin Bidney. Albany: SUNY Press, 2010 (1st edn 1819), inspired by the poetry of Hafez.
94 Sakr, Taha. 'Egyptian Dar al-Ifta Attacks "Liberal" Mosque in Germany'. *Egypt Independent*, 20 June, 2017. https://egyptindependent.com/dar-alifta-attacks-german-mosque/ (accessed 6 September 2018).
95 Dar al-Ifta' al-Misriyya. *Fatwa on Women Leading Women in Prayer*. www.dar-alifta.org/ar/ViewResearch.aspx?sec=fatwa&ID=2413&LangID=1 (accessed 11 April 2020); on the English language site, the *fatwa* about women leading prayer has been deleted (originally n.1635), Dar al-Ifta' al-Misriyya. *Fatwa on Women Praying in Mosques*. www.dar-alifta.org/Foreign/ViewFatwa.aspx?ID=7975 (accessed 11 April 2020), stating that for a woman to pray at home rather than at the mosque is 'in obedience to God's injunctions'.
96 Su, Alice. 'The German Mosque that Attracts Women Imams, Gays and Death Threats'. *Politico*, 27 July, 2017. https://www.politico.eu/article/berlin-feminist-mosque-ibn-rushd-goethe-germany-first-liberal-mosque-sparks-debate-in-berlin/(accessed 20 June 2018);

Pabst, Sabrina. 'Liberal Mosque in Berlin Draws Criticism'. *Deutsche Welle (DW)*, 21 June, 2017. www.dw.com/en/liberal-mosque-in-berlin-draws-criticism/a-39353066/21/6/2017 (accessed 20 June 2018).
97 Reda, *The Islamic Basis for Female-Led Prayer*; Eltahawy, Mona. 'Prayer toward Equality'. *The Washington Post*, 18 March 2005. https://www.washingtonpost.com/wp-dyn/articles/A45506-2005Mar17.html (accessed 5 August 2020).
98 Reda, *Women Leading Congregational Prayers*, then as 'What would the Prophet do? The Islamic basis for female-led prayer', 10 March 2005 in *Muslim Wakeup!*, re-published in several sites, including as Reda, *The Islamic Basis for Female-Led Prayer*.
99 Reda, *The Islamic Basis for Female-Led Prayer*, point 2 under Evidence, and point 7.
100 Assembly of Muslim Jurists of America, *A Collection of Fatwas and Legal Opinions on the Issue of Women Leading Prayer*. 5 April 2005 / 25 Safar 1426. www.abc.se/home/m9783/ir/d/fwlp_e.pdf (accessed 28 May 2020).
101 Azam, Hina. 'A Critique of the Argument for Woman-Led Friday Prayers'. In *A Collection of Fatwas and Legal Opinions on the Issue of Women Leading Prayer*. Assembly of Muslim Jurists of America. 5 April 2005 / 25 Safar 1426, 20-26. www.abc.se/home/m9783/ir/d/fwlp_e.pdf (accessed 28 May 2020).
102 Elewa and Silvers, '"I am one of the People"', 144–53.
103 al Qaradawi: 'I believe that any woman well-versed in the Qur'an like Umm Waraqa may lead her family members, including men, in both obligatory and supererogatory prayers ...', in Assembly of Muslim Jurists of America. *A Collection of Fatwas and Legal Opinions*, 28, 31.
104 Shakir, Zaid. 'An Examination of the Issue of Female Prayer Leadership'. In *A Collection of Fatwas and Legal Opinions on the Issue of Women Leading Prayer*. Assembly of Muslim Jurists of America. 5 April 2005 / 25 Safar 1426, 35–45. www.abc.se/home/m9783/ir/d/fwlp_e.pdf (accessed 28 May 2020), 44–5.
105 ibid., for al-Qaradawi's statement see 34, for Zaid Shakir 35.
106 For more details on context and arguments in the 2005 *Collection of Fatwas* see Calderini, Simonetta. 'Citing the Past to Address the Present: Authorities and Unexpected Interlocutors on Female Leadership of Salat'. Open access lecture. Fairfax, VA: Ali Vural Ak Center for Global Islamic Studies, George Mason University, 2014. https://islamicstudiescenter.gmu.edu/conferences-and-workshops/center-lecture-series/spring-2014 (accessed 8 July 2020).
107 A summary of the Indonesian scholars' *fatwa* is in Anwar, 'Sexing the Prayer', 203–4.
108 Prado, Abdennur. *About the Friday Prayer Led by Amina Wadud*. 10 March, 2005. https://abdennurprado.wordpress.com/2005/03/10/about-the-friday-prayer-led-by-amina-wadud/ (accessed 14 April 2020).
109 Abou El Fadl, Khaled. 'Fatwa: On Women Leading Prayer'. *The Search for Beauty: On Beauty and Reason in Islam*. 5 April 2010. www.searchforbeauty.org/2010/04/05/fatwa-on-women-leading-prayer/ (accessed 14 April 2020).
110 On Turabi's statements see Akec, John (transl.) 'Sudan's Turabi: Muslim Women can Marry Christian or Jew'. *Sudan Tribune*, 11 April, 2006. www.sudantribune.com/article.php3?id_article=15021 (accessed 14 April 2020).
111 For Sohaib Bencheikh's status see Schleifer, S. Abdallah (ed.). *The Muslim 500: The World's 500 Most Influential Muslims 2020*. Amman: The Royal Islamic Strategic Studies Centre, 2019. www.themuslim500.com/wp-content/uploads/2019/10/TheMuslim500-2020-low.pdf (accessed 9 June 2020); for attending a woman-led prayer see Taylor, Pamela. 'Canada: Leading the Mufti; Progress in the Islamic

Tradition'. *Women Living Under Muslim Laws*, 17 February, 2006. www.wluml.org/node/2843 (accessed 9 June 2020).
112 Al-Banna, *Jawaz Imamat al-Mar'a li'l-Rijal*, 9.
113 ibid., 90.
114 ibid., 47.
115 ibid., 45.
116 ibid., 48–9.
117 ibid., 52–3.
118 As an example of the textualists' 're-construction/re-elaboration' by selection and association of passages and tradition, Banna provides the example of the Umm Waraqa *hadith* and how, in time, the expression 'the people of her house' was understood. See ibid., 54–6.
119 Al-Banna uses *musawa* to indicate gender equality on several occasions, see ibid., 7, 11, 49 etc.
120 For an international reporter's assessment of al-Banna see Slackman, Michael. 'A Voice for "New Understanding" of Islam'. *The New York Times*, 20 October, 2006. www.nytimes.com/2006/10/20/world/africa/20iht-profile.3237674.html (accessed 15 April 2020).
121 See Khoirul Hadi, M. al-Asy Ari. 'Fiqh Renewal of Gamal Al-Banna and Its Relevance of Fiqh Developments in Indonesia'. *Millatī, Journal of Islamic Studies and Humanities* 2, 2 (2017), 221–37; and the works by Indonesian scholar Mukhammad Zamzami, such as Zamzami, Mukhammad. 'Metodologi Studi Hadis Jamâl al-Bannâ'. *Mutawâtir: Jurnal Keilmuan Tafsir Hadis* 4, 2 (2014), 211–42. For the USA media see Fleishman, Jeffrey. 'In the Library with a Leading Islamic Liberal'. *Los Angeles Times*, 6 May, 2008. www.latimes.com/world/la-fg-liberal6-2008may06-story.html (accessed 15 April 2020), and academic study Radhan, Luay. 'Gamal al-Banna's Islamic Feminism in The Muslim Woman'. *Journal of Women and Human Rights in the Middle East*, 2 (2014), 5–18.
122 Qur. 2.228 (*wa li'l-rijal 'alayhinna darajatun*), about divorce and *'idda*, after the assertion that the rights of the wives are equal to those used towards them, although men have 'precedence over them', in Eddouada, Souad and Renata Pepicelli. 'Maroc: Vers un "Féminisme Islamique d'État"'. *Critique Internationale* 46, 1 (2010): 87–100. www.cairn-int.info/article-E_CRII_046_0087--morocco-towards-an-islamic-state-feminis.htm (accessed 12 March 2018).
123 Cieślewska, *Islam with a Female Face*, 123 (*tarawih*) and 136 (*namaz/salat al-zuhr*).
124 ibid., 137–9.
125 Borrillo, Sara. *Femminismi e Islam in Marocco: Attiviste laiche, teologhe, predicatrici*. Napoli: Edizioni Scientifiche Italiane, 2017, 41; on the statement of the Moroccan Council see Arbaoui, L. 'Ani Zonneveld's Visit to Morocco Creates Controversy over Woman Imam'. *Morocco World News*, 3 November 2015, www.moroccoworldnews.com/2015/11/171818/ani-zonnevelds-visit-to-morocco-creates-controversy-over-woman-imam/ (accessed 12 March 2018).
126 About Malikism as expression of national and cultural Moroccan identity see the statements on the website of the Moroccan Ministry of Habous and Islamic Affairs, 'Maliki School is a Social and Psychological Culture'. *Habous.gov.ma*, 28 June, 2012. www.habous.gov.ma/2012-01-27-14-38-19/887-2012-06-28-13-14-48.html (accessed 13 March 2018). Though Malikism is the majority and state endorsed *madhhab* in Morocco, there are other legal schools, for the Twelver Shi'a see Zweiri, Mahjoob. 'Are Shias Rising in the Western Part of the Arab World? The Case of Morocco'. *The Journal of North African Studies* 13, 4 (2008): 513–29.

127 For some analytical remarks on the role of Malikism as a national unifier to avoid *fitna*, see Eddouada, Souad. 'Morocco's "Mourchidates" and Contradictions'. *Reset: Dialogues on Civilizations (ResetDOC)*, 17 April, 2009. www.resetdoc.org/story/moroccos-mourchidates-and-contradictions/ (accessed 12 March 2018).
128 Eddouada and Pepicelli, 'Maroc', 87–100.
129 Dar al-Ifta' al-Misriyya, *Fatwa on Women Leading Women in Prayer*.
130 For the *fatwa* in the Arabic version dated 8 October 2017, see ibid.
131 See the Muslim Women's Council efforts since 2015 to establish a woman-run mosque in Bradford, Britain, in Gani, Aisha. 'Meet Bana Gora, the Woman Planning Britain's First Female-Managed Mosque'. *The Guardian*, 31 July, 2015. www.theguardian.com/lifeandstyle/2015/jul/31/bana-gora-muslim-womens-council-bradford-mosque (accessed 11 April 2020); and the 2019 'response' by the Muslim Council of Britain to offer courses for women to develop skills to be in senior positions on a mosque committee at The Muslim Council of Britain. *Women in Mosques Development Programme*. 2019. https://mcb.org.uk/project/women-in-mosques-development-programme/ (accessed 17 April 2020).

CONCLUSION

The idea of writing this book on the history of debates about women leading prayer was triggered by the question of an inquisitive and perplexed man from a notable *shaykh*'s retinue asking me, back in 2009, whether women imams existed at all. The book does not provide a simple answer, but, for the first time, gathers together and scrutinizes a complex web of past and present narratives, arguments and cases, ranging from reported episodes in the past to well-known and copiously documented events in recent times. In the first Part of this book, I analysed, among others, *hadith*s that reported that two of the Prophet's wives and one of his female Companions had led women in prayer.

The *hadith*s, even when their authenticity was in doubt, came to be used as authoritative sources for law making. I have shown that *hadith*s on women leading prayer met all the criteria to be considered legally authoritative, thus in principle establishing that –on the basis of the example of the Prophetic *sunna* – a woman leading prayer should be an acceptable practice to adopt for Muslims. Thus, by the very methods and standards that male exegetes had established, these *hadith*s set a precedent for a woman to lead prayer. Instead, this seemingly straightforward logic did not survive the pressures resulting from the mores and socio-cultural contexts in which the exegetes and jurists operated.

This book has provided evidence that scholars commenting upon these narratives have engaged with the role of women in prayer as leaders and participants as part of wider ritual and doctrinal concerns. These concerns include, among others, the obligatory nature of prayer for believers, the circumstances under which prayer should be performed and what might invalidate it.

In pre-modern times, mores and socio-cultural factors had, to a degree, derailed exegetes from the same method of establishing the authoritativeness of the Prophetic *sunna* that they had devised as a source for the law. Today those same factors have instead created the conditions to reclaim those Prophetic traditions to validate the actions of the many female imams, who now exercise their leadership role across four continents.

So, the answer to the inquisitive and the perplexed would be that yes, indeed women leading prayer do exist now, as they did during and after the time of the Prophet. The Prophet himself ordered one of them to lead prayer and also instructed his wives to do so. This should have sealed (once and for all) the issue of the continued validity of female *imama*. Instead, as we have demonstrated in this book, the majority of pre-modern scholars did not consider those cases as a precedent to authenticate continued female leadership. By tracking down the trajectories these scholarly debates took, it was possible to establish when, why and where some ideas gained more currency than others. We therefore exposed the resulting polarization of opinions, with most scholars prohibiting or limiting female prayer leadership, and only a few who did not oppose it.

In the process of investigating these debates, we engaged in textual and historical analysis of relevant terms used by pre-modern sources, such as imam, mosque, *fitna* and others, drawing attention to semantic developments, as well as modifications and adjustments in their uses.

This book has shown some instances of the similarities and continuities between past and present scholars, writers and agents. One of the most prominent similarities is that they all share a recurrent use of their respective pasts, whether real or imagined, to support and validate their specific positions in favour or against the permissibility of women acting as imams.

For all those scholars, the perfect past is embodied in the times of the Prophet, as reported by subsequent sources of varied degrees of authority. The time of the Prophet's Companions, and generally the early centuries of Islam, can also be perceived as being normative. What constitutes 'the past' is relative to individual perspectives and agendas. Regarding today's scholars and female imams, more recent pasts can be referred to as constituting a precedent. In a time when information and news are 'instantaneous', the past is quickly moulded to contribute to a (regularly updated) shared narrative of the past. In turn, a shared narrative of the past can shape present and future communal and group identities. With reference to the 2005 prayer leadership event by amina wadud, this shaping is already taking place among supporters and founders of inclusive mosques and other initiatives. This event has, for them and many more, become the common starting point, the shared recent past on which to build present and future actions.

The recourse to what past and present scholars and activists – from their own respective standpoints – reconfigure to be the 'normative' past is strongly conditioned by their interpretation and application of the category of *bid'a* (innovation in religion). A practice, or a belief, for which there is no precedent during the Prophet's time, was – and still is today – considered to lead to innovation, a direction that, since the 10th century, was dogmatically decreed as departing from the *sunna* and, hence, to be avoided at all cost.

Despite the existence of textual evidence about women as imams during the Prophet's time, most scholars concluded that women should not lead prayer. They reached such a conclusion by being conditioned by their cultural and social environment and by the application of their exegetical methods for the formulation of the law. They resolved the discrepancy between textual evidence and social mores by resorting to a selective interpretation of the sources. As a result, they argued, and continue to do so to this day, that *hadiths* about women as imams are weak, or that they are not to be acted upon, because they report practices which were legitimate only for the specific women those *hadiths* mentioned. Alternatively, scholars explained that the practice of female ritual leadership had been abrogated at some point after the Prophet's demise.

One cannot fail to notice that, despite being the prime source of scriptural and legal authority in Islam, recourse to the Qur'an in these debates is marginal. Instead, the text of the Qur'an, read through the lens of principles of social and gender justice, is reclaimed by contemporary female imam exegetes, like amina wadud, to argue in support of female leadership, and so to restore the word of God against the work of men.

The underlying concern and preoccupation with *bid'a* has not abated in present times. In 2005, after wadud's New York *imama*, the Assembly of Muslim Jurists of America issued a collection of *fatwas* which decreed: 'The Assembly believes that the position taken [i.e. a woman leading the Friday prayer for a mixed congregation and delivering the Friday *khutba*] is a misguidance, *an innovation* in the religion, and it loathes it.'[1] Consequently, when a women-only mosque opens, when a woman leads mixed congregations in prayer, when women propose to manage or even share the management of mosques, those very same women, accused of introducing innovation, feel the need to assert that their leadership is 'nothing new' in Islam.[2] Since 2005, accusations of *bid'a* have escalated into threats or violence against women imams and their supporters. In the eyes of the opponents of female leadership, this *bid'a*, something that must be avoided at all cost, leads to *fitna*, that is community conflict bringing a disruption of social order and eventually leading to chaos.

Those who react violently against women imams ostensibly do so not because they are 'against women' *per se*, but because they see themselves as the defenders of what they consider to be the divinely decreed social order. In light of this, in their opinion, any minimal departure from this order would undermine it or destroy it, and so must be stopped. By arguing that female prayer leadership is an innovation that leads to *fitna*, they conflate the association of *fitna* with women, which is all but absent in the Qur'an. In those *hadith*s, where the association between *fitna* and women is explicitly made, *fitna* has been usually understood as 'tribulation' or 'temptation'.[3] Moreover, when stressing this association, they are voicing the shared memory of the role that 'A'isha is reported to have played in the first *fitna* (dissent, civil strife) in Islam.

This book demonstrates how, by engaging in scholarly debates across time, opposition to women as imams, and today's manifest hostility against them, are both the outcome of discourses where the approach to the issue of female leadership betrays an overarching concern with the preservation of social order. By contrast, modern scholarly and broader debates in favour of the legitimacy of female prayer leadership reflect discourses of social justice, human rights and spiritual gender equality. The latter was best articulated in pre-modern times by Ibn al-'Arabi when, consistent with his argument that spiritual leadership is bestowed by God irrespective of the gender of its recipient, he supported female prayer leadership for any type of congregation.

Current arguments based on a gender egalitarian reading of the Qur'an betray the additional agenda that reclaiming the right to lead is only one expression of restoring the authoritative voice of the Qur'an. A parallel claim is made to restore the original versions of Prophetic *hadiths* and the prescriptive ways in which *hadiths* should be used to endorse ritual practice. From this perspective, the very deniers of female leadership of prayer, on the basis of being an innovation, paradoxically, have themselves fallen into the trap of 'innovating' the way in which *hadiths* ought to be used!

As for the women who, in the past, are reported as having led prayer, it is undeniable that only a few examples have emerged from the sources. This is not something that has been a concern of this book. Whether one or many, these examples have been included in a much more significant framework: in that, as precedents, they have contributed to female leadership finding its way into scholarly discussions about prayer. One should also be aware of the fact that lack of reporting does not denote no activity. In this book we argued that the scarcity of past references could be due to social perceptions about the ritual role of women, the specific locations where this role was, or could have been, exercised, and the type of sources analysed. Classical writers, particularly historians and chroniclers, traditionally focused on reporting events taking place in official and urban settings at the expense of informal and rural ones, such as prayer rooms and shrines or local village mosques.

In early modern times sources do attest to the existence of women-only mosques in China and instances of female prayer leadership. In present times, debates on female *imama* are the result of documented events which are reported in academic studies as well as being covered by the media. Cases of Muslim women leading prayer did, and in some cases still do, take place globally, in cities such as New York, but also in Somali villages such as Gabiley, in an apartment in Berlin or in a mosque in the Henan province of China.

This brings us to the most striking difference between past and present narratives about female imams: present narratives are usually shaped, if not created, by the very actors or agents themselves. While the direct voice of Umm Salama in dialogue with the Prophet is, for example, recorded by Ibn Sallam, the narrative on her is not hers, but that of Ibn Sallam. On the other hand, today's female imams such as amina wadud or Sherin Khankan contribute to, or create, their own narrative. Even though they might not own the narrative about themselves, they are intellectually, academically, theologically competent and qualified to locate their actions and their roles within a wider interpretative framework to which they personally contribute. Moreover, the majority of today's women imams owe their status to their own efforts, competence, experience and qualities, and not to being related to authoritative men.

Above all, female imams today are fully self-aware of their roles and of the consequences – spiritual as well as social – that might derive from them. This is in contrast to the dynamics that led pre-modern women to passively respond and react to instructions given to them to lead prayer. A notable exception to this passivity is 'Amra bint 'Abd al-Rahman, the niece of 'A'isha, who took the lead, not so much in prayer *per se*, but in being assertive enough to dictate to other women the terms of the performance carried out by a female prayer leader.

The research carried out for this book has also identified a common feature that legitimizes female prayer leadership in the majority of past narratives about women imams and for present prayer leaders – namely religious knowledge. This can be understood as knowledge of the Qur'an and *hadith*s, as seen in the narratives on 'A'isha and Umm Waraqa, and the 'sacred knowledge' that Shi'i reports attribute to Umm Salama. It could be the knowledge of Islamic doctrine, as taught since the 17th century in the women's religious schools in China, the theological knowledge as proven by academic qualifications, as in the case of Sherin Khankan, or from obtaining the traditional *ijaza*, as in the case of Halima Krausen. Knowledge can indeed be identified as an 'egalitarian' criterion of excellence, which justifies holding a position of prayer leadership. As shown by several *hadith*s, and other texts analysed in this book, to possess religious knowledge gives a Muslim person legitimacy to be a prayer leader, irrespective of social status, age or gender.

There have been noticeable developments in Muslim minority countries in the imam's roles, which reflect an expansion of the functions of mosques there. Imams are not only leaders of prayer but faith leaders, counsellors, community representatives, 'chaplains', scholars, legal and moral guides. Faith leadership can be performed in non-conventional, at times makeshift or nomadic, mosques, as well as in virtual spaces (virtual mosques) where prayer leadership, preaching and religious instruction are widely accessible. These virtual platforms, though serving an important need at a time when many young people discover their faith online, or when people practice their faith online (during the quarantine caused by the Covid-19 pandemic at the time of writing), also raise important questions about balanced, accurate and responsible reporting and scholarship.

Imams and *mufti*s have been active on the internet for at least two decades, along with the availability of online *khutba*s (some as short as eight seconds on Snapchat), legal advice, and free courses on Islam, including Qur'anic recitation and multifarious *da'wa* activities.[4] There are iPhone and Android apps for iMosque services. Muslim women are very active online, with a varied agency in terms of the provision of scholarship and leadership. Most Islamic websites include menus dedicated to women's issues, especially concerning family matters, modesty, dress and the roles and contribution of women during the time of the Prophet. A few sites also include sub-menus on female leadership together with various news items, even on women in mosque management. Biographies and representations of past women acting as prayer leaders are numerous on the internet, and in the case of Umm Waraqa, an animated cartoon has been produced and is available on YouTube.[5] The scholars who answer doctrinal, ritual and legal questions posed by the public are categorized as imam (all male), '*alim* (male scholar) or '*alima* (i.e. female scholar), implying that while Islamic scholarship is gender neutral, *imama* is not. The positive aspect of this online presence is the range of audiences who can be reached; but exposure can also lead to heightened polarization of opinions, especially in terms of real-time responses.

One of the largest American online educational platforms, set up to explain and facilitate access to thousands of US colleges and schools, has the webpage 'Career Opportunities: Public and Social Services', which includes the career of 'imam'. Its page contains accessible and reader-friendly information, including the snappy *Did You Know?* One of them reads: 'Did You Know? Only men can serve as imams'.

With growing numbers of women leading prayers and delivering the *khutba* in women-only and inclusive mosques, with the discourse on inclusivity being increasingly adopted by some established Islamic organizations in Islamic countries and Muslim-minority countries, and with Muslim women-led initiatives, along with the outreach, educational and scholarly activities of existing women imams, surely this webpage will soon need updating.

Debate on female *imama* will not end with this book. It will be ongoing and continuously changing direction and it will be with us for many years to come. In these debates there are several actors and shades of opinion, as this book has shown. One of the recurrent past and present arguments against female prayer leadership conflates expressions of spirituality and religious piety with social constructs of gender. What this book has exposed is how those who are against the legitimacy of leadership of female imams are missing a fundamental point that lies behind the actions of these women. The mainly male vocal opponents see the woman first and the believer second, they confuse gender with biology.

However, in doing so they reduce the figure of the imam from being a person, who is the vicegerent of God on earth as *insan* (human being), to one of physicality as a male. What is missed – whether out of convenience or not – is that these women, instead, put themselves forward as believers first and then, and only then, as women. In compliance with the obligatory nature of the prayer, by prioritizing it for what it is ultimately meant to be – a practical manifestation of surrender to God – the women imams give priority to piety over male-constructed procedures and scenography. Women imams and their followers therefore put themselves forward as the ultimate example – no matter the circumstances or threats – of the faithful; those who put their love of God above all else, even men. They are symbolically not dissimilar from the female martyrs of the early days of Islam for whom to defend and practice their faith always came first. In short, the female imam who fronts a congregation today is not the prayer leader of men and women but the embodiment of piety that, beyond biological accident, leads *mu'minin* and *mu'minat*, who are equal in all respects in the eyes of God, as sanctioned in the Qur'an.

Notes

1 Assembly of Muslim Jurists of America. *A Collection of Fatwas and Legal Opinions*, 4.
2 About women's management of mosques see statements in Gani, 'Meet Bana Gora, the woman planning Britain's first female-managed mosque'.
3 See the use of this *hadith* in Shakir, 'An Examination of the Issue of Female Prayer Leadership', 42.
4 On Muslim communities online, Islamic cyber spaces, cyber imams, and more, see the academic works by Gary R. Bunt, including Bunt, Gary R. *Islam in the Digital Age: E-Jihad, Online Fatwas and Cyber Islamic Environments*. London: Pluto Books, 2003.
5 Kaprawi, Norhayati. *Ummu Waraqah Sang Imam Wanita [Umm Waraqa the Female Imam]*. YouTube, 19 November 2018. www.youtube.com/watch?v=9pweF0iGNd4 (accessed 9 July 2020).

GLOSSARY

'Abbasids dynasty of caliphs (750–1258), descendants from the uncle of the Prophet Muhammad al-'Abbas.

ahad (Ar. Pl.) single strand *hadith*s, that is *hadith*s handed down by a single transmitter who passed on a tradition to only one single pupil, who in turn transmitted it to only one single pupil.

ahong (Ch.) generic title for men and women equivalent to imam (as teacher, religious leader, community representative).

'alim (fem. *'alima*) learned person, particularly in religious sciences. Plural is *'ulama'* as a generic term to indicate the religiously learned.

Ansar the Meccan 'Helpers of the Prophet', second in precedence to the *Muhajirun* who migrated to Medina.

Asbab al-nuzul 'occasions of revelation' of the Qur'an (literary genre).

'awra a) something exposed (See Qur. 33.13); b) in legal discourse a part of the body to be concealed (see Qur. 24.31); c) private parts, *pudenda*. Specifically, for men and slave women the area between the navel and the knees; for free women, either the private parts, or most of the body except the face, or the whole body except the eyes, or the whole body and her voice.

baligh legal term to indicate maturity and legal competence.

batin esoteric meaning behind the exoteric wording of sacred texts and religious laws.

dar house, abode; area; tribe.

da'wa mission or propaganda. In Isma'ili context an invitation to uphold the right of an individual or a family to the imamate; also the entire hierarchy of ranks within the religious organization.

dawla the state apparatus, state as an institution.

dhikr 'remembrance', rhythmic devotional invocation of God's names.

du'a lit. invocation; for Isma'ilis it is the daily prayer which invokes Allah, the Prophet and the Imams.

fadila excellence.

faqih (pl. *fuqaha'*) jurist or specialist in Islamic jurisprudence, *fiqh*.

fard (leg.) obligatory; one of the five legal statuses (*ahkam*); *fard kifaya* – communal obligation.

farida (pl. *fara'id*) the obligatory prayers.

fatwa a legal opinion by an authoritative legal Muslim scholar, such as a *mufti*, in response to a specific juristic question.

fiqh Islamic jurisprudence, explanation and application of the shari'a (q.v.).

fitna dissent, division or sedition within a society, perceived as disruption of the 'natural' order; also used to indicate seduction.

ghayba occultation or concealment, the condition of anyone believed to have been absconded by God from human vision and whose life is miraculously prolonged while in occultation until his reappearance at a pre-ordained time before the Day of Resurrection. For Twelver Shi'is, *ghayba* historically refers to the occultation of their

12th Imam in its two phases of the 'lesser occultation' (873–4) and the 'greater occultation' (941).

ghusl (rit.) major ritual ablution for major impurities (sexual intercourse, menstruation etc.).

hadith 'report'; tradition relating the deeds and sayings of the Prophet Muhammad or of his Companions; collectively the second major source of Islamic law. For Shi'is also report of an action or statement by one of the Imams.

hajj annual pilgrimage to Mecca that every Muslim must perform at least once in his or her lifetime. It takes place in the month of *Dhu'l-hijja*, the last month of the Islamic calendar.

haram (leg.) forbidden action; one of the five legal statuses (*ahkam*); something sacred to which access is forbidden (haram mosque).

hasab noble descent, merit.

hayd menstruation, one of the causes of major impurity.

Hijra the Prophet Muhammad's migration from Mecca to Medina in 622 CE / 1 AH.

'ibadat 'acts of service', religious duties.

'id religious festival; the most celebrated are *'id al-fitr* (the breaking of the fast at the end of Ramadan) *and 'id al-adha* (the festival of sacrifice, during the *hajj* month); there are also other festivals celebrated for example by Shi'is.

imam prayer leader, guide; master.

Imam In Shi'i context, the person recognized as the spiritual and political head of the Muslim community after the Prophet. 'Ali ibn Abi Talib and some of his descendants are considered to be such leaders, Imams, as legitimate successors to Muhammad. The Imams are regarded as infallible, sinless, divinely appointed, divinely guided in their special spiritual functions and as the ultimate repositories of all esoteric knowledge.

imama leadership; *imama kubra*, lit. the greater leadership, i.e. political leadership; *imama sughra*, lit. the lesser leadership, i.e. ritual prayer leadership.

'isma immunity from error, sinlessness of the Prophets; for Shi'is (Twelvers and Isma'ilis), also infallibility of the Imams and the People of House of the Prophet (see Qur. 33.33), including Fatima.

isnad the chain of authorities through whom a *hadith* narrative is transmitted.

Isra'iliyyat literature; i.e. narratives derived from religions other than Islam, especially from Judaism.

ittisaliyya relationship of connectedness or continuity with the past.

Ja'farite (leg.) the Shi'i legal school referring to teachings and traditions going back to the Shi'i Imam (q. v.) Ja'far al-Sadiq.

jama'a congregational prayers.

jama'at khana (lit. 'house of the community') for Nizari Isma'ilis it is the primary space of communal gathering and ritual performance, including the daily *du'a* prayer.

jami'a congregational mosque; a large space of worship for the daily *salat* and especially for the Friday congregational prayer.

jihad striving, effort, struggle; greater *jihad* is the inner strife; lesser *jihad* is the external fight (of the sword, of the pen, social *jihad*) in the path of Allah.

jum'a Friday noon prayer, in congregation, usually, for men in the mosque.

junub major impurity which can be remedied by a full bath or full cleansing (*ghusl*) for ritual, esp. for *salat*. According to Muslim jurists, two main causes of *junub* are sexual activity and menstruation (*hayd*).

khanaqa a space used by Sufi groups for teaching and communal worship, and at times the burial site of a Sufi master.

khatib lit. deliverer of a sermon, esp the Friday *khutba* (q.v.); preacher.

khuntha an umbrella Arabic term used to indicate a range of identities from hermaphrodite and intersex to an effeminate person.

khutba sermon delivered during the Friday midday public prayer in a mosque, usually inclusive of blessings upon the caliph (and his family) or the ruler.

kuriha/yukrah (leg.) undesirable/repugnant action [one of the five legal statuses – *ahkam*].

la ba's (leg.) not objectionable, legally permissible.

madhhab (pl. *madhahib*) a system of belief within Islam; a school of religious law.

madrasa religious college or school for the study of the law, often attached to the mosque.

mahr dowry or gift promised by the prospective husband and included in a marriage contract.

makruh (leg.) an act which is 'disliked' but still legally permissible.

malika (masc. *malik*) sovereign, queen.

masjid (lit. a place of prostration) a mosque, a space for the performance of ritual prayers; also a community/communal centre for social and educational gatherings.

mihrab mosque prayer niche, indicating the direction of prayer towards Mecca.

minbar pulpit in a mosque from where the imam or the *khatib* delivers the *khutba* (q.v.).

mu'amalat legal social matters (marriage, inheritance etc.).

mubah (leg.) neutral, permissible (one of the five legal statuses – *ahkam*).

mudahim female religious leaders in women's mosques in the Maldives.

Muhajirun Supporters of the Prophet who migrated to Medina.

muqaddama/muqaddamat (fem. religious leader; lit. one who is sent forth) esp. in Sufi context; someone holding an *ijaza*, or authorization, to represent a Sufi order; can also provide religious/spiritual education and oversee religious associations.

musalla an open space, usually outside the mosque, used for prayer; a prayer area.

nafila (pl. *nawafil*) optional prayer.

nasab genealogy, descent.

nu ahong woman imam in China (usually presiding over a women mosque (*nüsi*). Among her functions are teaching, praying, ritual guidance, giving sermons, counselling and in some mosques to lead women in prayer.

nüsi Chinese women's mosque, a place of worship, of ritual instruction, religious education, led by a *nu ahong* and usually for the exclusive use of women.

qibla the direction towards Mecca which Muslims face during prayer. It is marked by a niche inside a mosque.

rak'a (rit.) bending of the body followed by two prostrations; a cycle of postures in performing *salat*.

sabiqa precedence in Islam; length of adherence to the faith.

salat prescribed prayer for Muslims; among the required prayers are the five daily prayers.

salat al-jama'a congregational prayer.

shahid/shahida witness, martyr.

shari'a the Islamic law.

shaykh lit. an elder; honorific term used for a scholar, a master, a leader.

Sira nabawiyya the life and times of the Prophet Muhammad. Literary genre.

sunna 'custom' the way Muhammad acted; the source material for the *sunna* are the *hadith*s. *Sunna* is one of the four sources of shari'a; also (leg.) highly recommended action.

sura a chapter of the Qur'an, which comprises of 114 *sura*s.

tafsir exegesis of the Qur'an.

tahara (rit.) ritual purity, the required state for prayer; (leg.) the major washing required to cleanse from a state of major impurity (*junub*) in order to achieve cleanliness.

taqiyya precautionary religious dissimulation to escape persecution or danger.

tawhid doctrine of the unity of Allah.
'ulama' learned individuals, scholars in Islamic religious sciences; the religious class.
umm al-walad term commonly used to refer to a concubine, whether free or a slave, who would acquire rights upon giving birth to her master's child.
walad zina child conceived through unlawful sexual union; illegitimate child.
wali guardian, governor, defender; also a title used for the imams.
wudu' (rit.) minor ritual ablution for minor impurities.
zahir the outer, exoteric meaning of sacred texts and religious laws; counterbalancing the *batin* (q.v.).
ziyara visitation of tombs and shrines.

BIBLIOGRAPHY

Primary sources

Abu Dawud, Sulayman ibn al-Ash'ath. *Sunan Abi Dawud*. Edited by 'Aziz 'Abd al-Ra'as. Hums: Muhammad 'Ali al-Sayyid, 1969.

Abu Dawud, Sulayman ibn al-Ash'ath. *Sunan Abi Da'ud*. Edited by Hamd ibn Muhammad Da'as, 'Izzat 'Ubayd Khattabi. Hums: Muhammad 'Ali al-Sayyid, 1969–74.

Abu Dawud, Sulayman ibn al-Ash'ath. *Sunan Abi Dawud*. Translated by Ahmad Hasan (as *Sunan Abu Dawud*). New Delhi: al-Madina Publications, 1985, 3 vols.

Abu Dawud, Sulayman ibn al-Ash'ath. *Sunan Abi Dawud*. In *Jam' Jawami' al-Ahadith*. Vaduz: Thesaurus Islamicus Foundation, 2000.

al-Baghdadi, 'Abd al-Qahir. *Al-Farq Bayna al-Firaq*. Translated by K. Chambers Seelye as *Moslem Schisms and Sects: Al-Farq Bayna al-Firaq*. New York: Ams, 1966.

al-Baghdadi, 'Abd al-Qahir. *Al-Farq Bayna al-Firaq*. Beirut: Dar al-Ma'rifa, 1970.

al-Baji, Sulayman ibn Khalaf. *Kitab al-Muntaqa Sharh Muwatta'*. Edited by M. Shaqrun. Cairo: Matba'a al-Sa'ada bi Jawar Muhafiza Misr, 1912–13, 5 vols.

al-Bukhari, Muhammad. *Sahih al-Bukhari*. Translated by Muhammad Muhsin Khan as *The Translation of the Meanings of Sahih al-Bukhari*. Beirut: Dar al-Fikr, n.d.

al-Bukhari, Muhammad. *Sahih al-Bukhari*. Translated by Muhammad Muhsin Khan as *The Translation of the Meanings of Sahih al-Bukhari*. Riyadh: Dar al-Salam, 1984.

al-Bukhari, Muhammad. *Sahih al-Bukhari*. Translated by Muhammad Muhsin Khan as *The Translation of the Meanings of Sahih al-Bukhari*. Riyadh: Dar al-Salam, 1997, 9 vols.

al-Daraqutni, 'Ali ibn 'Umar. *Sunan al-Daraqutni*. Edited by Majdi ibn Mansur al-Shura. Beirut: Dar al-Kutub al-'Ilmiyya, 1996.

al-Hilli, Hasan ibn Yusuf Ibn al-Mutahhar al-'Allama. *Mukhtalif al-Shi'a fi Ahkam al-Shari'a*. Qum: Markaz al-Abhath wa-al-Dirasat al-Islamiyya, 1995–99, 10 vols.

Ibn Abi Shayba, 'Abdallah ibn Muhammad. *Al-Musannaf*. Edited by Muhammad 'Awwama. Jidda: Sharika Dar al-Qiblah, 2006, 6 vols.

Ibn al-'Arabi, Muhyi al-Din. *Al-Futuhat al-Makkiyya*. Cairo: Dar al-Kutub al-'Arabiyya, 1329 [1911], 4 vols.

Ibn al-'Arabi, Muhyi al-Din. *Al-Futuhat al-Makkiyya*. Edited by 'Uthman Yahya, Ibrahim Madkur. Cairo: al-Hay'a al-Misriyya al-'Amma li'l-Kitab, 1972–92. 14 vols.

Ibn al-'Arabi, Muhyi al-Din. *Tafsir al-Qur'an al-Karim*. Edited by Mustafa Ghalib. Beirut: Dar al-Andalus, 1978, 2 vols.

Ibn Babawayh, Abu Ja'far Muhammad ibn 'Ali. *Man la Yahdaruhu al-Faqih*. Tehran: Dar al-Kutub al-Islamiyya, 1970.

Ibn Hanbal, Ahmad. *Masa'il al-Imam Ahmad ibn Hanbal*. Edited by Shawish Zuhayr. Beirut: al-Maktab al-Islami, 1981.

Ibn Hanbal, Ahmad. *Musnad al-Imam Ahmad ibn Hanbal*. Edited by Samir Taha al-Majdhub. Beirut: al-Maktab al-Islami, 1993, 8 vols.

Ibn Hazm, 'Ali b. Ahmad. *Al-Muhalla bi'l-Athar*. Beirut: Dar Ihya Turath al-'Arabi, 2003.

Ibn Hisham, 'Abd al-Malik. *Al-Sira al-Nabawiyya*. Edited by Suhayl Zakkar. Beirut: Dar al-Fikr, 1992.
Ibn al-'Imad 'Abd al-Hayyi ibn Ahmad al-Ikri al-Hanbali. *Shadharat al-Dhahab*. Beirut: Al-Maktab al-Tijari li'l-Tiba'a wa-al-Nashr wa-al-Tawzi', 1380 / 1960, 8 vols.
Ibn Ishaq, Muhammad. *Sirat Rasul Allah*. Translated by Alfred Guillaume as *The Life of Muhammad: A Translation of Ibn Ishaq's Sirat Rasul Allah*. Karachi: Oxford University Press, 1978.
Ibn al-Jawzi, 'Abd al-Rahman. *Ahkam al-Nisa'*. Beirut: Dar al-Kutub al-'Ilmiyya, 1985.
Ibn Khayyat, Khalifa. *Ta'rikh khalifat ibn Khayyat*. Edited by Akran Diya al-'Umari. Beirut: Mu'assasat al-risala, 1977.
Ibn Khuzayma, al-Sulami al-Nisaburi. *Sahih Ibn Khuzayma*. Edited by Muhammad Mustafa al-A'zami. Beirut: Al-Maktab al-Islami, 1970.
Ibn Maja, Muhammad ibn Yazid. *Sunan al-Hafiz Abi 'Abdallah*. Edited by Muhammad Fu'ad 'Abd al-Baqi. Cairo: Dar Ihya' al-Kutub al-'Arabiyya, 1952–3, 2 vols.
Ibn al-Murtada, Ahmad ibn Yahya. *Al-Bahr al-Zakhkhar*, quoted and annotated in *Al-Manar fi'l-Mukhtar*, edited by al-Maqbali, Salih ibn Mahdi. Beirut: Mu'assasat al-Risala, 1988.
Ibn Qudama, Muwaffaq al-Din. *Al-Mughni*. Beirut: Dar al-Kitab al-'Arabi, 1972, 12 vols.
Ibn Rahwayh, Ishaq ibn Ibrahim. *Musnad Ishaq ibn Rahwayh*. Beirut: Dar al-Kutub al-'Arabi, 2002.
Ibn Rushd, Abu al-Walid Muhammad. *Bidayat al-Mujtahid*. Translated by Imran Ahsan Khan Nyazee as *The Distinguished Jurist's Primer*. Reading: Garnet, 1994.
Ibn Rushd, Abu al-Walid Muhammad. *Sharh Bidayat al-Mujtahid wa Nihayat al-Muqtasid* (3rd edn). Edited by 'Abdallah al-'Abadi. Cairo: Dar al-Salam, 2006.
Ibn Sa'd, Muhammad. *Kitab al-Tabaqat al-Kabir [Ibn Saad: Biographien: Band 8, Biographien der Frauen]* (Vol. 8). Edited by Carl Brockleman and Eduard Sachau. Leiden: Brill, 1904.
Ibn Sa'd, Muhammad. *Kitab al-Tabaqat al-Kabir*. Beirut: Dar Sadir, [1968], 9 vols.
Ibn Sa'd, Muhammad. *Kitab al-Tabaqat al-Kabir* (Vol. 8). Translated by Aisha Bewley as *The Women of Madina*. London: Ta-Ha, 1995.
Ibn Sa'd, Muhammad. *Kitab al-Tabaqat al-Kabir*. Edited by 'Ali Muhammad 'Umar. Cairo: Maktabat al-Khaniji, 2001, 11 vols.
Ibn Sallam, Abu 'Ubayd al-Qasim. *Kitab al-Nasikh wa-l-Mansukh (MS Istanbul, Topkapi, Ahmet III A 143)*. Edited by John Burton. Cambridge: Gibb Memorial Trust Arabic Studies, 1987.
Ibn Taymiyya, Ahmad. *Majmu' al-Fatawa*. Edited by Mustafa 'Abd al-Qadir 'Ata. Beirut: Dar al-Kutub al-'Ilmiyya, 2000.
Ibn Taymiyya, Ahmad. *Naqd Maratib al-Ijma'*. Beirut: Dar al-Kutub al-'Ilmiyyah, 1970.
Al-Jahiz, 'Amr ibn Bahr Abu Uthman. *Kitab al-Hayawan*. Beirut: al-Majma' al-'Ilmi al-'Arabi al-Islami, 1969.
al-Kulayni, Abu Ja'far Muhammad al-Razi. *Al-Furu' min al-Kafi*. Edited by 'Ali Akbar Ghaffari. Beirut: Dar Sa'b – Dar al-Ta'aruf, 1980–1, 6 vols.
Al-Malati, Muhammad ibn Ihmad Abu'l-Husayn. *Al-Tanbih wa'l-Radd 'ala ahl al-Ahwa' wa'l-Bid'a*. Edited by Muhammad Zahid Kawthari. Baghdad: Maktabat al-Muthanna, 1968.
al-Mas'udi, 'Ali ibn al-Husayn. *Muruj al-Dhahab wa Ma'adin al-Jawhar*. Beirut: Dar al-Kutub al-'Ilmiyya, 2004, 4 vols.
al-Mawardi, Abu al-Hasan 'Ali ibn Muhammad. *Al-Ahkam al-Sultaniyya*. Translated by

Wafa H. Wahba as *The Ordinances of Government: A Translation of al-Aḥkam al-Sultaniyya wa al-Wilayat al-Diniyya*. Reading: Garnet, 1996.

al-Mawardi, Abu al-Hasan 'Ali ibn Muhammad. *Al-Hawi al-Kabir fi Fiqh Madhhab al-Imam al-Shafi'i, wa Huwa Sharh Mukhtasar al-Muzani*. Edited by 'Abd al-Fattah Khalid Shibl. Beirut: Dar al-Kutub al-'Ilmiyya, 1999, 5 vols.

al-Mizzi, Yusuf ibn 'Abd al-Rahman. *Tahdhib al-Kamal fi Asma' al-Rijal*. Edited by 'Awwad Ma'ruf Bashshar. Beirut: Mu'assasat al-Risala, 1992.

Muhaqqiq al-Hilli, Ja'far ibn al-Hasan, Abu'l-Qasim. *Shara'i' al-Islam fi Masa'il al-Halal wa'l-Haram*. Edited by Muhammad 'Ali 'Abd al-Husayn. Tehran: Manshurat al-A'lami, 1969.

al-Murtada al-Zabidi. *Taj al-'Arus min Jawahir al-Qamus*. Beirut: Manshurat Dar Maktabat al-Hay'a, 1888.

Muslim, ibn al-Hajjaj. 'Sahih Muslim'. In *Jam' Jawami' al-Ahadith* (Vol. 4). Vaduz: Thesaurus Islamicus Foundation, 2000.

Muslim, ibn al-Hajjaj. *Sahih Muslim*. Translated by 'Abdul Hamid Siddiqi as *Sahih Muslim: Being Traditions of the Sayings and Doings of the Prophet Muhammad as Narrated by his Companions and Compiled under the Title of al-Jami'-us-Sahih*. Lahore: Muhammad Ashraf, 1976.

Muslim, ibn al-Hajjaj. *Sahih Muslim*. Translated by Nasiruddin al-Khattab as *The Translation of the Meanings of Sahih Muslim*. Riyad: Dar al-Salam, 2007.

al-Muzani, Isma'il ibn Yahya. *Mukhtasar al-Muzani*. Edited by Muhammad 'Abd al-Qadir Shahin. Beirut: Dar al-Kutub al-'Ilmiyya, 1993.

al-Nawawi, Muhyi al-din. *Kitab al-Majmu'*. Edited by Muhammad Najib al-Muti'i. Beirut: Dar Ihya al-Turath al-'Arabi, 2001.

al-Qadi al-Nu'man, Ibn Hayyun Ibn Muhammad (Abu Hanifa). *Da'a'im al-Islam* (3rd edn). Cairo: Dar al-Ma'arif, 1969.

al-Qadi al-Nu'man, Ibn Hayyun Ibn Muhammad (Abu Hanifa). *Da'a'im al-Islam*. Translated by Asaf Ali Asghar Fyzee as *The Pillars of Islam: Da'a'im al-Islam of al-Qadi al-Nu'man*. Oxford: Oxford University Press, 2002–4, 2 vols.

al-Qadi al-Nu'man, Ibn Hayyun Ibn Muhammad (Abu Hanifa) *Kitab al-Idah*. Edited by Muhammad Kazim Rahmati. Beirut: Mu'assasat al-A'lami lil-Matbu'at, 2007.

al-Qadi al-Nu'man, Ibn Hayyun Ibn Muhammad (Abu Hanifa). *Kitab al-Idah*. Tübingen University Library, MS Ma vi 322, n.d.

al-Qadi al-Nu'man, Ibn Hayyun Ibn Muhammad (Abu Hanifa). *Ta'wil al-Da'a'im*. Edited by al-A'zami. Cairo: Dar al-Ma'arif, 1969–72. 3 vols. (vol 3 2nd edn 1982).

al-Rafi'i, 'Abd al-Karim, al-Qazwini Abu'l-Qasim. *Al-'Aziz, Sharh al-Wajiz*, known as *al-Sharh al-Kabir*. Edited by 'Ali Mu'awwad and 'Adil 'Abd al-Mawjud. Beirut: Dar al-Kutub al-'Ilmiyya, 1997.

al-Rumi, Yaqut ibn 'Abd Allāh al-Hamawi. *Kitab Irshad al-Arib ila Ma'rifat al-Adib al-Ma'ruf bi-Mu'jam al-Udaba', aw, Ṭabaqat al-Udaba'*. Edited by David Samuel Margoliouth. Leiden: Brill, 1907–26, 7 vols.

al-Safadi, Khalil ibn Aybak. *A'yan al-'Asr wa A'wan al-Nasr*. Edited by Falih Ahmad Bakkur. Beirut: Dar al-Fikr, 1998, 4 vols.

al-Safadi, Khalil ibn Aybak. *Kitab al-Wafi bi'l-Wafayat*. Wiesbaden/Beirut: Franz Steiner Gerlach, 1931–2013, 32 vols.

Sahnun Ibn Sa'id, al-Tanukhi. *Al-Mudawwana al-Kubra li'l-Imam Malik ibn Anas*. Beirut: Dar al-Kutub al-'Ilmiyya, [1994], 5 vols.

al-Shafi'i, Muhammad ibn Idris. *Kitab al-Umm*. Edited by Muhammad Zahra al-Najjar. Beirut: Dar al-Ma'rifa li'l-Tiba'a wa-al-Nashr, [1400-/1980s], 8 vols.

Al-Shaybani, Muhammad ibn al-Hasan. *Kitab al-Athar*. Translated by Hafiz Riyad Ahmad as *Kitab al-Athar of Imam Abu Hanifa: The Narration of Muhammad ibn al-Hasan ash-Shaybani*. London: Turath, 2006.

al-Tabari, Abu Ja'far Muhammad ibn Jarir. *Ta'rikh al-Rusul wa'l-Muluk* (Vol. 1). Translated and annotated by Franz Rosenthal as *The History of al-Tabari: General Introduction and From the Creation to the Flood*. Albany: SUNY Press, 1989.

al-Tabari, Abu Ja'far Muhammad ibn Jarir. *Ta'rikh al-Rusul wa'l-Muluk* (Vol. 6). Translated by W. Montgomery Watt and M. V. McDonald as *The History of al-Tabari: Muḥammad at Mecca*. Albany: SUNY Press, 1988.

al-Tabari, Abu Ja'far Muhammad ibn Jarir. *Ta'rikh al-Rusul wa'l-Muluk* (Vol. 7). Translated by W. Montgomery Watt and M. V. Mcdonald as *The History of al-Tabari: The Foundation of the Community*. Albany: SUNY Press, 1988.

al-Tabari, Abu Ja'far Muhammad ibn Jarir. *Ta'rikh al-Rusul wa'l-Muluk* (Vol. 8). Translated by Michael Fishbein as *The History of al-Tabari: The Victory of Islam: Muhammad at Medina A.D. 626–630 / A.H. 5–8*. Albany: SUNY Press, 1997.

al-Tabari, Abu Ja'far Muhammad ibn Jarir. *Ta'rikh al-Rusul wa'l-Muluk* (Vol. 11). Translated by Khalid Yahya Blankinship as *The History of al-Tabari: The Challenge to the Empires A.D. 633–635 / A.H. 12–13*. Albany: SUNY Press, 1993.

al-Tabari, Abu Ja'far Muhammad ibn Jarir. *Ta'rikh al-Rusul wa'l-Muluk* (Vol. 12). Translated by Yohanan Friedmann as *The History of al-Tabari: The Battle of al-Qadisiyyah and the Conquest of Syria and Palestine A.D. 635–637 / A.H. 14–15*. Albany: SUNY Press, 1992.

al-Tabari, Abu Ja'far Muhammad ibn Jarir. *Ta'rikh al-Rusul wa'l-Muluk* (Vol. 16). Translated by Adrian Brockett as *The History of al-Tabari: The Community Divided*. Albany: SUNY Press, 1997.

al-Tabari, Abu Ja'far Muhammad ibn Jarir. *Ta'rikh al-Rusul wa'l-Muluk* (Vol. 17). Translated by Gerald Hawting as *The History of al-Tabari: The First Civil War*. Albany: SUNY Press, 1996.

al-Tabari, Abu Ja'far Muhammad ibn Jarir. *Ta'rikh al-Rusul wa'l-Muluk* (Vol. 19). Translated by I. K. A. Howard as *The History of al-Tabari: The Caliphate of Yazid b. Mu'awiyah A.D. 680–683 / A.H. 60–64*. Albany: SUNY Press, 1990.

al-Tabari, Abu Ja'far Muhammad ibn Jarir. *Ta'rikh al-Rusul wa'l-Muluk* (Vol. 22). Translated by Everett K. Rowson as *The History of al-Tabari: The Marwanid Restoration: The Caliphate of 'Abd al-Malik A.D. 693–701 / A.H. 74–81*. Albany: SUNY Press, 1989.

al-Tabari, Abu Ja'far Muhammad ibn Jarir. *Ta'rikh al-Rusul wa'l-Muluk* (Vol. 39). Translated by Ella Landau-Tasseron as *The History of al-Tabari: Biographies of the Prophet's Companions and Their Successors: al-Tabari's Supplement to His History*. Albany: SUNY Press, 1998.

al-Tusi, Muhammad ibn al-Hasan, Shaykh al-Ta'ifa. *Kitab al-Khilaf*. Qum: Dar al-Kutub al-'Aliya, n.d., 3 vols.

al-Tusi, Muhammad ibn al-Hasan, Shaykh al-Ta'ifa. *Al-Mabsut fi Fiqh al-Imamiyya*. Edited by Al-Sayyid Muhammad al-Kashfi. Tehran: al-Matba'a al-Haydariyya, 1958.

al-Tusi, Muhammad ibn al-Hasan, Shaykh al-Ta'ifa. *Tahdhib al-Ahkam fi Sharh al-Muqni'a li'l-Shaykh al-Mufid*. Edited by Hasan al-Musawi Kharsan. Najaf: Dar al-Kutub al-Islamiyya, 1958, 6 vols.

Zayd ibn 'Ali. *Musnad al-Imam Zayd (Majmu' al-Fiqh)*. Translated by Eugenio Griffini as *Corpus Iuris di Zaid Ibn Ali*. Milano: Hoepli, 1919.

Secondary sources

Abou El Fadl, Khaled. 'Fatwa: On Women Leading Prayer'. *The Search for Beauty: On Beauty and Reason in Islam*. 5 April 2010. www.searchforbeauty.org/2010/04/05/fatwa-on-women-leading-prayer/ (accessed 14 April 2020).
Adang, C. 'The Beginnings of the Zahiri Madhhab in al-Andalus'. In *The Islamic School of Law: Evolution, Devolution and Progress*, edited by P. Bearman, 117–25. Cambridge, MA: Harvard University Press, 2005.
Afsaruddin, Asma. *Excellence and Precedence: Medieval Islamic Discourse on Legitimate Leadership*. Leiden: Brill, 2002.
Afsaruddin, Asma. *The First Muslims: History and Memory*. Oxford: Oneworld, 2007.
Afsaruddin, Asma. *Striving in the Path of God*. Oxford: Oxford University Press, 2013.
Afzalur, Rahman (ed.). *Encyclopaedia of Seerah*. London: Seerah Foundation / Muslim Schools Trust, 1981–1987, 7 vols.
Ahmed Leila. *Women and Gender in Islam: Historical Roots of a Modern Debate*. New Haven, CT: Yale University Press, 1992.
Akec, John (transl.) 'Sudan's Turabi: Muslim Women can Marry Christian or Jew'. *Sudan Tribune*, 11 April, 2006. www.sudantribune.com/article.php3?id_article=15021 (accessed 14 April 2020).
Algar, Hamid. 'Emam-e Jom'a'. *Encyclopaedia Iranica* (Vol. 8), edited by Ehsan Yarshater, 386–391. London, Boston: Routledge & Kegan Paul, 1998.
Ali, Kecia (ed.). *A Jihad for Justice: Honouring the Work and Life of amina wadud*. 2012. www.keciaali.com/a-jihad-for-justice (accessed 13 June 2020).
Alipour, Mehrdad. 'Transgender Identity, The Sex-Reassignment Surgery Fatwas and Islamic Theology of a Third Gender', *Religion and Gender* 7, 2 (2017): 164–179.
Allen-Ebrahimian, Bethany. 'China: The Best and the Worst Place to Be a Muslim Woman'. *Foreign Policy*, 17 July 2015. https://foreignpolicy.com/2015/07/17/china-feminism-islam-muslim-women-xinjiang-uighurs/ (accessed 2 November 2018).
Allès, Elisabeth. *Musulmans de Chine: Une Anthropologie des Hui de Henan*. Paris: Éditions de l'École des Hautes Études en Sciences Socials, 2000.
Amin, Yasmin. *Umm Salama and her Hadith*. MA thesis, American University in Cairo, 2011.
Amin, Yasmin. 'Wives of the Prophet'. In *The Oxford Encyclopedia of Islam and Women* (OEIW) (Vol. 2), edited by Natana J. Delong-Bas, 426–30. Oxford: Oxford University Press, 2013.
Antoun, R. T. *Muslim Preacher in the Modern World: A Jordanian Case Study in Comparative Perspective*. Princeton, NJ: Princeton University Press, 1989.
Anwar, Etin. 'Sexing the Prayer: The Politics of Ritual and Feminist Activism in Indonesia'. In *Muslima Theology: The Voices of Muslim Women Theologians*, edited by E. Aslan, Marcia Hermansen and E. Medeni, 197–216. Frankfurt: Lang, 2013.
Arbaoui, L. 'Ani Zonneveld's Visit to Morocco Creates Controversy over Woman Imam'. *Morocco World News*, 3 November 2015, www.moroccoworldnews.com/2015/11/171818/ani-zonnevelds-visit-to-morocco-creates-controversy-over-woman-imam/ (accessed 12 March 2018).
Arberry, Arthur J. *The Koran Interpreted*. London: Oxford University Press, 1964.
Arnaldez, Roger. 'Ibn Hazm'. In *Encyclopaedia of Islam* (2nd edn; EI2) (Vol. 3), edited by Bernard Lewis, Victor Louis Ménage, Charles Pellat and Joseph Schacht, 790–99. Leiden: Brill, 1986.
Asad, Muhammad. *The Message of the Qur'an*. Gibraltar: Dar al-Andalus, 1980.

Asad, Talal. *The Idea of an Anthropology of Islam*. Washington, DC: Center for Contemporary Arab Studies, Georgetown University, 1986.

Asani, Ali. 'From Satpanthi to Ismaili Muslim: The Articulation of Ismaili Khoja Identity in South Asia'. In *A Modern History of the Ismailis: Continuity and Change in a Muslim Community*, edited by Farhad Daftary, 95–128. London: IB Tauris, 2011.

Assembly of Muslim Jurists of America. *A Collection of Fatwas and Legal Opinions on the Issue of Women Leading Prayer*. 5 April 2005 / 25 Safar 1426. www.abc.se/home/m9783/ir/d/fwlp_e.pdf (accessed 28 May 2020).

Ateş, Seyran. *Selam, Frau Imamin: Wie ich in Berlin eine Liberale Moschee Gründete (Salam, Mrs Imam: How I Founded a Liberal Mosque in Berlin)*. Berlin: Ullstein, 2017.

Auda, Jasser. *Maqasid Al-Shari'ah: A Beginner's Guide*. London, Washington: The International Institute of Islamic Thought, 2008.

Auda, Jasser. *Reclaiming the Mosque: The Role of Women in Islam's House of Worship*. Swansea: Claritas Books, 2017.

Ayyad, Essam, S. 'An Historiographical Analysis of the Arabic Accounts of Early Mosques: with Special Reference to those at Madina, Baṣra and Kūfa'. *Journal of Islamic Studies* 30, 1 (2019): 1–33.

Ayyad, Essam S. 'The "House of the Prophet" or the "Mosque of the Prophet"?' *Journal of Islamic Studies* 24, 3 (2013): 273–334.

Azam, Hina. 'A Critique of the Argument for Woman-Led Friday Prayers'. In *A Collection of Fatwas and Legal Opinions on the Issue of Women Leading Prayer*. Assembly of Muslim Jurists of America. 5 April 2005 / 25 Safar 1426, 20–26. www.abc.se/home/m9783/ir/d/fwlp_e.pdf (accessed 28 May 2020).

al-Azmeh, Aziz. *The Times of History: Universal Topics in Islamic Historiography*. Budapest and New York: Central European University Press, 2007.

Bakhtiar, Laleh. *The Sublime Quran*. Chicago: Kazi, 2007.

Baksi-Lahiri, Sudeshna. *Women's Power and Ritual Politics in the Maldives*. Ithaca, NY: Cornell University, 2004.

Al-Banna, Jamal. *Jawaz Imamat al-Mar'a li'l-Rijal*. Cairo: Dar al-Fikr al-Islami, 2005.

Bano, Masooda and Hilary Kalmbach (eds.). *Women, Leadership, and Mosques: Changes in Contemporary Islamic Authority*. Leiden: Brill, 2012.

Barazangi, Nimat Hafez. *Woman's Identity and Rethinking the Hadith*. London: Routledge, 2015.

Bauer, Karen. 'Debates on Women's Status as Judges and Witnesses in Post-Formative Islamic Law'. *Journal of the American Oriental Society* 130, 1 (2010): 1–21.

Baugh, Carolyn. 'Revolting Women? Early Kharijite Women in Islamic Sources'. *Journal of Islamic and Muslim Studies* 2, 1 (2017): 36–55.

BBC News. 'Iranian Women to Lead Prayers'. BBC News Online World Middle East, 1 August, 2000. http://news.bbc.co.uk/1/hi/world/middle_east/861819.stm (accessed 29 March 2018).

Bearman, Peri, J., Bianquis, Th. et al. *Encyclopaedia of Islam* (2nd edn; EI2). Leiden: Brill, 1960–2005. 12 vols.

Bearman, Peri, Rudolph Peters and Frank Vogel (eds.). *The Islamic School of Law: Evolution, Devolution and Progress*. Cambridge, MA: Harvard University Press, 2005.

Becker, C. H. 'On the History of Muslim Worship'. In *The Development of Islamic Ritual*, edited by Gerald Hawting, 49–74. Aldershot: Ashgate, 2006.

Bedi, R. J. 'Sisters in Islam files for judicial review on fatwa', *The Star*, 31 October 2014. www.thestar.com.my/news/nation/2014/10/31/sisters-in-islam-files-for-judicial-review-on-fatwa/ (accessed 20 April 2020).

Bernama. 'In Sisters in Islam Case, High Court says Fatwa is Syariah Court's Jurisdiction'. *New Straits Times*, 27 August 2019. www.nst.com.my/news/crime-courts/2019/08/516547/sisters-islam-case-high-court-says-fatwa-syariah-courts (accessed 9 April 2020).

Bhol, Asma. 'I'm a female imam'. *FT.com Magazine*, 14 May 2016. www.ft.com/content/2ccda9ea-17c7-11e6-bb7d-ee563a5a1cc1 (accessed 12 May 2018).

Bloom, Jonathan. 'Mosque'. In *Encyclopaedia of the Qur'an* (EQ) (Vol. 3), edited by Jane Dammen McAuliffe, 426–38. Leiden: Brill, 2003.

Borrillo, Sara. *Femminismi e Islam in Marocco: Attiviste laiche, teologhe, predicatrici*. Napoli: Edizioni Scientifiche Italiane, 2017.

Bowering, Gerald. 'Prayer'. In *Encyclopaedia of the Qur'an* (EQ) (Vol. 4), edited by Jane Dammen McAuliffe, 215–31. Leiden: Brill, 2004.

Brink, Judy. 'Lost Rituals: Sunni Muslim Women in Rural Egypt'. In *Mixed Blessings, Gender and Religious Fundamentalism Cross Culturally*, edited by Judy Brink and Joan Mencher, 199–208. London, New York: Routledge, 1997.

Brown, Jonathan. 'Did the Prophet Say It or Not? The Literal, Historical, and Effective Truth of *Hadith*s in Early Sunnism'. *Journal of the American Oriental Society* 129, 2 (2009): 259–85.

Bulliet, Richard W. *Conversion to Islam in the Medieval Period: An Essay in Quantitative History*. Cambridge, MA: Harvard University Press, 1979.

Bunt, Gary R. *Islam in the Digital Age: E-Jihad, Online Fatwas and Cyber Islamic Environments*. London: Pluto Books, 2003.

Butler, Judith. *Bodies That Matter: On the Discursive Limits of 'Sex'*. New York: Routledge, 1993.

Caetani, Leone. *Annali dell'Islam* (1st edn 1905–7). Hildesheim, New York: Olms, 1972, 10 vols.

Calder, Norman 'Friday Prayer and the Juristic Theory of Government: Sarakhsi, Shirazi, Mawardi'. In *Norman Calder: Interpretation and Jurisprudence in Medieval Islam*, edited by J. Mojaddedi and A. Rippin, 35–47. Aldershot: Ashgate Variorum, 2006.

Calder, Norman. *Studies in Early Muslim Jurisprudence*. Oxford: Clarendon Press, 1993.

Calder, Norman, Jawid Ahmad Mojaddedi and Andrew Rippin (eds.). *Interpretation and Jurisprudence in Medieval Islam*. Aldershot: Ashgate, 2006.

Calderini, Simonetta. 'Citing the Past to Address the Present: Authorities and Unexpected Interlocutors on Female Leadership of Salat'. Open access lecture. Fairfax, VA: Ali Vural Ak Center for Global Islamic Studies, George Mason University, 2014. https://islamicstudiescenter.gmu.edu/conferences-and-workshops/center-lecture-series/spring-2014 (accessed 8 July 2020).

Calderini, Simonetta. 'Classical Sources on the Permissibility of Female Imams: An Analysis of some *Hadith*s about Umm Waraqa'. In *Sources and Approaches across Near Eastern Disciplines*, edited by Verena Klemm and Nuha al-Sha'ar, 53–70. Leuven: Peeters, 2013.

Calderini, Simonetta. 'Contextualising Arguments about Female Ritual Leadership (Women Imams) in Classical Islamic Sources'. *Comparative Islamic Studies* 5, 1 (2009): 5–32.

Calderini, Simonetta. 'Female Seclusion and the Veil: Two Issues in Political and Social Discourse. The Reforms of Sultan Muhammad Shah'. In *Islam and the Veil: Theoretical and Regional Contexts*, edited by Theodore Gabriel and Rabiha Hannan, 48–62. London: Continuum, 2011.

Calderini, Simonetta 'Islam and Diversity: Alternative Voices within Contemporary Islam'. *New Blackfriars*, 89, 1021 (2008): 324–36.

Calderini, Simonetta. '"Leading from the Middle": Qadi al-Nu'man on Female Prayer Leadership'. In *The Fatimid Caliphate: Diversity of Traditions*, edited by Farhad Daftary and Shainool Jiwa, 94–117. London: IB Tauris, 2018.

Calderini, Simonetta. 'Mary and Prayer in the Qur'an, *Tafsir* and Interpretation'. *Studi Magrebini*, 13 (2014–15): 129–55.

Cantone, Cleo. 'Women Claiming Space in Mosques'. *International Institute for the Study of Islam in the Modern World – ISIM Newsletter*, 11, 2 (2002): 29.

Cesari, Jocelyne (ed.). *The Oxford Handbook of European Islam*. Oxford: Oxford University Press, 2015.

Chakanetsa, Kim. 'Women Leading Muslim Communities'. *The Conversation, BBC World Service Online*, radio interview with Halima Krausen and Sherin Khankan, 2 April, 2018, www.bbc.co.uk/programmes/w3cswp16 (accessed 13 June 2020).

Cieślewska, Anna. *Islam with a Female Face: How Women are Changing the Religious Landscape in Tajikistan and Kyrgyzstan*. Krakow: Ksiegarnia Akademicka, 2017.

Cooke, Miriam. 'Ungendering Peace Talk'. In *Women and Peace in the Islamic World: Gender, Agency, Influence*, edited by Yasmin Saikia and Chad Haines, 25–42. London: IB Tauris, 2015.

The Copenhagen Post. 'Danish mosque continues to make history', *Copenhagen Post Online*, 10 August, 2016. http://cphpost.dk/?p=66605 (accessed 10 November 2018).

Cortese, Delia. 'Transmitting Sunni Learning in Fatimid Egypt: The Female Voices'. In *The Fatimid Caliphate: Diversity of Traditions*, edited by Farhad Daftary and Shainool Jiwa, 164–191. London: IB Tauris, 2018.

Cortese, Delia and Simonetta Calderini. *Women and the Fatimids in the World of Islam*. Edinburgh: Edinburgh University Press, 2006.

Daftary, Farhad. *The Isma'ilis: Their History and Doctrines*. Cambridge: Cambridge University Press, 2007.

Dar al-Ifta' al-Misriyya. *Fatwa on a Woman Leading Men in Congregational Prayers*. n.d. www.dar-alifta.org/Foreign/ViewFatwa.aspx?ID=10803 (accessed 28 May 2020).

Dar al-Ifta' al-Misriyya. *Fatwa on Women Leading Women in Prayer*. n.d. www.dar-alifta.org/ar/ViewResearch.aspx?sec=fatwa&ID=2413&LangID=1 (accessed 11 April 2020).

Dar al-Ifta' al-Misriyya. *Fatwa on Women Praying in Mosques*. n.d. www.dar-alifta.org/Foreign/ViewFatwa.aspx?ID=7975 (accessed 11 April 2020).

Deeb, Lara. *An Enchanted Modern: Gender and Public Piety in Shi'ite Lebanon*. Princeton, NJ: Princeton University Press, 2006.

Delong-Bas, Natana J. (ed.). *The Oxford Encyclopedia of Islam and Women* (OEIW). Oxford: Oxford University Press, 2013, 2 vols.

Demiray, Suleyman, Helms Barbara and Serap Bulsen. 'CAF [Canadian Armed Forces] Welcomes First Muslim Female Chaplain and Chaplain Candidate' *The Maple Leaf*, 12 April, 2018. https://ml-fd.caf-fac.ca/en/2018/04/12195 (accessed 18 June 2018).

Dixon, 'Abd al-Ameer 'Abd. *The Umayyad Caliphate 65–86 / 684–705: A Political Study*. London: Luzac, 1971.

Dossa, Parin Aziz. *Ritual and Daily Life: Transmission and Interpretation of the Ismaili Tradition in Vancouver*. PhD thesis, University of British Columbia, 1985.

Dutton, Yasin. *The Origins of Islamic Law: The Qur'an, the Muwatta' and Madinan 'Amal*. Abingdon: Routledge Curzon, 2002.

Eccel, A. Chris. 'Female and Feminine in Islamic Mysticism'. *The Muslim World* 78, 3–4 (1988): 209–24.

Eddouada, Souad and Renata Pepicelli. 'Maroc: Vers un "Féminisme Islamique d'État"'. *Critique Internationale* 46, 1 (2010): 87–100. www.cairn-int.info/article-E_

CRII_046_0087--morocco-towards-an-islamic-state-feminis.htm (accessed 12 March 2018).
Eddouada, Souad. 'Morocco's "Mourchidates" and Contradictions'. *Reset: Dialogues on Civilizations (ResetDOC)*, 17 April, 2009. www.resetdoc.org/story/moroccos-mourchidates-and-contradictions/ (accessed 12 March 2018).
Elewa, Ahmed and Laury Silvers. '"I Am One of the People": A Survey and Analysis of Legal Arguments on Women-led Prayer in Islam'. *Journal of Law and Religion* 26, 1 (2010–11): 141–171.
Eltahawy, Mona. 'Prayer toward Equality'. *The Washington Post*, 18 March 2005. www.miftah.org/display.cfm?DocId=6919&CategoryId=5 (accessed 28 May 2020).
Faith Matters. *Developing Diversity: Meeting the Needs of Muslim Women, A Directory of Mosques in England*. Faith Matters, 2010. www.faith-matters.org/images/stories/publications/Developing_Diversity.pdf (accessed 13 June 2019).
Farahat, Omar. 'Review of B. Sadeghi's *The Logic of Law Making in Islam*'. *Journal of Law and Religion* (2014): 1–4. www.academia.edu/7331550/Review_of_Sadeghis_The_Logic_of_Law_Making_in_Islam (accessed 28 May 2020).
al-Fassi, Hatoon Awjad, 'Women in Eastern Arabia, Myth and Representation'. In *Gulf Women*, edited by A. Sonbol and K. Dreher, 25–47. London: Bloomsbury, 2012.
Fatoohi, Louay. *Abrogation in the Qur'an and Islamic Law*. Abingdon, New York: Routledge, 2013.
Fekete, Liz. *A Suitable Enemy: Racism, Migration and Islamophobia in Europe*. London: Pluto, 2009.
Fentress, James and Chris Wickham. *Social Memory: New Perspectives on the Past*. Oxford: Blackwell, 1992.
Ferghana. 'Uzbekistan: Women in Bukhara are Prohibited to Go to Mosques'. *Ferghananews.com*, 17 August, 2009. http://enews.fergananews.com/news.php?id=1324 (accessed 13 May 2019).
Fernea, Elizabeth. *Guests of the Sheik: An Ethnography of an Iraqi Village*. New York: Doubleday Anchor Books, 1965.
Fewkes, Jacqueline H. *Locating Maldivian Women's Mosques in Global Discourses*. Cham: Palgrave Macmillan, 2019.
Fewkes, Jacqueline H. 'A "Women's Space" at the Indian Ocean Crossroads: Women's Mosques in the Maldives'. In *Gender at the Crossroads: Multi-disciplinary Perspectives*, edited by Nurten Kara, 277–84. Famagusta: Eastern Mediterranean University Press, 2009.
Fleet, Kate, Gudrun Krämer, et al. *Encyclopaedia of Islam 3 Online* (3rd edn; EI3 Online). Leiden: Brill online. https://referenceworks.brillonline.com/browse/encyclopaedia-of-islam-3 (accessed 20 June 2020).
Fleishman, Jeffrey. 'In the Library with a Leading Islamic Liberal'. *Los Angeles Times*, 6 May, 2008. www.latimes.com/world/la-fg-liberal6-2008may06-story.html (accessed 15 April 2020).
Forbes, A. D. W. 'The Mosque in the Maldive Islands: A Preliminary Historical Survey'. *Archipel* 26 (1983): 43–74.
Frisk, Sylva. *Submitting to God: Women and Islam in Urban Malaysia*. Seattle: University of Washington Press, 2009.
Gaborieau, Marc, Roger Allen et al. *Encyclopaedia of Islam 3* (3rd edn; EI3). Leiden: Brill, 2007–13.
Gaffney, Patrick D. *The Prophet's Pulpit: Islamic Preaching in Contemporary Egypt*. Berkeley: University of California Press, 1994.

Gaiser, A. R. 'Imamate in Kharijism and Ibadism'. In *Encyclopaedia of Islam 3 Online* (3rd edn; EI3 Online), edited by Kate Fleet, Gudrun Krämer, et al. Leiden: Brill online. Article published 2017. http://dx.doi.org/10.1163/1573-3912_ei3_COM_32433 (accessed 7 November 2019).

Gallup American Muslim Report. *Muslim Americans: A National Portrait*. Gallup & Muslim West Facts Project, 2009. www.themosqueinmorgantown.com/pdfs/ GallupAmericanMuslimReport.pdf (accessed 18 May 2018).

Gani, Aisha. 'Meet Bana Gora, the Woman Planning Britain's First Female-Managed Mosque'. *The Guardian*, 31 July, 2015. www.theguardian.com/lifeandstyle/2015/jul/31/bana-gora-muslim-womens-council-bradford-mosque (accessed 11 April 2020).

Gauvain, Richard. 'Ritual Rewards: A Consideration of Three Recent Approaches to Sunni Purity Law'. *Islamic Law and Society* 12, 3 (2005): 333–93.

Gilliat-Ray, Sophie, Mansur Ali and Stephen Pattison. *Understanding Muslim Chaplaincy*. London, New York: Routledge, 2013.

Gleave, Robert. *Inevitable Doubt: Two Theories of Shi ʿi Jurisprudence*. Leiden: Brill, 2000.

Gleave, Robert (PI). *Uses of the Past: Sharia and Gender in Legal Theory and Practice*. Bergen, Exeter: Gottingen and Leiden, 2016–18. www.usppip.eu/ (accessed 14 June 2020).

Goethe, Johann, Wolfgang von. *West-Östlicher Divan*. Translated by Martin Bidney as *West-East Divan: Poems, with 'Notes and Essays': Goethe's Intercultural Dialogues*. Albany: SUNY Press, 2010 (1st edn 1819).

Goffman, Erving. *The Presentation of Self in Everyday Life*. New York: Doubleday, 1959.

Goitein, Shelomo Dov. 'The Origin and Nature of the Muslim Friday Worship'. In *Studies in Islamic History and Institutions*, edited by Shelomo Dov Goitein, 111–25. Leiden: Brill, 1966.

Gopalan, Jayalakshmi. *Women in Politics in South Asia* (Background Paper Series Number 1). Chennai: The Prajnya Resource Centre on Women in Politics and Policy, 2012. http://retro.prajnya.in/prcbg1.pdf (accessed 7 July 2020).

Gorke, Andreas. "Abdallah b. ʿUmar b. al-Khattab'. In *Encyclopaedia of Islam 3 Online* (3rd edn; EI3 Online), edited by Kate Fleet, Gudrun Krämer, et al. Leiden: Brill, 2012. http://dx.doi.org/10.1163/1573-3912_ei3_COM_32433 (accessed 11 February 2019).

Grabar, Oleg (ed.). *The Formation of Islamic Art*. New Haven, CT: Yale University Press, 1987.

Graham, William A. 'Traditionalism in Islam: An Essay in Interpretation'. *Journal of Interdisciplinary History* 23, 3 (1993): 495–522.

Grossman, Susan. 'Women and the Jerusalem Temple'. In *Daughters of the King: Women and the Synagogue*, edited by Susan Grossman and Rivka Haut, 15–38. Philadelphia, PA: The Jewish Publication Society, 1992.

Guardi, Jolanda and Renata Bedendo. *Teologhe, Musulmane, Femministe*. Cantalupa (To): Effata' Editrice, 2009.

Haddad, Yvonne Yazbeck, Jane I. Smith and Kathleen M. Moore. *Muslim Women in America: The Challenge of Islamic Identity Today*. New York: Oxford University Press, 2006.

Halevi, Leor. 'Wailing for the Dead: The Role of Women in Early Islamic Funerals'. *Past & Present*, 183 (2004): 3–39.

Halici, Nihat. 'Female Imams in German Mosques Get a Mixed Reception'. *Deutsche Welle*, 7 October 2006. www.dw.com/en/female-imams-in-german-mosques-get-a-mixed-reception/a-2195419 (accessed 13 June 2020).

Hallaq, Wael B. *The Origins and Evolution of Islamic Law*. Cambridge: Cambridge University Press, 2005.
Hallaq, Wael B. 'Was al-Shafi'i the Master Architect of Islamic Jurisprudence?' In *Islamic Law* (Vol. 2) (Critical Concepts in Islamic Studies Series), edited by G. Picken, 105–26. New York: Routledge, 2011 [originally published 1993].
Hammer, Juliane. *American Muslim Women, Religious Authority and Activism: More Than a Prayer*. Austin, TX: University of Texas Press, 2012.
Hammer, Juliane. 'A (Friday) Prayer of Their Own: American Muslim Women, Religious Space, and Equal Rights'. *University of North Carolina, Religious Studies News, American Academy of Religion*, 24 March 2015. http://rsn.aarweb.org/articles/friday-prayer-their-own (accessed 18 May 2018).
Haneef, Sayed Sikandar Shah. 'Sex Reassignment in Islamic Law: The Dilemma of Transsexuals'. *International Journal of Business, Humanities and Technology*, 1, 1 (2011): 1–10.
Hassan, Mona. 'Women Preaching for the Secular State: Official Female Preachers (Bayan Vaizler) in Contemporary Turkey'. *International Journal of Middle East Studies* 43, 3 (2011): 451–473.
Hassan, Mona. 'Women-Only Masjid Opens in California'. *The Khilafah*, 4 February 2015. www.khilafah.com/women-only-masjid-opens-in-california/ (accessed 18 May 2018).
Hawting, Gerald R. (ed.). *The Development of Islamic Ritual*. Aldershot: Ashgate, 2006.
Hawting, Gerald R. *The First Dynasty of Islam*. London, New York: Routledge, 2000.
Hill, Joseph. *Wrapping Authority: Women Islamic Leaders in a Sufi Movement in Dakar, Senegal*. Toronto: University of Toronto Press, 2018.
Hillenbrand, Robert. *Islamic Architecture: Form, Function and Meaning*. New York: Columbia University Press, 1994.
Hobsbawm, Eric and Terence Ranger (eds.). *The Invention of Tradition*. Cambridge: Cambridge University Press, 1983.
Howard, I. K. A. 'The Development of the *Adhan* and *Iqama* of the *Salat* in Early Islam'. In *The Development of Islamic Ritual*, edited by Gerald Hawting, 95–104. Aldershot: Ashgate, 2006.
Huey Fern Tay. 'China's Female Imams Carrying on Ancient Islamic Tradition'. *Australia Broadcasting Corporation (ABC)*, 6 March, 2014. www.abc.net.au/news/2014-03-05/an-china-female-imams-feature/5298860 (accessed 2 November 2018).
Hummel, Ulrike. 'Female Imams in Germany: The Call of the Muezzin Women'. *Qantara. de*, 14 September, 2009. https://en.qantara.de/content/female-imams-in-germany-the-call-of-the-muezzin-women (accessed 4 September 2019).
Inclusive Mosque Initiative. *About*. http://inclusivemosqueinitiative.org/about/ (accessed 5 October 2018).
Inclusive Mosque Initiative. *IMI Is Not Doing Anything New*. http://inclusivemosqueinitiative.org/imi-isnt-doing-anything-new/ (accessed 5 October 2018).
Iqbal, Nosheen. 'Raise Your Gaze: "Islamic Feminism is Overlooked in the Mainstream"'. *The Observer*, 16 September 2018. www.theguardian.com/world/2018/sep/16/new-radicals-2018-raise-your-gaze-muslim-feminists-mosque (accessed 10 November 2019).
Jalajel, David Solomon. *Women and Leadership in Islamic Law: A Critical Analysis of Classical Legal Texts*. Oxford, New York: Routledge, 2017.
Jaschok, Maria. 'Nü ahong'. In *The Oxford Encyclopedia of Islam and Women* (OEIW) (Vol. 2), edited by Natana J. Delong-Bas, 15. Oxford: Oxford University Press, 2013.

Jaschok, Maria. 'Sources of Authority: Female Ahong and Qingshen Nusi (Women's Mosques) in China'. In *Women, Leadership, and Mosques: Changes in Contemporary Islamic Authority*, edited by Masooda Bano and Hilary Kalmbach, 37–58. Leiden: Brill, 2012.

Jaschok, Maria and Shui Jingjun. *The History of Women's Mosques in Chinese Islam*. Richmond: Curzon, 2012 (1st edn 2000).

Jaschok, Maria and Shui Jingjun. *Women, Religion and Space in China*. New York, London: Routledge, 2011.

Johansen, Baber. 'Casuistry: Between Legal Concept and Social Praxis'. *Islamic Law and Society* 2, 2 (1995): 135–56.

Judd, Steven C. 'Abu Thawr', In *Encyclopaedia of Islam 3 Online* (3rd edn; EI3 Online), edited by Kate Fleet, Gudrun Krämer, et al. Leiden: Brill, 2012. http://dx.doi.org/10.1163/1573-3912_ei3_COM_24754 (accessed 3 March 2020).

Juynboll, G. H. A. *Encyclopedia of Canonical Hadith*. Leiden: Brill, 2007.

Kaegi, Walter E. *Byzantium and the Early Islamic Conquests*. Cambridge: Cambridge University Press, 1992.

Kahhalah, 'Umar Rida. *A'lam al-Nisa'*. Beirut: Mu'assasat al-Risala, 1977, 5 vols.

Kaprawi, Norhayati. *Ummu Waraqah Sang Imam Wanita [Umm Waraqa the Female Imam]*. YouTube, 19 November 2018. www.youtube.com/watch?v=9pweF0iGNd4 (accessed 9 July 2020).

Kar, Mehrangiz. 'Women's Political Rights after the Islamic Revolution'. In *Religion and Politics in Modern Iran: A Reader*, edited by Lloyd Ridgeon, 253–65. London: IB Tauris, 2005.

Karim, Jamillah. *American Muslim Women: Negotiating Race, Class, and Gender within the Ummah*. New York: New York University Press, 2009.

Kassam, Tazim. 'The Daily Prayer (*Du'a*) of Shi'a Isma'ili Muslims'. In *Religions of the United States in Practice* (Vol. 2), edited by Colleen McDannell, 32–43. Princeton, NJ: Princeton University Press, 2001.

Katz, Marion Holmes. *Body of Text: The Emergence of Sunni Law of Ritual Purity*. New York: SUNY Press, 2002.

Katz, Marion Holmes. *Prayer in Islamic Thought and Practice*. Cambridge: Cambridge University Press, 2013.

Katz, Marion Holmes. *Women in the Mosque: A History of Legal Thought and Social Practice*. New York: Columbia University Press, 2014.

Kenney, Jeffrey T. *Muslim Rebels: Kharijites and the Politics of Extremism in Egypt*. Oxford: Oxford University Press, 2006.

Khankan, Sherin. *Sherin Khankan on Islam*. Interview by Bart Schols on Belgian TV, 2017. https://mimeticmargins.com/2017/05/31/sherin-khankan-on-islam/ (accessed 10 November 2018).

Khankan, Sherin. *Women are the Future of Islam: A Memoir of Hope*. London: Rider, 2018.

Khoirul Hadi, M. al-Asy Ari. 'Fiqh Renewal of Gamal Al-Banna and Its Relevance of Fiqh Developments in Indonesia'. *Millatī, Journal of Islamic Studies and Humanities* 2, 2 (2017), 221–37. https://pdfs.semanticscholar.org/c4c8/dda50989ec471f720c32dfdc512324360b5a.pdf (accessed 15 April 2020).

Khoja-Moolji, Shenila S. *An Emerging Model of Muslim Leadership: Chaplaincy on University Campuses*. The Pluralism Project at Harvard University. 2011. http://pluralism.org/wp-content/uploads/2015/08/Khoja_Moolji_Muslim_Chaplaincy_2011.pdf (accessed 20 June 2020).

Kohlberg, Etan. 'The Position of the *Walad Zina* in Imami Shi'ism'. In *Belief and Law in Imami Shi'ism*, edited by Etan Kohlberg, 237–66. Aldershot: Ashgate, 1991.
Kohlberg, Etan. 'Shahid'. In *Encyclopaedia of Islam* (2nd edn; EI2) (Vol. 9), edited by Peri J. Bearman, Th. Bianquis et al., 203–7. Leiden: Brill, 1997.
Krämer, Gudrun and Sabine Schmidke (eds.). *Speaking for Islam: Religious Authorities in Muslim Societies*. Leiden: Brill, 2006.
Kreuter, Kiron. 'Turkey: Women Want Equality in the Mosque'. *Deutsche Welle*, 10 November, 2011. www.dw.com/en/turkey-women-want-equality-in-the-mosque/av-6656710 (accessed 13 June 2019).
Kroissnbrunner, Sabine. 'Turkish Imams in Vienna'. In *Intercultural Relations and Religious Authorities: Muslim in the European Union*, edited by W. Shadid and P. van Koningsveld, 181–207. Leuven: Peeters, 2002.
Kruk, Remke. *The Warrior Women of Islam: Female Empowerment in Arabic Popular Literature*. London: IB Tauris, 2014.
Kugle, Scott Siraj al-Haqq. *Homosexuality in Islam: Critical Reflection on Gay, Lesbian and Transgender Muslims*. Oxford: Oneworld, 2010.
Kunkler, Mirjam and Roja Fazaeli. 'The Life of Two *Mujtahidahs*: Female Religious Authority in Twentieth-Century Iran'. In *Women, Leadership and Mosques*, edited by Masooda Bano and Hilary Kalmbach, 127–60. Leiden: Brill, 2012.
Lahaj, Mary. 'Making It Up As I Go Along: The Formation of a Muslim Chaplain'. *Reflective Practice Formation and Supervision in Ministry*, 29 (2009): 148–53.
Lambek, Michael. 'Localizing Islamic Performances in Mayotte'. In *Islamic Prayer across the Indian Ocean: Inside and Outside the Mosque*, edited by David Parkin and Stephen Headley, 63–98. London: Curzon, 2000.
Lane, Edward William. *An Arabic-English Lexicon*. Lahore: Suhayl Academy, 2003, 2 vols.
Lange, Christian and Maribel Fierro (eds.). *Public Violence in Islamic Societies: Power, Discipline, and the Construction of the Public Sphere, 7th–19th Centuries CE*. Edinburgh: Edinburgh University Press, 2009.
Langer, Lorenz. *Religious Offence and Human Rights: The Implications of Defamation of Religions*. Cambridge: Cambridge University Press, 2014.
Laoust, Henri. *La Politique de Ġazali*. Alger: Société Nationale d'Édition et de Diffusion, 1971.
Le Goff, Jacques. *History and Memory*. New York: Columbia University Press, 1992.
Le Renard, Amélie. 'From Qur'anic Circles to the Internet: Gender Segregation and the Rise of Female Preachers in Saudi Arabia'. In *Women, Leadership, and Mosques: Changes in Contemporary Islamic Authority*, edited by Masooda Bano and Hilary Kalmbach, 105–126. Leiden: Brill, 2012.
Lekovic, Edina. *Stepping Up*. Full video of her first *khutba* at the Women's Mosque of America, 30 January, 2015. http://womensmosque.com/videos/ (accessed 18 April 2018).
Levine, Jihad, S. E. *Out from Darkness. . .into Light: A Grief and Bereavement Booklet for Muslims in Prisons and Jails*. S. E. Jihad Levine and the Pennsylvania Prison Chaplains Association, 2010. http://paprisonchaplains.org/Content/out-from-darkness-into-light.pdf (accessed 22 March 2018).
Lim, Louisa. 'Female Imam Blaze Trail Amid China's Muslims'. *npr.org (National Public Radio USA)*, 21 July 2010. www.npr.org/2010/07/21/128628514/female-imams-blaze-trail-amid-chinas-muslims (accessed 15 April 2019).
Long, Ibrahim J. 'Muslim Chaplains: Serving in Diversity'. *AMC [Association of Muslim Chaplains]*, 2010. https://associationofmuslimchaplains.com/muslim-chaplains-serving-in-diversity (accessed 4 July 2017).

Lowry, Joseph E. 'Ibn Qutayba: The Earliest Witness to al-Shafi'i and his Legal Doctrines'. In *Islamic Law* (Vol. 2) (Critical Concepts in Islamic Studies Series), edited by G. Picken, 150–65. New York: Routledge, 2011.

Lowry, Joseph E. 'Ritual Purity'. In *Encyclopaedia of the Qur'an* (EQ) (Vol. 4), edited by Jane Dammen McAuliffe, 506–7. Leiden: Brill, 2004.

Madelung, Wilferd. "'Ali b. al-Hosayn'. In *Encyclopaedia Iranica* (Vol. 1), edited by Ehsan Yarshater, 849–50. London, Boston: Routledge & Kegan Paul, 1998.

Madelung, Wilferd. 'The Sources of Isma'ili Law'. *Journal of Near Eastern Studies* 35, 1 (1976): 29–40.

Mahmood, Saba. *Politics of Piety: The Islamic Revival and the Feminist Subject*. Princeton, NJ: Princeton University Press, 2005.

Makdisi, George, Dominique Sourdel and Janine Sourdel-Thomine (eds.). *La Notion d'Autorité au Moyen Age: Islam, Byzance, Occident*. Paris: Presses Universitaires de France, 1982.

Mandaville, Peter. 'Globalization and the Politics of Religious Knowledge'. *Theory, Culture & Society* 24, 2 (2007): 101–115.

Marçais, George. 'Dar'. In *Encyclopaedia of Islam* (2nd edn; EI2) (Vol. 2), edited by Peri J. Bearman, Th. Bianquis et al., 113–15. Leiden: Brill, 1965.

Marsden, Magnus. *Living Islam: Muslim Religious Experience in Pakistan's North-West Frontier*. Cambridge: Cambridge University Press, 2005.

Massignon, Louis. 'La Mubahala de Medine et l'Hyperdulie de Fatima'. In *Opera Minora: Textes Recueillis, Classés et Présentés avec une Bibliographie*, edited by Youakim Moubarac. Paris: Presses Universitaire de France, 1969, 3 vols.

Mattson, Ingrid. *Can a Woman be an Imam?* 2005. http://ingridmattson.org/article/can-a-woman-be-an-imam/ (accessed 10 May 2018).

Mawani, Rizwan. *Beyond the Mosque: Diverse Spaces of Muslim Worship*. London: IB Tauris, 2019.

McAuliffe, Jane Dammen (ed.). *Encyclopaedia of the Qur'an* (EQ). Leiden: Brill, 2001–6, 6 vols.

Mediano, Fernando Rodriguez. 'Justice, Crime and Punishment in 10th/16th Century Morocco'. In *Public Violence in Islamic Societies: Power, Discipline, and the Construction of the Public Sphere, 7th–19th Centuries CE*, edited by Christian Lange and Maribel Fierro, 179–202. Edinburgh: Edinburgh University Press, 2009.

Melchert, Christopher. 'Dawud b. Khalaf'. In *Encyclopaedia of Islam 3 Online* (3rd edn; EI3 Online), edited by Kate Fleet, Gudrun Krämer, et al. Leiden: Brill online, 2012. http://dx.doi.org/10.1163/1573-3912_ei3_COM_32433 (accessed 2 March 2020).

Melchert, Christopher. 'How Hanafism Came to Originate in Kufa and Traditionalism in Medina'. *Islamic Law and Society* 6, 3 (1999): 318–47.

Melchert, Christopher. 'Traditionists-Jurisprudents and the Framing of Islamic Law'. *Islamic Law and Society* 38, 3 (2001): 383–406.

Melchert, Christopher. 'Whether to Keep Women out of the Mosque: A Survey of Medieval Islamic Law'. In *Authority, Privacy and Public Order in Islam*, edited by Barbara Michalak-Pikulska and A Pikulski. Leuven: Peeters, 2006.

Mernissi, Fatima. *The Veil and the Male Elite: A Feminist Interpretation of Women's Rights in Islam*. Cambridge: Perseus Books, 1991.

Mernissi, Fatima. *Women and Islam: An Historical and Theological Enquiry*. Oxford: Blackwell, 1991.

Michalak-Pikulska, Barbara and A. Pikulski (eds.). *Authority, Privacy and Public Order in Islam*. Leuven: Peeters, 2006.

Ministry of Habous and Islamic Affairs, Morocco. 'Maliki School is a Social and Psychological Culture'. *Habous.gov.ma*, 28 June, 2012. www.habous.gov.ma/2012-01-27-14-38-19/887-2012-06-28-13-14-48.html (accessed 13 March 2018).
Morony, Michael G. *Iraq after the Muslim Conquest*. Princeton, NJ: Princeton University Press, 1984.
Mottahedeh, Roy P. *Loyalty and Leadership in an Early Islamic Society*. London, New York: IB Tauris, 2001.
Motzki, Harald. *Analysing Muslim Traditions: Studies in Legal, Exegetical and Maghazi Ḥadith*. Leiden: Brill, 2010.
Motzki, Harald (ed.). *The Biography of Muhammad: The Issue of the Sources*. Leiden: Brill, 2000.
Mourad, Suleiman Ali. 'al-Ḥasan al-Baṣrī'. In *Encyclopaedia of Islam 3 Online* (3rd edn; EI3 Online), edited by Kate Fleet, Gudrun Krämer, et al. Leiden: Brill online, 2012. http://dx.doi.org/10.1163/1573-3912_ei3_COM_32433 (accessed 6 December 2019).
Musa, Aisha Y. 'Al-Shafi'i, the Ḥadith, and the Concept of the Duality of Revelation'. *Islamic Studies* 46, 2 (2007): 163–197.
The Muslim Council of Britain. *Women in Mosques Development Programme*. 2019. https://mcb.org.uk/project/women-in-mosques-development-programme/ (accessed 17 April 2020).
Naguib, Shuruq. 'And Your Garments Purify: Tahara in the Light of Tafsir'. *Journal of Qur'anic Studies* 9, 1 (2007): 59–77.
Nanji, Afroza and Alykhan Nanji. 'Charting a Family's Journey'. *The.Ismaili: United Kingdom*, 6 January, 2008. https://the.ismaili/our-stories/charting-familys-journey (accessed 11 April 2018).
Neuwirth, Angelika. 'The House of Abraham and the House of Amram: Genealogy, Patriarchal Authority, and Exegetical Professionalism'. In *The Qur'an in Context*, edited by Angelika Neuwirth, 499–532. Leiden: Brill, 2010.
Neuwirth, Angelika. *Scripture, Poetry and the Making of a Community: Reading the Qur'an as a Literary Text*. Oxford: Oxford University Press, 2014.
Newman, Andrew J. *The Formative Period of Twelver Shi'ism: Hadith as Discourse between Qum and Baghdad*. Richmond: Curzon, 2000.
Nicolle, David. *Yarmuk AD 636: The Muslim Conquest of Syria*. London: Osprey, 1994.
Northwestern. 'Associate Chaplain Recognized as Leading Female Muslim: Tahera Ahmad Honored at the White House During Women's History Month'. *Northwestern Now*, 28 March, 2014. https://news.northwestern.edu/stories/2014/03/chaplain-ahmad-white-house-honor/ (accessed 22 March 2018).
Osanloo, Arzoo. *The Politics of Women's Rights in Iran*. Princeton, NJ: Princeton University Press, 2009.
Ovamir, Anjum. 'Islam as a Discursive Tradition: Talal Asad and His Interlocutors'. *Comparative Studies of South Asia, Africa and the Middle East*, 27, 3 (2007): 656–72.
Pabst, Sabrina. 'Liberal Mosque in Berlin Draws Criticism'. *Deutsche Welle (DW)*, 21 June, 2017. www.dw.com/en/liberal-mosque-in-berlin-draws-criticism/a-39353066/21/6/2017 (accessed 20 June 2018).
Pedersen, Johannes. 'Masdjid'. In *Encyclopaedia of Islam* (2nd edn; EI2) (Vol. 6), edited by Peri J. Bearman, Th. Bianquis et al., 644–5. Leiden: Brill, 1991.
Pedersen, Johannes. 'Minbar'. In *Encyclopaedia of Islam* (2nd edn; EI2) (Vol. 7), edited by Peri J. Bearman, Th. Bianquis et al., 74–5. Leiden: Brill, 1993.
Pedersen, Johannes. 'Nadhr'. In *Encyclopaedia of Islam* (2nd edn; EI2) (Vol. 7), edited by Peri J. Bearman, Th. Bianquis et al., 846–7. Leiden: Brill, 1993.

Penn, Michael Philip. *Envisioning Islam: Syriac Christians and the Early Muslim World*. Philadelphia, PA: University of Pennsylvania Press, 2015.
Petersen, Jesper. 'Media and the Female Imam'. *Religions* 10, 3 (2019), 159.
Pickthall, Marmaduke. *The Meaning of the Glorious Koran*. London: Allen & Unwin, 1976.
Pico Union Project. *Reimagining Religion: Stories of Religious Creativity in Los Angeles*. 9 October, 2017. Edited by Elliot Lockwood. USC, Dornsife, Centre of Religion and Civic Culture. www.youtube.com/watch?v=csujYp3cZQE (accessed 18 May 2018).
Pierce, Matthew. 'Remembering Fatimah: New Means of Legitimizing Female Authority in Contemporary Shi'i Discourse'. In *Women, Leadership and Mosques*, edited by Masooda Bano and Hilary Kalmbach, 345–62. Leiden: Brill, 2012.
Plumb, John Harold. *The Death of the Past*. Basingstoke, New York: Palgrave/Macmillan, 2004 (1st edn 1969).
Prado, Abdennur. *About the Friday Prayer Led by Amina Wadud*. 10 March, 2005. https://abdennurprado.wordpress.com/2005/03/10/about-the-friday-prayer-led-by-amina-wadud/ (accessed 14 April 2020).
Quinn, Ingrid. *Women in Public Life in the Maldives: Situational Analysis*. Malé: UNDP (United Nations Development Programme), 2011.
Radhan, Luay. 'Gamal al-Banna's Islamic Feminism in The Muslim Woman'. *Journal of Women and Human Rights in the Middle East*, 2 (2014), 5–18.
Rahman, Fazlur. *Islam*. Chicago and London: University of Chicago Press, 1979 (1st edn 1966).
Rahman, Fazlur. *Islamic Methodology in History*. Karachi: Central Institute of Islamic Research, 1965.
Ratbil, Shamel. 'First Mosque for Women in Kabul'. *Deutsche Welle (DW)*, 9 February 2006. www.dw.com/de/erstemoschee-f%C3%BCr-frauen-in-kabul/a-1890595 (accessed 2 November 2018).
Raudvere, Catharina. *The Book and the Roses: Sufi Women, Visibility, and Zikir in Contemporary Istanbul*. London: IB Tauris, 2002.
Raven Wim. 'Martyrs'. In *Encyclopaedia of the Qur'an* (EQ) (Vol. 3), edited by Jane Dammen McAuliffe, 281–6. Leiden: Brill, 2003.
Reda, Nevin. *The Islamic Basis for Female-Led Prayer*. [2005]. www.irfi.org/articles/articles_351_400/islamic_basis_for_femaleled.htm (accessed 27 May 2020).
Reda, Nevin. 'Women in the Mosque: Historical Perspectives on Segregation'. *American Journal of Islamic Social Sciences* 21, 2 (2004): 77–97.
Reda, Nevin. *Women Leading Congregational Prayers*. Canadian Council for Muslim Women. [2005]. www.ccmw.com/documents/WomenLeadership.doc (accessed 31 May 2005).
Reinhart, A. Kevin. 'Impurity/No Danger'. *History of Religions* 30, 1 (1990): 1–24.
Reinhart, A. Kevin. 'Ritual Action and Practical Action'. In *Islamic Law in Theory*, edited by Kevin A. Reinhart and Robert Gleave, 55–103. Leiden, Boston: Brill, 2014.
Reynolds, Gabriel Said (ed.). *The Qur'an in its Historical Context*. London: Routledge, 2008.
Rippin, Andrew. 'The Function of *Asbab al-Nuzul* in Qur'anic Exegesis'. *Bulletin of the School of Oriental and African Studies* 51, 1 (1988): 1–20.
Ritchie, Megan, Terry Ann Rogers and Lauren Sauer. *Women's Empowerment in Political Processes in the Maldives*. Washington: IFES, 2014. www.ifes.org/publications/womens-empowerment-political-process-maldives (Accessed 26 May 2020).
Robinson, Chase F. *Empire and Elites after the Muslim Conquest: The Transformation of Northern Mesopotamia*. Cambridge: Cambridge University Press, 2000.
Robinson, Chase F. 'The Ideological Uses of Early Islam'. *Past & Present* 203, 1 (2009): 205–28.

Roded, Ruth. 'Umm Salama Hind'. In *Encyclopaedia of Islam* (2nd edn; EI2) (Vol. 10), edited by Peri J. Bearman, Th. Bianquis et al., 856. Leiden: Brill, 2000.

Roded, Ruth. *Women in Islamic Biographical Collections*. Boulder, London: Lynn Rienner, 1994.

Sachedina, Abdulaziz Abdulhussein. *The Just Ruler in Shiʿite Islam: The Comprehensive Authority of the Jurist in Imamite Jurisprudence*. New York: Oxford University Press, 1988.

Sadeghi, Benham. *The Logic of Law Making in Islam: Women and Prayer in the Legal Tradition*. Cambridge: Cambridge University Press, 2013.

Sadeghi, Benham. 'The Traveling Tradition Test: A Method for Dating Traditions'. *Der Islam* 85, 1 (2010): 203–42.

Safi, Omid (ed.). *Progressive Muslims: On Justice, Gender and Pluralism*. Oxford: Oneworld, 2003.

Sakr, Taha. 'Egyptian Dar al-Ifta Attacks "Liberal" Mosque in Germany'. *Egypt Independent*, 20 June, 2017. https://egyptindependent.com/dar-alifta-attacks-german-mosque/ (accessed 6 September 2018).

Salem, Elie Adib. *The Political Theory and Institutions of the Khawarij*. Baltimore, MD: John Hopkins University Press, 1956.

Sisters in Islam. 2007. www.sistersinislam.org.my/BM/mission.htm (accessed 9 April 2020).

Samatar, Abdi Ismail. 'Social Transformation and Islamic Reinterpretation in Northern Somalia: The Women's Mosque in Gabiley'. In *Geographies of Muslim Women: Gender, Religion, and Space*, edited by Ghazi Walid Falah and Caroline Nagel, 226–48. New York, London: The Guilford Press, 2005.

Sanders, Paula. 'Gendering the Ungendered Body: Hermaphrodites in Medieval Islamic Law'. In *Women in Middle Eastern History*, edited by Nikki Keddie and Beth Baron, 74–95. New Haven, CT: Yale University Press, 1991.

Sayeed, Asma. *Women and the Transmission of Religious Knowledge in Islam*. Cambridge: Cambridge University Press, 2013.

Schleifer, S. Abdallah (ed.). *The Muslim 500: The World's 500 Most Influential Muslims 2020*. Amman: The Royal Islamic Strategic Studies Centre, 2019. www.themuslim500.com/wp-content/uploads/2019/10/TheMuslim500-2020-low.pdf (accessed 9 June 2020).

Scott-Baumann, Alison and Sariya Cheruvallil-Contractor. *Islamic Education in Britain: New Pluralist Paradigms*. London: Bloomsbury, 2015.

Şenses Ozyurt, Saba. 'Bridge Builders or Boundary Markers? The Role of the Mosque in the Acculturation Process of Immigrant Muslim Women in the United States'. *Journal of Muslim Minority Affairs* 30, 3 (2010): 295–315.

Shakir, Zaid. 'An Examination of the Issue of Female Prayer Leadership'. In *A Collection of Fatwas and Legal Opinions on the Issue of Women Leading Prayer*. Assembly of Muslim Jurists of America. 5 April 2005 / 25 Safar 1426, 35–45. www.abc.se/home/m9783/ir/d/fwlp_e.pdf (accessed 28 May 2020).

Shannahan, Dervla, S. 'Gender, Sexuality and Inclusivity in UK Mosques'. In *Studying Islam in Practice*, edited by Gabriele Marranci, 124–134. London and New York: Routledge, 2014.

Sharify-Funk, Meena, William Rory Dickson and Merin Shobhana Xavier. *Contemporary Sufism: Piety, Politics, and Popular Culture*. London: Routledge, 2018.

Shaykh, Saʿdiyya. *Sufi Narratives of Intimacy: Ibn ʿArabi, Gender, and Sexuality*. Chapel Hill, NC: The University of North Carolina Press, 2012.

Side Entrance: Photos from Mosques around the World, Showcasing Women's Sacred Spaces. https://sideentrance.tumblr.com/ (accessed 13 June 2019).

Slackman, Michael. 'A Voice for "New Understanding" of Islam'. *The New York Times*, 20 October, 2006. www.nytimes.com/2006/10/20/world/africa/20iht-profile.3237674.html (accessed 15 April 2020).

Sonbol El-Azhari, Amira and Kira Dreher (eds.). *Gulf Women*. London: Bloomsbury, 2012.

Spellberg, Denise A. *Politics, Gender and the Islamic Past: The Legacy of 'A'isha bint Abi Bakr*. New York: Columbia University Press, 1994.

Spielhaus, Riem. 'Making Islam Relevant: Female Authority and Representation of Islam in Germany'. In *Women, Leadership, and Mosques: Changes in Contemporary Islamic Authority*, edited by Masooda Bano and Hilary Kalmbach, 437–55. Leiden: Brill, 2012.

Stewart, Devin J. *Islamic Legal Orthodoxy: Twelver Shiite Responses to the Sunni Legal System*. Salt Lake City, UT: The University of Utah Press, 1998.

Stewart, Devin J. 'Polemics and Patronage in Safavid Iran: The Debate on Friday Prayer During the Reign of Shah Tahmasb'. *Bulletin of the School of Oriental and African Studies* 72, 3 (2009): 425–57.

Stowasser, Barbara F. *Women in the Qur'an: Traditions and Interpretation*. New York, Oxford: Oxford University Press, 1994.

Street, Nick. 'First All-Female Mosque Opens in Los Angeles'. *Al-Jazeera America*, 3 February 2015. http://america.aljazeera.com/articles/2015/2/3/first-all-female-mosque-opens-in-los-angeles.html (accessed 8 May 2018).

Su, Alice. 'The German Mosque that Attracts Women Imams, Gays and Death Threats'. *Politico*, 27 July, 2017. www.politico.eu/article/berlin-feminist-mosque-ibn-rushd-goethe-germany-first-liberal-mosque-sparks-debate-in-berlin/ (accessed 20 June 2018).

Sultan Muhammad Shah. *Message to the World of Islam*. Karachi: Ismailia Association for Pakistan, 1977.

Talmon-Heller, Daniella J. *Islamic Piety in Medieval Syria: Mosques, Cemeteries and Sermons Under the Zangids and Ayyūbids (1146–1260)*. Leiden, Boston: Brill, 2007.

El-Tawhid Juma Circle. www.jumacircle.com/ (accessed 5 October 2018).

Taylor, Pamela. 'Canada: Leading the Mufti; Progress in the Islamic Tradition'. *Women Living Under Muslim Laws*, 17 February, 2006. www.wluml.org/node/2843 (accessed 9 June 2020).

Timani, Hussam S. *Modern Intellectual Readings of the Kharijites*. New York: Lang, 2007.

Torab, Azam. *Performing Islam: Gender and Ritual in Iran*. Leiden, Boston: Brill, 2006.

Torab, Azam. 'Piety as Gendered Agency: A Study of Jalaseh Ritual Discourse in an Urban Neighbourhood in Iran'. *The Journal of the Royal Anthropological Institute* 2, 2 (1996): 235–252.

Tucker, Judith E. *Women, Family, and Gender in Islamic Law*. Cambridge: Cambridge University Press, 2008.

Van Dijk, Teun A. 'Principles of Critical Discourse Analysis', *Discourse and Society* 4, 2 (1993): 249–83.

Van Doorn-Harder, Pieternella. *Women Shaping Islam: Reading the Qur'an in Indonesia*. Urbana and Chicago, IL: University of Illinois Press, 2006.

Versteegh, Kees. 'Zayd Ibn 'Alī's Commentary on the Qur'ān'. In *Arabic Grammar and Linguistics*, edited by Yasir Suleiman, 9–29. Abingdon: Routledge, 1999.

Vinding, Niels Valdemar. 'Churchification of Islam in Europe'. In *Exploring the Multitude of Muslims in Europe*, edited by Niels Valdemar Vinding, Egdunas Račius and Jörn Thielmann, 50–66. Leiden: Brill, 2018.

wadud, amina. *Inside the Gender Jihad: Women's Reform in Islam*. Oxford: Oneworld, 2006.
wadud, amina. *Qur'an and Woman: Rereading the Sacred Text from a Woman's Perspective*. Oxford: Oxford University Press, 1999.
Watt, Montgomery W. 'Abu Bakr'. In *Encyclopaedia of Islam* (2nd edn; EI2) (Vol. 1), edited by Peri J. Bearman, Th. Bianquis et al., 109–11. Leiden: Brill, 1960.
Wensinck, Arent Jan. 'The Origin of the Muslim Laws of Ritual Purity'. In *The Development of Islamic Ritual*, edited by Gerald Hawting, 75–94. Aldershot: Ashgate, 2006.
Winkel, Eric. *Islam and the Living Law: The Ibn al-Arabi Approach*. New York: Oxford University Press, 1997.
Winston, Brian. *A Right to Offend*. London: Bloomsbury, 2012.
Wodak, Ruth and M. Meyer. 'Critical Discourse Analysis: History, Agenda, Theory and Methodology'. In *Methods for Critical Discourse Analysis*, edited by Ruth Wodak and M. Meyer, 1–33. London: Sage, 2009.
The Women's Mosque of America. https://womensmosque.com/about-2/ (accessed 2 November 2018.
Yusuf, Imtiyaz. 'Imam'. In *Encyclopaedia of the Qur'an* (EQ) (Vol. 2), edited by Jane Dammen McAuliffe, 502–4. Leiden: Brill, 2002.
Zaman, Muhammad Qasim. *The 'Ulama in Contemporary Islam: Custodians of Change*. Princeton, NJ: Princeton University Press, 2002.
Zamzami, Mukhammad. 'Metodologi Studi Hadis Jamâl al-Bannâ'. *Mutawâtir: Jurnal Keilmuan Tafsir Hadis* 4, 2 (2014), 211–42.
Zweiri, Mahjoob. 'Are Shias Rising in the Western Part of the Arab World? The Case of Morocco'. *The Journal of North African Studies* 13, 4 (2008): 513–29.

INDEX

'Abbasid dynasty 4, 62, 65, 86, 108
al-'Abidin, Zayn ibn 'Ali 53, 58
Abou El-Fadl, Khaled 169
abrogation 67–8, 75–6, 193
Abu Bakr 27–8, 33, 41, 112
Abu Bakra 116, 117
Abu Dawud, Sulayman 2
    Sunan 100–1
Abu Hanifa 3, 65–6, 75
Abu Hurayra 48 n. 64
Abu Salama 54
Abu Thawr al-Baghdadi 119, 120, 121, 125
Afghanistan 141
Afsaruddin, Asma 11, 27, 41
agency (female) 10, 150, 159, 176
    Umm Salama 105
    Umm Waraqa 105
ahl al-hadith 98, 119
ahl al-ra'y 98, 119–20
ahongs/nu ahongs (female religious leaders in China) 142–7, 175
'A'isha bint Abi Bakr (Prophet's wife) 56, 58, 84
    Camel, Battle of 56, 112
    Du Ahong 145
    as *hadith* transmitter 53, 56, 84
    hadiths 52, 54, 56, 64, 66, 174
    Kharijis and 111
    Liu Zhi 145
    mosques 86
    prayer leadership 56, 63, 64, 66, 67
    Turabi, Hassan 169
algorithms 178
'Ali ibn Abi Talib 28, 55, 56, 58, 106–7
'Ali ibn al-Husayn
    female slave of 53, 69, 70, 84
'alima (female scholar) 32, 159, 172, 195
Allès, Élisabeth 15
Aly, Marwa (American university chaplain) 156–7
'Amra, bint 'Abd al-Rahman (*hadith* transmitter) 53, 69, 194

al-Andalus 62
al-Ansari, 'Abd al-Rahman ibn Khallad 101
Anwar, Ghazala 160
Archangel Gabriel 24, 32
Asad, Talal 7, 15, 65, 126
Asbab al-nuzul 12, 46 n. 39
Asma ('A'isha's sister) 84
al-'Asqalani, Ibn Hajar 52, 68
Assembly of Muslim Jurists of America (AMJA) 193
    Collection of Fatwas 13, 166–8, 193
Ateş, Seyran (female imam) 164–5, 176
'awra (concealment) 63, 71–2, 74, 75
    China 145
    coverings 74
    female slaves 71, 80, 93 n. 75
    female voice 63, 79–80, 145
    free women 69, 71–2, 80, 93 n. 75
    interpretations/meanings 74
    legal discourse 63, 74, 75, 79–80, 117
    status 80
auctoritas (authority). *See* authority
audiences 177–8
    responses 178
authority 8, 27, 77, 182 *see also* leadership
    changing conception of 37
    definitions 27
    hadiths 2
    sources of 2, 78
    wadud, amina 177
al-'Ayni, Badr al-din 68
Ayyad, Essam. S. 30
Azam, Hina 167
al-Azmeh, Aziz 7, 105

al-Babarti, Akmal 67–8
Badr, Battle of 7–8, 99, 105
al-Baghdadi, Abu Mansur Ibn Tahir 107, 111–12, 113
    Al-Farq Bayna al-Firaq 111
Al-Bahr al-Zakhkhar (Ibn al-Murtada) 131 n. 72

al-Baji, Sulayman ibn Khalaf 62, 64
    Kitab al-muntaqa 63
al-Banna, Hasan 169
al-Banna, Jamal 13, 169–71
    Permissibility of Female Prayer Leadership of Men, The (*Jawaz Imamat al-Mar'a li'l-Rijal*) 169–70
Bano, Masooda/Kalmbach, Hilary 15
Banu Najjar clan 30, 99, 103
Barlas, Asma
Basra 60, 61
Baugh, Carolyn 108
al-Bayhaqi, Abu Bakr 52
ben Cheikh, Sohaib 169
Bhol, Asma 164
Bibi Seshanbe 172–3
bid'a (innovation) 117, 192, 193
    China 144
    Lekovic, Edina 148
    Reda, Nevin 166
    Sisters of Islam 162
bid'a hasana (good innovation) 170
Bidayat al-Mujtahid (*The Distinguished Jurist's Primer*) (Ibn Rushd) 104
blessing 83
Book of Guidance (*Kitab al-Umm*) (al-Shafi'i) 51, 53, 57, 69, 70, 71
Books (Ibn Sallam ibn Sayyar, Abu 'Abdallah Muhammad) 51–2, 58
booty sharing 116, 131 n. 66
Böwering, Gerald 104
al-Bukhari, Muhammad 2, 14, 64, 103
    Sahih by Muhmmad al-Bukhari 68, 91 n. 50
Butler, Judith 11
Buyids, the 77

Calder, Norman 14, 57
Camel, Battle of 56, 112
Canada 163
Central Asia 172–3
chaplains 156–7
childbirth 43 n. 11, 161
China 142–7
'churchification of Islam' 139
Clermont mosque, Cape Town 160
Collection of Fatwas (AMJA) 13, 166–8, 193
communal prayer 10, 28–31, 33, 125–6 *see also* congregational prayer

Communism 143, 145
congregational prayer 8, 10, 35, 37, 45 n. 23, 71, 78, 157 *see also jama'a* and *jum'a*
    hadiths on female prayer leadership 62–74
    Shi'ism 77–83
    Sunni jurisprudence 74–7
    women leading men 97–8, 116–26 *see also* Ghazala al-Haruriyya *and* Umm Waraqa bint Nawfal
    women leading women 57–61, 83–7 *see also* 'A'isha bint Abi Bakr *and* Umm Salama Hind bint Abi Umayya
consensus 33, 36, 63, 76, 117, 121, 173 *see also Collection of Fatwas*
    Bhol, Asma 164
    *hadith*s 11, 60
    Khankan, Sherin 150
contemporary interpretations 165–177

dar 101, 102–4, 126, 166, 175 *see also* home
Dar al-Ifta' 165, 174
al-Daraqutni, Abu'l-Hasan'Ali 52
al-Daraqutni, 'Ali b. 'Umar
    Sunan 102
Denmark 149–50
Douglas, Mary 25
dress (women's) 74, 148
Du Ahong (Chinese female religious leader) 145
du'a (prayer for Isma'ilis) 157, 158
al-Duhni, 'Ammar 59, 60

education 177
    female 153, 155–6, 158
    religious education 142, 143, 153, 158
Egypt 33, 34, 155
    Dar al-Ifta' 165, 174
Elewa, Ahmed/Silvers, Laury 167
Eltahawy, Mona 166
ethnicity 30, 160, 163
exegetical sources 11–12

fadila (excellence) 23, 41
fara'id/fard (religious obligation/s) 29, 70, 71, 79
Al-Farq Bayna al-Firaq (al-Baghdadi, Abu Mansur Ibn Tahir) 111

Index

Fatima (Prophet's daughter) 82–3, 145
Fatima bint ʿAbbas ʿUmm Zaynab al-Baghdadiyya' (female preacher) 124
Fatima bint al-Muthanna (*shaykha*) 123
Fatima Khatun (Ayyubid patroness) 125
Fatimids, the 34–5, 77
fatwa/fatwas 162 see also *Collection of Fatwas*
    female prayer leadership 155–6, 165, 166–9, 174–5, 178
Fentress, James/Wickham, Chris 15
Fewkes, Jacqueline 152
fiqh 3, 164
fitna (temptation) 102, 126, 193
    female *imama* and 72, 166
    Hanafi school 67, 125
    Hanbali school 73–4
    legal discourse 75, 76, 80, 85, 86
    Maliki school 173
    Reda, Nevin 166
    Shafiʿi school 71, 72
    women's mosques 176
Friday congregational prayer. See *jumʿa*
funerals 68, 92 n. 71, 118, 146
al-Futuhat al-Makkiyya (*The Meccan Revelations*) (Ibn al-ʿArabi, Muhyi'l-din) 122, 123, 167

Gabiley mosque 153–5
Gabriel. *See* Archangel Gabriel
Gauvain, Richard 25
gender/s 5, 9, 14, 39, 40, 86, 120 see also gender equality
    al-Banna, Jamal 169–71
    chaplains 156
    China 143–6
    discrimination 10
    Ghazala al-Haruriyya 116
    hermaphrodite/intersex 39, 40 see also *mukhannath*
    Ibn al-ʿArabi, Muhyi'l-din 123, 193
    impurity/purity 25–6
    language 118
    mosques 150–1
    online 195
    peace/war 130 n. 56
    performativity 11

al-Qadi al-Nuʿman 118
Qurʾan 54–5
gender equality 10, 24, 124, 143, 145, 168, 174–5 see also wadud, amina
    Abou El-Fadl, Khaled 169
    al-Banna, Jamal 171
    China 143, 145–6
    Ibn al-ʿArabi, Muhyi'l-din 193
    inclusivity 163–5, 176–7
    Ismaʿilis 158
    Morocco 173–4
    Somalia 154
    women's mosques 150, 176
Germany 150, 165
ghada prayer 110
Ghazala al-Haruriyya 97, 98, 106–16, 125
Gilliat-Ray, Sophie 156, 157
Gleave, Robert 15
Goethe, Johann Wolfgang von 165
Grabar, Oleg 45 n. 29
Graham, William 7, 15
Great Book of the Classes (*Tabaqat*) (Ibn Saʿd) 51, 57–8

hadith transmitters (female) 52–3, 55, 56, 57, 58–9 see also Umm Salama Hind bint Abi Umayya
hadiths 1, 11–12, 52–3, 57–9, 62–77
    ʿAʾisha bint Abu Bakr 52, 54, 56, 64, 66, 174
    Abu Bakra 116, 117
    ahad/single strand hadiths 59, 64, 81, 101, 121
    authority of 76
    compilations 2, 52, 81, 85
    female prayer leadership 62–74
    Inclusive Mosque Initiative 164
    Indonesian Scholars' Assembly 168–9
    al-Qaradawi, Yusuf 168
    Reda, Nevin 166
    regional 60–1
    reliability 11, 59–60, 76 see also *isnads*
    Shiʿi 77, 80–1
    studies 11, 59
    Umm Salama 53, 54–6, 57–8, 84
    Umm Waraqa 62, 76, 99–106, 119, 124, 166, 168, 174
    weak 11–12, 90 n. 36, 117, 168, 192
    women leading men in prayer 97–126

hajj (women's *jihad*) 115
Hajja Faiza (female religious and prayer leader in Egypt) 155
al-Hajjaj (Umayyad commander) 107, 108, 109–10, 114
Hamdanids, the 77
Hanafi school 3, 60, 65–8, 75, 76, 85, 120
    China 144
    women leading prayer 60, 65–8, 118, 144
    women's mosque attendance 125
Hanbali school 3, 60, 72–4, 85, 122
    women leading prayer 60, 72–4, 75–6, 85, 118
    women's mosque attendance 73, 74, 122
haram (sacredness) 31, 168
hasab (noble descent) 27
Hawting, Gerald 14
hayd (menstruation) 25, 91 n. 50, 117
hermaphrodite 39 see also *mukhannath*
al-Hilli, al-'Allama 3, 79, 81–2
al-Hilli, al-Muhaqqiq 36, 38
Hind bint 'Utba 115
historical female figures as legitimizing precedents 124, 147, 154, 172 see also 'A'isha bint Abi Bakr *and* Ghazala al-Haruriyya *and* Umm Salama *and* Umm Waraqa
History (al-'Usfuri, Khalifa Ibn Khayyat) 108
Hobsbawm, Eric/Ranger, Terence 15
home 100–1 see also *dar*
    women's prayer leadership 76, 105
    women's worship 71, 73–4, 75, 76, 80
Hui (Muslim community in China) 142, 143
Hujayra bint Husayn (*hadith* transmitter) 51, 57, 59, 60, 84

'ibadat 3, 9, 75, 167
Ibn Abi Shayba, Abu Bakr 52, 59, 66
    al-Musannaf 52, 61
Ibn al-'Arabi, Muhyi'l-din 13, 98, 119, 122–4, 149
    al-Futuhat al-Makkiyya (*The Meccan Revelations*) 122, 123, 167
    Tafsir al-Shaykh al-Akbar 123
Ibn Babawayh, Abu Ja'far Muhammad ibn 'Ali 2, 80
Ibn al-Hajjaj, Muslim 2

Ibn Hanbal, Ahmad 3, 56, 72, 73, 118, 120
    Masa'il 72
    Musnad 56, 72, 100
Ibn Hazm, 'Ali b. Ahmad 53
Ibn Hisham, 'Abd al-Malik 12, 24
Ibn al-Humam 68
Ibn Idris, Abu 'Abdullah Muhammed 81
Ibn al-'Imad al-Hayyi ibn Ahmad al-Ikri al-Hanbali 112–13
Ibn Ishaq, Muhammad
    Sirat al-Nabi 23–4
Ibn al-Jawzi, 'Abd al-Rahman 72–3, 74
Ibn Khayyat, Khalifa 107
Ibn Khuzayma al-Nisaburi 101–2
Ibn al-Murtada, Ahmad ibn Yahya
    Al-Bahr al-Zakhkhar 131 n. 72
Ibn Qudama al-Maqdisi 73, 93 n. 86, 119
Ibn Rushd, Abu al-Walid Muhammad 104, 119, 165
    Bidayat al-Mujtahid (*The Distinguished Jurist's Primer*) 104
Ibn Rushd-Goethe mosque 165, 174
Ibn Sa'd, Muhammad 51, 57, 59, 66, 85
    Great Book of the Classes (*Tabaqat*) 51, 57–8
    Umm Waraqa bint Nawfal 99, 100, 102, 103
Ibn Salama, 'Amr 38
Ibn Sallam ibn Sayyar, Abu 'Abdallah Muhammad 51–2, 58, 82
    Books 51, 58
Ibn Taymiyya, Ahmad 73–4, 118
Ibn 'Umar, 'Abdullah 53, 174
Ibn Umm Maktum (blind imam) 39
Ibn 'Urwa, Hisham 63, 64
Ibn 'Uyayna, Sufyan 59, 60, 72
Ibu Uswatun (prayer leader in Java) 141
'id (festival) prayers 29
    and female leadership 73
ijaza 150
ijtihad (legal reasoning) 77, 81–2, 170–1
illegitimacy 26
imama (leadership) 2, 4, 53, 116, 163–5 see also leadership
    Ibn al-'Arabi, Muhyi'l-din 122–4
    imama kubra (political leadership) 27, 28, 113
    imama sughra (ritual prayer leadership) 27–8, 114

Shi'ism 77–83
  use of term 27
imams 11, 23, 31–41 *see also* prayer leadership
  choosing 33–4, 36–8, 40–1
  hierarchy 123
  Ibn al-'Arabi, Muhyi'l-din 123
  in history 33–5
  meaning 11, 31–2, 53, 137, 138, 139, 179 n. 2
  modern roles of 138–9
  modern uses of term 139–40
  qualities/requirements of 26, 29, 36–40, 86, 106, 113, 138
  roles of 35–6, 86, 138
  Shi'ism 77, 78, 79
  status 139
  term in hadiths 11, 33
  term in Qur'an 11, 32
  women 40–1, 122–4, 140–2 see also *ahongs/nu ahongs*
impurity 24–6, 62, 117, 120, 163, 166
Inclusive Mosque Initiative (IMI) 163–4, 176
inclusivity 163–5, 176–7
India xi, 159, 164
Indonesia 141, 156, 168–9
Indonesian Scholars' Assembly 168–9
innovation. See *bid'a*
Inside the Gender Jihad (wadud, amina) 160
intersex 39, 40 see also *mukhannath*
Iran 77, 79, 108, 155–6
Iraq 3, 31, 60–1, 67, 70, 107–9
Islamophobia 150
'isma (infallibility/sinlessness) 34, 78
Isma'ilis 35, 118, 157–8 *see also* al-Qadi al-Nu'man, Ibn Hayyun Ibn Muhammad
*isnad*s (*hadith* transmission chain) 58–9, 61, 90 n. 36
Isra'iliyyat literature 26
ittisaliyya (connectedness) 7

Jackson, Nakia 160
Jackson, Troy 163
Ja'far al-Sadiq 77, 78
Ja'fari school 3, 77
al-Jahiz 108
  Kitab al-Bayan 113

Jahziya (Khariji woman)
Jalajel, David 14
jama'a (congregational prayer) 45 n. 23 *see also* congregational prayer
jama'at khana: (place of worship for Isma'ilis) 157
jami'a (congregational mosque) 29, 109
Jaririyya school 121
jariya (slave girl)
  of 'Ali ibn al-Husayn 53, 69, 70, 84
  of Ibn 'Umar, 'Abdullah 174
Jaschok, Maria 142, 143
Jaschok, Maria/Jingjun, Shui 15, 142
Java 141
jihad (striving, effort) 55, 105, 106, 155
Jingjun, Shui/Jaschok, Maria 15, 142
Judaism 96 n. 126
jum'a (Friday congregational prayer) 29, 40, 70, 79, 93 n. 85 *see also* communal prayer
  first *jum'a* prayer in Medina 29
  inclusivity 163, 164
  led by women 155, 161, 163, 164–5, 167, 169, 193
  women and 125, 140, 147–8, 156–7, 169
junub (major impurity) 24, 25
Juwayriyya (daughter of Abu Sufyan) 115

Kahhalah, 'Umar Rida 113
kamadia (Isma'ili male religious leaders) 157
kamadiani (Isma'ili female religious leaders) 157
kamal (spiritual perfection) 122–3
al-Kasani, Ala' al-Din 67
Kassam, Tazim 157
Katz, Marion 5–6, 14, 125
Khadija (Prophet's wife) 24, 26, 30, 32, 145
Khaki, El-Farouk 163
Khankan, Sherin 149–50, 176–7
Kharijis/Kharijism 35, 106–14
Khatami, Muhammad (president of Iran) 155
khatib/khatiba (sermon preacher) 34, 147, 152, 161, 164
al-Khattab, al-Sultan 82
Khawla bint al-Azwar 115
khuntha 5, 41
khutba (Friday sermon) 193

Edina Lekovic 148
inclusivity 164
Krausen, Halima 150
Maldives, the 152
online 195
wadud, amina 160, 161, 164
women and 70, 94 n. 98
Kitab al-Athar (al-Shaybani, Muhammad ibn al-Hasan) 66
Kitab al-Bayan (al-Jahiz) 113
Kitab al-idah (al-Qadi al-Nu'man) 58
Kitab al-Khilaf (al-Ta'ifa, Shaykh) 80, 81
Kitab al-Majmu (al-Nawawi, Muhyi al-din) 71
Kitab al-muntaqa (al-Baji, Sulayman ibn Khalaf) 63
Kitab al-Muwatta' (Malik ibn Abbas) 62, 63, 64
Kitab al-Umm (*Book of Guidance*) (al-Shafi'i) 51, 53, 57, 69, 70, 71
knowledge 27, 37, 40–1, 118, 155 see also *hadith*s
  female prayer leadership 195
  as source of authority 27
  transmission of 55, 84, 143
Krausen, Halima (female leader and imam) 149, 150, 195
Kufa 3, 60–1, 109
Kufa, great mosque 109
  'Ali ibn Abi Talib 107, 109
  Ghazala al-Haruriyya 106, 107, 108, 109–13
al-Kulayni, Muhammad 2

leadership 26–8, 100, 106, 112 see also *imama*
  Ghazala al-Haruriyya 113–14
  prayer. *See* prayer leadersip
legal arguments 155, 160
  precedents 173
  women leading men in prayer 116–26
legal schools 3, 37, 74–7, 120–1, 177 see also Hanafi school *and* Hanbali school *and* Maliki school *and* Shafi'i school
  Ja'fari school 3, 77
  Jaririyya school 121
  Zahiriyya school 120–1
  Zaydi school 3, 77

legal sources 12–13, 125
legal structure 28
Lekovic, Edina (female imam and preacher) 148
Liu Zhi 145
Lowry, Joseph 57

Mabsut (al-Ta'ifa, Shaykh) 79
madhahib. *See* legal schools
madrasas (religious college) 156 see also education
Mahmood, Saba 15, 155
mahram (unmarriageable family member) 70
al-Malati, Abu'l-Husaym Muhammad 110–11, 113
Malaysia 151, 162
Maldives, the 151–3, 176, 178
Malik ibn Abbas 3, 61
  Kitab al-Muwatta' 62, 63, 64
Maliki school 3, 40, 62–5, 173
  women's mosque attendance 155
  women leading prayer 60, 61, 62–5, 74–5, 76–7, 85, 116
maqasid al-shari'a 160
Mariam Mosque 149–50, 176
martyrdom 99, 113 see also *shahada*
Mary (mother of Jesus) 12, 122, 123–4, 149
Masa'il (Ibn Hanbal, Ahmad) 72
masjid (place of prostration/ mosque) 29–30, 31, 101, 103, 147 see also mosques
al-Mas'udi 107, 110
Mattson, Ingrid 144–5
maturity 62, 70
al-Mawardi, Abu Hasan 29, 34, 38, 39, 112, 131 n. 73
  Ordinances of Government 34
Al-Maziri, Abu 'Abdallah 116
Medina 3, 60–1, 64–5, 164
Medinan practice 64–5
Mekkaoui, Raja Naji 173
Melchert, Christopher 14, 61, 65, 66, 121
menstruation 25, 91 n. 50, 117
minbar (pulpit in a mosque) 107, 113, 124
mixed congregations 159
modesty 70, 75, 76, 80, 117, 167, 168 see also *'awra*
Moroccan Fatwa Council 173

Morocco 173-4
mothers of believers 54, 55
Mottahedeh, Roy 26-7
mosques 6, 29-31 *see also* women's mosques
  architecture 31
  Clermont mosque, Cape Town 160
  Companions mosques in Medina 30
  El-Tawhid Juma Circle 163
  Ghazala al-Haruriyya 106, 107, 108, 109-11
  government 29, 37
  Ibn Rushd-Goethe mosque 165, 174
  imams and 37-8
  Inclusive Mosque Initiative (IMI) 163-4
  inclusivity 163-5
  institutionalization 86
  Kufa 106, 107, 108, 109-13
  Mariam Mosque 149-50, 176
  masjid 29-30, 31, 101, 103, 147
  meaning of term 31, 137
  Mecca 30
  nomadic 195
  Prophet's mosque in Medina 30, 164
  segregation 85-6
  temporary 159
  tribal mosques in Medina 30
  al-Tusi, Muhammad ibn al-Hasan 80
  Umm Waraqa bint Nawfal 101, 103
  urban 6, 86, 194
  village 6, 126, 194
  virtual 195
mu'amalat 3, 9
Mu'awiya (Governor of Syria) 106-7
Mubahala episode 82-3
mudahim (female religious leaders in the Maldives) 151-3
Mudawwana (Sahnun ibn Sa'id, al-Tanukhi) 62, 63, 64
muezzin 101, 103, 104
mufti (jurist issuing *fatwas*) 174, 175, 195
Muhammad. *See* Prophet Muhammad
al-Muhaqqiq al-Hilli 36, 38
mukhannath 49 n. 75 *see also* intersex
mukhi (Isma'ili male religious leaders) 157
mukhiani (Isma'ili female religious leaders) 157
Mukhtasar (al-Muzani, Abu Ibrahim) 120

mulk (political power) 27
al-Murtada, Sharif 81
musalla (prayer area) 30, 31, 141
al-Musannaf (Ibn Abi Shayba, Abu Bakr) 52, 61
Muslim, ibn al-Hajjaj 2
Musnad (Ibn Hanbal) 56, 72, 100
al-Muzani, Abu Ibrahim 53, 119, 120
  Mukhtasar 120
al Muzani, Isma'il b. Yahya 70

Nafisa bint al-Hasan (prayer leader) 118, 124
narrators 59, 84, 88 n. 18, 98
nasab (genealogy) 27
naskh (abrogation) 67
nawafil (optional prayer) 29, 37, 55, 79
al-Nawawi, Muhyi al-din 71
  Kitab al-Majmu 71
Nicolle, David 115
nu ahongs (woman imams in China) See *ahongs/nu ahongs*
nüsi (Chinese women's mosque) 142-3, 144, 150

Omid, Mrs (Iranian female preacher) 184 n. 59
Ordinances of Government (al-Mawardi, Abu Hasan) 34
otun/otyncha (Central Asian female religious leader) 172
Ottoman dynasty/ Ottomans 4

past, the 7-8, 73, 76, 86, 171-5
  al-Banna, Jamal 170
Permissibility of Female Prayer Leadership of Men, The (Jawaz Imamat al-Mar'a li'l-Rijal) (al-Banna, Jamal) 169-70
Pesantren (Islamic boarding schools in Indonesia) 156
piety 27, 41, 113
Pirandello, Luigi
  Six Characters in Search of an Author 126
Plumb, John 15
political authority 28, 34-5
potestas (power) 27
power 27

Prado, Abdennur 169
prayer 10–11, 33 see also congregational prayer and salat
  communal 10, 28–31, 33, 125–6
  compulsory nature of 121
  du'a 157, 158
  fara'id/fard 29, 70, 71, 79
  ghada 110
  'id 29, 73
  nawafil 29, 37, 55, 79
  tarawih 66, 118, 141
  tasbih Fatima 83
  validity 120
prayer leadership 5, 24, 26–8, 86 see also imams and women's prayer leadership
  ethnicity 86
  al-Hajjaj 109
  illegitimacy 26
  imama sughra 27–8, 114
  imams 31–2, 33
  Maldives, the 151–2
  maturity 62
  Prophet Muhammad 32–3, 37
  purity 24–6
  al-Rajraji, Hasan 116
  requirements 28–9, 100
  Shabib ibn Yazid al-Shaybani al-Haruri 109
  Shi'i 78–9
  women leading men 97–126, 159, 166–71 see also Ghazala al-Haruriyya and Umm Waraqa bint Nawfal
  women leading women 51–87, 104, 149, 155–6, 158–9, 165, 174 see also 'A'isha bint Abi Bakr and Umm Salama Hind bint Abi Umayya
preachers (female) 2, 15, 124
precedents 23, 41, 171, 172, 173–4
Progressive Muslim Union 161
Prophet Muhammad 37, 85
  choosing imams 28, 32, 39, 103, 108, 112
  Companions of 162, 172
  gender equality 170
  Mubahala episode 82–3
  ordering a woman to lead prayer 100
  permitting a woman to lead prayer 99, 101–2, 105
  as prayer instructor 16, 24, 26, 32–3, 83, 191
  prayer leadership model 32–3, 37
  Prophet's mosque in Medina 30, 164
  Umm Waraqa bint Nawfal 99–101
purity/impurity 24–6, 120

al-Qadi al-Nu'man, Ibn Hayyun Ibn Muhammad 3, 58, 82, 83, 117–18, 158
  Ta'wil al-Da'a'im 118
  Kitab al-idah 58
al-Qaradawi, Yusuf 167, 168
Qatam ibna al-Shijna (Khariji woman) 109
Qur'an, the 1, 11, 14, 172, 193
  al-Banna, Jamal 170
  feminist interpretation 149, 160
  knowledge 41
  principles 162
  wadud, amina 160, 177
Quran and Women (wadud, amina) 160

al-Rafi'i, Abu'l-Qasim 71
Rahman, Fazlur 11
al-Rajraji, Hasan 116
rak'a (ritual prostration) 55, 109, 110
Raza, Raheel (female imam) 160
Reda, Nevin 13, 102, 161, 166, 167, 168
Reinhart, Kevin 25
religious obligations. See fara'id
ritual prayer. See salat
rulers 27–8, 29, 31, 33–4, 86, 172 see also leadership

sabiqa (precedence) 23, 41 see also precedents
Sa'da bint Qamama (female Companion prayer leader) 53, 84
Sadeghi, Benham 14, 61, 66, 67, 75
Sahaba (the Prophet's Companions) 162, 172
Sahih by Muhmmad al-Bukhari (al-Bukhari, Muhammad) 68, 91 n. 50
Sahnun ibn Sa'id, al-Tanukhi
  Mudawwana 62, 63, 64
salafi fiqh 170
Salafi Islam 146
salat (prescribed ritual prayer) 1, 3, 6, 8, 32, 104, 157 see also prayer

daily prayers 10, 29, 35, 37, 125, 139
'id 29, 73
inclusivity 163–5
'jum'a See jum'a
Khadija 24
leadership 26–7, 37 see also prayer leadership
purity 24–6
al-Qadi al-Nu'man, Ibn Hayyun Ibn Muhammad 82
salat al-jama'a. See congregational prayer
tarawih 66, 118, 141
Salim Mawla Abi Hudhayfa 29
Samatar, Abdi 154–5
al-Sarakhsi, Muhammad ibn Ahmad 38, 67
Saudi Arabia 141
Sayeed, Asma 52, 56, 84
Sayyida Arwa (queen of Yemen) 82
scriptural exegesis 171–2
scriptural sources 11–12
selectivity 10
Senegal 19 n. 27, 151
Sevener school 3, 34–5, 77, 78
Seyed Mehdi Razvi (imam of Hamburg community) 150
Shabib ibn Yazid al-Shaybani al-Haruri (Khariji leader, Ghazala's husband) 107–12, 113, 114
Shadeer, Yasmin (female imam) 160
al-Shafi'i, Abu 'Abdallah Muhammad ibn Idris 3, 37, 51, 69–70, 120, 121
  'Amra 53
  'awra 71–2
  Book of Guidance (Kitab al-Umm) 51, 53, 57, 69, 70, 71
  jariya (slave girl) 53
  tahara 25
  Umm Salama Hind bint Abi Umayya 59, 60
Shafi'i school 37, 68–72, 120, 121, 122
  women leading prayer 53, 60, 68–72, 74–5, 76, 85
  women's mosque attendance 122, 154
Shah Karim al-Husayni, Prince (Aga Khan IV) 158
shahada (martyrdom) 83, 99 *see also* martyrdom
shahid/shahida (witness, martyr) 99

Shakir, Zaid 168
Shams Umm al-Fuqara' (*shaykha*) 123
shari'a (Islamic law) 3, 9
al-Shaybani, Abu Bakr 101
al-Shaybani, Muhammad ibn al-Hasan 67, 85
  Kitab al-Athar 66
*Shaykha*s (female leaders, learned women)123, 149, 150
Sheba, Queen of 27, 172
Sheikh Marian (female prayer leader in Somalia) 153, 154–5, 175–6
Shi'ism 77–83
Silvers, Laury (female imam) 160, 163
Silvers, Laury/ Elewa, Ahmed 167
al-Sira al-Nabawiyya (Ibn Hisham, 'Abd al-Malik) 12, 32
Sirat al-Nabi (Ibn Ishaq) 23–4
Sisters in Islam 162
Six Characters in Search of an Author (Pirandello, Luigi) 126
siyada (personal authority) 27
social media 138, 141, 164, 165, 178, 179
  i-preachers 171
  Ibn Rushd-Goethe mosque 165, 174
  Reda, Nevin 161, 166
  virtual platforms 195
  wadud, amina 161–2
social structure 28
Somalia 153–5, 175–6
sources 11–13
South Africa 160, 161
spiritual perfection 122–3
storytellers. *See* narrators
studies on women imams 13–15
Sudan 151, 169
Sufism 14–15, 97, 123, 143, 153, 172–3
al Sufiya, Hammada 130 n. 57
Sultan Muhammad (Mahomed) Shah (Aga Khan III) 158
Sumayya bint al-Khattab 55, 99, 145
Sun Chenying (Chinese female religious leader) 146
Sunan (Abu Dawud, Sulayman) 100–1
Sunan (al-Daraqutni, 'Ali b. 'Umar) 102
sunna 38, 69, 120, 150, 191
  female military action 112, 115
  as a highly recommended action 71
  as legal source 2, 3, 11, 55, 67, 112

Sunni jurisprudence 74–7
suras (Quranic chapters) 32, 46 n. 39
    surat al-Ahzab 148
    surat al-Baqara 109, 110
    surat Al al-'Imran 109, 110
    surat al-Tawba 28

al-Tabari, Abu Ja'far Muhammad Ibn Jarir 23–4, 36–7, 119, 121
    Ghazala al-Haruriyya 107–9
    leadership 26
    purity 25
tafsir (Qur'anic exegesis) 12, 24–5
Tafsir al-Shaykh al-Akbar (Ibn al-'Arabi, Muhyi'l-din) 123
tahara (ritual purity) 24–5
al-Tahawi, Ahmad 66, 67
Tahdhib al-Ahkam (al-Ta'ifa, Shaykh) 81
al-Ta'ifa, Shaykh 3, 79, 80, 81 *see also* al-Tusi, Muhammad ibn al-Hasan
    Kitab al-Khilaf 80, 81
    Mabsut 79
    Tahdhib al-Ahkam 81
Talmon-Heller, Daniella 14
al-Tantawi, Muhammad 'Ali 170
tarawih (Ramadan night prayers) 66, 118, 141
tasbih Fatima 83
tawhid (doctrine of the unity of Allah) 160
El-Tawhid Juma Circle 163
tawhidic paradigm 14, 160, 161–2, 163, 164
Ta'wil al-Da'a'im (al-Qadi al-Nu'man) 118
taxation 49 n. 75
Taylor, Pamela (female imam) 160
temptation 67, 73, 76, 85, 193 *see also fitna*
The Women's Mosque of America 147–9
tradition 7, 172
    precedents 171, 172
Tucker, Judith
    Women, Family and Gender in Islamic Law 10
Turabi, Hassan 169
Turkey 141, 179 n. 3
al-Tusi, Muhammad ibn al-Hasan 2, 79, 80 *see also* al-Ta'ifa, Shaykh
Twelver school 3, 34, 77, 78

UK 156, 163–4
'Umar ibn al-Khattab 54, 64, 85–6
Umayyad dynasty/Umayyads 4, 107–8
Umm Hakim bint al-Harith 115
Umm al-Hasan (*hadith* transmitter) 58–9, 84
Umm Salama Hind bint Abi Umayya (Prophet's wife) 54–6, 84, 105–6
    first marriage 54
    as *hadith* transmitter 53, 55, 56, 57, 84
    Lekovic, Edina 148
    personality 54
    prayer leadership 51–2, 53, 54–6, 80, 174
    as precedent 172
    sources 57–8
    status 58
    war and 115
Umm 'Umara 115
umm al-walad (concubine) 80, 87 n. 6
Umm Waraqa bint Nawfal 84, 97, 99–106, 114–15
    hadiths 62, 76, 99–106, 119, 124, 166, 168, 174
    prayer leadership 53, 84, 87, 98–106, 124, 126, 174, 175
    Turabi, Hassan 169
'Understanding Shari'a' project 15
al-'Usfuri, Khalifa Ibn Khayyat 108, 110
    History 108

Vinding, Niels 139

wadud, amina 13, 14, 159–64, 165–6, 177
    influence 17
    Inside the Gender Jihad 160
    khutbas 160–1, 164
    as precedent 174
    Quran and Women 160
    reaction to 166–9
walad zina (illegitimate child) 26
war 113–16
women 161 *see also* women's mosque attendance *and* women's mosques *and* women's prayer leadership
    age 71–2, 80
    al-Banna, Jamal 169–71
    attractiveness 70, 71, 72, 125
    categories 71–2
    chaplains 156–7

childbirth 43 n. 11, 161
coverings 74
deficiencies 63, 116
desirable 80
dress 74, 148
female voice 63, 73, 79, 80
freeborn 71, 72
groups 162
imams 155–63, 165–6 see also *imama*
legal debates 10
marriage 108, 118
menstruation 25, 91 n. 50, 117
modesty 70, 75, 76, 80, 117, 167, 168 see also *'awra*
pious 100, 105, 113, 123, 173, 177
prayer rooms 141, 151, 159
preachers 124
rulers 27
silencing 10
slaves 53, 69, 70, 71, 80, 84, 93 n. 75, 174
social attitudes 75–6
spaces 141–2, 176 see also home
status 71–2, 82, 86, 118, 125
temptation. See *fitna*
threats against 161, 162, 176, 193
war and 113–16
Women, Family and Gender in Islamic Law (Tucker, Judith) 10
women's mosque attendance 5–6, 70, 71, 85–6, 140–1
  Hanafi school 125
  Hanbali school 73, 74, 122
  Maliki 155
  Shafi'i school 122, 154

Women's Mosque of America, The 147–9
women's mosques 140–2, 150–1, 176
  in Europe 142, 149–51, 163
  Egypt 154
  in USA 147–9
  in Canada 163
  in China 142–7, 150, 176
  in the Maldives 151–3, 176
  in Saudi Arabia 141
  Indonesia 141
  in Afghanistan 141
  in Somalia 153–5
  nüsi 142–3, 144, 150
women's prayer leadership 1, 4–5, 10, 32, 53, 60, 62–77 see also Umm Salama Hind bint Abi Umayya *and* Umm Waraqa bint Nawfal
  leading men 97–126, 159, 166–71 see also Ghazala al-Haruriyya *and* Umm Waraqa bint Nawfal
  leading women 51–87, 104, 149, 155–6, 158–9, 165, 174

Xiuti (Chinese) 145

Yang Huizhen (Chinese female *ahong*) 144, 145
Yarmuk, Battle of 115

al-Zahiri, Abu Sulayman Dawud 119–21
Zahiri/Zahiriyya school 120–1
Zayd ibn 'Ali 58
Zaydi school 3, 77

www.ingramcontent.com/pod-product-compliance
Lightning Source LLC
Chambersburg PA
CBHW072107010526
44111CB00037B/2016